TWENTIETH-CENTURY DOCTOR

Number Four:
*Sara and John Lindsey Series
in the Arts and Humanities*

TWENTIETH-CENTURY CENTURY DOCTOR

House Calls to Space Medicine

MAVIS P. KELSEY, SR.

Texas A&M University Press
College Station

The paper used in this book meets the
minimum requirements of the American
National Standard for Permanence of Paper
for Printed Library Materials, z39.48-1984.
Binding materials have been chosen for durability.

Library of Congress Cataloging-in-Publication Data

Kelsey, Mavis Parrott, 1912–
     Twentieth-century doctor : house calls to space medicine /
Mavis P. Kelsey, Sr.
       p.   cm. — (Sara and John Lindsey series in the arts and
humanities ; no. 4)
   Includes bibliographical references and index.
   ISBN 0-89096-866-7 (cloth)
   1. Kelsey, Mavis Parrott, 1912– 2. Physicians—Texas—
Houston—Biography. I. Title. II. Series.
R154.5.K45 A3   1999
610'.92—ddc21
[b]   98-44065
                                         CIP

CONTENTS

PREFACE AND ACKNOWLEDGMENTS

My Mormon friend Donald Dyal tells me that all of us should keep journals and write our memoirs. Our personal records help our descendants to know from whence they came. For most of us, our family members are the most important people in our lives. We count on them to support us when we need help and to celebrate with us when we succeed. I started out in 1995 to write fifty pages of memoirs. When I finished I had written six hundred pages. I published the memoirs privately in a limited edition of two volumes, *The Making of a Doctor* (1995) and *Doctoring in Houston* (1996). Written exclusively for my family, these volumes contained much family history, letters, and photographs. Many anecdotes were included to illustrate or impart the flavor of the time. Sometimes one brief anecdote will tell more than several pages of description.

Now the two volumes have been condensed into one. I was advised to omit a lot of the letters and family information, yet I have included some of the letters of my recently deceased wife, Mary. These letters portray Mary's character better than I can. In some sense this is also Mary's autobiography. I'm sorry that illness prevented her from writing her own. She would have some memories which are contrary to mine. I'm an old cranky opinionated conservative. I didn't hold back in expressing my beliefs in the original volumes. I have reluctantly left most of this out since my publisher said the general public wasn't interested in my opinions—some of which would certainly inflame the readers. This book is only intended to describe the life and times of a doctor whose life spans the twentieth century.

I was fortunate to have Elisabeth O'Kane as editor. Elisabeth has the unusual talent of correcting my errors and condensing stories, while still leaving my style exactly as written. We had to omit a lot of good tales to reduce the number of pages.

I thank my former partner William D. Seybold for saving the correspondence among him, William V. Leary in Rochester, Minnesota, and me in Houston. Written between 1949 and 1950, these letters describe our plans to join in forming a partnership to develop a multispeciality clinic. My memory was also refreshed by a study of my appointment books and papers, as well as the papers of Seybold and my brother, John Kelsey. These papers are in the

John P. McGovern Historical Collections and Research Center, Academy of Medicine, Jessie Jones Library, Texas Medical Center, under the direction of Elizabeth White. Elizabeth and her staff have been very helpful in providing the papers and early photographs of doctors, early leaders, and views of the Texas Medical Center.

I remember many stories told me by the founders and leaders of the Texas Medical Center: E. W. Bertner; the M. D. Anderson Foundation trustees Horace M. Wilkins, Colonel William Bates, and Judge John Freeman; Leland Anderson; Bishop Clinton S. Quin; Fred Elliott; Judge J. A. Elkins; Thomas Monroe; Wesley West; and Lee Clark. My good friend Tommy Anderson has told me the story of his uncle Monroe D. Anderson and the history of the Anderson family. Other informants were Mary Lou King, original director of the Harris County unit of the American Cancer Society; Governor and Mrs. W. P. Hobby; George Butler; Cooper Ragan; and Miss Ima Hogg. Randolph Lovelace provided information as well as leadership, which lead to the clinic's contracts with the National Space Agency. Jacqueline McCord, recently deceased, the former administrative assistant of the University of Texas Post Graduate School of Medicine, provided the official early history of the school. *Texas Medical Center News* published a series of articles about the fifty years of the Texas Medical Center which also provided a great deal of information.

While collecting material for the book I have been helped by Drs. C. C. Shullenberger; Clifton Howe; Grant Taylor; Bob Moreton; Ed Blackburn; Carson Williams; Sam Barnes; Mickey LeMaistre; Dick Wainerdi; and Dr. Leary's widow, Margaret Mallory. Information from many of my former partners at the Kelsey-Seybold Clinic has been credited to them in the text. Among the employees of the clinic, Jackie Greer, Aggie Greer, Jim Bakken, Betty Wilcox, and Joyce Burch have been very helpful. Dorothy Teall, Nell Barnette, and Vickie Buxton have each written brief yet valuable histories of the clinic and its role in the National Aeronautics and Space Agency (NASA). Terry Litchfield provided the minutes of the trustees meetings of the Kelsey-Seybold Foundation. *Kelsey-Seybold Review,* published as a periodical since the 1960s, also proved a useful source on the history of the clinic

Most of this book was written from memory. For some background facts I have referred to a few published sources: the catalogues of Texas A&M University, 1929–32, and the University of Texas Medical Branch in Galveston, 1932–36; *The University of Texas Medical Branch at Galveston, A Seventy-Five Year History of the Faculty and Staff* (1967); *The Doctors Mayo* (1941), by Helen Clapesattle; *The First Twenty Years of the University of Texas, M.D. Anderson Hospital and Tumor Institute* (1964); *A History of the Texas Medical Center, 50th Anniversary Edition* (1994), by Don N. Macon, in association with Thomas

Dunaway Anderson; *A History of Baylor University College of Medicine* (1956), by Walter H. Moursund, Sr.; and *Remembrances and Reflections* (1991), by Grant Harvey Taylor, edited by N. Don Macon and John P. McGovern. I also consulted *The Handbook of Texas* (1952), published by the Texas State Historical Association, and several Texas almanacs published by the *Dallas Morning News*.

This is the twelfth book I have taken a part in writing. My dear wife, Mary, and I labored together for many years producing these books. On December 4, 1997, our good Lord took Mary in his arms for a better world. This would have been a better book if she had been able to help me write it. Mary would have enjoyed seeing this book come off the press. Many thanks also to our sons John, Tom, and Mavis and their wives for their contributions and their patience. I'm sorry my editors would not let me tell more about them and their achievements. Our secretary Pat Marburger has typed and corrected, time after time, our manuscripts and indexed and helped design most of our books. She has my undying gratitude.

Part 1

The American
Medical Scene,
1890s–1930s

CHAPTER I

Beginnings

My Family Ancestry

Most people agree that a reasonably healthy ego is necessary for a happy life. However our normal egocentricity leads most of us to ignore the importance of our individual heritage, the very source of our being. For this reason my autobiography should tell why I, Mavis Parrott Kelsey, was born in Deport, Texas, on October 7, 1912. That story sets the stage for my life, how I lived it, and how it will influence my descendants.[1]

Our Kelseys are descended from Samuel Kelso/Kelsey (1720–96), who was probably born in Scotland. With his Scotch wife, Susannah Mills (1723–1804), and seven children, including my ancestor, Samuel Kelsey, Jr., he migrated in 1767 to Chester District, in the Piedmont area of South Carolina. Samuel fought in the American Revolution and had his whiskers shot off by the British in the Battle of Fishing Creek. After arriving in America, the spelling of the family name for most members was changed from Kelso to Kelsey.

By the fourth generation following their immigration, Samuel and Susannah had more than three hundred descendants. Most of the Kelsey family remained in the South and retained the southern culture, although a few family members migrated to the Midwest, and a fair number continued to the American West.

Many young men in the Kelsey family were killed in the Civil War. At least three of my four great-grandfathers fought in the Confederate army. I heard many Civil War stories from people who lived through it. The annual Civil War–Veterans squirrel stew was still being held in Deport, Texas, when I was a boy, and we sat around a lantern at night time listening to tales about the war. When my grandfather Joseph Benson Kelsey (1856–1923) moved his family to Milton, Texas, from Red Banks, Mississippi, in 1901, my grandmother Mary Emma "Jessie" McAlexander Kelsey (1862–1935) brought a trunk holding bundles of worthless Confederate money. Even as a small boy, I was fond of these Confederate bills. She would send me to town on errands, sometimes trumped up I think, and reward me with one. Saving these bills was probably my first experience in collecting, a bothersome habit that has taken up so much of my life and caused every closet and shelf in my house to be filled with books, papers, and pictures. Virtually none of this Confederate money survived, however. While I was away at college my brother John Roger Kelsey, Jr., traded the collection away for fishing tackle. John continues to fish, and I continue to collect.

My grandfather Joseph was widely known as J. B. His entire family called him Papa. Even though I was only ten years old when J.B. died, he had a profound influence on my life. He inspired me to become a doctor. He, in turn, had been motivated by two of his uncles who became doctors: Jasper and George Enoch Kelsey, who had attended a medical school in Nashville, Tennessee, which later became part of Vanderbilt University. Both had been doctors in the Confederate army. J.B. married Jessie, a school teacher, in 1880 when he was twenty-four years old. Her father, J. P. McAlexander, gave them a house and a farm when they married. Before going to medical school, J. B. occupied himself by farming and helping his uncle George Enoch Kelsey practice medicine. He also attended a course of lectures at the Memphis Hospital Medical School, and in April 1888 my grandfather obtained a license to practice medicine in Mississippi, but he wanted to improve his professional capabilities by earning a medical degree. He registered at Vanderbilt and—working his way through medical school by practicing medicine—he earned his degree in 1889. He opened his own practice, first in Barton, Mississippi, and then in nearby Red Banks. The practice of medicine was not lucrative in Marshall County, Mississippi, in the 1890s, however. The land was worn out, and the people were too poor to pay the doctor. Added to this, J. B. never tried to collect his bills. Against his wishes, Jessie went out in a buggy and collected medical bills in money or in farm produce so that the family could eat and buy clothes.

In 1900, J. B. made a trip to Texas to look for a new location. He decided on Milton in Lamar County, where several families from Marshall County had already moved. There, he found the land more fertile and the people more prosperous. Lamar County at the turn of the century had premium Texas black land—considered to be the best for producing cotton. J.B. bought several lots, built a two story house and a drug store adjoining, and opened the remaining land to the public as a park. He also bought a farm near Milton. He returned to Mississippi to get Jessie and their four children—James Russell, Joseph Benson, Jr., Lillian Lucille, and my father, John Roger. A few years later, in

Dr. Joseph Benson Kelsey, 1856–1923

1907, a new Texas law required many doctors to take a three-month license renewal course. To take the course, J.B. went to a medical school in Fort Worth, and stayed in the dormitory with John Roger, who at the time was attending Polytechnic College (today, Texas Wesleyan College). There was a severe measles epidemic with several deaths at Poly, as the school was known, while J. B. was there. He became exhausted treating the students, including my father.

My grandfather practiced in Milton until 1908, when he and his family moved six miles away to Deport.[2] A new railroad—the Paris and Mount Pleasant—that bypassed Milton, but went through Deport, had resulted in the decline of Milton. In Deport, J. B. partially retired from his medical practice and opened a buggy and hardware store to provide a career for his three sons. He also purchased fourteen acres and opened a real estate development. Here, he built his house and enticed his friends to do likewise so that he would have them as neighbors. I never understood how J. B. was always out of money but was able to build a nice two-story house in Milton and a large two-story house when he moved to Deport. He had a large barn and outbuildings for his livestock, a large garden, an orchard, and a smokehouse. It is possible J. B. was being financed by his wife Jessie, who came from a wealthy family and had her own money and property.

My grandfather had taken a leading role in the community when he moved to Deport. He was chairman of the school board in 1912 when the new three-story brick school was built, and chairman of the Stewards when the new Methodist Church was finished in the same year. His name is still on the school and church cornerstones. In Deport, he gradually reduced his medical practice, and his sons ran the buggy and hardware business while he developed a fine garden and orchard and raised domestic animals. Although virtually retired, J. B. still had a large bay horse and buggy and made house calls, and I occasionally would ride with him. At home, he still prescribed calomel followed by a "through" of Castor oil for all the family each spring, painted our wounds with iodine, and vaccinated us for smallpox. He gave bismuth and paregoric for diarrhea, Epsom Salts or Crazy Water Crystals for constipation. He treated our malaria with quinine. He braced us with a tonic of iron, quinine, and strychnine—a bitter dose—given before each meal. He tied a sachet of asafetida around our necks to ward off contagious diseases. It smelled so bad that a contagious person wouldn't come near.

My grandfather was not a large man, probably about five feet, eight inches tall. He always had a mustache. When he died on April 23, 1923, he was sixty-nine, and I was ten years old. I had returned home from school that afternoon and visited with my grandfather working in his flower bed next door. He spoke cheerfully, as usual. About 7:30 that night, after we had finished supper, we got an urgent call to come to J. B.'s house. We arrived to see him sitting in his rocker dead. He had been playing with his little granddaughter Mary Dean Oliver. The cause of death was said to be acute indigestion, which had killed my great-grandfather Judge J. B. Massie while eating oysters in 1910 and my wife's grandfather T. W. Randolph while eating cherry pie in 1885. So-called acute indigestion was the most common diagnosis for sudden death until well into the twentieth century, when the condition became recognized as the angina pectoris (chest pain) of coronary artery occlusion. In today's world, these men would have been treated earlier by coronary by-pass and might have lived several more years.[3]

My father, John Roger Kelsey, who went by the name of Roger, was born November 14, 1890, the first of J. B. and Jessie's four children. On October 4,

1911, he married my mother, Bonita Parrott (1892–1980). Her father, Elijah Thomas Parrott, called E. T., was a rancher and an owner of several general stores, a lumber yard, and a wagon sales business in Throckmorton, Texas. Her mother, Virginia Ann, was the daughter of Judge John Bramwell Massie, a rancher who had been elected the first judge of Throckmorton County in 1879.[4]

As an only daughter, Bonita was the pet of her father and four brothers. They called her Missy. She was sent to Polytechnic College in Fort Worth when she was fourteen and attended for four years, from 1906–10. One Sunday night at Poly, she and her roommate, Mavis Graham, were cooking on a chafing dish in their room when Bonita's nightgown caught fire. She ran down the hall screaming, but Mavis displayed great presence of mind when she grabbed a blanket and threw it around Bonita and brought her to the floor, smothering the fire. Bonita suffered some light scars, but her life was saved. When Bonita's mother learned of this, she said that Bonita's firstborn child should be named Mavis. I am her firstborn and have since carried the name Mavis Parrott Kelsey.

Roger had already attended Texas Military Academy and Paris Commercial College before studying at Poly for two years, from 1909 to 1910. While at Poly, he was also working in the hardware business with his father and brothers. Boys and girls were strictly separated at Poly in 1910, when Roger and Bonita began a romance by passing notes. They had their first date on February 11, which was Suspension Day—a day when all classes and rules were suspended, and boys and girls could spend the day together. They finally became engaged and married when Mother was nineteen and Dad was twenty years old. Roger Kelsey brought his bride to Deport in October of 1911, where they found Dr. Kelsey building a house for the young couple as a wedding present.

I was born in this house on October 7, 1912, as were my sisters Mary Virginia, on September 6, 1914, and Elizabeth Lillian, in January 1916 (who died of infectious diarrhea in 1918), and my brother, John Roger, Jr., on May 2, 1922.[5] Since the family doctor was unable to get to the house soon enough, J. B. came over from next door and ushered me into this world.

Bonita and Roger went to Throckmorton that Christmas to show off their firstborn son. Years later they told me the story of how they arrived by train in Seymour on a rainy night and hired a rig, two mules, and a man to drive them twenty-five miles to Throckmorton. About ten miles out, the driver got stuck in the mud and tore up the harness. With three-month-old Mavis carried on one of the mules, the Kelseys trudged back to Self's ranch house, where they spent the night. Christmas eggnog and cake were served the next morning. After repairing the harness the group started out again. My mother's brother

Mavis and his mother, Bonita Kelsey

Bramwell met them in the Parrotts's Buick touring car. It was very cold, so Bramwell took out the floor board to get heat from the engine. First the blanket Mavis was wrapped up in caught fire. Then it got caught in the clutch, nearly killing Mavis before they could get him out. They carried sugar to throw into the clutch to keep it from slipping. The people at home were kept informed by a telephone, which was carried along and used by throwing a wire over the party line that ran along the road. The group finally arrived in Throckmorton at midnight, nearly frozen to death. Mavis was placed in front of the fireplace where he could be admired, the first of his generation on both sides of his family. This was the first of several instances when my life must have been spared for some purpose.

My grandfather J. B. had sent Roger and, later, his brother Russell to the

Paris Commercial College to learn management and accounting so they could help him operate his new wagon and buggy store, which had opened in Deport in 1908. One year later, J. B. added a general hardware store, named himself president, and put his sons to work in it. Russell and Roger alternated duties while one or the other attended college. Russell, only eighteen years old, made $3000 profit the first year while Roger was at Poly. In 1911, J. B. announced his retirement and appointed Roger president of the Deport Hardware Company. Roger was twenty years old and still a student at Poly. The event was written up in the *Deport Times,* and Roger's picture was shown. He held that position until the family business dissolved in 1960. His other brother, Joe Kelsey, entered the business in his teens as a bicycle salesman and repairman. When their sister, my Aunt Lucille, married Dean Oliver, Dean came in as a partner representing her interest.

The Deport Hardware Company soon became the largest business in Deport. It occupied a brick building, a large warehouse, and a wagon and implement yard. An additional warehouse was built near the railroad tracks. Hundreds of bicycles, buggies, and wagons were sold, along with harness, fancy buggy whips, and leather goods. The store carried a complete stock of hardware— everything a farm or household needed, from a cow yoke to a coffee grinder; any tool a carpenter used; every piece of equipment a hunter, fisherman, or sportsman could want, from traps, guns, and ammunition, to cane poles and fly rods, and from boxing gloves and baseball bats to croquet sets. The warehouse held things such as unassembled wagons, cans of paint, and barrels of axle grease. The wagon yard was full of farm implements. I loved to be in the store where I had run of the place and could handle all these wonderful things.

Modernization would change the inventory. Automobiles were becoming popular and before World War I the Deport Hardware Company started selling various makes. Wagons and buggies were replaced by Dort and Maxwell automobiles. The company Brush delivery truck replaced the horse dray. Within a few years, the auto manufacturers began selling their cars through exclusive auto dealer franchises. In the early 1920s Deport Hardware obtained a franchise from Ford Motor Company and opened the Kelsey Motor Company to sell and service Model Ts. A new building was built with showroom offices, a parts department, garage, and car wash, a gasoline service station and a railroad side warehouse. The wagon yard became a car lot, and the hardware store was left with a warehouse full of unassembled new Peter Shuttler wagons, the best money could buy. They were sold off gradually during the next twenty years.

In later years, after the Model A Ford had come out in 1928 and enjoyed an era of great success, the General Motors Chevrolet began to outsell the Fords and became the most popular car in America. Kelsey Motor Company dropped the Ford franchise for a Chevrolet franchise in the 1930s. Deport Hardware went out of business in the 1920s, but Joe Kelsey later revived it with his own hardware and lumber company. Russell Kelsey expanded the car business, opening a Chevrolet agency in Bonham, Texas, and later in Leonard, Texas. Dean Oliver moved to Grand Prairie, Texas, to open a real estate and insurance business. Roger Kelsey kept the Kelsey Motor Company until he retired in 1958, sold the business, and pursued his ranching and investing interests.

As a young boy, I always wanted to work at Deport Hardware Company and the Kelsey Motor Company. In my teens, after the Kelseys got the Ford dealership, I began working in the garage without being invited, hired, or paid. Mechanics Tom Ferguson and Johnny McLemore taught me to be a fairly good mechanic. I built myself a car from the wreckage of several others, and I finally got on the payroll by washing and greasing cars. Once we were to deliver several Model Ts to Pittsburgh, Texas, about fifty miles away. By this time I had learned to drive and was allowed to drive one of the open cars. Somehow near Talco I managed to run off the road into a deep ditch. The car turned over on top of me. The engine was running, and gasoline poured on me from the tank under the seat. I turned off the engine, finally got a door open and crawled out before the other cars caught up. Dad was driving one. The several other drivers righted the car. Dad drove it on and his bottom got blistered by the gasoline soaked seat. This was another narrow escape for me.

Although my father was very frugal, he was always the largest contributor to the church, the school, and other civic endeavors. He gave a lot of his time to the Stewards of the Methodist Church, the school board, and the city government, serving numerous chairmanships and as mayor of Deport. My father was also interested in various investments outside the hardware and motor companies, including the First National Bank and the Farmers Gin, land, farming, ranching, and oil leases. He was an active stock and bond investor all his adult life and ran what amounted to a private bank—loaning dozens of farmers money for raising crops or buying farms. He was also an avid fisherman and hunter. He nearly always camped out on fishing trips and kept complete camping equipment neatly packed and ready at all times. When our family doctor, Stephen Grant, could get away from his practice, he and Roger would journey the seventy-five miles to the cold swift streams in the rugged mountains of southeast Oklahoma for three days of fishing. Indeed, among my most pleasant memories are those of fishing and hunting trips with my father, beginning in early boyhood. I remember one when I got badly sunburned by swimming nude all day in the full sun and had to sit up a day or two. Dad poured dairy cream on my back to reduce the pain.

My brother John also went on many trips to the southeast Oklahoma mountains. The journey involved crossing the Red River on a cable ferry, powered by the river current. The roads were gravel or dirt. We camped on the banks of several mountain streams that we forded in our cars. Big bass, perch, and catfish could be seen in the crystal clear pools. Cool waters tumbled through the rocky shallows where we teens waded in the nude and built rock dams and caught crawfish and minnows to use for fish bait. Back in the draws were a few cabins where Choctaw Indians lived.

This was also moonshine country. One morning my friend Mahlon Grant and I, while wandering in the woods, found a still. No one was around, but the moonshiners were probably watching us from the bushes with rifles cocked. We walked on and soon came upon a large secluded house with several tough looking men on the porch. After exchanging cautious greetings we were given directions to the road, and we hastened on our way. Mahlon and I walked several miles before we found our camp in the late afternoon. There were a lot of outlaws who hid out in these mountains. "Hanging Judge" Parker at Fort Smith, Arkansas, had eradicated the older ones some years before, but there was a new crop, such as Pretty Boy Floyd who robbed banks in several surrounding states.

The fishing friends also made trips to fish in Canada; Yellowstone Park; Colorado; White River, Arkansas; and Mexico. Hunting trips always included an annual deer hunt in the Texas Hill Country and elk hunts in the Rockies. Maudie Dinwoody served faithfully as camp cook on these longer trips for over forty years. I wish I had his recipes and know-how for cooking camp food. For breakfast we always had hot biscuits cooked in a Dutch oven, and for dessert Maudie made peach and blackberry cobblers. The fish were fried in cornmeal. No "store bought" food was allowed, except peppermint stick candy and apples.

In 1973 Roger and Bonita moved to Paris, Texas, to enjoy their retirement. The onset of arteriosclerosis, however, meant a gradual decline in both of their healths. My sister Virginia Gibbs looked after them for the next several years. My father died October 5, 1978, and my mother less than two years later on May 30, 1980. They are both buried in Deport and share the same tombstone. In life, my father was prominent and successful in his community. He was always busy and worked long hours, but he was not the human dynamo my mother was. Bonita was a very warm hearted person with a fierce love for all her family. I soon learned that the slightest criticism of one of hers would bring her to tears. Likewise, the slightest indiscretion or vulgar word by one of her children would bring a stern rebuke, sometimes tears, and, when we were small, a switching with a peach tree switch.

My mother was a great cook, but she never cooked anything that measured to her standard of perfection. She had prodigious energy. Except for the traditional brief afternoon nap, she was busy twelve hours a day in and out of the house, canning, cooking, cleaning, gardening, painting, wallpapering, fixing furniture, making lye soap, making all our clothes, bathing children and cutting their hair, hosting church and social club functions, entertaining neighbors, friends, and visiting relatives who often stayed for days, and traveling by car to Paris for a spool of thread that couldn't be found in Deport. She even upholstered the car seats. She kept the storm cellar full of canned fruit and vegetables, giving much of it away. She got tired but never really complained. Some might say she lived a life of drudgery, but she wouldn't have agreed. She didn't have to do it—she had help and her own income from oil wells; she just wanted to, and she thoroughly enjoyed what she was doing. When I came home from school, she ran out to me with a warm kiss and a strong embrace. My mother wore her affection on her sleeve; she didn't hide it like I do, like Dad did. She was very generous, while I am frugal, like my dad was. Dad and Mother both had strong opinions, many of which they shared, and did not hide them. They were a devoted a couple, but sometimes there were fireworks.

I grew to manhood in the house where I was born. My childhood, spent in a country town, was a happy and normal one—free of hardship, abuse, and misfortune. My relatives were devoted, loving, kind, and gentle people who played an important and attentive role in the upbringing of the grandchildren. We lived in prosperity, relative to the times. About all I can do is tell of life in a country town during the first quarter of the twentieth century.

CHAPTER 2

Texas Country Boy

Deport was and still is a town of a few hundred people in southeast Lamar County. It was twenty-one miles by a poor dirt road from Paris, the county seat with eighteen thousand people. This dirt road happened to be the old Choctaw Indian Trail from Louisiana to Oklahoma.[1] The town is located in Texas' Black Land Belt, an area extending from Northeast Texas to San Antonio and containing some of the best land in America for growing cotton. The terrain attracted settlers beginning in the 1820s, and by 1901, when my family arrived, the area was completely settled by farmers who had abandoned their worn-out cotton farms in the Deep South. Deport is on the west side of the Blossom Prairie—prior to settlement, a beautiful treeless ten-by-twenty-mile sea of native grass and wild flowers. Here, the first travelers found buffalo, elk, and deer roaming the land, hunted by the native Caddo Indians.

When I was a boy, only a few acres of the virgin Blossom Prairie still existed as hay meadows. The rest of the prairie had been divided into cotton farms. The first settlers had marked off their borders by planting switches from bois d'arc (bodark) trees, which rapidly took root and developed, with other trees, shrubs, weeds, and blackberry bushes, into long hedge rows. This was before barbed wire. A bodark hedge was said to be "pig tight, horse high, and bull strong." Many of these hedges still existed when I was a boy and had grown to be twenty feet wide or more, providing cover for wildlife: quail, doves, rabbits, squirrels, coons, possums, skunks, and snakes. My friends and I walked many miles hunting these hedge rows. Several creeks with wooded bottom lands traversed the prairie. This land, subject to overflow, was fenced in as pasture and provided wonderful rabbit hunting. When I was a young boy, local owners never complained about boys hunting on their land.

The farms were small tracts, usually not more than 160 acres, an amount of land a farmer with one or two teams of mules could cultivate. Even the larger plantations were divided among several tenants. The economy was based on mule power; there virtually were no tractors then. All the implements such as plows, wagons, and cultivators were pulled by a team of two mules. The black land was so productive that farmers used every available acre for cotton production. Consequently, there was little diversification and very little land for pastures, gardening, or fruit orchards. For these cotton farmers it was more economical to buy their produce from the sandy land farmers (sandlappers) who couldn't grow cotton. This sandy land, just outside the Blossom Prairie, was good for small truck farming, fruit, berries, watermelons, sweet potatoes, and the like. Much of it was wooded. In the bottoms were walnut, hickory, pecan, and persimmon trees for gathering nuts in season. These woods were great for hunting possums and coons with hounds at night.

The Choctaw Trail as it passes through Deport today, is busy U.S. Highway 271, a far cry from the late 1800s, when J. R. Westbrook of Deport got his start hauling freight over it by ox-drawn wagons. When I was a boy, many families were still traveling the Choctaw Trail in covered wagons, migrating from Mississippi and Louisiana to the Choctaw country of southeastern Oklahoma. The trail was a dusty dirt road that passed by our house. Sometimes several families plodded by in one day.

Throughout my childhood, 90 percent of Americans were in agriculture and lived in the country, without paved roads and reliable rapid transportation. I knew grown people who never had been out of Lamar and Red River Counties their entire lives and didn't want to leave. In the early 1900s travel was a very slow process. For this reason when relatives came visiting they planned an extended stay. Two weeks was a short visit.

Deport was my home from 1912 until 1936, when I left Texas to intern at Bellevue Hospital in New York City. I have a vivid memory of the little town I was so proud of, where I spent a happy boyhood and youth with a loving family and gentle people. Unfortunately, I was born into a society of people who believed in racial segregation, an institution that was as real as any physical building standing in Deport. It is only now, as I look back on my past and review it, that I can see the prejudices of my youth. All the time I lived in Deport, my family employed blacks at home, in the store, and in the fields. We developed close friendships and as children played together. But we were segregated in hundreds of preposterous ways. Black women wet nursed white babies and blacks cooked and served our meals, but had to eat out of different utensils and never at our table in private or public. They used a separate drinking cup at water fountains. Blacks were not allowed on Main Street and entered the stores only by the rear entrance. Black people were called by their first names only.

In my mind's eye, I can see every street, every business, every church, the school, and the house of every relative and friend, which was just about everyone in town. You will wonder why I loved Deport when I describe some of its features. At first, there was not a paved street in town or one leading into town. Deport was virtually paralyzed after several days of rain, when every street became a bottomless quagmire of black waxy mud. Mule teams were kept busy pulling wagons and automobiles out of the mud. Mud clung to bare feet, shoes, or boots and was tracked into the house. The cow bogged down in the barnyard.

During the summer droughts, however, the streets turned into powdery dust that filled the air behind every passing vehicle. A pall of dust hung over the town. Dust seemed to seep through the walls into the house and settle on the beds and furniture. Sometimes the droughts lasted all summer, and drinking water had to be hauled into town. The ponds dried up, and the cattle couldn't find water. At other times, heavy rains filled Mustang Creek to overflowing. Water raced down Main Street. It scoured out the dirt street, flowed into the stores, and cut off the traffic between the north and south sides of town. After floods, the town was besieged by mosquitoes carrying malaria. We often slept inside mosquito netting.

In the summer the temperature often exceeded one hundred degrees for days. There was no air conditioning. We often tried to sleep on pallets on the porch or on the lawn. Blue northers struck during the winter. People said there was nothing between us and the North Pole but a barbwire fence. Going to the outdoor privy in winter could be a chilling experience. It was also extremely difficult to court your girlfriend in a parked car when both of you were bundled up and nearly freezing.

There was no electricity in Deport until 1926. Before then, we studied by kerosene lamp. Water and sewerage came a few years after electricity. No public water or sewerage or indoor toilets existed in Deport before then. Everyone had an outdoor privy, which was cleaned out periodically by the scavenger. He shoveled the human waste into his cart, and replaced it with a shovelful of lime. By the time I went to college the streets had been paved. But all of these hardships made us appreciate the good times when the weather was balmy; when wild flowers were blooming on the Blossom Prairie; when the green cotton fields covered the landscape; when the wagons lumbered in laden with cotton, and the gins hummed all night; when the trees were heavy with pecans and walnuts ready to pick; when frosty, sunshiny Saturday mornings arrived, perfect for a rabbit hunt; when the school or church was filled with the prettiest girls in the world; when hundreds of interesting people and things invited fun and adventure.

I liked to go to town and walk up and down Main Street, dropping in to visit the owner of any store I wished. Dad often sent me to the other end of Main Street to the post office where the people stood around gossiping and waiting for Broadie Bell to put the mail in our boxes. I lingered over the candy counter in Glover's Grocery hoping to snitch a chewy caramel. I sat in the barber shop and listened to the sex stories and looked at pictures of naked girls which were passed around. During the holidays I clerked in the men's section of Hudson Davis Dry Goods. I gossiped at the City Drug Store soda fountain. There were a few dozen loafers who had staked out their territory on the storefront sidewalks, and could always be found there, sometimes saying nothing for hours, spitting tobacco juice.

The business district, along Main Street, was two blocks long with businesses on both sides. Stores on the east side backed up to Mustang Creek. Stores on the west side backed up to Gray Street (always called Back Street).[2] Main Street was rather wide, providing room for cars to park into the curb and still leave space for many more cars and wagons to park when it was crowded. The store sidewalks were about three feet high, an attempt to bridge the flood waters of Mustang Creek. Most of the stores were one-story brick with a metal shade covering the sidewalk. On Saturday, all the farmers came to town to shop, and the streets were packed. When I was young, the town had a surprising number of businesses: two banks, five groceries, two restaurants, a barber shop, two drug stores, three dry goods stores, a jewelry, a dry cleaner, two hardware stores, two blacksmiths, a leather and shoe repair shop, the post office, a lumber yard, two filling stations, a feed store, a picture show, a two-story wooden hotel, two auto garages, a livery stable, a calaboose, a furniture store and funeral home combined, a feed store, a grist mill, a tinner's shop, a weekly newspaper, a Masonic lodge, a hospital, an ice house, and, when I was older, a beauty shop for women.

The numerous small businesses in Deport in the 1920s were thriving. Most of the stores, businesses, and hotels are gone today, and the countryside population has diminished with the advent of mechanized farming. Our family's small 160-acre farm at Shadowland on the Blossom Prairie, for example, had supported a family for a hundred years. Now we rent the farm to a nearby farmer who has acquired several family farms for his own—the families having long ago moved to the cities. He farms about 1000 rented acres, including ours, with a million dollars worth of labor saving implements and, during part of the year, with hired help. Also gone is the horse-and-buggy economy, for which Texas counties were organized. With some exceptions, the counties by law had to be small enough for every citizen to ride horseback on a dirt road to the county seat and return in the same day. This limited the counties to about thirty miles square. Now, people can easily drive fifty miles to a regional shopping center and spend a day at a mall. These new economic centers thrive, while other towns shrivel. Between 1980 and 1990, ninety Texas counties lost in population, even though the state population grew more than 10 percent. So far, even though many towns its size have become ghost towns, Deport is hanging in there and may survive that fate.

Other important institutions in Deport included the town's public school, a three-story brick building with eight classrooms, built in 1912. Each classroom had a cloakroom and a large coal burning stove. Large windows provided light, as there was no electricity. There were rows of school desks; the seat of one desk faced the next which had a shelf for books under the writing surface. There was an open space between the bottom and the back of the seat. Through this opening a student could goose the student in front with a sharp pencil. Goosing a student could be very a risky and tempting adventure, especially if the student was a girl. The victim may squirm and try to be quiet or could let out a scream which would disrupt the entire room. The instigator could get in deep trouble.

On the third floor of the Deport School was a gas-lit auditorium, seating six hundred people, with an elevated stage. On this stage I played the role of a clown in the senior class play. The auditorium was used for many public functions and as a meeting place for various churches. The faculty held religious chapel services there on a regular schedule, with the entire student body attending. The entire population was Protestant, so there was no diversity of religious ideas. Argument about separation of church and state was never heard of. People considered many of the purposes of both institutions to be the same, with the two acting in unison and without conflict.

A one-room school, operated by the Deport school board, was provided for black children. When my father was school board chairman, I remember he had difficulty locating a black teacher. The strict segregation of blacks was a terrible blight. Like most of the people at the time I would have rejected integration, and it took years for most of us to realize our intolerance.

There were some poverty stricken people in Deport. In those days the federal government left it to state and local institutions and people to take care of charity. Lamar County supported a poor house in Paris. The state supported a few efficiently run mental hospitals and a school for the blind and deaf. The churches operated several orphanages. There were three churches in Deport, Baptist, Methodist, and Presbyterian. I was a Methodist. The churches were about the same size, each occupying a wooden building with seating for about two hundred. Each church had a full-time pastor and provided him and his family a parsonage.

The cotton yard was another public institution, located down by the railroad tracks. Hundreds of bales of cotton were stored there, awaiting buyers or shippers who loaded the bales into boxcars for transport to New England textile mills. As children, we romped on these cotton bales, jumping from bale to bale. Eventually, the city built a large warehouse to store the cotton off the ground and under roof. Cotton bales had to be weighed by a bonded weigher. Our cotton weigher was elected at the same time as other local officials such as the judge, the sheriff, the constable, and the county school superintendent. The position of cotton weigher was hotly contested, since it received a fee for every bale weighed.

I have a few very vivid memories from my early childhood growing up in Deport: some sad, some tragic, some exciting, and some just very ordinary. When I was about three years old, while visiting my Parrott grandparents in Throckmorton, I remember running out of the house into the yard in my bare feet. I stepped into a yard full of grass burrs, an event made memorable probably because it was extremely painful. I had to endure more pain while my mother extracted these burrs, which hung from the skin on nasty little hooks. Someone had a camera and took snapshots of this episode. Even now, looking at these faded pictures provokes pangs and chuckles.

My most striking early memory with a proven date is of the great Paris, Texas, fire of March 12, 1916. I was three-and-a-half years old. This fire is best described on the historical marker on the city square of Paris:

> Although Paris was founded in the mid-1840s many of its historic structures were lost in a fire that destroyed almost half the town in 1916. Winds estimated at 50 miles per hour soon blew the fire out of control as it burned a funnel-shaped path to the northeast edge of Paris. Firemen from Bonham, Cooper, Dallas, Honey Grove and Hugo, Oklahoma helped the Paris Fire Department battle the flames, which were visible up to 40 miles away. The blaze destroyed most of the central business district and swept through a residential area before it was controlled. Property damage from the fire was estimated at $11,000,000.

Viewed from Deport, seventeen miles away, the fire, I remember, lit the entire northwest sky that night. Many in Deport stood outdoors watching in great excitement. Dad and other men in town drove to Paris to offer help. I heard much talk about the fire for days and would hear more for years to come, as Paris was rebuilt.

I distinctly remember a little Brush delivery truck owned by the Deport Hardware Company. I loved to ride in it. Often I could recognize the sound of its motor as it was driven to the depot several blocks from home. I remember taking off running across a cotton patch toward the depot with my mother chasing after me and catching me. I was still wearing a dress, as boys did then until they were four or five years old, before graduating to knee pants. I also recall when my baby sister Elizabeth Lillian died in 1918, and when my uncle Russell was wounded at the Battle of Château Thierry in France in World War I. The family sat by the fireplace at my grandfather's house and prayed for him. The adults often talked about the war and how mean Kaiser Bill was. I have a visual memory of sitting on the back steps with my sister Virginia. We were throwing bread to the chickens when Mother came out and scolded us for wasting food while the Armenians were starving. Many of my contemporaries remember that same admonition.

I remember the first radio I ever saw. In the 1910s there may have been some radios for retail sale, but many were custom-made by their owners. My uncle Russell was something of a self-trained electrician. He and several friends rented a vacant store building, where they undertook to build a radio in their spare time. They bought a collection of electric tubes, condensers, ear phones, and other mysterious items—batteries, yards of wires, an aerial, and sheaves of blueprints. The various parts, all connected by wires, occupied the top of a long table. Russell and his friends welcomed visitors to come and observe their undertaking. Finally, they had a radio that occasionally received a signal. The group held an open house one Sunday afternoon. Our family was invited. I remember Uncle Russell telling us how the radio worked. When I put on the ear phones, I heard a lot of crackling sounds but wasn't sure whether I heard WLS in Saint Louis, WGN in Chicago, or just static. Technology developed rapidly, however. For our family, Uncle Russell soon built a radio on which I listened to as many stations as I could count. I'd stay up past midnight listening, competing with other boys to see who heard the most stations.

I was sent to the Deport public school at age six. I started a year early and was moved up a year, so most of my classmates were two years older. This, plus my natural awkwardness, put me at a physical disadvantage, which accompanied me through school. As I look back on my early schooling, I believe I was somewhat dyslexic. I seemed to learn quickly enough in some ways, but my grandmother Kelsey, a former school teacher, in spite of great effort, could hardly teach me to read or write. Nevertheless, I went to school.

My first grade teacher, Miss Prudence Haun, was a sweet loving person who later married my uncle Russell. She worked very diligently, until she taught me to write. I remember standing at the blackboard in front of the class, totally unable to write the simplest words, so frustrated that I cried. My parents and grandparents believed the problem may have been because I was left-handed and thought this should be corrected as soon as possible. Although I finally learned to write with my right hand, I couldn't be taught to throw or swing a bat right-handed.

After Aunt Prudence finally taught me to write I did fairly well in school, not that I liked to study. My eleven years in public school were a wonderful experience. I learned all about sex, by conversation only. I fell in love with several girls, but they never knew it. I learned how to smoke, and I learned all the vulgarities that I never heard at home. I made a lot of friends, and we often spent the night at each other's houses. I learned to play all the sports, but was never good enough to be on a team. I was very active in shinny, mudball fights, and corncob fights. I could never learn to play any kind of musical instrument, although I was given a few piano lessons and had a harmonica. This was odd because all the adults in my family could play something. The only musical number I recognized in music appreciation was "The Anvil Chorus." I identified the scaling of anvils, not the music. We marched to the school chapel singing "Onward Christian Soldiers," and the service opened with a prayer. There was no separation of church and state in those days.

I was often a disciplinary problem. I liked to sail paper airplanes, make vulgar noises, pinch girls, put rubber bands on the coal stove to cause smoke and bad odors—anything that raised my prestige in the eyes of my classmates. I often had to stay in at recess or after school.[3] The worst offenses meant being punished by the superintendent, who had authority to paddle bad boys. But I soon discovered that his paddle wasn't as bad as Mother's peach tree switches. Those switches were more painful than Dad's razor strap. I never got a whipping I didn't deserve, however, and I deserved a lot more than I got.

We went to school each year for nine months, from 8:00 A.M. to 4:00 P.M., five days a week. The only holidays were Thanksgiving, Christmas, and Easter. School was a place to learn the basics, "readin', writin', and 'rithmetic." The only extracurricular activities were sports, not taken as seriously as today, and interscholastic league competition, which was serious. We practiced for weeks in preparation for interscholastics, held in Paris for all Lamar County school pupils. I was in debate but never won. We had much homework. When I left school in the afternoon I had a little relaxation—after supper at six it was "on the books" for a couple of hours. Spelling matches occurred in every grade. We got plenty of coaching at home. Declamation meant making speeches to your classmates. We were required to memorize and recite poetry, Lincoln's Gettysburg Address, and the like. Math performance at the blackboard was a daily assignment. There was an honor roll for each class published regularly in the *Deport Times*. I still have a copy of the paper with my name on it. At the Kelseys you had better be on the honor roll.

At our house no one slept late, even after we went to college. It was completely unthinkable for any of the children to be in bed after Dad and Mother had gotten up to do the cooking and chores, put breakfast on the table, and say morning prayers. Our family did most of the many chores as a group. We did have some outside help, however. Shorty, a hired man, worked for our family, and we employed a washwoman to do the laundry and ironing. She built a wood fire under a large iron washpot full of water, boiled the dirty clothes, scrubbed them on a rubbing board, and hung them on the clothesline to dry, before ironing them. I especially remember Bess, who rotated among the Kelsey families. She kidded the children and got along fine with all our family.

Our family divided chores along traditional lines. The men and boys took care of the milk cow. Our tomcat, Tiger, always came to the barn during milking. He stood on his hind legs while I served a few jets of warm milk into his mouth. We milked before breakfast and before supper without fail or the milk would cake in the cow's bag. It was my duty to lead the cow to the pasture in the morning and lead her home in the afternoon. My brother John assumed these duties when I went away to college. The men also took care of the firewood. After several cords of wood were delivered and stacked, a man came with a gasoline powered saw, built for the sole purpose of cutting cord wood into stove wood. Cooking stove wood was split by the men or boys. The stove wood was stacked neatly in the backyard. We believed only shiftless people left their wood in a pile.

The garden was a cooperative family project. I remember picking beans when I could hardly walk. In the spring everyone in the family liked to till the soil, plant the potatoes, radishes, peas, and beans, set out tomatoes, onion sprouts, and other vegetables, then watch them grow. There were no fresh vegetables in the stores. After we had weathered a winter of eating dried beans, salt pork, and stewed dried fruit, we were starved for vitamins. Nothing could taste better than new creamed potatoes with fresh shelled English peas, garnished with green onions.

Our enclosed backyard was home to a flock of chickens. A henhouse held ten to twenty hens; the hens, rooster, and half-grown chickens roosted on horizontal wooden poles. There were several box-like nests for the hens to lay their eggs, which we collected daily. A proud rooster, who guarded his harem, woke us every morning with his crowing. We children loved to pet the little chicks, but when they grew, in spite of our affection for them, they ended up on the table, fried and accompanied by cream gravy and hot rice or biscuits. Old hens who quit laying were grabbed by Mother, who wrung their heads off, plucked them, and baked them filled with cornbread dressing. When the big old rooster could no longer perform, Dad chopped his head off with an ax, and Mother and the neighbors made him into a few dozen hot tamales.

Deport was almost exclusively a cotton growing community. In the summer, just after school was out, the recently planted cotton needed chopping, hoeing, and cultivating. The chopping thinned the young plants, leaving one to three plants every six inches, or the width of a hoe. Hoeing cotton was cutting the weeds and grass around the plants, often done one to three times after the chopping. Cultivating was done with a riding or walking cultivator that plowed the furrows to kill the weeds and grass and loosen the soil. I soon learned that riding a cultivator was much less tiring than walking all day behind one and handling the mules. I hired myself out to do these jobs, as well as to pull corn and help in baling hay.

I also had my own cotton crop, which I raised on two acres of vacant lots leased to me for that purpose by my grandmother. I farmed the patch for several years during summer vacations while I was in high school and college. I chopped, hoed, and picked the cotton entirely by myself. Each year I produced at least 1500 pounds of seed cotton, which when ginned produced a 500-pound bale of lint cotton and 1000 pounds of cotton seed. In good years lint cotton usually sold for about 30 cents a pound or $150 a bale. I sold my bale for the highest bid (often to an Anderson Clayton Cotton Company buyer) and usually made about $100, after the expenses of seed and ginning. I promptly deposited the check in the First National Bank, where Dad was a director.

My friends and I had a lot of fun picking cotton. Several of us would get together to take jobs in other fields. We picked the cotton from the bolls, row after row—sometimes stooping over, sometimes on our knees—and stuffed it into a long canvas sack strapped over one shoulder and dragging behind. On our farm, I weighed the cotton of all the pickers. A good picker could gather over 300 pounds in a day; a few picked more than 400 pounds. I could pick 200 pounds; my brother John picked 200 pounds in one afternoon. I took my first chew of tobacco in the cotton patch. You could chew tobacco or dip snuff in the cotton patch but your hands were too busy to smoke. The usual pay was 1 cent a pound, paid on Friday afternoon, so we had money on Saturday to take to town.

Deport had three cotton gins and one cotton seed oil mill. The ginners needed plenty of water to run their steam engines, so the gin ponds were the largest pools in town and were a great place to fish for perch or snag a bullfrog—or take a fine swim. One sad memory is of watching from the banks of Deport Oil Mill pool as adults searched the water for the body of Leonard Guest, a school friend who occasionally spent the night with me. I will never forget when his nude cold body was pulled from the depths.

Each ginning season, a great competition was held to see who would produce the first bale of cotton weighing 500 pounds or more. The gin whistle blew to announce the event to the entire town, and the local paper had an article describing the farmer, when he planted, what the bale weighed, and the prize awarded him. Once the ginning season got under way the gins went day and night. I have spent many a night, windows open, listening to the gins hum, the mockingbirds sing, and the cotton wagons rumbling home in the wee hours, after the farmers had finally got their turn for ginning their cotton. There was an air of excitement in the town during ginning season, especially if there was a good crop. The farmers could pay their debts and buy new clothes and supplies.

Dietary habits and customs were very different when I was a boy. Meals were rather formal in our house. The entire family sat down together for all three meals. After the blessing, the food was politely passed around. A pitcher of sweet milk was also passed. Then we started eating. There were two courses—the meat and vegetables first—then a dessert course. We came to the table on time, fully dressed with our hats off, our hands and faces freshly washed. Mother was very strict about table manners. We took modest servings. We didn't take big bites or talk with food in our mouth. We put the knife down before using the fork with our right hand. Putting food in the mouth using the left hand was bad manners; only coarse people would do it. I am grateful for the good manners I was taught at home and took for granted.

Since there were no supermarkets, fresh food was available only in season from one's own garden or local produce. A Saturday event for me was to go to the corn crib and pick out some fine yellow ears free of weevils, shell a sack full, and take the corn to the grist mill to be ground into cornmeal. Cornmeal mush, served with sugar and cream, was a favorite breakfast cereal. Fresh speckled butterbeans were cooked with ham hock and served on crumbled cornbread with chopped onions, a pickle, and a glass of buttermilk. We also needed cornmeal to make hot tamales and tamale pie. We picked wild grapes in the woods to make wine and jelly. There were many varieties of wild grapes in the Red River Valley. Thomas V. Munson of Dension, Texas, cultivated these grapes and developed a root stock that was immune to phylloxera, which was destroying France's grape and wine industry until the French obtained Munson's root stock for their vineyards.

Much of our food came from our sandy land neighbors: peanuts, sweet potatoes, strawberries, apples, sorghum molasses, and sugar cane stalks to chew on. Refrigeration was inadequate, so everything had to be cooked from the basic supplies, although commercial canned food was available. Milk and dairy products came from one's own cow. There was no knowledge about the role of fats in causing arteriosclerosis. All kinds of fats were produced—in butter and cream, salt pork, pork lard, greasy sausage, heavy fatted beef, fat baking hens—and eaten in large quantities.

Grandfather Kelsey fattened hogs for slaughter on the first good freeze in December. All the family plus some outside help would gather. First a large wash pot was filled with water and brought to boil over a wood fire. The hog, ranging from 200 to 500 pounds, was killed by a well placed blow to the head with the blunt end of a single blade axe. It was hung up by the hind legs, disemboweled, and bled. The hog was completely shaven of all bristles, and the body cavity cleaned out with hot water. The liver was saved, and fat was stripped from the intestines. We gave the heart, sweetbreads, lungs, stomach, intestines, feet and other offal to our help. Then the hog was butchered into hams, shoulders, bacon sides, chops and other serving cuts. The skin was removed from many parts with a thick layer of fat to be cut into small pieces. The pieces were boiled in their own fat in a large wash pot to make lard and cracklings. The cracklings were cooked until they were golden brown, taken out, and thoroughly drained of fat while they were hot, leaving them crisp, then salted. After they dried and cooled, they were then placed in a stone jar to be used for flavoring. Crackling cornbread was especially tasty. Mother often put cracklings into our school lunch boxes with a piece of cornbread or a biscuit.

We had a great variety of food, even though it came seasonally. There was always plenty for growing kids. Since the main meal of the day was at noon, it was called dinner. Dad came home for dinner, and we children walked home from school, returning afterward. A meat dish was served at the noon meal. Mother came from ranch country, so she often served beef roasts and steaks and fried steak with gravy (before it was called chicken fried steak). Mother pounded a round steak and dipped it in flour and black pepper to fry. Occasionally we had fried liver with onions. I often heard Mother quote her father about good beef: "The best is from a big steer off the range. There shouldn't be too much fat and it should be bright yellow from the steer eating fresh grass." Mother laid down the law about game, however. She cooked quail, doves, venison, squirrels, ducks, and geese, but no possums, coons, cottontails, or crawdads were allowed in the house.

I loved fish fries. Groups of family or friends would catch a large mess of catfish, perch, and bass, or would buy a large catfish weighing up to forty pounds and go to the woods. The men would clean the fish, season with salt and pepper, coat with cornmeal, and deep fry them in a large iron wash pot. The women would bring potato salad, sliced onions and pickles, watermelon, homemade light bread, and summer salad. If a table wasn't available, a cloth was spread on the ground. We waved the flies, bees, and mosquitoes away while we feasted.

We went strong on vegetables, such as stewed tomatoes, squash, and snap beans with potatoes. We had lots of legumes, both fresh and dried, including speckled butter beans, black-eyed peas, English peas, navy beans, and pinto beans. In the winter, we ate boiled cabbage, creamed onions, mustard greens, buttered turnips, potato salad, creamed sweet potatoes with marshmallows, and Irish potatoes cooked many ways, preferably whipped with butter or gravy. We had never heard of broccoli, Brussels sprouts, artichokes, leeks or avocados. Spring salad in season included sliced onions, green peppers, cucumbers, and tomatoes in a vinegar dressing. Bib lettuce and radishes were available from the spring and fall garden. Dried fruits were more popular than they are today, as were stewed fruits such as prunes, figs, apples, apricots, and peaches. We usually only saw fresh oranges at Christmas, when we would all sit around the stove while Dad peeled one and passed around the sections. Native blackberries grew wild in every weed patch, hedge row, and pasture.

Dessert and sweets were a major part of every meal, beginning with jams and jellies for breakfast. The desserts included many dishes we still have today. Mother made great cakes, pies, custards, and cookies. Layer cakes were best with thick icings or fillings containing black walnuts, hickory nuts, or pecans. Angel food was great with orange icing, served with ice cream. Mother liked to make pineapple upside down cake. There were no mail-order fruit cakes. We made our own. We started by accumulating all the candied fruits and nuts and spices. Then Mother spent a whole day making several cakes, soaked with homemade nectar, plus a box of fruitcake cookies. The cakes were usually for Sunday or special events, but pies were everyday food. Blackberry and peach cobblers were made during the fruit season, and pecan pies were also prepared when in season. Mother also made lemon, chocolate, banana, caramel, chess, buttermilk, strawberry, cherry, plum, custard, pumpkin, sweet potato, and apple pies. Occasionally Mother made her own mince meat. No complicated recipe was too great a challenge for her.

Every family had its own cow, otherwise it couldn't claim a proper household. The milk was strained when it came from the barn. Before iceboxes, we cooled our milk on a special table that had a metal top and a three-inch rim around the sides. The table top was filled with water; pails of milk were set in the water, and a white cotton sheet was placed over the milk, with the edges of the sheet tucked into the water. Capillary attraction soon drew water up into the sheet. The water evaporated on the wet surface of the sheet to cause cooling. With plenty of milk we had regular custard to eat with a spoon, a liquid custard to drink, and custard puddings with rice or bread and raisins, seasoned with cinnamon and nutmeg. Ice cream and sherbet were Sunday dishes. Fresh peach ice cream was my favorite, but banana and strawberry ice creams were never refused.

Cookies, or tea cakes as we called them, were great to carry in school lunches but we rarely carried a lunch. We ate cookies when we came home in the afternoon. If there weren't any cookies we would punch a hole in a cold biscuit and fill it with molasses. Favorite cookies were oatmeal, nut, sugar, and peanut butter. Brownies, sand tarts, Cream puffs, and candy were special treats. My favorite homemade candy was chocolate fudge with black walnuts. A finer type candy was divinity. We made molasses taffy, popcorn balls, stuffed dates, and date roll. We had what is known widely as pralines, but I never heard them called that until I was older.

A new food fad was sweeping the country when I was a boy. Hamburgers had just become widely known. They were made by the original recipe first used in Athens, Texas, and popularized at the Saint Louis World's Fair in 1904, where, for some reason, they acquired the name hamburger. I remember Rankin Bell's hamburger stand in Deport. It was a typical one-man operation in a small oblong wood building with the kitchen on one end. The kitchen was separated by a counter from the other end, where there was a board seat against the back wall for customers. There was also a serving counter between the kitchen and the street. The owner-cook used a kerosene burner under a solid iron griddle to fry thoroughly a greasy round beef patty and scorch the buns. Fortunately no one in the country would eat rare meat, or half of the customers may have died of food poisoning. He'd charge a dime for the hamburger and a nickel for a Coke or maybe a sour lemon soda to wash it down with. Ordering that hamburger was the major event on Saturday afternoon after working in the cotton field all week. My mother was a great cook and could never understand why I wanted to get a hamburger at a greasy joint and drink those awful soda pops when I could get a chicken salad sandwich and a glass of sweet milk at home.

My memories of food—growing it, preparing it, and eating it—are clearest when remembering family get-togethers, especially during the holiday season. The entire Kelsey family, altogether more than twenty people, plus a few visitors had Thanksgiving and Christmas noon dinners together. We had the same holiday dinner for Thanksgiving and Christmas. Preparations began several days in advance. The biggest turkey available was purchased and released in the backyard with the chickens. One of the big tom's wings was clipped to prevent him from flying over the fence. He was fed generously, and after several days of fattening he was sacrificed the day before Christmas when the men chopped his head off, then plucked and dressed Tom Turkey.

At another Kelsey house, family members prepared big bowls of potatoes, legumes, buttered turnips, creamed onions, creamed sweet potatoes topped with melted marshmallows, and cranberry sauce. Hot rolls, pumpkin pies, pecan pies, and cream puffs were cooked at another house. Fruit cake had been made many days before. Special delicacies included scalloped oysters, celery sticks stuffed with pimento cheese, stuffed olives, pickled onions, spiced peaches, and roasted almonds. A big tray held chocolate fudge, divinity, stuffed dates, and fruit cake cookies. Ambrosia was made with fresh grated coconut and orange segments. As if that wasn't enough there was fruit salad. The custom was to cook every possible dish for these events—a custom going back for generations. Leftovers were good for days. Food was served from the dining table, the side board, and the kitchen. After blessings the senior members ate at the dining table while the others sat around the parlor, living room, and kitchen. Dinner started promptly at noon with lots of talk and lasted until two or three in the afternoon before everyone finished eating, talking, and cleaning up. By this time the kids were all out in the yard throwing a football or playing other games.

I did not lack recreation or entertainment during my childhood. Even after doing homework, numerous chores, and work in the cotton fields during summer, we boys found time for a wide variety of physical outdoor activity. Looking back I realize that I was extremely busy as I grew up, something I was not aware of at the time but that likely began a life pattern. I can't stand being idle and find it difficult to sit and talk or play cards, things I do only if I'm laid up sick in bed.

There were all the children's games still played today such as hide and seek, jump rope, tag, and roller skating. Favorite games at school were snap the whip, jacks, marbles, and shinny. I tried hard at ball games but being left-handed had poor coordination and was younger and smaller than my classmates. We enjoyed scrub baseball, where the player rotated positions until it came his turn to bat. As few as three could play. Outside school I enjoyed mudball fights. We chose partners, made egg-sized balls from the mud on the streets and threw them at each other until the losing team retreated with mud-stained clothes and bruises. We often had Corncob fights on Sunday afternoons in the barn. The combatants chose sides. The defenders collected a bucket full of corncobs and forted up in the barn loft. The attackers besieged the defenders by throwing cobs at them through the barn loft doors. When the defenders ran out of corncobs, the attackers stormed the barn, and the defenders hid in the loft behind bales of hay until they finally surrendered. After a surrender, the teams changed sides and started over. Mudball and corncob fights resulted in some eye injuries.

I participated in other risky activities. Very few people today have heard of shooting off anvils, a dangerous form of celebration dating back to Colonial days. People in the country around Deport shot off anvils on the Fourth of July, Armistice Day, and during the Christmas holidays. An anvil, often weighing more than a hundred pounds, has a hole on the bottom about one cubic inch in size. The holes of two anvils were filled with gun powder. One anvil was then placed upright on the other so that the two holes were opposite each other. A line of gun powder in the form of a fuse was poured from the center of the first anvil and was lit by a torch on the end of a long pole by the anvil shooter, who then would run like hell to get out of the way. The earthshaking explosion could be heard for miles away. The anvil could fly off in any direction. Shooting an anvil crippled for life one of the DeBerry boys from Bogota. Tom DeBerry became a popular and prominent Texas senator in the 1920s and 1930s.

Unless I was kept in as punishment for some mischief or bad grades, I spent nearly every Saturday during the winter hunting with my friends. After graduating from air guns, we each carried a single-shot shotgun, usually 20 gauge, or a .22 caliber single-shot target rifle, we called a target. Ammunition was very expensive. We didn't shoot many tin cans for fun. We were lucky to leave home with four shotgun shells or twenty target shots. We learned to aim well and preferred our game to be sitting. On a rare occasion I'd come in with a kill for every shotgun shell. My friend Ford Baughn was an excellent shot. Eventually he could hit a rabbit running with a .22 rifle. We also hunted doves. I've crawled on my stomach a quarter of a mile to shoot a dove on a barbwire fence and have the bird fly away just as I took aim. Our Saturday hunts lasted all day. We walked miles in the woods and along bois d'arc hedge rows. During our hikes we encountered several ancient Indian campsites, where we collected arrow heads to add to our bag of game. We frequently took a mixed-breed dog to chase rabbits. My uncle Tom Parrott once gave me a Russian wolf hound for that purpose.

Hunting coons and possums at night was also fun. We were usually taken by an older man who had one or more hounds. We'd walk for miles in the woods, then stop to build a fire and tell stories. Occasionally we treed a coon or possum. We often got lost, wandering in circles then emerging from the woods to find a house miles from home; we'd straggle home after daylight. Some boys set traps for coons and possums, skinned them, and stretched the skins over boards to dry. They got a fairly good price for coonskins, which were then used for fur coats popular among college boys.

The local creeks and ponds had many fishing holes. But to really fish we went to Oklahoma with Dad or to Sulphur River about twenty miles away for big catfish caught on a trout line or, illegally, by poisoning or netting. Some intrepid woodsmen swam along under the banks to pull by hand these big cats out of holes. Some catfish weighed forty pounds and could scrape the skin off of a hand put in their mouth. Plenty of big water moccasins also inhabited those holes. Many remember their favorite swimming hole. Mine was about a mile north of Deport on Mustang Creek, but it wasn't much to brag about. The water was about as muddy as it could get. Many boys didn't know how to swim and were ashamed to acknowledge it. They were thrown in, and it was sink or swim. We didn't have formal swimming lessons. My dad taught me to swim in the clear waters of Little River of Oklahoma, where my friends and I spent many days getting thoroughly sunburned.[4]

In addition to the hunting and fishing trips with Dad, I made many other camping journeys. A trip to the Arkansas Ozarks was a favorite excursion for the people who lived on the prairies of Northeast Texas. Many people carried the camping equipment on the running boards and the rear luggage rack of their touring cars. Spare tires, tubes, patching kits and tools were needed to fix the frequent flats and blow outs. Cool drinking water was provided by a desert water bag, tied outside the car to catch the breeze. Water seeping through the canvas bag cooled the contents by evaporation. Mud chains were a must on the unpaved roads. Breakdowns were common, caused by broken axles, blown gaskets, leaking radiators, stripped gears, and drowned-out engines after attempting to ford swollen streams.

Some of the larger towns had campgrounds, but motor courts were few and far apart. We wouldn't think of staying in the luxury hotels of Hot Springs or Eureka Springs. There were boarding houses, but mostly we camped off the roadside in wooded spots near a spring or by a clear running stream, where the children could wade. Dad would set up the tent, unfold the cots and start a fire, while Mother got out the pans and made biscuits and fried bacon and eggs, maybe open a can of corned beef or vegetables, and for dessert pass out homemade cookies. On extended trips we bought fresh fruit and vegetables, ham, pork sausage, or live chickens from farmers or roadside stands.

Among my fondest memories are those of summer vacations in Throckmorton with my mother's family. They lived in town but had ranches in the country. Life there was horse oriented. Everyone in town had horses in the barn. If they wanted to go downtown a quarter mile away, they saddled up and went on horseback. Many boys had a favorite gentle pony on which they'd learn how to ride bareback. There were plenty of hitching posts in this town of nine hundred people. I spent most of my time in Throckmorton with Uncle Gee Parrott's family. There was no one I admired more than his son Jake. He was a year or two younger than I, but even as a teen he was a real cowboy.

As we got older, my friends and I lost interest in outdoor life. Girls were our new interest. Our voices changed, and we got pimples and pubic hair. Conversations were all about sex. At school recess we gathered in a car and listened to the old hands tell about their sexual experiences—or more likely to tell stories that had been told them. Our sex life was limited to talk. We had dates, parked and necked and came home with stone ache. That was about it. In spite of this preoccupation with sex, we did have wholesome fun on dates at picnics and at church and school parties. We wrote notes, gave presents, and went to square dances, on hayrides and horseback rides, and to watermelon and ice cream parties. There were some wonderful mothers and chaperons who let us dance at their houses. Even Mother relented. I fell in love several times.

Our family was very religious and lived by the Ten Commandments. We said our prayers every night. We did not eat a meal without first saying a blessing. The Kelsey family spent much time in the Deport Methodist Church, at Sunday school, the morning church service and sermon, the Sunday night service for adults, and the Epworth League for young people, followed by another service and prayer meeting on Wednesday night. Mother took part in the missionary society, and Dad was a church steward. Covered dish dinners were served at noon on Sunday for various events, such as special services at Easter, Thanksgiving, and Christmas, housewarmings and "poundings" for new pastors, and district meetings. Our family often entertained the parson for dinner and hosted a visiting evangelist who held a revival each night for a week or ten days.

Our Methodist Church usually had a "protracted meeting," or a revival, each summer after the cotton was laid by to await cotton picking season. During this slack period the farmers had time to relax. They would not be dog-tired from field work, and their wives could talk them into driving into town in their shirt sleeves to hear an evangelist. This was the hottest time of summer, and the revivals were held outdoors or in the Deport open tabernacle. The tabernacle had a corrugated iron roof and was enclosed by wire netting so the breeze could get in but the chickens could not. Sometimes revivals were held on the back lawn of the Methodist Church. Palm leaf fans advertising Garrett's and Rooster snuff were passed out. The residing pastor often held the revival or an out of town evangelist was engaged who had a reputation for bringing souls to the Lord. Rarely, a famous traveling evangelist came through who was crusading through the state or region. This type always attracted huge crowds.

Local talent furnished the music, with Kelsey family musicians in the forefront. Songs included, "Amazing Grace," "Nearer My God to Thee," and

"Come to the Church in the Wildwood." The evangelist preached a roaring hellfire-and-damnation sermon, telling about the wages of sin. To me, he made God and the Devil real people. After his sermon, the evangelist softened his voice and pleaded for us to come forward and confess. There were a sizable number in the congregation who had already confessed or perhaps felt they had never sinned. They looked around to see if the backsliders or sinners, whom everyone knew, were coming forward. Sometimes one or two would leave their seats and descend on a helpless sinner and badger him to come forward and confess—or simply take him by the arms and lead him forward. Some wary husbands would not sit on the benches with their wives but stood in the background. When they heard the call to confess these husbands quietly disappeared in the darkness, probably to catch hell from their wives later on the way home.

My parents made me go to all these revivals. Boys my age sat together off to the side. Some of the young people especially were responsive to the entreaties of the evangelists. Mahlon Grant always answered the call promptly, and eventually the other boys were coaxed down the aisle. My sister Virginia said I always followed Mahlon down to the altar, which amused her a great deal. As I got older, and went to college at age sixteen and when my friends and I could get a car, we would sneak out and drive around trying to find a date or drive out in the country to find a square dance or buy a fruit jar of home brew. We liked to observe Holy Roller revivals. They were held in an open tent on the outskirts of town by the charismatic Nazarene Church, whose members would express their religious fervor in unknown tongues and roll on the hay-covered dirt floor. I never knew where these people came from, but they did muster large crowds. Today this is a popular church but has shed most of its "charisma."

My mother and her parents never touched alcohol. My grandfather J. B. Kelsey also opposed the use of alcohol and tobacco. He thought it was a sin to drink and that tobacco destroyed your health. But he made "nectar" by placing fresh peaches, mustang grapes, or blackberries in a five gallon crock and covering the fruit with sugar. A cloth was placed over the crock, which was put in the cool storm cellar to ferment for weeks or months. This produced a sweet syrupy fruit flavored drink containing a little alcohol. It was served to everyone including children during holidays. No one sipped more than an ounce. It was a custom, probably passed down in the family for generations, that other Deport families also followed. The nectar was not considered an alcoholic drink, just a tonic, but Mother wouldn't touch it.

For the most part, I followed my parents' advice and avoided alcohol, until I entered college.[5] In bull sessions our admirable and experienced upperclassmen liked to tell about how great it felt to get tight and how much fun they had at drinking parties. Finally someone offered me a swallow of white lighting. It was magic. In a few minutes I was on a great high, loud and silly. I think that first intoxication was 90 percent imagination, something I had plenty of. Later, as medical students during Prohibition, we made home brew and bought bootleg whiskey and grain alcohol to make gin. After the Volstead Act was repealed while I was still in medical school, we could get plenty of good beer and blended whiskey, my favorite being Old Quaker. Without any sense of guilt, I was disobeying a rule in our family that stood for generations. I continued to drink without my parents' knowledge, sometimes too much.

Beginning in the 1920s cigarettes were widely advertised and women soon started smoking, even in public. The tobacco industry lead people to believe that smoking was a harmless relaxing recreation. Hostesses put out cigarettes, matches, and ash trays. Cigarette boxes, ash trays, and cigarette lighters were favorite presents. This went on unabated for fifty years, until the public finally was convinced that smoking caused lung cancer.

I started smoking a little in high school. Dad smoked a pipe and wasn't upset when he learned that I smoked occasionally. Mother thought it was terrible. I thought I was smart to smoke and chew tobacco. Older guys did it. I learned to roll my own cigarettes, using a little cigarette rolling device. We liked to go around with a Bull Durham label hanging out of our shirt pocket with a ready roll cigarette hanging from our lips. As a college senior and a medical school senior, I demonstrated my dignity and maturity by smoking a pipe. I quit smoking years later, while president of the Harris County Cancer Society. Once, the society held a luncheon at the Houston Club, and I sat at the head table smoking. After the meeting, a lady came up to me and criticized me for smoking at the head table while president. I quit and haven't smoked since, except for a puff from a cigar to celebrate a friend becoming a father.

Chewing tobacco was a tougher habit to learn. The first chew tasted terrible and made me vomit. But I toughened up and learned to chew and squirt tobacco juice in the cotton patch. Thick Tinsley and Thin Tinsley were two popular brands. Thin Tinsley was strong as a mule's hind leg. Brown's Mule was another brand, equally strong. I never chewed after I went to college, except when studying for finals at A&M and Galveston. Chewing tobacco to stay awake and study was a long established custom. A country boy had to show that he could handle it.

I started college in 1929, the year the Great Depression began. During the depths of this country's severest economic crisis, my parents—at great effort—

sent all of us through college without interruption. We are forever grateful to them for their sacrifices for us. As I look back on those days I realize that only a loving mother and father could tolerate the many crazy, selfish, thoughtless things I did, yet still make the sacrifices to give me an education. Their efforts made my life better: my parents gave me a career in medicine which I enjoyed for fifty years before a lengthy busy retirement.

CHAPTER 3

Texas Agricultural and Mechanical College, 1929–32

The Great Depression was devastating to the majority of Americans, but it was not as bad for those who were frugal, raised most of their own food, and lived close to the earth as we did. We were also fortunate to have an additional source of income. My mother was getting a check each month from oil wells on the E. T. Parrott ranch. In the early 1920s, the Throckmorton ranches of Uncle Dick Parrott, grandfather E. T. Parrott's brother, became valuable oil fields. In 1926 our family drove out to Throckmorton to watch a gusher. We stood closely around the well. I asked why we didn't stand back because we would be drenched with oil. The answer was, "I hope we get drenched in oil. If this is a gusher, we can get new clothes." We were disappointed; the well was dry. Before E. T. died, he made a provision in his will that income from oil found on his ranch which adjoined that of Uncle Dick would be divided: half to his widow and the remainder split equally among his children. Up to twenty wells were producing at one time; some were gushers. The Parrotts went through some flush times. Mother got a significant royalty check each month for years, which helped put her three children through college, eventually making doctors of my brother and me.[1]

Not so many country people went to college when I was young. My grandparents and parents had received varying amounts of college education, and both grandmothers had taught school. It was taken for granted that I would go to college. Dad wanted me to go to the University of Texas at Austin and take premedical courses. He registered me and even got a dormitory room assignment. My choice for college, however, was Texas Agricultural and Mechanical College (A&M) at College Station. I thought a military college was by far the greatest thing. Uniforms, marching, parades! Cousin Madison Wright from Throckmorton was going there. Finally, Dad relented and helped me apply at A&M. The 1929 catalogue listed the fixed expenses for an annual session, paid in advance—no checks—as follows:

maintenance, per term	*$125.00*
room rent, per term	*30.00*
matriculation fee	*17.00*
medical service fee	*10.00*
refundable room key deposit	*1.00*
	$338.00

Additional expenses included:

approximate laboratory fees	*$10.00*
text books	*15.00–25.00*
student activity fee (voluntary)	*15.00*
post office box rent (voluntary)	*.50*
physical training	*3.75*

Maintenance included room, board, heat, light, and laundry. Rooms were furnished for each student with a single bedstead (overhead bunk for two roommates), mattress, linens, a table, and chairs. The matriculation fee included use of the library. The medical service fee covered the professional services of the college physician and the hospital staff. The student activity fee entitled the student to attend all intercollegiate contests held at College Station and to receive a copy of the *Longhorn,* the college annual, and the *Battalion,* the weekly college newspaper.

When it came time to leave home for college, Mother got all my things together and packed them in the trunk she had used when she went to Polytechnic. She also prepared a shoebox lunch with fried chicken for me to eat on the train. Dad took me to Paris and checked my trunk through to College Station. Mother and Dad were concerned about whether I could change trains in Dallas. I rode the Cotton Belt to Dallas and changed without incident to the Houston and Texas Central for College Station. In 1929, such a train trip was a major adventure for a sixteen-year-old country boy. I got off the train at College Station in September and found my way to the registrar's office in the Main Building (today, the Academic Building). I requested and was assigned to ROTC Troop D Cavalry in the new Puryear Hall dormitory. I was advised to go back to the station, borrow a Railway Express baggage cart and haul my trunk up to my dormitory.

The school required reserve officer training for the first two years. I bought my uniform at the Exchange Store. Only foreign, graduate, and disabled students were not required to dress in the regulation uniform approved by the professor of Military Science and Tactics. This included a complete woolen uniform with an extra pair of breeches; three o.d. (olive drab) shirts, at least two of which had to be woolen; a white dress shirt; a waist belt; one suit of unionalls; a black tie; two pairs of leather leggings; one pair of service shoes; one cap with insignia; one cavalry hat with a yellow silk cord; one Sam Browne belt; insignia for shirt collar and coat; and four ROTC shields. The complete uniform, which cost $85.00, was economical, we were told: if we took good care, we could wear these clothes all the way through college. Seniors needed riding boots and a saber.

The history and physical setting of Texas A&M played an important role in determining the college's character. The Morrill Act of 1861 donated public lands to the states to provide for colleges for the benefit of agriculture and mechanic arts. In 1871, the Texas legislature established the Agricultural and Mechanical College of Texas and appropriated $75,000 for buildings. The legislature issued script for 180,000 acres of land to raise $174,000 for investment in gold bonds, constituting the original endowment for the college. One year later, the college was located in Brazos County, in the country on a site of 2,416 acres of land donated to the state by the citizens of the county. The Missouri and Pacific and the Southern Pacific Railroads traversed the property. Railroad stations were constructed and the stop was named College Station. The town and post office that grew up around the campus also took that name. The Texas Constitution of 1876 contained provisions for the support and regulation of A&M. By September of that year, the Main Building and Gathright Hall had been completed, and the first students entered on October 4, 1876.[2]

When I arrived, on a large open lawn in front of the Main Building stood the bugle stand and the bronze monument of former school president Lawrence S. Ross sculpted by Pompeo Coppini. To the right of the Main Building was Guion Hall, a handsome building in the classical revival style that seated about three thousand people on the main floor and large balcony. On the back wall of the stage was a huge flag, a gift of the U.S. Government commemorating the Aggies who fought in World War I. There was one star for each Aggie who served. In a center panel of the flag was a gold star for each Aggie who had given his life in the war. Many formal meetings occurred in Guion Hall, including graduation ceremonies for my class. Unfortunately, Guion Hall was later razed to make way for the Rudder Building. The school lost an architectural treasure when Guion Hall was destroyed.

Bernard Sbisa Hall, or the mess hall, was built in 1912 and expanded in 1926 to seat more than 2,750. All campus students were required to eat there. The college had its own dairy that supplied Sbisa Hall with sweetmilk, buttermilk, cottage cheese, and ice cream. The dairy also supplied the town of College Station. The Military Walk, extending from Guion Hall to Sbisa Hall with numerous buildings on each side, created a dramatic view when the Aggies paraded to meals. Other important structures on the main campus housed studies for agriculture, veterinary medicine, horticulture, textile and petroleum engineering, military science and armory, and civil, electrical, and mechanical engineering. The A&M band, one hundred strong, lived in Goodwin Hall, facing the drill field. Famous for its precision drills during halftime at football games, the band also played for important social and military occasions, gave open air concerts, lead the corps in marching to the mess hall or to Guion Hall for chapel, and played at dress parade.

Extensive athletic facilities on the southwest quadrant of the campus included the newly constructed Kyle Field (1927–29), seating over thirty-three thousand people, the Memorial Gymnasium (1924) for basketball, seating three thousand, and the Baseball Grandstand (1923). All students were expected to attend all athletic events, and all were required to take physical education. I took wrestling, boxing, handball, volleyball, mile running, and golf at various times. Frank Anderson was director of athletics and taught me in one physical education class. At one time during a controversy about hazing, he was the commandant of cadets, and the students tried to get him fired because he was enforcing the prohibition of hazing. There could not have been a kinder man, more dedicated to the welfare of A&M. I renewed his acquaintance when his son Frank Jr., studied medicine and trained at the Mayo Clinic. Frank Jr., later worked at the Kelsey-Seybold Clinic for a few years before returning to College Station to practice.

Across the railroad tracks from the main campus were 350 acres of agricultural facilities. A large creamery, where students bought ice cream, sat close to the railroad stations. There were poultry, cattle, horse, swine, sheep, and goat barns and lots, as well as the cavalry barracks, horse pens, and equitation halls for ROTC and a large cavalry drill field. Beyond the barns were various experimental orchards, gardens, and fields and several thousand acres of fine farm land extending toward the Brazos River, six miles from the main campus.

College Station did not have an airfield while I was a student. Planes landed in a pasture or on the cavalry drill field. I always wanted to ride in a plane. When an airplane flew over Deport, people ran outside to look at it. I had never been up close to an airplane until a barnstorming single-engine, two-seat biplane came to College Station. Word spread rapidly that the pilot was selling rides, so I ran out to the pasture and got in line. When my turn came I paid the pilot a few dollars for a short flight over the campus. Little did I know then that I would become a flight surgeon in a world war and later fly all over the world in commercial planes carrying several hundred people.

About 1930, the Fireman's Training School was instituted. Firemen came from all over the state and stayed in vacant dormitories during the summer. While in summer school in 1931, I was standing at the West Gate to hitch a ride to Bryan. Two women drove up in a Ford roadster with a rumble seat. I started to get in the back, when the women informed me they were prostitutes and were not offering me a free ride. They seemed eager to talk and told me they were single mothers from Waco in town for the Fireman's School. They were making a lot of money from the firemen to buy nice things for their little ones. They were not alone in this enterprise.

Texas A&M had been preparing students for medical school since the college began. Although designed for agriculture and engineering students, the school emphasized biology, chemistry, physics, and mathematics, providing ideal curricula for the study of medicine. In 1924, Arts and Science was organized as a separate department with a degree program. For years the faculty and administration had worried that cultural subjects had been neglected. Many students came to A&M with limited opportunity for cultural development: the college was isolated in the country and agriculture and engineering studies did not require cultural subjects. In an effort to overcome this weakness, the faculty required basic courses in English, history, and public speaking for all students.

What little A&M offered in the liberal arts was good. The few English professors there were competent and highly motivated. Thomas Mayo, an Oxford graduate in English literature, read poetry every afternoon in the billiard room at the YMCA. Professor Mayo was instrumental in building the Cushing Memorial Library. When he became library director there were only fifteen thousand books, today there are more than four million. He also organized the Juntos Club in 1925. This was an informal group of faculty and students who met regularly at a faculty house. Professor Mayo must have seen me spending much time in the library—or observed how I needed more exposure to culture—because he invited me to be a member. The club promoted literary and philosophical discussions between students and faculty in an informal setting. Usually about twenty people attended. At the time, a popular subject for discussion was improving the human race through eugenics. We reviewed the works of Friedrich Nietzsche, George Bernard Shaw, and Henrik Ibsen. We discussed the controversial subject of group medical practice. For a doctor to join such a practice, at the time, was to violate the ethics of the

American Medical Association. Our debates on this issue stayed with me and influenced my thinking on the role of clinical practice in the medical profession.

Academic standards at A&M were high. Students' grades were reported to parents and study hours enforced. Soon after supper each night, the students had to be in their rooms studying until lights went out at 11:00 P.M. There was no wandering in the halls, and students were not disturbed by visitors. Upperclassmen maintained discipline in the dormitories, discipline being one of the few benefits of hazing. Another fine tradition was for students to help others who were having trouble with classes. By the time students became juniors and seniors, they were supposed to have developed good study habits and had freedom of movement during study hours. We went to classes five-and-a-half days a week. We had few school holidays and no spring break. Professors strongly discouraged absences and took poor attendance into account when grading. Absences had to be made up, and too many resulted in a failing grade. Good grades brought honor points, and a student who made sixty or more grade points in a year became a "Distinguished Student." Rules for graduation required that a student make more than half his grades above a C.

I registered for the School of Science program. During the first year I studied general zoology and learned the various phyla of the animal kingdom and dissected type specimens in the laboratory. In my sophomore year I studied comparative vertebrate zoology and learned the anatomy of chordates and the progressive development and evolution of the organ systems. This course was most helpful in medical school for studying embryology and congenital defects. In summer school I took introductory bacteriology, which included busy laboratory work in staining, microscopic technique, and identification of bacteria. While taking this course, I was given a part time job that included cleaning the glassware—but there was a real fun part to the job. I went with the professor to the area farms to test well water for bacterial contaminants.

In the third year I took general physiology. I also took courses in entomology and parasitology in the science department and the School of Veterinary Medicine. The veterinarians said I was the first premed student to apply for a course at their school. They gave me special attention, and I learned a lot. At the end of my sophomore year I had accumulated many grade points. I realized that if I attended summer school I could easily graduate in three years. At that time one could be accepted in medical school with only two years of college, if the premedical course requirements had been met. However, I felt that having a Bachelor of Science degree was much better than scraping through with minimal requirements. My professors encouraged me to pursue a three-year graduation track, and the dean approved my plan.

For the summer, I rented space in a large room over the college pharmacy and shared it with three or four other students. During summer school I took genetics and eugenics under Drs. Humbert, Horlacher, and Godby. These courses were especially interesting to me, given that we had debated the issue of genetically improving the human race at the Juntos Club. Francis Galton, who coined the term eugenics, was not the first to advocate improving the human race by selective breeding. Belief in the hereditary aspects of human behavior and intelligence has been long held, and the discoveries of Mendel and Darwin encouraged geneticists to search for proof of behavioral heredity. As examples, in the 1920s, musical ability and temperament were thought to be controlled by single genes. These human traits were subjected to statistical study, while intensive breeding experiments were carried out on fruit flies, mice, dogs, and other animals seeking a genetic basis for behavior. Eugenics was thus a popular subject before Hitler attempted to eradicate the Jews and develop Germany into a super race. The resulting Holocaust revealed the dangers of eugenics. The study of genetics at college, however, proved valuable to me—and was the only formal education on the subject I ever had. My knowledge of genetics, although limited, has helped me understand hereditary diseases. The more we learn about genetics, the more we realize its importance.

I took several chemistry courses that also proved useful. The first was a year of inorganic chemistry, to be followed by courses in qualitative and quantitative analysis and physical chemistry, a new course in a new chemistry building. Here I learned about pH and ionization, helping me understand the body electrolytes. My chemistry professors included M. T. Harrington, a young man at the time who would have an outstanding career at A&M, becoming head of the chemistry department and eventually president of the college. We renewed our acquaintance years later when we were on the Development Council of the A&M library. I took one term in general psychology in the agricultural administration department and college physics for the entire second year. Math courses included algebra, trigonometry and geometry.

I also had to fulfill my liberal arts requirements. The college did not accept my high school English credit, and I'm sure my deficiency in that subject was noticeable to students and professors. Nevertheless, I had passed the entrance exam. At A&M I studied rhetoric and composition for a year and then took several courses in English literature, public speaking, argumentation, contemporary literature, and commercial correspondence. Professor Mayo taught a course in contemporary literature, covering the most significant British and American novelists, poets, and dramatists after 1800. I chose two years of German and had only one required history course. To fill out my curriculum, I also took several elective courses outside of science—some said to be crip courses—such as commercial law, insurance, corporate finance, money and banking, economics, and sociology. One of my physical education subjects was boxing. As a boy in Deport, I was always getting in fights with older, bigger boys. I wanted to know how to protect myself.

Aside from my studies, a good part of my three years at Texas A&M involved my activities with the Reserve Officer Training Corps (ROTC). At A&M the ROTC had control of student discipline and life outside the classroom. The line of authority resulted from an agreement between the college administration and the U.S. Army. The army provided a contingent of tactical officers, personnel, equipment, and financial support to operate an ROTC program for every able bodied student at A&M. The commandant of the Corps of Cadets was assigned very broad authority, including disciplinary procedures. Any furlough—a permit to leave the campus for a day or more—had to be approved by Colonel Nelson, the commandant when I was an undergraduate. These requests had to be signed by a parent. Sometimes cadets forged their parents' signature, a cause for expulsion. Colonel Nelson was irritated by the numerous requests to leave early for corps trips. He was famous for saying that if there was a corps trip to hell many students would apply to leave for it early.

The hierarchy of discipline passed from the commandant through his tactical officers to the cadet staff officers to cadet company or troop officers and, finally, to the individual cadets in their dormitories. Not needing house mothers, the students disciplined themselves. The cadet officers were required to maintain discipline. This system, also found at the U.S. military academies and at state supported military schools such as the Virginia Military Institute and the Citadel in South Carolina, taught leadership and responsibility to those who moved up in the ranks. It also relieved the administration of many disciplinary chores. The commandant, through the ROTC, directed the daily life of the cadets. The bugler woke the students with reveille every morning and put them to bed every night with taps. Every movement of the student body was scheduled. The bugle blew to fall into formation and march to Sbisa Hall for every meal, to assemble for drill, or to march to chapel. In short, we lived by sound of the bugle.

On Sunday morning we had room inspection. The cadet senior officers and the regular army officers marched into our rooms like Prussians, scowled, and ran their white-gloved hands over the door and window sills looking for dust. They checked our bunks to be certain they were made according to regulation. The officers inspected our uniforms to be sure they were neat, with shoes shining and brass buttons polished. We stood at rigid attention answering their questions with a crisp "Yes Sir!" or "No Sir!" and tried to get as few demerits (rams) as possible. Once or twice a week we had intensive drill and learned to march in perfect formation, carrying our rifles and answering commands in unison. We had to be in top shape so that we could parade the streets of Dallas, Fort Worth, or Austin during football season. In 1930, we went to Fort Worth to play TCU. The trip was highly publicized in the *Battalion*. The railroad round trip ticket was $3.00. Almost the entire student body arose early, got into dress uniform, marched in formation to the station and boarded. We filled an entire train of passenger cars, maybe two trainloads. We arrived in Fort Worth, disembarked, got into formation and paraded through downtown Fort Worth, led by the Aggie Band. There were thousands of spectators—we were very proud.

Many an Aggie experienced sex for the first time during a corps trip. Prostitutes did a land office business providing an initiation into manhood. In Dallas, I was among the cadets who went to see a girlie movie and hear a lecture on topics such as how to get a prophylactic, how to make your date want to have sex, and how to perform. Shown in one of the less respectable movie houses, with barkers outside to promote it, the entire program was extremely disappointing. Today, I can see more explicit programs on television every night.

We in the four cavalry troops considered ourselves to be the elite. In 1929–30, we were housed in Law and Puryear Halls. We had distinguishing uniforms and special facilities—horses, barns, riding halls, and barracks for enlisted cavalry soldiers. The cavalry summer camp was the most desirable of all, down on the Mexican border at Fort Clark, near Bracketville. I missed summer camp when I dropped out of the ROTC to graduate in three years. The four cavalry troops were supervised by regular army cavalry major John Wheeler, Captain Isaac Walker and two or three lieutenants. We were issued Springfield army rifles that we kept in our rooms and used at drill. We kept them shining clean. All freshmen were privates. One in eight privates was made corporal the second year. I was fortunate to be promoted to this exalted rank. All seniors not in military science were second lieutenants. I also held this exalted rank.

The greatest fun was equitation. I soon learned that meant learning to ride horseback. Every week we went to the cavalry stables, where a tough sergeant taught us how to ride in the rough old army saddles on hard-mouthed big rugged horses. Fortunately, the horses were well broken. We learned how to control the horse's gait, to post, to jump, to ride in formation, to form the rifle troop, and to conduct fire. We learned care of the horse and saddlery and the use and care of the saber, machine rifle, and pistol. Many of the students were West Texas cowboys who could ride a bucking bronco but had trouble posting and jumping. During mounted drill, pranksters liked to goose your horse out of formation. Loosening another cadet's cinch strap was grounds for expulsion.

I liked my regular army tactical officers, with the exception of one captain, a strict and humorless man who walked with a clipped gait, gave sharp commands, and issued many rams for minor infractions. For my senior year, my Dad bought me some custom-made light colored slacks, called pinks, of which I was very proud. As soon as I strutted out on campus in my new pinks I was spied by this captain, who stopped me and said my slacks weren't regulation. He ordered me to go back to my room and change. I protested that seniors were wearing pinks all over the campus. He replied that it was not regulation in the cavalry, and he would not allow it. I tried to wear my fine pants on a corps trip where this captain wouldn't see me, but darned if I didn't run into him on the street. He gave me a thorough dressing down and a bunch of rams. I had to give up wearing my beloved pinks. I finally wore them out as hunting clothes.

The disciplinary system that flowed through the ROTC had its good and bad points. The 1932 catalogue expressed the good: "Every student is expected at all times to conform to the ordinary rules of gentlemanly conduct: to be truthful; to respect the rights of others; to be punctual and regular in attendance upon all required exercises; to apply himself diligently to his studies; and to have regard for the preservation of college property." Students were not permitted to keep motor vehicles. The upperclassmen taught us to be neat in appearance, greet everyone, look people in the eye and introduce one's self with a smile and a firm handshake, and to be polite and helpful to others, especially while hitchhiking—the principle mode of transportation for cadets off campus.

The bad part was hazing. Many students in authority over underclassmen did not know how to restrain themselves, and they abused the privilege. This led to an entrenched system of abuse. Hazing came to a head at A&M in 1910. A student was dismissed for placing burning sulphur near a sleeping cadet, resulting in serious burns to the victim. During the next four years many students were expelled, twenty-three at one time in January 1913, and others were put on probation for hazing. The faculty took a strong stand against hazing because it disrupted study. Governor Calquitt warned the college about numerous complaints from irate parents. Even so, 466 students signed a petition demanding reinstatement of the twenty-three dismissed students. The faculty struck the names of the 466 petitioners from the college rolls because, in their petition, the students admitted hazing. The student body then went on strike, refusing to go to class. About 150 of the 466 students who were dismissed went home. The others claimed they were persuaded or coerced to sign the petition and were allowed to stay. Classes resumed. This was not the last hazing scandal at A&M. Others occurred in 1928, 1930, 1932, 1937, 1942, and later. One boy drowned in a hazing episode. Texas newspapers published letters from irate parents, and more students were dismissed. Alumni were divided on the issue.[3]

Enrollment, which had been about 4000 students in the mid-twenties, had dropped significantly by the time I had begun school in 1929.[4] In that year the senior class numbered only 393. As I entered A&M, I did not know that there was a public outcry about hazing. The complaints certainly had not reduced hazing when I arrived. The upperclassmen had their boards or paddles prominently displayed on their walls. The boards were varnished and decorated with A&M emblems, class years, and unit designations. Any tactical officer could see them during inspection. I mounted my own board on the wall when I became a sophomore. I had my butt thoroughly beaten black and blue many times in my freshman year, and even a few times in my sophomore year. The safest, least painful, way to take a beating was to stand almost straight up and hold the buttocks as tight as possible. Most of the hazing was done by a very few sadists who inflicted their cruelty on defenseless "fish." Being a fish amounted to serving as an upperclassman's housekeeper and valet. The fish cleaned the upperclassman's room, made his bed, and ran his errands. He delivered his mail and delivered him a Coke or ice cream before taps. Some upperclassmen were very demanding and kept the fish from his own studies. There was a rule, however, that no fish would polish an upperclassman's shoes or boots.

I got very mad at some upperclassmen and swore revenge but never carried it out except on Fish Day. Then the roles were reversed, and fish could order upperclassmen around and punish them. Another practice was "drowning out," a way of revenge if you could put it over. When someone became very unpopular for being too harsh, one or more students would sneak into his room in the dead of night and suddenly dash several buckets of water on the sleeping villain. The trick was to race back to your bunk and pretend to be asleep. Next morning some sheets would be seen hanging out the victim's window to dry. If too many upperclassmen were being drowned out, they would "air out" the fish by getting them out of bed and marching them sometimes as far as the Brazos River, about six miles away. Or the upperclassmen would have an "Ass Tear": all the fish would be lined up in the dormitory hall, and each upperclassman would give each fish a swat. Some upperclassmen gave you a light tap while others would try to "knock your butt off." There were many upperclassmen who did little or no hazing, however. I was lucky enough to be the fish for Cadet Captain Mark Focke who never administered more than a gesture of hazing. We became good friends. When I became a sophomore, Bob Rutledge was my fish. I hope I was as kind to him as Mark Focke was to me.[5]

A&M had dozens of other traditions that could not be violated. The annual muster, for example, had its beginning in 1903 when the students organized an annual ceremony to celebrate the Battle of San Jacinto on April 21. On that day, students would also pay homage to all A&M men who died in the preceding year. At muster, some living comrade would answer "here" for the departed Aggie when the roll was called. I attended a muster at the Brown Convention Center in Houston in 1990, when 1,500 attended. Hundreds of musters go on all over the world. The musters have brought Aggies together on the battlefronts of many wars.[6]

The bonfire on the campus the night before the football game between A&M and the University of Texas also began in the early twentieth century, in 1908. Originally, small bonfires were built on cold nights for students to stand around and keep warm the night before a football game. Apparently, around 1928, the Texas game became the "official" reason for a bonfire. I remember yell practice in front of a small bonfire built of accumulated trash in 1929. I don't remember seeing a privy in the fire, but they did appear later, along with dismantled chicken houses. Many a local farmer was outraged when his outbuildings disappeared to be sacrificed on the bonfire. Numerous other traditions related to Southwest Conference football games. School spirit ran high before ball games. Fist fights were common. In 1926, during the Baylor–A&M game at Waco, a riot erupted between Baylor and A&M students on the field at halftime. An A&M student was killed. Cadets in the field artillery wanted to move their cannons to Waco and level Baylor University. When I was a freshman, this tragedy was the subject of much conversation. No football game was held with Baylor for two years while tempers cooled off.

There must be hundreds of nicknames for all the objects, events, and attitudes at A&M. The most colorful are for mess hall food. I remember my first few meals in Sbisa Hall: I wasn't fast enough to get any food, and I didn't know how to ask for what was available. The waiters quickly passed out several platters of each item on the menu. The fastest students, or mealhounds, were the first to grab a huge serving before passing the platter. There was plenty of food, but the favorite dishes didn't make it around. I was appalled at the gluttony, but soon learned about the survival of the fittest. I didn't lose any weight. Rabbit was salad; dope was coffee; reg was syrup; spuds were potatoes; bull neck was meat; cow was milk; cush was dessert; and grease was butter. Gunwadding was bread; Dad had learned that term at Texas Military Academy and liked to tease Mother by asking for gunwadding, the light bread she so proudly made.

I had entered A&M just one month before the October 1929 stock market collapse and panic on Wall Street. Although I was more fortunate than many college students because my parents paid my entire way through, I was still on a very tight budget. I'm sure my allowance was a very few dollars for each year. I hitchhiked home for the holidays to save money. Hundreds of A&M boys were working their way through. The 1929 catalogue announced that the college would hire as many students as possible, but no student should expect more than forty dollars a term. I found various paying jobs at A&M to supplement the small allowance Dad gave me, but I didn't bother to tell him I was making extra money. The first job I remember was selling peanuts at the 1929 A&M–Texas Thanksgiving football game. I had read a "Peanut Sellers Wanted" sign on a bulletin board and reported to a stand under the new Kyle Field stadium. Several fellow students were given a shoulder bag filled with paper sacks of roasted peanuts. I walked all over the stadium selling sack after sack. By the end of the game my pockets were stuffed with money. I was dog-tired. I went to cash in my profits, but when I got through paying for the peanuts I was five dollars in debt. Such a disappointment! I don't know whether I lost the money, got short changed, or had my peanuts stolen.

I had an interesting job copying music for "Doc" Samuel E. Asbury, one of the all time great personalities at A&M. Born in 1875, Doc Asbury came to A&M in the early 1900s as a chemist, but his life revolved around his love of poetry, music, drama, and Texas history. He was recognized as an authority in each of these fields. Doc combined his knowledge in an effort to produce what he told me was an opera based on Texas history. He began working on the Battle of San Jacinto, but he soon decided to have dramas of eight events performed simultaneously on different stages in historically correct sequence. For example, the Battle of the Alamo would be performed on one stage while the meeting that went on in Washington on the Brazos would be performed on another stage. Eventually Doc Asbury had architectural plans drawn for his "composition house," an octagonal building with a stage in each section for the simultaneous performance. The only audience would be the actors themselves. When I started working for him he had written a master score and had employed students to make a total of eight copies. There were usually two or three student copyists, each copying a separate score. I didn't know how to read music, however. Doc Asbury told me just to copy exactly what I saw. His little house was on the north side of campus and was covered with vines on the outside, the inside stuffed with books and phonograph records. There were several pianos, and pictures covered the walls and the ceilings. There was a table large enough for three of us to copy. I heard later that his opera was never performed but his papers were preserved in the Asbury Room of the library.

In my sophomore and senior years I waited tables in Sbisa Hall as a "Sbisa Volunteer," in return for meals and possibly some small wage. I wore a white serving jacket and learned to race through a crowd, balancing over my head a huge metal tray loaded with several platters of food. I had very few crashes, spilling food and platters over a wide area of students. We waiters lined up at food counters in the giant kitchen and loaded our trays for delivery to the long tables, each seating about twenty boys. I remember watching the lightning fast chefs flip hot cakes by the hundreds on the huge grills. Serving twenty-five hundred hungry boys a hot meal in less than an hour was a miracle that happened three times a day. That made Mr. Sbisa famous.

All of these activities—jobs, ROTC training, and studies—kept me too busy to do much else, which was a good thing, because I was prone to get in trouble. During summer school, I lived with some students who had a Model T. The car got us into criminal mischief—if we want to excuse ourselves that way. We slipped into garages and siphoned gasoline out of cars at night. At a dance in Brenham we jacked up the wheels of a car and removed the rims with the tires. We were lucky not to get caught. No wonder there was a strict rule against students owning cars. Another group of us had a bad habit of nocturnal chicken theft. We preyed on the neighboring farmers, who in those days didn't use shotguns to discourage intruders. We also climbed the fences of the poultry farm and stole some of the prize breeding hens. We took our game into the woods, built a campfire, and feasted on grilled chicken. I think these chicken roasts were inspired by my boyhood campfires on rabbit hunts.

I had other outdoor adventures as well. My troopmate and one time room-mate "Buck" Moore lived in Oakwood, Leon County, which was a stop on the railroad about a hundred miles from College Station. Several Aggies in that part of the state used to "ride the blinds" of the passenger trains to their hometown. I made a couple of these nighttime trips with Buck to spend a weekend with his parents. The blinds between passenger cars had hand and foot holds, so railroad tramps and Aggies would run and jump on after the train had started, often unseen by the conductor. In those days, a two or three car "local" would stop at every village, where we were usually caught and run off, but we invariably got right back on. I remember one trip when the engineer and conductor got tired of chasing us off, so they stopped the train out in the country, alongside a road, so we could hitchhike in. While they were searching for us, Buck and I slipped into one of the passenger coaches and took seats. The windows were open, and we could hear the conductor and engineer talking outside: "Where did those boys go? We can't find them. They must have gone to the road. Go start the train. I'll keep them off and catch on when the train is moving." Soon the conductor came down the aisle taking tickets from the amused passengers. He looked at us with surprise and disgust. We told him we wanted to buy a ticket to Oakwood. The other passengers laughed, and finally the conductor joined in and sold Buck and me tickets priced for the remainder of the mileage to Oakwood.

I survived that and many other escapades. Eventually, on June 4, 1932, at age nineteen, I received a Bachelor of Science degree with a major in biology from Texas A&M. I was on the list of those eligible for valedictorian, an honor elected by the senior class. I didn't attend the voting and may not have received a single vote. I marched in the final review at graduation but I was not especially excited about graduating. My classmates considered me sort of an interloper who belonged in the class of '33, a nineteen-year-old kid assuming senior privileges. Even my family did not come down. I was so intent on medical school that college graduation was only a step.

Earlier, our premed club had talked Raymond Berry, our biology professor, into taking us to Galveston to see the University of Texas Medical School. About six or eight of us were allowed a furlough and went down on the train. Professor Berry had arranged for us to meet Dean George Bethel, who gave us an encouraging talk about the virtues of being a doctor. Then we were shown through the medical school laboratories, including the anatomy lab where medical students were dissecting human bodies. On the train going down to Galveston, premed student Jim Little, who lived in the country six miles out of Gilmer, told us he had never been in a town with an elevator and he wanted to ride one. During our tour we went to see the inside of the new outpatient building, starting on the top floor. Our little group gathered in front of the elevator, all waiting to see how Jim would react. We got on together and the operator closed the door, turned his lever, and up we went. Jim seemed pleased. As we ascended Jim remarked, "Hell this ain't nothing!" Soon after our trip to Galveston I applied there for medical school and was accepted.[7]

After graduation, I packed my belongings in Mother's old trunk, borrowed a Railway Express cart, as I had when I arrived at A&M in 1929, and pulled the trunk to the railroad station to ship it home. I hitchhiked all night, arriving home in Deport the next morning to show my diploma to Mother and Dad. I spent the summer of 1932, like the previous ones, taking care of my cotton crop and doing common labor. I worked for a Deport contractor building a new brick house. I remember pushing wheelbarrows full of wet concrete in the hot sun to build the foundation and slab—at least until Mahlon Grant and I decided to hitchhike to California.

People always listen in disbelief when I tell them about riding a freight train to California in 1932 to see the Olympics I didn't see. That summer was one of the hottest on record, with temperatures over 100°F. day after day. My friend

Mahlon Grant and I decided to hitchhike to Los Angeles to see the Games. Our parents did not approve. They wouldn't even take us to Paris [Texas] to get on the highway. We stood together on Deport's Main Street with our small bags containing a change of clothes. We each had about $100 but we tucked $50 in bills inside one shoe so it couldn't be stolen.

Hitchhiking went fairly well but I no longer had the advantage of a Texas A&M cadet uniform and many drivers passed us by. On the second day we were just west of Fort Worth when a car stopped. It contained two women and a back seat full of small kids and luggage. We crowded into the car and soon found that our hostesses were wives of two enlisted sailors who were being transferred from Norfolk, Virginia, Naval Yards to San Diego, California, Naval Yards. The men were being moved by ship, while their women were following in an automobile. All of a sudden we had caught one ride all the way to California and the Olympic Games.

The ride was a mixed blessing, however. Small kids were crawling over us. There was no room to move. The women were happy and cheerful, plump and mature, about ten years older than we. As the day wore on they became extremely friendly, even cuddling up to us. This was before air conditioned automobiles and we were getting pretty sweaty. The ladies took complete charge of us. By late afternoon we arrived at Sweetwater. Without consulting us our hostesses sought out a motor court, as motels were then called. They registered for two rooms, drove up to the rooms and started unloading. It became apparent that I was to stay in the room with one family and Mahlon in the room with the other. Without having said a word to each other Mahlon and I told the ladies we were going downtown to look around a little. We were told to hurry back. We didn't have the nerve to tell them we were declining their hospitality.

Mahlon and I had just given up a free ride, room and board, and warm affectionate companionship all the way to California. I don't remember where we slept that night, probably on a park bench after eating some cheese and crackers. Next morning we stood on the highway waiting for a ride. The highway ran next to and parallel to the Texas & Pacific Railroad freight yard. While we waited a long westbound freight train pulled into the yard and stopped. There must have been fifty hobos in the cars. Some stood in open container cars; some sat, with their feet and legs hanging out, in the open doorways of empty freight cars. Some hobos alighted to stretch their legs and look the town over for a possible handout.

Some hobos were veterans of the road. Most were obviously new at the game, however. There were teenage boys and fifty-year old men, but most of these passengers were in their twenties and thirties. There were many "Okies" but they didn't come from Oklahoma alone. They came from Texas, Kansas, Ohio, Iowa—all the drought stricken farm states—the Dust Bowl. They were country people. Also there were city people out of jobs. This was in the depths of the Great Depression. One could have witnessed this scene at any freight yard in the Western United States. The railroad brakemen walked around doing their duties and ignoring the hobos.

Mahlon and I watched this scene with increasing interest. No ride was forthcoming on the highway. We walked over to the freight train and talked to a few of the easy riders. In summary their message was: "We are out of work, we're going to California to get a job or be in a better climate. If you're not working you can at least go to a nice place to hang out. The trainmen treat us nice. Come on and join us. We will show you how." When the train pulled out those of us not aboard started running along. Mahlon and I grabbed on to an empty container car and crawled in. There must have been ten people standing in the car. I can remember it vividly to this day. We felt as strangers but soon found there was a camaraderie among these travelers, much as there is among fellow travelers all over the world, be it in a 400 passenger transoceanic jet airplane or in a life boat full of shipwreck survivors.

The old professional hobos seemed to stand apart. We avoided them. The majority of the riders were restless unemployed young men. Upon looking over our fellow passengers I was amazed to see an A&M Senior ring on one. I walked up to him and flashed my own ring. We were both class of '32. I don't remember his name, but he was out of work. Not a single A&M engineering student had a job in engineering when he graduated. I saw my classmate several times on the way to California. I hope he found a good job and had a successful career.

During the first day riding the freight cars Mahlon and I learned our way around. That afternoon we were sitting on top of a box car as the train ran alongside the highway. Cars were zipping along past us. Who should pass us but our friends, the Navy wives. There they went, car loaded with kids and luggage, looking neither right or left. They could have seen us easily as they slowly pulled ahead. Mahlon and I turned our heads and sat perfectly still until our friends were well past.

We pulled in to El Paso about 1:00 A.M. We left the freight yard and walked through downtown with a group of hobos who knew where there was free lodging and food. We came to a huge makeshift shelter for wandering men. We showered off the layers of grime and smoke from the oil burning train engines, shaved, and slept until noon. We got up to find hundreds of wanderers around the place and surrounding grounds. There was a soup kitchen serving all you could eat for fifteen cents. There were so many homeless hungry men entering and leaving El Paso that a charitable agency had opened the facility. They even had a barber shop with ten cent haircuts.

This was during Prohibition. Drinking beer in an open bar in Juárez, Mexico, was about the most exciting adventure we could imagine, so Mahlon and I walked across the International Bridge and drank a mug of cool foaming beer. We then headed back to the freight yards to swing a ride in a box car for Tucson, Arizona. There was wonderful scenery all the way through the Big Bend, New Mexico, and Arizona. We pulled into the yards at Tucson one late afternoon, walked to the railroad station and called Mahlon's aunt and uncle who was a leading doctor in the city. They were expecting us and thought we had come in on a passenger train. They drove out to meet us at the station. Imagine their surprise when they found two grimy hobos. After overcoming their shock, they welcomed us cordially and drove us to their fine home where we bathed and slept until afternoon the next day. Mahlon's aunt got our clothes laundered.

Next day the doctor showed us his office and took us to lunch at an elegant downtown private club. I will never forget the green corn tamales we were served. After a couple of days we hopped a freight train for California. I can remember going through Yuma, Arizona, said to be the hottest city in America. Here we entered California and went west to El Centro. Suddenly we were no longer tolerated on the freight trains. California already had too many unemployed men. The police and trainmen carried big sticks and drove us off. Once when we got away from the police we followed a group of hobos to a genuine hobo camp. Here were some very tough, dangerous looking characters boiling water in a tin can over a campfire.

When the brakemen tried to prevent us from getting on there were so many they couldn't stop all of us. If they kept us off one train usually we could catch the next. I remember going north from El Centro and skirting the west side of the Salton Sea. Never have I seen more desolate country. We eventually arrived in the lush irrigated citrus orchards. Every time the train stopped we jumped off, ran into the orchards and gathered as many oranges as we could carry back to the train. For many this was the first food in twenty four hours.

Mahlon and I stayed in a YMCA in Los Angeles. We were eager to see the Pacific Ocean and swim in it. We took a street car to Santa Monica beach, rented bathing suits, and swam and loafed around for hours. It was hazy and we couldn't see the sun. We never thought about sunburn but for the next couple of days, we suffered from terrible burns and later peeled off.

Much to our disappointment we got to Los Angeles before the Olympics started and we couldn't wait. We called my lovable great Aunt Annie Britain who lived on a fruit farm near Hanford. She was excited to hear from me. She had not seen any Texas relatives for a long time. Mahlon and I caught a north-bound freight train. When we pulled into Bakersfield there were policemen and trainmen with sticks just about everywhere. They rounded up about twenty of us and lined us up at the passenger station while someone tried to decide what to do with us. There was talk about putting us in jail. As we stood there under guard a passenger train pulled into the station. Passengers stared at us from the windows. Some well-dressed men and women got out of the Pull-man cars and walked around looking us over like we were captured varmints. It was a degrading experience.

I don't remember how we got away but we decided it was safer to hitch-hike the remaining eighty miles to Hanford. We arrived in good time. Aunt Annie and Uncle Bob Britain met us at the train station. They were as sur-prised as Mahlon's aunt was in Tucson when they picked up two hobos, but Aunt Annie gave us a warm, hugging and kissing welcome. She had our laun-dry done, let us sleep late, and talked a lot about all the folks in Texas.

Aunt Annie and Uncle Bob had an irrigated fruit farm with houses for two Japanese families who did the work. There was a profusion of plants, includ-ing vegetables, berries, and just about every fruit. Their commercial crop was mainly apricots. Of course they had their own milk cow and chickens, ducks, guineas, and work horses. Aunt Annie was a great cook and served us fruit pies and homemade ice cream. They entertained us for three or four days before we left to make our way back to Texas on the freight trains. We were seasoned travelers. We knew the lingo of the road. We advised the less experienced how to ride the cars. We became accustomed to being dirty. We slept comfortably on the hard floors of box cars or in the reefers (ice compartments for refriger-ating produce). We could walk on top of box cars while the train was going at full speed. We could even jump off the train when it was going fast and hit the ground in a roll without getting hurt. We knew how to slip onto the train and hide from the brakemen. Our main diet was cheese and crackers and fruit. We never got sick a day, never got robbed, never got hurt.

On our way home I remember Tucson where several hundred unemployed World War I veterans, calling themselves the Bonus Army, were encamped in a public park. They were on their way to Washington, D.C. as a group to protest the postponement of their Veteran's bonus until 1945. The men were camping out. They had old cars or no transportation. Certainly many had ridden the freight trains. Speeches were being made when we went by to see them. This was a national movement. Fifteen thousand veterans reached Washington. A riot ensued with several people killed. President Hoover used the U.S. Army to drive the Veterans out of Washington.

Back in Texas, we stopped at Abilene to visit a high school classmate who attended Abilene Christian College. Our friend was studying journalism and had a job publishing the school paper. Mahlon and I then hitchhiked about seventy miles north of Abilene and visited my relatives in Throckmorton. I brought them news from Aunt Annie.

Our final leg of the journey was a hitchhike from Throckmorton to Deport. We were glad to see our parents and other family. I don't remember how glad they were to see us, but I've always been welcome at home in Deport. It's a tradition. We were gone a month. We only spent the money in our pockets. We never touched the $50.00 we had concealed in a shoe.

Perhaps my Aggie experiences of riding the blinds had put into my head the idea of riding freight trains like hobos across half the country. In any event, Mahlon and I witnessed first hand the devastating effects of the depression on peoples' lives: the poverty and misery, as well as the anger. It was a journey that I would never forget. Looking back, I do not think that such a carefree and potentially dangerous adventure just happened when it did without a reason. The trip occurred after having just finished experiencing the tight discipline and control of A&M and right before I was to embark on a new and different path—one equally as structured and disciplined, as I planned to pursue my dream of entering the medical profession and becoming a doctor.

Part 2

The Modernization
of Medicine, 1930s–40s

CHAPTER 4

University of Texas Medical Branch, Galveston, 1932–36

From an early age, I wanted to be a doctor. Next to the influence of my grand-father J. B. Kelsey, Dr. Stephen H. Grant was the most important person in finalizing that decision.[1] He was the leading general physician–surgeon in Deport and surrounding communities and had built a small hospital, the Deport Sanitarium. Dr. Grant was very advanced for a country doctor. He had graduated from the University of Texas Medical Branch (UTMB) in Galveston in 1903 and had spent a year or two interning and in residency under James E. Thompson—an English surgeon of the original faculty. Dr. Grant could take out tonsils or lance a quinsy, set fractures, and remove a big goiter, a gallbladder full of stones, a large fibroid uterus, a hot appendix, a kidney stone, a cancerous breast or a cancer of the colon—and all in the tiny wooden two-story Deport Sanitarium. I personally saw him perform these operations.

Dr. Grant was our family physician. While in my early teens he lanced a deep nail puncture on my foot. I had stepped on a big nail that penetrated my foot by an inch, and by bedtime the foot was badly swollen and painful, and I had a fever. Dad and Mother got Dr. Grant out of bed to meet us at the sanitarium. He mopped the area with iodine and then suddenly made a cru-ciate incision, then swabbed the deep wound with tincture of iodine. He used no anesthetic, but he worked so fast that it was over almost before I could resist and begin screaming from the unbearable pain. He applied a wet Ep-som salts dressing and gave me an oral dose of codeine. I was taken home and slept well. Within a day or two I was limping to school and bragging about my experience. Dr. Grant's skill and acumen made a lasting impression on me: I used this treatment for infected wounds for many years before antibiotics were introduced.

I started hanging around the Deport Sanitarium, and Dr. Grant often took me on house calls out in the country in his Model T. He used to make calls in a buggy. He tried a motorcycle but had too many falls because of ruts in the road. Once he saw a man in the country who had his skull split open by a blow with a heavy hoe. Brains were showing and falling out. Dr. Grant pushed the brains back in, then pushed the skull and scalp together the best he could. His antiseptic was probably iodine or silver nitrate. He bandaged the head tightly. The man survived and lived for years as a somewhat retarded worker who died of some other cause.

I learned a great deal from Dr. Grant. He said tincture of capsicum was the best treatment for delirium tremors. He depended on calomel for many ailments and used mercury rubs for syphilis. I learned from his observations, too. The diagnosis of internal cancer was very primitive then, for example, and Dr. Grant told me how to recognize the disease from late signs and symptoms, such as a mass in the abdomen, jaundice, bowel obstruction, massive bleeding, advanced emaciation, or metastatic bone pain. Dr. Grant took me into the profession of medicine, relating how he dealt with patients and showing that a good doctor was also a good counselor. He enjoyed the utmost respect.

The lessons continued. After I had been in medical school a couple of years I performed some tests in Dr. Grant's limited laboratory, taking blood counts, malaria smears, and acid fast smears for TB; I also tested for sugar in the urine and made H.E. (Hematoxylin Eosin) stains for gonorrhea and streptococci and dark fields for syphilis. I also helped him do proctoscopies, urethral dilatations for gonorrheal stricture, and uterine dilatations and curettements.

I do not remember helping with deliveries, but Dr. Grant did hundreds, maybe thousands, all in the home. Caesareans were done in the sanitarium, but he did quite a bit of surgery at home. One summer day, for example, Dr. Grant asked me to scrub with him for a hysterectomy to be performed in the patient's house. His nurse, Miss Rhoda Oliver, had all the sterilized instruments, swabs, towels, and sheets in a large metal container. We drove about five miles out to a nice farm house, where an operating room—a converted table—was set up in the dining room. Large pots of water were boiled. The family and relatives were on hand to follow orders and help when needed. Miss Rhoda draped the patient for surgery while we scrubbed and donned surgical gowns, caps, and masks. Miss Rhoda gave the anesthetic. Dr. Grant went to work, while I held clamps and hemostats. In an amazingly brief time, he removed a huge fibroid uterus, about the size of a cantaloupe, and closed the wound. I believe Dr. Grant had the technical skill of Denton Cooley. After surgery we went out in the yard and dissected the uterus and multiple fibroids to be sure there was no malignancy. Grant had the family dig a deep hole and bury the surgical specimen. Miss Rhoda packed up the equipment. When the patient began overcoming the anesthesia and seemed safe we drove back to Deport. The patient recovered completely. I saw her in Deport many times thereafter.

All of these early influences and experiences crystallized in September 1932, when I entered UTMB in Galveston to pursue my goal of becoming a doctor. The professors at A&M had prepared me well. I cannot emphasize how important an intensive pre-medical education can be to help a student confront the rigors of medical school. After three fruitful years at A&M and a summer of hitching rides on freight trains, I was ready for Galveston. Dad expressed Mother's trunk with my belongings and arranged a ride for me on top of a trailer load of cotton bales bound for Galveston. My high school classmate Ralph Ladd was driving the large truck, and he let me off at the Kempner Cotton Compress in Galveston. I caught a Broadway street car and found my way to the AKK fraternity house, where I stayed as a guest of Malcom Johnson of Paris. Malcom was a sophomore and "rushed" me for membership in the fraternity. I visited other fraternities and joined AKK, my first choice. It might have been my only choice.

As a freshman medical student in 1932, I found Galveston, located on the east end of Galveston Island, to be an exciting city of forty-five thousand people. Galveston was reached by a rail and vehicular causeway, built in 1912. A drawbridge on the causeway allowed boats to pass, delaying auto and rail traffic. The city at the time was the second largest port in the United States. Only New York was greater. I loved to loaf on the waterfront and see the ships from all over the world. Galveston's greatest export was cotton. A huge old grain elevator has since disappeared. Banana boats were unloaded by an army of men carrying one stalk at a time. Dr. Brinkley, the "goat gland doctor" from Del Rio, had two elegant white yachts, each over a hundred feet long. Dr. Brinkley made a fortune by radio advertising that his goat gland injections would restore men's sexual potency and cure prostate trouble. The Morgan and the Mallory Steamship Lines operated passenger ships to New York with stops in Havana and elsewhere. Dozens of fishing, shrimping, and oystering boats comprised the Mosquito Fleet. Their crews sold their catch at dockside.

Galveston was also a popular resort town for Texans. In addition to the big hotels such as the Galvez and the Buccaneer, a few motor courts and numerous boarding houses were near the seawall, as well as the usual beach front

University of Texas Medical Branch, Galveston, ca. 1930. Courtesy Moody Medical Library, The University of Texas Medical Branch at Galveston

clutter of curio shops, drive-ins, and restaurants. Galveston was wide open for gambling, said to be operated by the Maceo family. The Sui Jen restaurant and gambling club was at the end of a long pier opposite the Galvez Hotel. Its gambling paraphernalia could be hidden before officers could get down the pier to catch gamblers in the act. In the west residential area was the Hollywood Club, a swank casino where leading entertainers performed. In the business district were at least two gambling halls, one the elegant private Turf Club and the other a plain hall open to the general public. My friends and I occasionally stopped at the latter hall to watch or take a few rolls of the dice while on our after-dinner walk from the AKK house. Slot machines were in restaurants and bars all over town. A red light district extended a few blocks on the west end of Post Office Street. We students would walk through the district and be invited into every house. Occasionally, we went into the parlors and bought beer and danced with the women after putting money in the jukebox. The madams seemed to enjoy having us, just to sell us beer and play the music. Since violent crime was rare, we felt safe to walk anywhere in town, day or night.

When I entered the Medical Branch, as UTMB was then called, the school was forty-one years old.[2] Old Red, the original medical school building located on the Strand between Ninth and Tenth Streets, was built in 1891. It was in full use, as was the original John Sealy Hospital, built next door in

1890. By 1932, John Sealy Hospital expanded to include wings on each end of the original building. Old Red and John Sealy Hospital had been badly damaged but survived the 1900 hurricane that devastated the city. In fact, a large number of people had been saved by taking refuge in those buildings.

By 1932 the campus broadened to include the Laboratory or Kieller Building on the Strand, across the street from Old Red. The Out-Clinic Building was built across the street from John Sealy. The original building, like that of John Sealy Hospital, is now completely swallowed by a massive brick structure. The University Hall—a women's dormitory—was also across the street from John Sealy, just east of the Out-Clinic Building. This building, long since destroyed, was an architectural masterpiece. Between John Sealy and Galveston Bay sat several small buildings, including the Children's Hospital, the Negro Hospital, and the Isolation Ward, all soon to be replaced by larger structures. The U.S. Public Health Hospital, or U.S. Marine Hospital, razed in 1938, was located in the west end of town. The new State Psychopathic Hospital, still standing, was located on the Strand just west of Old Red on the same side of the street. The new Rebecca Sealy Nurses Home, no longer standing, was across the street, south of the Out-Clinic Building. St. Mary's Catholic Hospital was about two or three blocks south of the Medical School. Over the years, the Medical School and St. Mary's expanded until they were directly across the street from each other. In 1996 UTMB purchased St. Mary's.

Diagonally across the streets from the southeast corner of the campus on Ninth Street was the College Inn, operated by Mr. Christy. He was the uncle of the yet to be famous Mitchell brothers, Christy, John, and George, and of their sister Maria. The College Inn was the most popular hangout for medical students. Christy served good inexpensive meals. There was seating at a counter and booths along the wall. These booths were a favorite place for medical students to play pitch, a popular card game. The fraternity houses were scattered through the east Galveston residential neighborhoods, where two- or three-story box-like buildings sat on raised foundations to prevent flooding inside. Quite a few fine old houses still stood and represented a variety of styles, Victorian, French Second Empire, Italianate, and Greek revival. There were three-story houses—most of wood, some of brick—with large verandas, bay windows, or widow's walks. Students walked past these houses and neighborhood stores or down the back alleys on their way from the fraternity houses to the medical school, eight blocks from the AKK house. About 10:00 P.M. every night students at our AKK house were interrupted by the hot tamale man ringing his bell, as his horse-drawn cart moved slowly down the darkened street. Several of us pitched in a dime or so to buy a few dozen hot tamales to eat in our rooms. Five-cent bags of newly invented Fritos from San Antonio came on the market about this time, and the tamale man added these to the menu for students studying late at night.

The Medical Branch enjoyed a national reputation based on its faculty, its fine museums in anatomy and pathology, and its outstanding laboratory facilities. The library in 1932 had 22,000 volumes, complete copies of 252 medical periodicals, and a number of rare medical books. Today, UTMB library has one of the finest rare medical book collections in the world. Most of the lecture classes and laboratory sessions were held in Old Red and the Kieller Building. Clinical teaching took place in the Out-Clinic Building and the John Sealy Hospital, with its 385 beds. Compared to today, the medical school faculty was amazingly small. In 1932–33 there were only forty-three professors, fourteen instructors, and eight interns. The staffing did not change significantly during my four years as a student or when I was an instructor of pathology in 1937–38. A reason for this was the effects of the Great Depression on state funding of UTMB. The budget was very tight: the general biennial appropriation by the state legislature was $498,560 for 1931–32; $345,324 for 1933–34; and $415,000 for 1936–37. Consequently, faculty salaries during the depression were nothing to brag about. I was paid $150 as an instructor, and the majority of adjunct and associate professors were paid no more than $5,000 to $10,000 a year.

It cost $30.00 to register as a medical student at the Medical Branch. Applicants had to be at least eighteen years old and have a minimum of two years of college credits with passing grades and proper premedical courses. The first class I recall was anatomy. It may not have been the first, but it was the most shocking, even though I knew what I was getting into. The students were seated in an amphitheater facing a wall covered with anatomical charts. The professor, H. O. (Daddy) Knight, entered the well. With him came Associate Professors Felix Bute and Donald Duncan and Instructor F. J. L. Blassingame, and Scotty, the deaner or laboratory assistant. Dr. Knight introduced the staff and outlined the course. After telling us we would start by dissecting the upper extremity of our cadaver, he pointed to charts showing us what we would find when the skin was removed—the muscles, the arteries and veins, the nerves—and how these structures were positioned. Scotty then rolled into the room a table with a cadaver whose upper arm had been dissected. Dr. Knight pointed out the structures, his hands becoming greasy with human fat from the cadaver. Dr. Knight had a habit of rubbing his hands over his head. Soon his bald head was shining from the fat on his hands. Fortunately, the cadaver was completely sterilized with formalin, so there was no risk of Knight contracting a scalp infection. He did smell of formalin, however.[3]

We then marched to the huge dissecting room, where some fifty tables sat, each bearing a nude cadaver covered by an oilcloth sheet. This scene confirmed the school's promise in its catalogue that "dissecting material was abundant and thoroughly preserved." The department used 250 bodies a year. My partner and I were assigned the body of a young woman. Near the tables were large vats of formalin for storing the bodies. The atmosphere was redolent of formaldehyde. I understand that William Kieller, the original professor of anatomy, developed the formalin method of preserving cadavers and specimens—a method adopted by all anatomy laboratories. We worked in groups of two in carrying out the dissection of each part. Cunningham's *Manual of Practical Anatomy* was used in the laboratory and Cunningham's fifteen-hundred page *Textbook of Anatomy* was used for reference. After three years of studying anatomy my books were badly worn and I had memorized and forgotten, several times, nearly every word in those texts. I made 100 on several examinations, however, so I did retain some useful information. Galveston had the most intensive anatomy courses of any medical school in America.

Dr. Knight and the other teachers started with a lecture and demonstration of what we would be dissecting that day. Students were often called on to recite. In the laboratory, the teachers walked from table to table, helping students with their dissections. In addition to dissecting our cadaver we were issued human bones for the region we were dissecting. We took the bones to the fraternity house and learned the names of the features—the joints, the tubercles, and the sites of muscle origins and insertions. This part of anatomy is called osteology. We also brought home the odor of formalin. In the anatomy lab we plugged away day after day working with our bare hands, a scalpel, and forceps. We removed the fat and carefully located every little vessel and nerve in the arm. We finished this dissection the first semester and spent the next semester dissecting the thorax and abdomen to learn all about the internal organs, giving us more useful information than did the arm.

The anatomy faculty were fine men, all popular with the students. An air of congeniality existed among students and teachers, and I found this to be true for virtually every course in medical school. I cannot remember a single professor I disliked. Admittedly we made fun of some for their eccentricities and we feared some because they were so demanding. Dr. Byron M. Hendrix, professor of biochemistry, held his course on the top floor of Old Red, a space now occupied by anatomy. He had a seventh cranial nerve palsy that altered his face and speech. It didn't bother him a bit. We called him "Lumpy." Dr. Meyer Bodansky operated the clinical pathology laboratory in the Out-Clinic Building. His textbook, *Introduction of Physiological Chemistry*, was used by us and most medical schools in America. The worst job I ever had was in his clinical laboratory—analyzing feces. The students remember biological chemistry for the tests we performed on ourselves. We did chemistry on our own spit. We also carried gallon jars around to collect our urine to test while on special diets.

The next freshman course was embryology and histology, taught by Dr. John Sinclair in the Kieller Building. We dissected fish, frogs, and fetal pigs. In histology, now called microscopic anatomy, we learned to identify the tissues of the body. This class tended to be rowdy, with students throwing specimens at each other. Some macabre jokes were pulled in the anatomy lab, like putting human parts in people's lunch boxes. Physiology, the next major course, was held on the ground floor of Old Red with Dr. Eugene Lyman Porter as professor and Dr. W. A. Selle as associate. Here, in groups of four, we used live animals, including cats and dogs, that we anesthetized and operated on to study the function of different organs. The course in medical zoology I took with Wendell Gingrich was a study of the animal forms that infest humankind, beginning with the protozoans including malaria and amebiasis. We progressed to flukes, trichina, tapeworms, hook worms, and finally to the world of ticks, lice, and poisonous insects. These courses provided the rudiments of tropical medicine, which we studied our senior year.

In bacteriology, taught in Old Red by Professor William B. Sharp and Wendell Gingrich, we learned the general characteristics of bacteria of medical importance. We grew some pathogenic bacteria in test tubes. Viruses were hardly known, except for smallpox and rabies; the virus for poliomyelitis would be discovered twenty years later. Many pathogenic bacteria were yet to be discovered. Viruses, too small for our microscope, were called ultra-filtrable because they could be strained through a filter so fine that bacteria could not pass through. We learned how to diagnose a few bad bacteria by culture and by microscope. We learned about sanitation and bacterial contamination of food—lessons that later helped me as a field surgeon in Alaska during World War II. I had a brief course in preventive medicine, offered by the bacteriology department, that was limited entirely to sanitation. There was no mention of nutrition, tobacco, alcohol, toxic agents, exercise, or living habits. Indeed, the field of preventive medicine was not even in its infancy.

Our sophomore year largely focused on pathology, taught by Dr. Paul Brindley. The course was well organized and very intense, the most important course I had before entering clinical medicine. We spent many hours in lecture and laboratory, using Boyd's *Pathology* as our text. After Dr. Brindley lectured and projected gross specimen on the screen, we went to the laboratory to lay our hands on preserved specimens and study microscopic slides of the diseased tissue. The museum was one of the finest in the country, containing examples of virtually every disease. I often wondered where they ob-

tained the specimens of Madura foot. These were human feet partially destroyed by a fungus disease. The name comes from Madura, India, where the
disease was common. The specimens of bubonic plague were collected in
Galveston from bodies of twelve patients who had died of the disease at John
Sealy Hospital in 1920. There were six survivors. We attended one hour of
lecture and two hours of laboratory three times a week for the entire school
year and autopsies the second semester.

Pharmacology was taught by W. T. Dawson and Charles H. Taft, Jr. During the 1930s pharmacists were still compounding prescriptions. We were
taught how to write prescriptions in Latin, instructing the pharmacists exactly what ingredients were to be included and in what form the medication
was to be dispensed. For example, the pharmacist may be instructed to make
up a syrup so that one teaspoonful would contain a single dose of the active
ingredient. A single dose might be contained in ten drops or in a powder,
folded into a paper, or placed in a capsule. We learned tinctures, elixirs, infu-
sions, solutions, syrups, pulvules, capsules, poultices, and ointments—obsolete knowledge today, since medications are prepackaged. All pharmacists have
to do now is count the pills or capsules, put them in a plastic vial, and paste
on a label. However, their responsibilities are greater because there are so many
more drugs to dispense, and they are responsible for knowing all of them as
well as their hazards. Mr. Dawson taught us the pharmacologic action of most
of the drugs then in use. Description of these drugs wouldn't fill a hundred
pages of today's twenty-seven hundred page *Physician's Drug Reference.*

Finally, during the second half of our sophomore year, we were introduced
to hands-on patient contact with brief courses in minor surgery and physical
diagnosis. Today, students see and interact with patients during their first year
of medical school. Minor surgery was taught by G. W. N. Eggers, then an
adjunct professor. I remember well the day he gave me the final examination
in minor surgery. The examination was oral questioning and performing various complicated bandages. I didn't do well, probably because I am a frustrated
left-hander. Physical diagnosis, although classed as a minor, was important. It
laid the groundwork for the practice of medicine. The course was intense:
one teacher for each four students instructed us in the elements of clinical
diagnosis at the bedside with actual patients, and each student examined the
patient under the direction of the professor. For the first time we used a stetho-
scope. We learned to recognize the normal breath sounds and heart sounds.
Then we examined patients with lung and heart disease. Some of the old favorite patients with easily recognizable heart murmurs were brought in for
demonstration. We examined the abdomen to feel the liver, the kidneys, the
spleen. This was real doctoring, an exciting experience after studying for years

just to reach this stage of medical education. We felt as if we were almost doctors. Little did I realize that it would be fourteen more years (with four years as a military doctor included) before I completed my training and saw a private patient of my own!

Gynecology and obstetrics were popular courses that we studied for two years under Willard R. Cooke, the professor, H. Reid Robinson, associate, and Don Paton, resident in obstetrics. In addition to heavy teaching loads, these doctors had busy practices. Dr. Cooke was a memorable figure. He was a native Galvestonian and a graduate of the Medical Branch, where he had also trained. A seventh generation physician, his father was a member of the original faculty. What better credentials could a professor at the Medical Branch have? He was silver haired, easy going, and smoked constantly while he talked informally and without notes, interspersing his lectures with medical anecdotes such as the one in which George Washington never had any children because he had hypospadias. Washington had an active sex life. He and Jefferson traded mulatto girls. Cooke was instrumental in the development of the American Board of Obstetrics and Gynecology, of which he was chairman for twenty years. He delivered two of my sons—Cooke in 1942 and Thomas in 1944. He served on the faculty for fifty-three years before his death in 1966. Dr. H. Reid Robinson was a staid, dedicated teacher. He lectured to us in Old Red. We misbehaved by sailing paper airplanes or shooting paper wads across the amphitheater during his class. His lectures in obstetrics were well organized and easy to learn.

I remember the first gynecology clinic I attended. There was a row of examining stalls facing an open passage. The only privacy the patients had was a curtain, which was often pulled aside leaving the patient's genitalia exposed as she lay with her legs in stirrups. It took a little getting used to doing gynecological examinations, especially for the male students. However, quite a few of the patients were relaxed and friendly. They were prostitutes from the red light district in for periodic examinations to rule out venereal disease. They knew we were medical students. Some of the women invited us down to see them. Many of the black women worried about "bad blood"; many of the white women worried about "syphs," terms they used to designate syphillis.

Two events stand out in my memory of obstetrics. The service had a program for the few women who wanted to deliver their babies at home. I was one of the students who had a car and volunteered for the service. One night I got the call that a woman was in labor at home, and my classmates at the AKK house wanted to go with me. About six brothers loaded into my car and we drove to John Sealy to pick up a large metal container filled with sterilized linens and instruments. We raced over to the patient's house, where we found

Dr. Willard Cooke, professor of gynecology and obstetrics, Galveston.
Courtesy Moody Medical Library, The University of Texas Medical
Branch at Galveston

the family sitting quietly on the front porch in darkness, the intended patient
among them. Without asking questions we unloaded our equipment, got the
family busy boiling water, and unpacked our linens and instruments. With
these preparations going on I started to get the patient ready. Some questioning of the patient and family revealed that the patient was five months pregnant. She had called in because she had "a little indigestion." Disappointed,
we loaded our equipment, returned it to John Sealy, and drove to the fraternity house, where our brothers made fun of us for responding to a false alarm.

The second incident occurred one hot night in the OB ward after I had
observed several deliveries and was on call to do a hospital delivery. Dr. Paton,
the resident, instructed us how to proceed in delivering the baby. The process
went along fine, with the mother groaning and straining and the baby's head

appearing. I began to feel weak. I knew I had to do something in a hurry or I would faint. Without excusing myself I rushed out of the delivery room, out of the building, and on to the lawn where I lay down. Fortunately, I wasn't needed for that delivery, which was completed long before I regained my cardiovascular equilibrium!

My junior and senior years were almost exclusively devoted to learning clinical medicine and surgery. There were lectures, demonstrations, and hands-on care of patients in the out-clinics, the delivery rooms, the operating rooms, and at the bedside in the hospital. All courses required heavy textbooks, which we sat up reading until midnight, night after night, and quizzing our roommates. We memorized by mnemonics: "On old Olympus Table Top a Finn and German Viewed Some Hops" was the way to remember the cranial nerves, if I remember correctly sixty-five years later!

The most important course during this time was titled the practice of medicine. The class bible was Cecil's *Textbook of Medicine.* Drs. Charles T. Stone and George Herrmann gave us valuable lectures for two years.[4] The junior year covered infections and diseases of the gastrointestinal, respiratory, renal, and cardiac systems. The senior year covered diseases of metabolism, the blood and ductless glands, and more cardiovascular diseases. The lectures were accompanied by service in the out-clinics and in the hospital. From our professors and Herrmann's *Clinical Case Taking* we learned, on actual patients, how to do a thorough history and physical examination. I believe learning to do a proper examination was the most useful single lesson I learned in four years of medical school. Our teachers repeatedly emphasized the importance of a careful history and physical examination in making a proper diagnosis, and, probably just as important, in not overlooking other serious conditions. The importance of a careful examination was emphasized in every institution where I would later train—at Bellevue Hospital, at the Scott and White Clinic, and at the Mayo Clinic.[5]

In addition to learning how to do examinations, most of us learned the bedside manner—in other words, how to treat patients gently with compassion and respect. A few students never grasped this, however, even though some made good grades. I enjoyed a close relationship with medical patients I saw in the hospital or clinic repeatedly. One patient named a baby after me and had me to her house for a special dinner. We also learned what clinical tests and X rays we needed to reach a proper diagnosis. Finally, we learned how to treat the patient; what medications or what psychological support to give; when to call the surgeon; and when to send the patient home. We trained in small groups under the leadership of a dedicated faculty who also served as great role models.[6]

William F. Spiller was adjunct professor of dermatology and syphilology. Lectures and out-clinics emphasized some diseases not common today. Pellagra was caused by vitamin B deficiency and was common among poor people who subsisted on salt pork and cream gravy. At around this time it was discovered that vitamin B prevents pellagra. We saw some cases of leprosy among the local population. Itch or scabies and pediculosis or crabs were common. Syphilis was seen in all its manifestations. The textbook on syphilis was several hundred pages long. Spiller described both the internal and external manifestations of syphilis, beginning with the chancre, which we learned to identify by visual inspection and prove by dark field microscopic examination. Then came the secondary rash. After this cleared there was a latent period until the spirochete attacked in the tertiary stage nearly every organ of the body. Spiller warned us: "Know syphilis and you know medicine. It mimics every disease." The blood Wassermann soon became positive, and many cases came to the clinic for treatment. Before penicillin, however, syphilis was extremely resistant to all treatments. Bismuth and mercury rubs helped a little, and arsphenamine given by injection over a one or two year period sometimes cured it. Cerebral syphilis, however, was incurable.

I also took several courses in surgery, which included lectures, ward classes, demonstrations in surgical pathology, out-clinics, and operative clinics. We learned the causes and diagnoses of surgical problems, as well as surgical techniques and procedures. We enjoyed the physical act of surgery: doing dressings, passing catheters, suturing wounds, and assisting the staff by holding retractors during surgical procedures. We also observed surgery in the amphitheater; the surgeon described the procedure, and an assistant summarized the history and demonstrated the X rays. I watched as A. O. Singleton, professor of surgery, open the chest and pericardium of a stab wound victim whose life was ebbing away from cardiac tamponade. He moved rapidly to find the stab wound in the left ventricle and close it by placing sutures into the throbbing heart, thus stopping the gush of blood and saving a life under desperate circumstances. It was the most exciting surgical event I observed as a student. Dr. Singleton, native Texan and Texas-trained, became nationally famous.[7] He was among the last of the great general surgeons who operated in every field. Abdominal surgery was his forte but he performed many thoracic operations, removing lung cancers, tuberculous lobes, and closing lung and heart wounds. He performed plastic surgery, many orthopedic procedures, radical mastectomies, thyroidectomies, and nephrectomies. He did all the neurosurgery in Galveston until Dr. Snodgrass came in 1937.

In 1932 most medical students were single young men. Only eight women were in our class of one hundred. I remember only one married man, but at graduation we learned that there was another in our AKK fraternity. Edgar T. Jones had been secretly married for four years. I believe probably ninety percent of the men joined one of the eight fraternities. Indeed, my first experience with medical student life was joining Alpha Kappa Kappa. The fraternity relationship also influenced the rest of my life as a result of the friendship, advice, and support I received from alumni brothers. There was a congenial relationship among the fraternities. The only rivalry was during rush week, when there was competition to pledge the outstanding freshmen. All the fraternity houses were large old three story residences in walking distance of the medical school. The AKK house was a brick building; the other fraternities were housed in wooden, Victorian gingerbread structures.[8]

I stayed at the AKK house during the wild rush week. Bootleg liquor flowed freely. Home brew, made in the fraternity house, was served. There was a continuous open bar. People came and went, boys with dates, freshmen rushees, even Dean Bethel came and fraternized. There were beach parties and softball games. Some upperclassmen went to Sui Jen to gamble, and a group walked through the red light district at night. Even so, I encountered some sober students who talked seriously about classes and identified the good and bad professors. When rush week was over I was asked to join AKK, along with fifteen other freshmen, including Jim Little and Ross Margraves from A&M. About ten were from the University of Texas. All of us forgot about the traditional rivalry between A&M and Texas. We were a homogeneous group, with similar socioeconomic backgrounds, although some of us were from small towns and some from the city. Although we knew that twenty-five percent of the student body would fail, we were determined to graduate, and all of us did. We slept three in a room, many sleeping on the screened porches. More than forty were crowded into the house and the upstairs apartment of what was once a carriage house.

About my junior year, Dad let me have a Model A sedan. But I became too extravagant, so Dad thought it best for me to walk to classes. Later on, I went downtown to Dow Chevrolet Company to buy a secondhand car. I found a seven-passenger 1925 blue four-door Lincoln limousine in near perfect condition. The roll-up curtains and the jump seats were as good as new. The engine purred. The price was $60.00. Apparently there was no market for a big ten-year-old gas guzzler, so six of us contributed $10.00 each and drove it out. It was a great success. Everyone wanted to ride it to school or take their dates to dances in it. It often carried ten passengers.

During the 1935–36 Christmas vacation, AKK held a national convention in Richmond, Virginia. Ralph Letteer was elected the delegate from our chapter with expenses paid. Ralph took the family Chevrolet sedan and picked up

Howard Eberle and Cooper Conner. On the way to Richmond, Ralph stopped in Deport to invite me to join them. He proposed that all of us could make the trip on his paid expenses. We could go nonstop and alternate driving and sleeping, thus saving hotel costs. Dad was not a bit enthusiastic about me going but finally relented and replaced a couple of worn tires on Ralph's car.

An active social life revolved around the fraternities. Each fraternity had an annual dance, usually at the Galvez Hotel, and invited all the other fraternities and provided dates for the women students. Many of the nurses came as dates. The people of Galveston were very hospitable to the medical students. They invited us into their homes and clubs. Their daughters dated the medical students. The mothers were chaperons at our dances. Medical students were invited to the annual Mardi Gras celebrations. Many a medical student married a Galveston girl or a University of Texas nursing student.

Another event I remember was held at Osteon, an exclusive club with two seniors from each fraternity comprising its membership. They held an annual wild weekend party and dance. All fraternity members were invited, as well as a horde of people from Austin, Houston, and other cities. At our fraternity, we made bathtub gin from a gallon of grain alcohol, purchased from the Maceos, combined with juniper berry juice and water. One tin was enough for a huge party. People started drinking in the afternoon, "getting suited up," as they said, for the dance. One of the brothers, Raleigh Ross, got suited up too early and put on a scanty leopard skin costume and went to town to buy a pair of slippers. He was very noisy. The storekeeper called the police. I remember after the police brought Raleigh home, we bathed him and put him to bed for a while. He still made the dance. After such events, we often went to the Tremont Cafe, which was open all night, and ordered scrambled eggs doused with Worcestershire sauce. These eggs and a glass of buttermilk were proven to prevent a hangover.

As I look back on my medical school days it seemed that we studied hard all week and attended drinking parties on the weekends. On Saturday and Sunday afternoons we had beach parties, to which we often invited girls. We swam and played softball until it got dark, then boiled a washtub of shrimp in seawater over a driftwood fire. We bought shrimp at the Mosquito Fleet for ten cents a pound. We sat around peeling and eating shrimp, drinking home brew, and singing. Cooper Conner and Frank Ashburn had beautiful voices, and we joined them in "My Wild Irish Rose" and "When Irish Eyes are Smiling." One of our favorites was "Let's Get Stinkin', Says Old Abe Linkin, Cause a Little Bit of Drinkin' Will Do a World of Good." And another favorite: "I'd Rather Get Drunk with an AKK, and Anyone Else I Know." Repeal of the federal liquor laws occurred in 1933. Before this we bought Mrs. Bee's Honey:

a phone call to Mrs. Beebe and $4.00 pooled by the brothers brought delivery of a one-half gallon fruit jar of her "honey," a fairly good moonshine. After repeal, which put Mrs. Beebe out of business, we bought blended bourbon for $1.00 a pint: Crab Orchard, Four Roses, and Old Quaker are brands I remember. We also drank Magnolia beer brewed in Galveston, Lone Star brewed in Houston, or Jax brewed in New Orleans.

There was more to fraternity life than hard study and drinking. We held bull sessions, discussing medicine, our families, our sweethearts, our goals in life. I sat up more than once all night talking with my roommates Ralph Letteer and Jim Little. Our annual initiation party was also an important event. Several alumni came down from San Antonio, Houston, and Dallas to join in our fun. They inspired us and advised us about internships. In fact, the AKK house was supported financially by the doctors in Houston, the leading one being E. W. Bertner, an individual who would later play an instrumental role in the development of the Texas Medical Center in Houston. Dr. Bertner graduated from the Medical Branch in 1911 and was a charter member of the Galveston chapter of AKK. He always came to the annual initiation banquet and was considered one of the boys. He even walked through the red light district with some of the brothers. While I was there, the chapter sank deep in debt, as young medical students tried to run the house. The grocery bill alone was $1,000 a month, about the same as the total monthly dues. Gengler's Grocery, the utilities, the phone company, and numerous other creditors were about to shut us down. Dr. Bertner organized a group of AKK doctors in Houston who bailed us out and put us on a strict budget. He personally gave us money every month and carried us through the crisis. He later told me the chapter paid him back, although I wonder if his payment was the satisfaction of doing a good deed. Some of my friends spent the summer between their junior and senior years as externs, a title designating a medical student, not yet graduated, working full-time as house staff in a hospital. After medical school, the doctor's first full-time hospital training assignment was called an internship, lasting from one to three years. After the internship the doctor may be appointed as a resident—a position having authority over interns and responsibility for treatment of patients under the supervision of the attending physician. While in medical school, I had participated in a National Youth Administration program in the pediatrics department under Boyd Reading. The blood sedimentation rate was being developed as a test for evidence for infection. My job was to do sedimentation rates and blood counts on pediatric hospital patients, the results to be compared with the clinical course of the patients. I obtained blood by puncturing a finger. You can imagine how popular

I was, going around the ward sticking kids. But nurses were great; it wasn't long before they had most of the children lined up wanting to be stuck to show how brave they were. The project was successful. Reading published an important paper confirming the value of the blood sedimentation rates submitted by his brave young "volunteers." I next wrote to Texas senator Tom DeBerry asking for his recommendation for an externship in one of the seven state mental hospitals. He was a family friend from Bogota and recommended me for an externship at the Wichita Falls State Hospital. Like my work with Reading, this also proved to be a worthwhile experience.

As I recall, Wichita Falls State Hospital had nearly a thousand patients at the time. Most were confined in two-story buildings with open wards. Violent patients were held in single rooms. The campus was divided into two halves, one for men, the other for women. Each ward opened to a large veranda where the patients sat or walked around and visited. Each ward had its own toilets, baths, and dining room. There was a separate hospital for physically ill patents or those undergoing surgery. The patients were taken care of by attendants who lived on the grounds and were dedicated, compassionate people. I never saw an instance of patient abuse the entire time I was there. When family members came to visit, an attendant brought the patient to a private room in the headquarters building. Although the ward entrances were locked and guarded by an attendant, many of the patients who were physically and mentally able worked both inside and outside the wards. The male patients were glad to work in the vegetable garden, dairy, and power plant and on the spacious grounds. Women liked to do housekeeping, cooking, laundry, and sewing.

I was given a private room and bath in the headquarters building, which had a dining room for professional staff. The medical staff met nearly every night for a medical program, reviewing cases, discussing medical articles, and quizzing me. During the depression, doctors' salaries were about $150 a month. Mine was an outrageously high $50 a month. I learned to diagnose various mental diseases and helped in surgery and the dental office. I made rounds on the wards and was introduced to the patients as Dr. Kelsey, a charade I enjoyed. I performed physical examinations and psychiatric interviews. I was assigned patients to work up and present to the staff for consideration to dismiss. Many patients were able to go home, although some relapsed and required readmission. This was especially true among manic depressive patients. Some patients had general paresis, a progressive dementia caused by syphilis of the central nervous system. I encountered all types of schizophrenia at the state hospital and collected letters written by a few of the patients with true paranoia. Several maniacal patients had to be isolated and restrained. Other patients had been there for years and wanted to stay because the hospital had become home to them and they had no other home.

Most of the patients were from the country or small towns of North Texas and represented all socioeconomic levels. All received the same care. Treatment consisted mainly of sympathetic supportive care and the passage of time to do its work. There were no drugs to treat mental illness, at least nothing more effective than phenobarbital. Texas had very few full-time psychiatrists. Practically the only beds for psychiatric patients were in the several state mental hospitals, commonly known as insane asylums. Titus Harris, professor of neuropsychiatry at Galveston, was among the first to treat psychiatric patients in a private hospital. His practice grew rapidly as wealthy people learned they could get private care in Galveston. He eventually had one of the largest practices of any physician in Texas. Timberlawn Sanitarium in Dallas and the Greenwood Sanitarium in Houston were two other private mental hospitals.

I learned a lot of practical medicine that summer at Wichita Falls State Hospital—a useful experience in my senior year as the mad scramble for internships began. It was everyone for himself; there was no matching program at the time. I considered several hospitals where Galveston AKKs had established connections: Kansas City General; St. Vincent's in New York, where Dr. Bertner had interned; Santa Rosa in San Antonio; and Charity in New Orleans. I asked Dean Carter for advice. A few days later he called me in and asked if I would like to intern in Bellevue Hospital in New York City. Carter had spent years at the Rockefeller Institute and knew Dr. Wykoff, dean of New York University Medical College, who had agreed to accept a man of Carter's choice for internship in Bellevue. I accepted immediately. Bellevue was a famous hospital, the largest in America. It claimed to be the oldest. Many famous doctors had trained there.

My graduation from medical school in 1936 was an exciting event. We had good-bye dates and beach parties. The Magnolia Brewery invited us, as some of their best customers, for all the beer we could drink. My parents came down for the graduation; they had sacrificed a lot for me. Both were still young to have a son graduating from medical college: Mother was forty-four and Dad was forty-five years old. I didn't show them the gratitude I should have. I left them and went off on a party both nights they were in Galveston. The graduation ceremony was held in the City Auditorium. The address was given by the professor of jurisprudence, Brantley Harris, a highly respected Galveston lawyer. I still have transcripts of my medical school grades, which had been fairly uniform throughout and good enough to get me into Alpha Omega Alpha, the honorary medical fraternity. I doubt that I earned the honor. I

Mavis as University of Texas Medical Branch graduate, 1936

was out ratting around at night and sleeping in the daytime. At A&M and Galveston I had a reputation for making good grades with little study. I helped my fellow students with their studies. I was proud of being smart; my schoolmates just called me a smart ass.

After graduation, I shipped Mother's trunk home and visited some of my classmates. I went with Ralph Letteer to visit his father at Chapman Ranch, south of Corpus Christi. Mr. Letteer was a college-educated agriculturist who managed this large privately owned ranch. Ralph and I then went to San Antonio to visit Carl Goeth and Huard Hargis. I next went to Austin to take the state board examination for medical license in Texas. June was one of the hottest months on record. There was no air conditioning, and the examinations were held in the state capital in the hall of the House of Representatives. We sat at the desks and took the written examination. To prepare, we had studied copies of previous examinations, which were repeated nearly verbatim each year. I was issued license number B4216 and have kept it in force until 1998. After the state boards, Ralph Letteer drove with Cooper Conner, Howard Eberle, and me to Dallas for the Texas Centennial celebration, where we saw the Cab Calloway band and Sally Rand perform her famous fan dance. After good-bys, Ralph and I went for a final visit to see Jim Little in Gilmer, Ross Margraves in Paris, and the Kelseys in Deport. Then we went our separate ways for our internships. All of us eventually returned to Texas. We kept in touch with each other the rest of our lives.[9]

CHAPTER 5

Bellevue Hospital, 1936–37

In the summer of 1936, I packed Mother's trunk once again for the trip to Bellevue Hospital in New York City. It was the longest journey of my life so far, but I loved riding trains. I boarded the Texas and Pacific at Paris and changed to the Pennsylvania Railroad in Saint Louis. After two days' travel, I arrived at Pennsylvania Station in New York City at about ten o'clock one morning.

I had been warned to be cautious of people in New York. I stood outside the train station trying to decide what to do, when a taxi drove up. The driver asked me where he could take me. With some caution I told him I wanted to go to Bellevue and asked him what the fare would be. The driver immediately recognized me as a stranger from the sticks, but he was a nice man. His fare was reasonable, and he made me feel safe and welcome. On the way to Bellevue he offered me good advice and information about New York. It may seem strange that I remember this first encounter, but this taxi driver allayed my anxieties about New York and its people.

Bellevue Hospital had four teaching divisions. New York University ran the program in the Third Division, where I would serve my internship. New York University Medical School was directly across First Avenue from Bellevue. I was invited to a reception that first night to meet the new doctors and the staff. One of the residents introduced himself as Ray Banta, a second-year intern from Wisconsin and, until my arrival, "the only gentile on the New York University staff." I promptly learned that most of the house staff were Jews from New York City who graduated from N.Y.U. Medical College. They joked about me being a gentile country boy from Texas. They wanted me to fit the tradition of a Texas cowboy. I made up a story about growing up on a ranch as a cowboy instead of telling them I had grown up in a cotton patch. The more I embellished my story the more they enjoyed it, and the more they realized the story was a fraud. We all became lifetime friends.[1]

Bellevue, 1936

Bellevue had many traditions. Said to be the oldest hospital in America, the institution got its start as the almshouse for New York City in the original municipal building. My room, which I shared with three others, was a former patient ward in the original building. I was told that George Washington made his inaugural address from the first floor balcony of this building where I roomed. The balcony was still there, approached by winding iron stairs on each side, exactly as depicted in a lithograph I have which was printed in the early 1800s. The first elevator in New York City was still in the building, a cagelike structure that operated at a snail's pace between the floors. It was originally used to transport patients, but the building was later occupied by offices and quarters for Bellevue house staff. This building was gone when I visited Bellevue sixty years later.

At the time of my arrival, Bellevue, with three thousand beds, claimed to be the largest hospital in America. It was located on the East Side of lower Manhattan from about Twentieth to Thirtieth Streets, between First Avenue and the East River. There were several large seven- and eight-story hospital buildings with wards on each floor. Some lawn space existed between some of the buildings and a promenade along the East River. The entire system was connected by basements and underground tunnels. The first level basement was for passage of personnel and patients. The second level was for freight and dead bodies. There was a third level, a mysterious basement and tunnel where no one ventured. People went in never to return, or so the story went. Most of the buildings were of nineteenth- and early twentieth-century construction. The City Neuropsychiatric and Prison Hospital building was a new structure, however, and I would later spend six months of my internship there.

A number of East River piers were near the hospital, one for yachts and others abandoned and decaying where neighborhood kids went diving and swimming in the nude. The East River was an open sewer at the time. The boys avoided floating fecal matter as they swam in the river. On the hospital lawn was a large vat in which workers constantly dipped bed springs to kill bedbugs. The mattresses were treated inside in an autoclave-like heater. Bellevue never rid itself of bedbugs, however. I found them in my bed several times.

The house staffs of all four divisions were served in a common dining hall. There were about a hundred interns and residents, fewer than you will find in a three-thousand bed hospital today. In those days, too, there was not the narrow specialization we have today. There were no certification boards in the medical subspecialties. Currier McEwen was chief of medicine, a cardiologist and specialist in rheumatic fever. He became dean after Dr. Wykoff's death.[2] Charlie Kossman was a cardiologist. I met him later at the School of Aviation Medicine, where he taught electrocardiography and in the Air Surgeons Office in Washington, D.C., during World War II. I knew S. R. Snodgrass, a neurosurgeon in the neuropsychiatric hospital at Bellevue. When I returned to teach pathology in Galveston I was surprised to see Dr. Snodgrass, who had accepted the position as chief of neurosurgery at the medical school. Bellevue also had a large residence for registered and student nurses. Bellevue nurses wore an attractive and distinctive cap that originated with Florence Nightingale in England. The Florence Nightingale system of nursing was established at Bellevue Hospital in 1873 as the first school of nursing in America. It became the model for nursing training in this country. A distant relative of mine, Walker Gill Wylie, was instrumental in establishing the Bellevue Nursing School.[3]

Leading physicians of New York City were on Bellevue's attending staff. The nursing staff was superb. There was an intensive training program for interns. The hospital was open to everyone, and even the poor received good treatment. Bellevue was subject to the New York's patronage system: Tammany Hall really ran the city, and Bellevue was a part of the city. At the neighborhood level the political leader, the ward boss, often sent his sick constituents over to Bellevue. Others came in by ambulance called by the local police. The Bellevue ward boss's saloon was located within a block of Bellevue. On election day he served free beer to the Bellevue house staff. He'd also arrange to take you to the polls; if you liked to vote he would take you as often as you wished.

My salary as an intern was $15.00 a month with uniform, room, board, and laundry. At least we had a little spending money. Some teaching hospitals did not pay interns one cent. In addition, Dad sent me an allowance, and

Bellevue had numerous perks. I had a wonderful time. For a five cent fare, for example, one could travel all over New York City on the elevated railway and subway. When new plays opened on Broadway, the producers wanted a full house. On opening night they sent tickets to Bellevue Hospital for the doctors and nurses to help them fill the theater. They often sent us unsold tickets for later performances, so we saw most of the plays. We also received tickets for Yankee Stadium and other entertainment.

I thoroughly enjoyed New York City. I rode the subway and the elevated to sightsee: Central Park, Greenwich Village, Chinatown, Wall Street, and the Museum of Modern Art. I was fond of Winslow Homer's paintings in the Metropolitan. Later in life, my wife, Mary, and I collected all his wood engravings and gave them to the Museum of Fine Arts in Houston; I also published a book on his work, *Winslow Homer Graphics* (1977). I wished to go to the top of the Empire State Building, but my New York friends made fun of me, saying only tourists went there. Forty years later, I finally got my wish and went, as a tourist, to its top. We sometimes walked to restaurants in Greenwich Village when we were free on Sundays. I remember a Turkish restaurant where I had my first shish kabob. I had only eaten southern and Mexican food before I came to New York, so I enjoyed many foreign foods for the first time, including Chinese, Greek, Japanese, German, Russian, and a Scandinavian smorgasbord. We walked to a seafood restaurant in Grand Central Station at night where I ate my first lobster and clams.

While in New York, the Hindenburg disaster occurred in nearby Lakehurst, New Jersey. New York was preparing for a World Fair. Mayor LaGuardia, called the Little Flower, was very popular. Radio City and Rockefeller Center were new. George Gershwin was performing. *Tobacco Road* was playing on Broadway. The news was filled with stories about the Prince of Wales renouncing the throne to marry Wally Simpson. The wealthy eccentric Texan, Hetty Green, was enjoying great publicity. The Communist Party was legal. I knew several interns from New York City who were active Communists. Some interns had served in the Spanish Civil War that was still going on. They were members of the Abraham Lincoln Brigade, some twenty-eight hundred volunteers, mostly American Communists, who fought Spanish fascism. I partied and had long bull sessions with these people, most of whom were adventurers or zealots.

An intern's social life at Bellevue revolved mostly around the hospital and staff. Attending staff members and their spouses invited the interns to their homes, a hospitality shown interns everywhere I have trained. Organized social functions were held in the hospital or at hotels. Dean Wykoff had two handsome daughters who went to Bryn Mawr College. The daughters planned to study medicine, and I remember the older one later graduated from medical school. The Wykoffs asked me to escort the older daughter to several social functions and dances in some of the great New York hotels. I had to rent a top hat and white tie and tails for these events.

Most social activity was informal dating and parties among interns, nurses, and dietitians in the hospital reception rooms or in nearby bars or movies. A trip to the opera, Broadway, Rockefeller Center, a Chinese restaurant, or a night club would be a big date. As in Galveston, we had plenty of alcohol for our parties. We drank manhattans, old fashioneds, and martinis. Fellow interns sometimes invited me to their homes. Once I went by rail for a Sunday in the New York countryside with a female intern named Byrd. Her parents had moved from Virginia to a farm in New York, where they had cows, chickens, horses, a vegetable garden, and fruit trees. It was a wonderful day. The Maurice Moores were especially nice to me, inviting me to their home several times. Maurice was from Deport, the son of Dr. J. H. Moore, my grandfather's colleague and a family friend. Maurice was the same age as Dad. He had gone to law school at Columbia University.[4]

In the first year of my internship at Bellevue Hospital I spent six months in internal medicine and six months in surgery. My first assignment was in a large internal medicine ward for women. I examined each new patient and recorded a history. I did a complete blood count, sedimentation rate, and urinalysis in the small ward laboratory. In those days I had to boil the urine in a test tube over a Bunsen burner to test for sugar. I could do a few blood chemistries, such as urea and sugar. Other tests were sent to the central clinical laboratory. The intern did the electrocardiograms and other tests, including basal metabolic rates. After examining the patient, I wrote orders for other tests, medications, and diet. The middle-aged chief ward nurse helped me. She knew more medicine than I did but never let on. She just petted me and made me feel important. There was a little kitchen on each ward. My nurse cooked special dishes for me, including hamburgers. The attending doctor or the chief resident made rounds, quickly checking my history and physical examination, pointing out errors, and quizzing me. I made rounds every evening to order sedatives (chloral hydrate or amytal) and laxatives (cascara or magnesia). Every patient wanted something. They were of every race and every age and were grateful for my attention.[5]

Once or twice a week, the chief of medicine or sometimes the dean of the medical college, Dr. Wykoff, would come through with several followers and examine a patient. Other consultants might come through and order a patient off to surgery, or to the pneumonia ward, or to isolation for tuberculosis. Patients with lobar or pneumococcus pneumonia had their sputum typed and their blood cultured. They were isolated, placed in oxygen tents and given the recently developed pneumonia antitoxin. If a patient came in with diabetic coma, Dr. Elaine Ralli's team would start a well-organized treatment program with intravenous fluids, frequent insulin injections, and careful monitoring. Her patients enjoyed a high recovery rate. I was fortunate to be assigned to her team. I treated coma cases later, based on her principles. She believed in strict control of diabetes, with every effort made to keep the blood sugar normal. A well-known endocrinologist specializing in diabetes, Dr. Ralli was one of the important people I knew during my time at Bellevue. As a young doctor in about 1922, she gave the first dose of insulin in New York City at Bellevue Hospital. The patient, a black woman, had thus received the first dose of insulin in the United States. She was still a patient at Bellevue. Dr. Ralli turned this patient over to me to treat in the outpatient clinic.[6]

In the 1930s, sulfonamides or sulfa drugs were new. While I was a senior in medical school, Dr. C. T. Stone had told the class that one of President Roosevelt's sons was successfully treated with a sulfa drug at Johns Hopkins Hospital. My future brother-in-law, Cooke Wilson, Jr., was also treated with a sulfa drug for pneumonia by a Hopkins physician about the same time. As part of my internship, I was assigned to a special project to test the sulfa drugs at Bellevue. Dr. John Nelson was the attending physician in charge. Many patients entered Bellevue with erysipelas, a disease we never hear of today. Common in the winter among alcoholics, it is a streptococcus infection, often on the face, extending from the nose to both cheeks as a fiery red swelling, accompanied by high fever. The infection usually lasted one to several weeks and was often fatal. I was notified when every case of erysipelas entered the Third Division. I examined the patient and started half of the patients on neoprontosil, a red sulfa pill that caused red urine. The other half of the patients received the same supportive care but no sulfa. We collected more than fifty patients. The results were dramatic. The patients treated with sulfa improved within twenty-four hours and were free of fever in two or three days while the untreated ran the usual prolonged course. Our studies were published in the *Journal of the American Medical Association,* the first medical article I ever joined in publication. Word soon got around Bellevue that we were testing sulfa drugs. One day a nephrologist met me in the hall and asked, "What's all this silly stuff you are fooling around with? That drug doesn't work, you just think it works. There never will be a drug that will pick out and destroy bacteria in the body without destroying the normal cells of the body itself." Now that was a famous doctor who made that remark. When some people get smart in one field, they begin to think they're an expert in everything.

It was said that if you trained at Bellevue you would see every disease known to man. The hospital had a huge admission ward containing perhaps a hundred beds. The patients were given a cursory examination by admitting officers who, moving through them rapidly, assigned the patients to various services. These doctors became very proficient in making a quick diagnosis. Admission service was thus a choice assignment, because one got to see so many interesting patients and learn the diagnostic features of their diseases. Some of us hung around just to watch them work and see some rare diseases pass through. The admission office was credited with first identifying lumbar disc syndrome at Bellevue. This was a relatively new diagnosis while I was there. Some of the early surgery for lumbar disc protrusion was done at Bellevue Hospital. I was also lucky enough to see some of the first cardiac catheterizations ever done, which were performed at Bellevue by Dr. Cournand. At the same time, Dr. Norman Jollife and his assistant, Dr. Goodheart, were researching the action of vitamin B1, by injecting it into patients with pellagra. I watched this research project to see the patients recover completely, proving that pellagra was caused by vitamin B1 deficiency. These two doctors, along with a dietician, later developed the Weight Watchers Diet, one of the first scientifically planned weight reduction programs.

The most exciting experience I had at Bellevue was riding ambulance for a month. Four interns were always on ambulance service and rotated taking calls. You were allowed to take other intern's calls if they wanted off. I agreed to take every call that any other intern didn't want. As a result I set a record at that time for the most ambulance calls made by an intern in one month at Bellevue—four hundred as I recall. I enjoyed it because I got to see New York and its people. I read the new novel *Gone With the Wind* while I rode ambulance. A policeman accompanied the intern and the driver on every ambulance call. The intern wore a white uniform and a Union soldier's cap in memory of the Civil War, when Bellevue provided ambulance service to Union soldiers wounded in battle. Many calls were routine—someone sick in bed with a minor fever. Often we had to walk up four floors to see the patient. The patients who were seriously ill with heart failure, pneumonia, or other illness were brought to Bellevue. Many calls were for people injured in fights or accidents. Some were DOA—Dead On Arrival. Sometimes news reporters were on the scene taking pictures and stories. Several times I had my name in New York papers as the Bellevue doctor who attended a crime or accident victim. Once I got to a patient just in time to deliver a baby. I left the mother and baby at home in a slum dwelling. I made an ambulance call on her every day until she was able to be up and take herself and the baby to a clinic. Her husband gave me a bottle of whiskey.

Every night we rode an ambulance to a jail off Broadway to give the drug addicts a morphine injection so they and other inmates could get some sleep. Many calls were made on drunks who were found on the streets. We stuck a swab with aromatic ammonia up their nostrils. If the drunk woke up fighting we left him for the policeman to take to jail. If this stimulant didn't arouse the drunk we knew he was dangerously ill and took him to the hospital. Occasionally, our ambulance policeman would have us stop at a saloon and go in for a free beer and lunch at a huge counter. The saloon keepers welcomed us. We were good for business, because a Bellevue ambulance parked in front of a saloon soon attracted a crowd of customers. Once I was called to see a beautiful young woman in an attractive apartment. She was febrile, suffering from severe abdominal pains, and her abdomen was rigid—all signs of acute peritonitis. We rushed her to Bellevue, where an operation revealed gonorrheal peritonitis from a ruptured infected ovarian tube (salpingitis). The patient died. The following year, women with gonorrheal salpingitis were being cured with sulfa drugs. My Galveston classmate, R. P. McDonald, came to Bellevue for a residency in gynecology and obstetrics during my second year. He told me that Bellevue always had a ward full, two rows of twenty-five women each, with gonorrheal salpingitis being treated with sulfa drugs. This was a year after Dr. Nelson and I had proved the effectiveness of sulfa drugs for erysipelas.

The second six months of my internship was spent as surgical intern in the neuropsychiatric building that included the New York Prison Hospital. This wasn't much of a job. To compensate me, they flattered me by calling me the surgical resident of the neuropsychiatric building. Any significant surgical problem was sent to the main operating rooms where I took no part in the treatment. There were several hundred patients in the wards. I was kept busy sewing up lacerations, doing dressings, incising boils, and doing consultations. I rotated duty in the emergency room. An intern's duty shift at Bellevue was twelve hours. Even if you had a night shift and did not get much sleep you still worked a twelve-hour day shift the next day. Several times I worked thirty-six hours of duty with virtually no sleep. Much of my work was in the prison hospital, a regular jail with guards, barred doors, and cells. Within its confines was a treatment room, where prisoners were brought from their cells. I became interested in the burglars who made up a large percentage of the inmates. I learned something about their criminal minds. These men thought they were making an honest living. Most of them did not carry guns, they were no threat, they did as little damage as possible, only took valuables. These burglars were professionals, and they had a code of ethics. They had built up a sense of respectability. They weren't about to change careers. They had friends and family in the profession. I think they were beyond rehabilitation.

As I completed my first year of internship, I was selected for an internal medicine residency program that lasted three more years and fulfilled the training requirements for board certification in internal medicine. This was an honor I did not fully appreciate until later, however. My second year began with six months of general pathology in the New York morgue at Bellevue, perhaps the most famous morgue in America. There was a large room with tables where several autopsies were performed simultaneously, beginning early in the morning and lasting until noon or later when the last case was completed. Along with the dead from Bellevue Hospital, the morgue also received the bodies of New York's crime victims or of those having died of unexplained causes. In the morgue I witnessed the results of every known brutality: sex crimes, serial murders, death by torture, gang executions, poisonings, stranglings, bloaters, drownings, and many others. Bellevue morgue was the fountainhead of forensic pathology. Many unidentified or unclaimed bodies left the morgue on an East River barge for burial in Potter's Field.

My work in the morgue was to assist in autopsies of patients who died in the New York University Division. I wrote the protocol of the gross and microscopic findings, to be corrected by a staff pathologist. In those days autopsy pathology still played a large role in medical discovery and teaching. Every teaching hospital sought to get permission for autopsy of patients who died in their hospital. Hospitals were judged by the percentage of autopsies performed. Bellevue had a good record. Training of an internist always included an assignment in pathology where one could correlate his or her diagnoses and treatments with what actually happened to the patient. At staff conferences the clinician presented the history and treatment of the patient. Staff members predicted what should be found at autopsy. Pathologists had the last word when they presented their findings, and they took great glee in proving the clinician wrong.

By the late summer of 1937, I was well established in the pathology assignment at Bellevue. Everything was going smoothly. I liked New York. I had friends. I had an enviable appointment leading to the top residency at Bellevue Hospital. Suddenly, late one afternoon about the first of September, I received a long distance call from Galveston. A long distance call in those days was always important. People didn't call to chat. The call was from Dr. Paul Brindley, professor of pathology at the Medical Branch, who offered me a job as instructor in pathology to start immediately at $150 a month. He pointed out the advantages of being in Texas. As I recall, I accepted his offer during the call. That was an impulsive decision, but there must have been several factors which influenced me. I was homesick for Texas, I liked Dr. Brindley, and I liked Galveston. Being an instructor on the faculty of a medical school was a very prestigious position for a twenty-four-year-old intern. The pay was ten times my Bellevue salary.

When I reported to Dean Currier McEwen that I planned to leave I caught hell: "Here we have offered this program for you in good faith, which you accepted, and now you go back on your word." There was much more. Dr. McEwen felt that Dr. Carter, who sent me to Bellevue, should never have allowed Dr. Brindley to call. Later, when I asked Dr. McEwen for a recommendation to the Mayo Clinic, he wrote back that he would not recommend me for anything. I had gone back on my word. Had I realized how important my appointment had been, I would not have accepted Dr. Brindley's offer. But there was no turning back. This was another example of how a single brief event changed my life forever. I often wonder what my career would have been if Dr. Brindley had not called. Obviously I was not Dr. Brindley's first choice, otherwise I would have been called a few months in advance.[7]

CHAPTER 6

Instructor in Pathology, University of Texas Medical Branch, 1937–38

A few changes had taken place at the Medical Branch in the year since I graduated. Several of my schoolmates were assistants or on the faculty.[1] Virtually all the professors were still there, several having been promoted, and the title of adjunct had been replaced by assistant professor. Truman Blocker, class of 1933, had been at Columbia Medical Center in New York as instructor in surgery while I was interning at Bellevue. We had visited each other in New York. I came back to Galveston to find that Truman also had returned to become assistant professor in surgery and surgical pathology. As soon as I arrived, Truman asked if I'd like to share an apartment with him. I accepted. The apartment comprised upstairs rooms above the private practice offices of faculty members Dr. Willard Cooke in gynecology and obstetrics and Dr. Boyd Reading in pediatrics. The apartment had two bedrooms, a bath, and a living room. Truman and I were rarely at the house: there was no kitchen, and we worked long hours. About all we did there was come home late, go to bed, and get up early the next morning and go to work. I took most of my noon meals at the College Inn and suppers at a boarding house next door to it. Levin Hall now occupies the site of the College Inn and the boarding house. The landlady was a great cook. Her husband was a retired commercial fisherman whose fishing friends provided the table with an abundance of seafood. We were served fried shrimp and oysters, shrimp creole, deviled crabs, seafood gumbo, baked redfish and fried sea bass.

My job as instructor was a valuable experience, largely the result of Dr. Paul Brindley's leadership. Dr. Brindley had been appointed an instructor when he graduated in 1925. He went to the Mayo Clinic and Boston City Hospital for graduate training. He became a professor and chairman of the department of pathology in 1929 at age thirty-three and held the position until his death in 1954. He was a quiet, thoroughly organized teacher and administrator. His concise lectures should have been published as a book. He orchestrated the work of his professors and instructors so that the laboratory assignments and the conferences followed his lectures closely. A remarkable teacher, he made it easy for the students to study the vast knowledge of pathology. During his youth, Dr. Brindley was crippled by osteomyelitis of the hips and had to walk with crutches. His energy and dedication to his work made us unaware of his handicap. He was even-tempered. I never saw him get mad or raise his voice, but no one doubted that he was boss. Once he assigned our duties, he rarely had to give orders. Dr. Jarrett Williams was associate professor of pathology. He graduated from the Medical Branch, joined the pathology faculty in 1935, and spent most of the next twenty-three years in the department. Alongside me was one other instructor, John Shaver, a Texan and my fraternity brother and classmate. Truman Blocker also often joined with us in presenting the clinical and pathological conferences. I enjoyed working with this congenial group.

Our most important undertaking was teaching pathology to the sophomore class. The first semester of lectures and laboratory demonstrations covered the fundamentals of pathology, including retrograde and progressive tissue changes, circulatory disturbances, inflammation, infections, deficiency diseases, and neoplasms. We taught by lecture, lantern slides, microscopic slides, charts, gross wet specimens, and mounted museum specimens from our outstanding museum. The second semester was devoted to the cardiovascular, respiratory, digestive, genitourinary, skeletal, nervous, endocrine, and hematopoctic systems. In the junior year we presented a course limited to the surgical pathology of the female genital organs. We also had a joint course in surgical pathology with the surgical department. Under Dr. Brindley's direction, we prepared the material for presentation to the class. We circulated through the laboratory, assisting students in the identification of the diseased tissues by gross and microscopic demonstrations. I got to know every student well. After sixty years, I still stay in touch with a few. I recently attended a medical school reunion, where several alumni came to me and said they enjoyed their student days in pathology and complimented the department for a good teaching job.

Shaver and I performed autopsies on patients who died in John Sealy Hospital and the Marine Hospital and handled medical examiner's cases of those who died in Galveston County from violence or under suspicious circumstances. The autopsies took place in an amphitheater in the Out-Clinic

Building. Eugene Theim had become the deaner who handled the bodies before and after the autopsies. We were frequently called to do an autopsy during the night. Students and faculty who treated the deceased patient tried to be present in the amphitheater while the autopsy was performed. As I recall I did about a hundred and fifty autopsies. Performing the autopsy was only part of the work, however. We saved tissues for gross study, for museum and teaching specimens, and for microscopic study. After the tissues had been preserved in formalin we dissected the tissue and cut additional sections for microscopic study. The sections were fixed in paraffin, cut with a microtome into thin slices and stained to bring out the distinctive features of the diseased tissue. For every autopsy a box of fifty or more microscopic slides were prepared for examination and storage for possible future study.

With all this work done we prepared a lengthy protocol, first writing a summary of the clinical history, physical, laboratory, and X-ray findings, and the treatment rendered. Following the clinical summary, we reported the autopsy findings—the condition of the body as a whole, including height, weight, nutritional status, and abnormal external features such as wounds. Following this, we described the condition of all the organs, including the brain and spinal cord if required. We described the findings in the microscopic slides. A detailed description of the condition causing death was included. Finally, we summarized the entire findings and listed the diagnosis for every other abnormality found at the autopsy. Sometimes we did not find the cause of death immediately and had to wait for chemical studies. Even then, there were mysterious deaths. We did not have a forensic pathologist like we had at Bellevue. Dr. Brindley reviewed each autopsy report, checking our gross findings and reviewing our slides and protocols during an open session.

As was customary, I kept a personal copy of the protocol of every case I autopsied, as well as a summary of each case in a pocket notebook. I had copies of all the autopsies I performed at Bellevue, Galveston, and the Mayo Clinic. A few of the striking findings were deaths from swallowing lye or undiluted Lysol, which completely necrotized the esophagus and stomach—a terrible way to commit suicide. There were deaths from an infected or punctured uterus, the result of abortion, and deaths from ruptured appendices and peritonitis. Before antibiotics, the death rate from appendicitis was ten percent. Today this is a prohibitive death rate, even for doing a heart transplant. Infection was the most common cause of death and included pneumonia, empyema, brain abscesses following mastoiditis, endocarditis, meningitis, and tuberculosis. Human longevity was less than sixty years. Now it is approaching eighty years.

The sulfonamides were the first significant antibacterial drugs. Their use was expanding rapidly. The Massengill Pharmaceutical Company of Richmond, Virginia, was noted for making drugs palatable and attractive. Sulfanilamide was insoluble in water, so Massengill prepared a syrup of sulfonamide by dissolving it in diethylene glycol—a drug preparation which turned out to be a fatal mixture. Diethylene glycol is highly hygroscopic, meaning that it draws water. When a patient swallowed the sweet and harmless tasting syrup of sulfanilamide, the diethylene glycol became concentrated in the kidneys, where its hygroscopic action drew the water out of the kidney cells, destroying them, resulting in kidney failure, uremia, and death. Suddenly we were performing autopsies on several patients who died of this form of kidney failure. We soon learned the cause of the kidney destruction. Animal experiments quickly determined that large doses of the glycols, including glycerol and diethylene glycol, as a result of their hygroscopic action, caused renal necrosis. Dr. Brindley suggested that I study our cases and publish a report about them. The article, my second to be published, received considerable publicity. I had a third article published on hypoplasia of the aorta while at the pathology department.

Although extremely busy, I did manage to have a social life during my year as an instructor at the Medical Branch. I went to the fraternity dances and beach parties, as well as to the parties and picnics that Dr. and Mrs. Brindley organized for the pathology department. On one occasion, I was highly honored when Dr. A. O. Singleton invited Truman and me for a family dinner at his home. We were the only guests. We sat at the table with Dr. and Mrs. Singleton, and their two high school aged sons, Albert, Jr., and Edward.[2] I also remember the time when Eugene Thiem and I rented a row boat to go fishing. We rowed a couple of miles across Galveston Harbor, past the Quarantine Station, to two partially sunken concrete ships, relics of World War I. This was a favorite spot to tie up on one of the old wrecks and clamber up. On board was plenty of room to sit comfortably while throwing out a line and waiting for the fish to bite. We carried a picnic and caught a few fish. About 3:00 P.M. we decided to row back to Galveston. We got a few hundred feet out when a stiff wind blew in from the south. Instead of going forward we drifted toward the main ship channel. Things didn't look good. Fortunately a motor yacht passed by, and the skipper threw us a line and towed us into the still waters of Galveston Harbor. This was yet another close call.

While back in Galveston, the most important social event for me was the marriage on February 12, 1938, of my apartment mate Truman Blocker and Virginia Irvine, a junior medical student. Truman had always been outstanding. He had been president of the Medical Branch student body and Dr. Singleton's chief surgical resident and was on his way to becoming a full professor, chief of plastic and maxillofacial surgery and dean of the medical college.[3] He would become a famous plastic surgeon, receiving many honors and awards. Dr. Titus Harris hosted Truman's bachelor party at John's Seafood Restaurant. Most of the prominent and dignified members of the faculty were present for this elegant affair. Champagne was served and many toasts were made. Truman was feeling important. All of a sudden a naked girl ran into the room and plumped herself down in Truman's lap, hugging and kissing him and claiming to be his sweetheart. This was the only time I ever saw Truman fail to rise to the occasion. He was so embarrassed he could not speak, and didn't know what to do. Some of the dignified professors were also embarrassed, but the young ones roared with laughter.

During this time, I embarked on what would become a lifelong passion—collecting Texana. Occasionally I read books and articles about medical history, but had never collected any of the books. One of my fellow interns at Bellevue often went to book stalls on the Lower East Side and collected old seventeenth-century medical books. He claimed they were bargains and very rare. When I got to Galveston, I discovered that Dr. Brindley also had some interest in medical history books and that his wife, Ann Brindley, was an avid student of Texas history, especially of Galveston history. She had published an article about Jane Long living on Bolivar Peninsula in 1817 when Jean Lafitte occupied Galveston Island. Ann, a leading figure in the field of Texas history, became president of the Texas State Historical Society. She loaned me a popular biography of Jean Lafitte by Lyle Saxon, a New Orleans author. Soon I was reading Ann's Texas history books. I forgot about medical history books and started collecting Texas history. Ann Brindley told me about Herbert Fletcher, the Houston dealer of Texana and owner of the Anson Jones Press. I went to Houston every chance I had to visit Herbert Fletcher and browse in his bookstore. I always purchased a book or two I could afford and sometimes a book I could not afford.

Some of my first books, some of them $5.00 purchases, were Randolph Marcy's *Exploration of Red River,* ($5.00 then, worth $500.00 today); Mary Maverick's *Memoirs;* De Shields's *Border Wars of Texas;* Marquis James's biography of Sam Houston, *The Raven;* Kendall's *Santa Fe Expedition;* Mary Austin Holley's *Texas;* John Wesley Hardins's *Life;* Gregg's *Commerce of the Prairies;* Green's *Texan Expedition Against Meir;* Gillett's *Six Years With the Texas Rangers;* Anderson's *A Texas Surgeon in the C.S.A.;* and Roemer's *Texas.* The very rare books brought $25.00—a price I could not afford—but I bought many recently published titles for fifty cents, the going price for an average book. By the time I left Galveston, I had collected about fifty Texas books, the beginning of a collection which would total more than six thousand.[4]

Since I had given up my position at Bellevue, I next had to look for a residency in medicine for when I completed the instructorship in pathology. I considered several places, but my first choice was the Mayo Clinic. The Mayo doctors were publishing many articles, demonstrating their leadership in clinical medicine. Many of the Mayo doctors were famous. I told Dr. Brindley that I planned to apply to the Mayo Clinic. It would be hard to get in, however, since this prestigious institution had hundreds of applicants. Dr. Paul Brindley's brother, Dr. George Valter Brindley, Sr., was head of Scott and White Clinic and Hospital in Temple, Texas. He came to Galveston to recruit residents and visit his brother. Paul Brindley called me in his office to meet G. V. Brindley, who told me that if I came to Scott and White for a year, he would get me into the Mayo Clinic. He offered me a job as a junior staff member in medicine. Scott and White was one of the few large clinics in America and had close professional ties with the Mayo Clinic. Drs. Scott and White were friends of the brothers Mayo. The two clinics interchanged residents. Dr. Charlie Mayo's son Joe had interned at Scott and White. I accepted the job on the spot. As I write this I realize the influence that the Brindleys had on my life. One brought me back to the Medical Branch, and the other brought me to Scott and White, where I met my wife, Mary Randolph Wilson. Also while at Scott and White I first thought of organizing a clinic—an idea that determined the remainder of my professional career.

CHAPTER 7

Scott and White Clinic and Marriage, 1938–39

I arrived at the Scott and White Clinic, Temple, Texas, around July 1, 1938, and soon found a room three blocks from the clinic. I had the front bedroom with a door onto the front porch. The room was well ventilated with large screened windows—an important consideration since there was no air conditioning then and temperatures often reached and exceeded one hundred degrees. I shared a bathroom with two women technicians from the clinic and took my meals at a very nice boarding house two blocks away.

Temple, Bell County, is located in Central Texas, between Waco and Austin. The town was established in 1880 by the Santa Fe Railroad, which in 1892 built the Santa Fe Hospital for its employees. King's Daughters Hospital was erected in 1897 and Scott and White Hospital in 1904. The three facilities made Temple a leading medical center. In 1938 the population was about fifteen thousand. I found Temple to be a very pleasant small city. As in Galveston, the people and the clinic doctors were very friendly. To serve the out-of-town patients there were three hotels—the Kyle, the Hawn, and the Doehring, as well as numerous boarding houses around the clinic. Temple was a town of many churches, and I attended the Methodist Church. The Temple Country Club, where I played golf, had very low dues for the young doctors. The Moss Rose, a combination of nightclub, beer tavern, and restaurant done in art deco, was popular with the younger members of the Scott and White staff. We often drove twenty-five miles to the nearest Mexican restaurant in Rosebud and fifteen miles during the summer to a popular public swimming pool near Belton.

The clinic, located not far from the center of town, occupied about six brick or stucco buildings surrounded by well-kept lawns. Most of the buildings were connected by covered walkways. The largest building was the main hospital, which was two and three stories high, with large verandas on each floor. This building contained operating rooms and beds for patients. There were three other hospital buildings: an old one story, a newer four story, and the three-story Woodson Ear Nose and Throat and Dental Hospital. There were two wooden out-clinic buildings with central waiting rooms and elongated wings that housed examining rooms extending along each side of a long hall. Across the street from the main hospital was the interns' quarters and house staff reception room, a converted residence with a large veranda. The house staff sat on the veranda after hours and told each other wild stories about their medical school days, their hometowns, and the girls they had known. Incidentally, the interns from Tulane talked about Alton Oschner's surgical resident Mike DeBakey.

In 1938 Scott and White was, and is today, the largest private clinic in Texas. The King's Daughters Hospital and Clinic was a smaller organization in Temple. At this time, there were very few large clinics in America. Within the medical profession, even as late as the 1930s, physicians—especially general practitioners—were still opposed to clinics, since they represented a form of group practice.[1] The Lahey Clinic and the Joslin Diabetes Clinic were in Boston. The Crile Clinic, later named the Cleveland Clinic, was in Cleveland, Ohio. The Virginia Mason Clinic was in Seattle and the Lovelace Clinic was getting underway in Albuquerque, New Mexico. Many small clinics or sanitaria were scattered throughout America and in Europe. The Paris Texas Sanitarium, as an example, was a two-story clinic-hospital staffed by six or eight doctors. Most of these institutions had their beginning in the practice of a single leading doctor who had gained local fame.

Arthur Carroll Scott, Sr., developed the three hospitals in Temple. He was born in Gainesville, Texas, July 12, 1865, and began reading medicine in a doctor's office at seventeen years of age. In 1882 he entered New York's Bellevue Medical College, and received his medical degree in 1886. After two years of internship in Pittsburgh, Pennsylvania, he returned to Gainesville to practice. His progress was rapid. He was appointed local surgeon of the Santa Fe Railroad and in 1892 became chief surgeon and moved to Temple to work at the Santa Fe Hospital. In 1894 he appointed Raleigh R. White, Sr., house surgeon of the Santa Fe Hospital. Drs. Scott and White formed a partnership and in 1898 established King's Daughters Hospital. In 1904 they withdrew from it and established Scott and White Hospital, meanwhile continuing to operate the Santa Fe Hospital. White was born in Mississippi in 1871. His family moved to Texas in 1881. After receiving his M.D. from Tulane, in 1891 he started a private practice, which he continued until he joined Scott. The next member

Dr. A. C. Scott, Sr., and Mavis, 1939

of the early staff who was still practicing in 1938 was Dr. Olin Gober who came in 1905, followed by Dr. Claudia Potter in 1906, and Dr. M. W. Sherwood in 1908. In 1911, Dr. G. V. Brindley, Sr., arrived on the staff. He was the chief of surgery and the clinic when he brought me to Scott and White.[2]

Scott and White was a very popular clinic. Patients came from all over Texas and surrounding states, mainly from the country, small towns, and small cities. Many were referred by their local physician. Fees were very reasonable and the medical care was outstanding for that time. Much charitable care was given to the poor and those who were down on their luck due to illness. No one was sued for nonpayment of bills. By his own example, Dr. Scott, Sr., had inspired his staff to treat patients with compassion and respect. There was an air of hospitality and friendliness. During the hot summer the patient hostess, Mrs. A. R. (Dee) Dickinson and her assistants passed iced tea to patients in the waiting rooms. Wealthy ranchers and poor tenant farmers alike felt at ease. The families of the clergy and the medical profession were given courtesy care. Health insurance was practically nonexistent.

Most of my work at Scott and White involved examining new patients. But I had some important lessons to learn. Once, for example, I wrote a history and physical examination for one of Dr. Scott's patients. After he had seen the patient he called me in his office and politely criticized me for describing the patient as an old crock. I had picked up a lot of bad habits at Bellevue, where we described patients with derogatory words and abbreviations. PMB was a common diagnosis meaning Poor Miserable Bastard. On other occasions, after I had introduced myself to the patient, they often let me know that they had come to see Dr. Scott or Dr. Brindley or some other "grown-up" doctor. This was my first experience with handling private patients who had a choice of doctors. I explained that I was on hand to prepare the patient for the senior doctor. I soon learned that I could gain the patient's confidence by establishing a personal connection, such as having a mutual friend or knowing about the patient's hometown. After college and medical school I knew people all over Texas. I loved geography—at one time I could name all 254 counties of Texas as fast as anyone could count them. And I knew about farming and ranching, the occupations of most of these patients. After some pleasant conversation I was able to get the patient relaxed and willing to let me do my examination.

The rule at Scott and White was to do a thorough history and physical examination such as I had learned at medical school and at Bellevue. This included asking very personal questions and looking into every body opening. We used an otoscope to look at the ear drums; an ophthalmoscope to view the optic fundi; a rhinoscope to look into the nose; a tongue blade to look at the mouth and throat; a speculum for the vagina; and a proctoscope for the rectum. We always did a manual examination of the female pelvis and a digital examination of the anus, rectum, and prostate of male patients. After writing a complete report of our examination we attempted to make a correct diagnosis. Then a senior doctor came in the room to see the patient, review our record, and help us decide what tests and x-rays the patient should have. Two or three days later, after all tests had been performed, we saw the patient again with the senior doctor. He discussed the findings with the patient, made a final diagnosis, and prescribed treatment. When a patient was hospitalized, I came by and followed the treatment. After the patient had been dismissed, the final record was sent back for the junior doctor to review and learn how accurate his initial diagnosis had been. Often the senior doctor reviewed the final record with the junior doctor.

Fads have always been present in medical belief and practices, and the 1930s were no exception. In medical school, for example, I was taught that meno-pausal symptoms were purely psychological or imaginary in origin, a folklore passed down from mother to daughter. We sent these patients away with no treatment for their suffering. Many doctors believed that various pelvic pains, menstrual cramps, and painful sex were caused by a retroverted uterus. These symptoms were thought to be relieved by suspending the uterus to the ante-rior abdominal wall so that it would not tip backward into the pelvis. Hun-dreds of thousands of women were subjected to this operation. Whether it helped is doubtful. A very large percentage of women have a retroverted uterus and never suffer a symptom. Many women were having this uterine sus-pension operation while I was at Scott and White. There was gossip within the medical profession that Scott and White Hospital was built on uterine suspensions. If so, Scott and White was not alone. This operation was being performed in every medical center and hospital in America. Scott and White simply had a larger practice. This surgical procedure, which eventually be-came obsolete, had at least one redeeming result. The appendix was usually removed during the operation, thus sparing many women the risks of acute appendicitis, which had an operative mortality rate of ten percent.

Also in the 1930s, the so-called foci of infection caused much concern. Nearly every organ could be a focus, including the gall bladder, sinuses, and prostate, while tonsil and dental infections were the most common. Foci were respon-sible for arthritis, low grade fever, valvular heart disease, allergies, and other chronic conditions. At Scott and White and at the Mayo Clinic, many pa-tients had exhaustive studies to rule out foci. Many adults were sent back to remove a few tonsil tags that were overlooked at a previous tonsillectomy or they had all their teeth extracted. Today the pendulum has swung too far the other way—we don't believe in tonsillectomies, regardless of how much the patient suffers. If foci are important, we are missing some important causes of diseases, because many of today's doctors never heard of foci of infection. In June 1997, however, I read an article blaming infected teeth for heart valve disease. Perhaps the pendulum is swinging back.[3]

I enjoyed an active social life in Temple. The young doctors at the clinic formed a congenial social group. Many were married or, as I discovered, were soon to be. It seemed there was some social event every night, such as an in-vitation to dinner by a senior staff member; an informal party at a junior staff member's house; a picnic or a barbecue; or a swim at the pool in Belton. The Chautuaqua educational center in Chautuaqua, New York, sent lecturers, mu-sicians, magicians, and other entertainers on tour to cities around the country including Temple. Going to an air-conditioned movie theater served as relief from the summer heat. Some of our group usually met at the Moss Rose for conversation and a beer or dinner. The county medical society met at one of the hotels each month for dinner and a program. There were church activities. It seemed as if someone was always getting married. Out of town visitors had to be entertained. Temple was a typical southern town full of gregarious people.

While enjoying the professional and social life of Temple, I did not forget my goal of training at the Mayo Clinic. In January 1939, I sent in my application and went to Rochester, Minnesota, for an interview. The ground was covered with snow when I arrived. My classmate and AKK brother Huard Hargis had already become a fellow at the clinic. He met me early in the morning at the railroad station and drove me to his apartment, where I stayed. I was welcomed by Huard's wife Lucylle, a wonderful woman from Paris, Tennessee. My day was filled with interviews. I only remember Dr. Donald Balfour, head of the Mayo Foundation and Dr. Russell Wilder, chief of medicine. I hit it off well with both of these famous men. Balfour virtually promised me a fellowship, so I returned to Temple feeling exhilarated. I was in a good mood when the greatest event of my life occurred—meeting Mary Randolph Wilson.

"Would you like to take a very attractive young lady to the Chautuaqua tonight?" Mrs. Dee, the clinic hostess asked me, as I was completing a busy day at Scott and White in mid-February 1939. "Always," I replied. I had done this before. Mrs. Dee explained that the young lady had come to town from Beaumont to be with her sister, who had entered the hospital for surgery the next day. Mrs. Dee had tickets for the young lady and me and for Marcia Morrison and Raleigh Curtis. Mrs. Dee arranged for me to pick up my blind date in the lobby of the Kyle Hotel and join Marcia and Raleigh at the Chautuaqua.

I arrived in the hotel lobby on time, but no attractive young lady was waiting for me. I paced around the lobby until program time and still no young lady. Mrs. Dee said her name was Mary Randolph Wilson so I called her room and asked for Miss Wilson. Miss Wilson replied that she would be down in a minute. I paced the lobby a while longer. Finally the elevator opened, and Miss Mary Randolph Wilson walked out in no particular hurry. Mrs. Dee was right about her being very attractive. She was little, five feet tall she told me later, and not lacking in self-confidence; she offered no explanation for being late. It never occurred to me until writing this autobiography that the young lady may have been late because she was reading a book she couldn't put down. This situation occurred many times in the years to come.

There was an air of culture and refinement about her. We exchanged greetings, and she was friendly and polite. I knew immediately that there was something special about her and that this was no ordinary date. I do not remember a thing about the Chautuaqua program. I was busy thinking about Mary Randolph Wilson and anxious to know more about her. I wondered how old she was and what was her education. She seemed to be very smart. Did she have a sweetheart? Would she like me? Who was her family? I was thinking serious thoughts. After the program was over I asked my date if she would like to go to the Moss Rose for a drink. She accepted promptly. We each had a beer and the conversation started. We talked without stopping for two hours, five beers each, and many cigarettes before we were told to leave so they could close for the night. I was surprised to see that little girl handle five bottles of beer and maintain her composure throughout the evening.

I am amazed at what I remember of that night. Some kind of chemistry occurred to imprint it on my memory. That night we didn't talk much about our backgrounds. We talked politics and history, and about Yankees and Southerners, and religion and morals. She was romantic and idealistic, torn between long-held traditions of the south and liberal ideas learned as an undergraduate at Vassar College. Women should marry and have families, she felt—but they should do more, like Mrs. Eleanor Roosevelt was doing. She was concerned that she had led a sheltered life. We discussed art. I was reading an art history book by a popular art historian Hendrick Van Loon, who denigrated impressionist and abstract art in favor of what had been accomplished by the great Dutch masters. He claimed that the only great art was the result of infinite patience and detail. Mary disagreed with Van Loon. In years to come, I learned that Mary was usually right. She had a master's degree in history and had collected some favorite history books. I told her about my beginning collection of Texana. We both were interested in family genealogy.

That night I learned that Mary had graduated from Beaumont High School at fifteen years of age and from Vassar in 1932, the same year I graduated from A&M. So I decided we were about the same age. She didn't mention it that night but she had come to the same conclusion. Mary seemed to enjoy the evening; I certainly did. I wondered what she could see in me. She seemed to be very impressed that I was a doctor. Compared to her background, that was about all I had worth mentioning. Mary was unusually smart and well-educated but didn't brag about it. She had a warm outgoing personality. I was completely captivated by her. I took her to the hotel after midnight and told her that I wished her sister Fay a successful operation the next day and offered to help both of them while in Temple and that I would call on them in the hospital. I was trying to be a very professional doctor friend, trying not to show the least sign of being overwhelmed by her physical and personal beauty or of having any romantic interest in her. I was a deceitful liar.

Next day I was surprised to learn that every young doctor in the clinic knew about the two good-looking sisters from Beaumont. Mrs. Dee was besieged by doctors wanting her to get them a date with Mary. Doctors' wives were gossiping about it. Mrs. Dee obliged and arranged dates for Mary and the doctors. One I recall was Fred Hammond, a fellow junior staff man. I even double dated with another girl while Mary dated another doctor. It was tough. I had to do something. Being polite to Mary and her sister Fay in the hospital room was no way to start a romance. I told Mrs. Dee that I was very struck with Mary. "You'd better tell her" was Mrs. Dee's reply. So I went to Fay's hospital room again. Fay was recovering rapidly from Dr. Brindley's operation. I was greeted cheerfully by Fay Wilson and Mary, and their mother, Mrs. James Cooke Wilson, Sr. After a visit Mary followed me out in the hall. I unmasked my deceit and told her what a marvelous time I had with her on our date and that I wanted to see her again. I was pleasantly surprised when Mary said she also had a great time and that she had rather be with me than any of the other doctors. She was sorry she already had another date that night. But I did manage to get a date with Mary before she left Temple. I don't remember where we went on our second date except that I parked the car in a dark place and we were soon hugging and kissing and I was telling her how much I admired her and what a wonderful girl she was.

But that was only a second date, much too early for a couple to fall in love. We promised to write each other, and Mary planned to see me when she came back for Fay's follow-up visit. After Mary returned to Beaumont we had a warm but somewhat reserved correspondence. A romance had begun, however. I could hardly wait until Fay and Mary came back in a few weeks for Fay's follow-up examination. By their return visit, all our group of young doctors and friends knew Mary and Fay. Mrs. Dee was our chaperon. They were invited to all the social functions, at least one every night. I had several dates with Mary, but she had other dates as well. In those days young people, not yet engaged to marry, continued to have other dates, unlike today when young people seem to have only one girlfriend or boyfriend. Mary and I knew we were falling in love. Of our friends in Temple only Mrs. Dee knew of our mutual affection. More than a Scott and White hostess for patients, Mrs. Dee was a consummate matchmaker. She advised and encouraged me in courting Mary. She invited Mary to come to Temple and stay with her so we could be together, and she accompanied me on a trip to Beaumont. Mrs. Dee was a perceptive, attractive, friendly, genuine person, ideally suited for her job as clinic hostess and admired by everyone. Mary and I loved her and shared our confidences with her.

During Mary's second trip to Temple we began to learn more about each other. I took her to my room to see my Texana collection. We talked about history and books—we would join together in collecting thousands of books in the next half century. Mary was known to her family and close friends as Sister. She was well liked by people of all ages. When Mary graduated from high school in May 1926, her father thought she was too young to go to college, so he sent her to the Holton Arms School, a finishing school in Washington, D.C., for two years. Afterward, she entered Vassar. When I learned this, it dawned on me that Mary was two years older than I, but I didn't mention it since I thought she knew. She graduated from Vassar in June 1932 with a bachelor of arts degree, having majored in modern and European history and minored in art history. Her education continued with several periods of study in Europe. In 1933, Mary and her sister Fay spent six months in Europe attending the Institute of World Affairs in Mondsee, Austria, and a graduate institute of international studies in Geneva.

The institute in Mondsee was an international gathering of famous teachers and political leaders. Among the most prominent were Chancellor Engelbert Dolfuss of Austria and Roscoe Pound, dean of Harvard Law School. The speakers mainly discussed the means of preventing an impending war. Hitler was arming Germany, while France was soon building the Maginot line. In Mondsee, Mary met the family of Dorothy Canfield Fisher, well-known author, novelist, and one-time editor at the Book of the Month Club. While Mary and Fay were in Europe in 1933, the Fishers recommended they stay in Paris for continued study, Mary at the Musée Lycée, where only French was spoken, taking piano from a leading pianist, while Fay took harp lessons. Mrs. Fisher arranged for Mary and Fay to stay with the Fischbacher family, owners of a publishing firm and a bookstore. The sisters were having so much fun they were reluctant to come home. Finally, after sending several cablegrams urging them to come home, their father sailed to France, put them on a ship, and brought them back to Beaumont in time for Christmas.

In 1934, Mary and Fay spent another summer in France studying music at the Fountainbleu School at Fountainbleu Palace, outside Paris. Mary studied architecture and piano and Fay the harp. After they had completed the three-month classes at Fountainbleu, Mary and Fay moved to a pension in Paris where they planned to stay indefinitely to study music and more French. Again the girls were reluctant to come home, but their parents insisted that they return for prenuptial parties for their brother Waldo Wilson and his fiancée, Charlotte Strong. Later that year, Mary was offered a position to teach at the Holton Arms School for the 1935–36 school year. Mary was surprised when one of her teaching assignments was arithmetic, a subject she knew little about. She taught herself arithmetic, and was able to stay a day ahead of her class of teenage girls.

While teaching at Holton Arms, Mary decided to study for a masters degree in history at George Washington University for the 1937 fall term. Her course of study focused on contemporary European history. Her thesis, "Stanley and Brazza in the Congo," was a 110-page scholarly work containing maps drawn and colored by Mary. One of her professors, impressed by Mary, invited her to his home in Richmond, where they spent a day with Douglas Southall Freeman, the leading historian of the South. Mary obtained an autographed copy of Freeman's four-volume biography of Robert E. Lee. She read the whole thing in a few days and visited Robert E. Lee's home. She followed this by reading Southall's multi-volume history of the Civil War. Before I met Mary, I thought I was an authority on the Civil War, having visited Appomattox; Stone Mountain, Georgia; and the Cyclorama of the Battle of Atlanta. Mary soon straightened me out on that subject.

After earning her master's degree, Mary went to New York to work at the Book of the Month Club, where Dorothy Canfield Fisher was an editor. In New York she attended a charm school for several weeks while staying at the Barbizon Hotel. This school trained women as secretaries or administrators for leading business men or high government officials. Very few women achieved executive positions in business or government in those days. About the time I met Mary, she was hosting a successful radio program called *Women in the News* at station KRIC in Beaumont. She interviewed local women and reported the achievements of women everywhere. I was anxious to hear one of her programs and managed to do so one night while I was visiting the AKK house in Galveston. I proudly gathered some of my fraternity brothers around a radio to listen to my sweetheart's performance. Later after we married and moved to Rochester, Minnesota, Mary applied to host the same program on Rochester radio, but she was turned down because of her southern accent. This offended Mary, because she believed she had overcome her accent after spending several years in schools on the East Coast and in Europe.

After Fay's follow-up visit, there was no real medical reason for her and Mary to return to Temple. Fay used to tell the story that she made a great sacrifice for Mary and me, however, when she talked her parents into sending her back to Temple with Mary to have a wisdom tooth extracted. I remember the event well. Fay was admitted to Scott and White for the extraction. While Fay and Mary were there we went to several parties. Charades and question games like the "Sixty-four Dollar Question" were popular. Mary won every game. She was a walking encyclopedia, never forgetting a date or a telephone number. She was undoubtedly, the smartest, prettiest, loveliest girl I had ever met, and I was falling head-over-heels in love. I thought I had been in love before. I had some girlfriends I felt affection for, but this was a totally different phenomenon. I could not get Mary off my mind. Everything she did was complete perfection. I gazed at her in admiration. When we were alone, I gave her the tenderest kisses and the gentlest embraces. When she responded, I felt like I was in heaven. I could not find adequate words to praise her. I was lovesick for the first and last time of my life. We still have some of the letters we wrote each other. Reading these letters today provides ample proof of the diagnosis of lovesickness, since people think lovesick couples are silly. We had known each other only a couple of months. We expressed our love for each other, but as much as I would have liked, it seemed unthinkable for me to propose: it would have been presumptuous. Our parents had no idea about our serious condition. Our backgrounds were so disparate.

We did have help, however. Mrs. Dee was telling all the older Temple people, friends of Mary's mother, that I was a nice young man. Fay was providing opportunities for us to be together. She planned a weekend party at the Wilson's beach house. Claude Wilson of the junior staff was invited as Fay's date, and I was invited as Mary's date. Driving to the beach or to Beaumont for a weekend was an ordeal. I'd leave after work on Friday and drive six hours, arriving at 11:00 P.M. for a Friday night party. If the Sunday night party ended early at 10:00 P.M., I could get back to Temple by 4:00 A.M. for a few winks before appearing for work at 8:00 A.M. I made several of these exhausting runs while courting Mary.

Le Caprice, the Wilson beach house, was located at Caplen on Bolivar Peninsula. Caplen is at Rollover, the very narrow neck of the peninsula where Jean Lafitte's men were said to have rolled barrels of pirate's loot from the Gulf of Mexico to their small boats in Galveston Bay. The beach house, built in 1930, was a large square two-story wooden structure, raised a few feet above the ground on storm-proof piers. Wide-screened verandas, facing the cool gulf breeze on each floor and extending the full width of the house, were furnished with rockers and comfortable wicker chairs. For years, Mary's father and mother served scotch and sodas on the upstairs veranda before lunch and supper. Several double beds swung from the ceiling on each veranda, a perfect place for an afternoon nap or a cool night's sleep, while the rest of Texas sweltered from the summer heat. The house could sleep twenty people, and in the center of each floor was a large living room that extended from the veranda through the entire house with large windows on both ends allowing the breeze to pass through. Each of these living rooms had a fireplace. On the east side was a pantry and kitchen. A dining room extended out on the veranda. I will never forget the deviled crab casseroles that came from the kitchen. Sudden wind

Mary Wilson and Mavis on Joe Darby's horse at Le Caprice, 1939

and rain squalls would often wake the occupants in the middle of the night. Everyone jumped out of bed to roll down the canvas curtains, meanwhile getting thoroughly drenched. Such great fun![4]

The house sat on several acres between the highway and the gulf. A two-story garage, with servants quarters above, horse stalls, and a garden and watermelon patch were in the rear. A large fenced-in lawn surrounded the house and extended to the beach. The lot was landscaped with blooming yucca or desert flag and phlox drummondi, named for the botanist Drummond who discovered the plant on Bolivar Peninsula many years ago. Martins in the birdhouse amused us with their cheerful songs. In those days the beach was several hundred yards wide when the tide was out. One could walk on the open beach for several miles in each direction. Mary and I walked together; we swam together; we rode an old horse together; we played shuffleboard together. We spent hours alone talking to each other and making love. After one visit in the spring of 1939, we let everyone know we had a serious love affair. We told our parents. We both became jealous. I didn't want anyone having dates with Mary, even old harmless friends. Mary wouldn't put up with me having dates or even looking approvingly at other girls. This proved to be a lifelong attitude of hers, which I learned to respect.

Before my first visit to Le Caprice, Mary's mother had met me only briefly during Fay's operation in Temple. I think the Wilson family decided that this was no brief friendship of Mary's, that this persistent young doctor would not go away. It was about time to look him over. I am sure there were discussions. I drove down alone one weekend at the Wilson family's invitation. Mary wrote down directions telling me how to find their house. From her letter one would have concluded they lived in a little cottage. Late one beautiful afternoon, I drove in to find a magnificent house in a five-acre garden. Mary and Fay greeted me and showed me to my room. Then we walked around in a lovely garden with hundreds of camellias, azaleas, and jasmines. I can't remember the details of my first meeting with Mr. and Mrs. James Cooke Wilson, Sr., although I can say that they were friendly and cordial, soon making me feel at ease. We talked about friends in common at Scott and White, about my work as a doctor, and my hometown and folks in Deport. Mary seemed more anxious than I; she was probably afraid that my grammar would slip into its East Texas habits. We had a scotch and soda in the library together. After this visit, Mary and I went to the home of her brother Waldo and his wife, Charlotte, for dinner. They were very hospitable. Brother Cooke, Jr., was away; I later met him in Temple, when he came to bring Mary.

The next morning Mr. Wilson walked me through the gardens. Among his many camellias were several very large bushes transplanted from Louisiana. Then he drove off to the office in his air-conditioned Packard, one of the first air-conditioned cars in Texas. Mary said the house, built in 1935–36, was the first air-conditioned one in Texas. It was designed in Georgian style by John Staub of Houston. The library, full of books, many of which Mary had collected, was rather secluded—one had to walk down a hall to reach it—but there was a large sofa in the room. When everyone else had gone to bed Mary and I felt secure to embrace, kiss, caress, and say sweet things on this sofa. I learned that the other Wilson children had the same experience. Today that sofa is in our dining-living room. It needs reupholstering. Another generation has courted on it, and I hope still another one will. After the garden tour with Mr. Wilson, Mary drove me to meet some of her friends. She also took me to see the Junior Welfare League's work at St. Theresa Hospital. Mary had helped organize the league in 1937 and was its first president. Waldo then drove me out to Spindletop where the Wilson-Broach Company had a number of producing oil wells.

I soon learned that the Wilson family was very popular and very prominent in Beaumont. Born and raised in Meridian, Mississippi, Mary's father, James Cooke Wilson (1879–44), had invested his time and money in the great oil boom that followed the Lucas oil gusher of January 10, 1901, at Spindletop, near Beaumont. Groups of investors formed syndicates to invest in drilling oil wells at the site. The bankers who employed Cooke in Meridian put together a syndicate and invited Cooke, then twenty-two years old, to go to Beaumont and manage their investment. Cooke put some of his own money in the venture and caught the train for Beaumont. He had barely arrived before he located a well, already drilled to 150 feet, but shut down for lack of funds. He bought the lease and the well for the syndicate and managed to drill it to 1,300 feet and produce a gusher. This was the twenty-seventh well to be drilled at Spindletop. Within the first year, 140 wells were drilled. Anyone who knows about the risks and percentages of success in drilling oil wells will certainly consider Cooke's initial success a stroke of good fortune. Cooke resigned his position in the Meridian bank and devoted his career to producing oil. A few years later, he was one of several men who organized the Humble Oil and Refining Company, which applied for charter on March 1, 1917. He owned some fine oil production, which the group wanted him to put into the venture. Finally Cooke agreed to put in one of the leases that he held on the right-of-way of the interurban tracks through Goose Creek. In return Cooke received a block of the original capital stock in the Humble Oil Company. Humble Oil became the most successful oil producing company in the United States. Standard Oil of New Jersey began acquiring Humble Oil Company stock. Eventually they controlled and later merged Humble Oil into Standard of New Jersey, which is today Exxon. Cooke's original Humble Oil stock went through several stock splits and changes of name; most of the stock passed down in the family.

While I was busy learning about the family, Mr. and Mrs. Wilson—and Mary's friends—said not one word to me about our courtship. Everyone had extended me a warm welcome, however. Their remarks could be condensed as follows: I must be pretty nice; otherwise Mary would not have me as a beau. Mary and I reaffirmed our love for each other during my visit, and I departed for Temple with my head swimming and wondering why I was so fortunate to meet such a fabulous family as the Wilsons. Almost sixty years later, as I reflect on these events, I think Mary's parents were friendly with me because I was the choice of their daughter whom they loved dearly. I think they had plenty of doubts about me as a son-in-law. They probably wished that Mary had picked an older, successful, wealthy cultivated man instead of a country boy doctor whose only possessions were the clothes on his back and a Chevrolet.

On July 4, 1939, I went to Caplen to visit Mary. It must have been at this time that I proposed to her. We had pledged our eternal love for each other time after time, so it was the proposal came as no surprise. Amazingly, later neither of us could remember the exact event of my proposal—possibly because we had become engaged subconsciously over a period of weeks. I would take Mary up to Dallas and buy her an engagement ring and drive on to Deport for my family to meet her. We would make definite plans. Mary wanted us to have a home with a family of boys and girls. But first, I had to talk to Mr. Wilson, a most important immediate step.

Mary did not know what her parents' reaction would be when they learned of our engagement. She thought they approved of me as a person, but she wondered if they opposed their daughter getting married to a man with an unproven future. Mary loved and respected her parents, but she wanted to get married, approval or no approval. Mary and I decided that I should go to Mr. Wilson and tell him that we were deeply in love, had given it a lot of thought, and had decided to get married. Period. I would tell him about myself, my plans for a career, my finances, and my family background. As a matter of principle I was determined not to take any money from the Wilsons. I called Dad and told him we were engaged and asked him for a modest allowance so that I could support my future wife. He agreed. This meant living on a shoestring, but Mary agreed heartily. She thought she had been too sheltered and should join me in the sacrifices of building our own future. As I look back I realize how naïve and idealistic we were, but we lived up to our ideals. Only with Mary's determination could we have done it, though.

With these plans in mind, Mary invited me to visit her in Beaumont. I arrived in a state of anxiety. Mary and I reaffirmed our love for each other and reviewed our strategy. There was an air of something about to happen in the Wilson house. The Wilsons served their scotch and sodas as usual, and then we had dinner. I can't remember whether Fay and Cooke, Jr., were there. After dinner Mr. Wilson went upstairs to his study, Mrs. Wilson to their bedroom. Mary gave me a reassuring kiss and sent me on my way to see Daddy. I knocked on the door, Mr. Wilson invited me in, and we sat down together. He was smoking a Picayune cigarette and offered me one, but I declined. I saw Mr. Wilson as a charming, polite, friendly, true southern gentleman he intended to be. He made up his mind quickly and had firm opinions. I admired him greatly. He knew why I was coming to talk to him. My presentation went off exactly as planned—it paid to think ahead. Mr. Wilson listened. I could tell that he knew Mary and I were dead serious. He offered no objections but questioned me about the very things I had anticipated. I told him my father had given his approval and would give me an allowance. With that exception, Mary and I were going to make it on our own. When I told him that I had a five thousand dollar life insurance policy he didn't seem too impressed. He told me what a wonderful girl Mary was and how much he and Mrs. Wilson wanted to be sure that she was happy and well provided for. After more discussion and Picayune cigarettes he congratulated me and offered Mary and me his full approval and support in our plans to marry. We shook hands with a firm grip. Mr. Wilson had a warm cheerful look on his face. We went downstairs to be with Mary. Mrs. Wilson came down and we all hugged and kissed each other. It's strange that I can remember this so well while I can't remember the details of proposing to Mary. Tension must enhance one's memory.

The visit with Mr. Wilson marked a turning point, however. Whereas I had control or at least partial control of events before, I was now a vestigial appendage of no consequence. The ladies would be in charge of all events until we were married and had left Beaumont on our honeymoon. It was decided that our engagement be announced on Sunday, July 27, and we would be married on Sunday, September 17. The announcement was published in the Beaumont, Houston, Dallas, Temple, and Deport papers.

Mary came up to Temple, and the ladies entertained her. We went to Dallas to buy a diamond ring. One had to look carefully at the ring to see the stone. That's all the money I had. Everyone was disappointed. Mary didn't say anything, but I'm sure she was embarrassed by such a small diamond. She referred to the ring and my financial circumstances in a letter to her mother dated July 21, 1939: "marrying Mavis seems the securest thing in the world to me. He may never be rich but I know I can trust him always to do the right thing and I believe that is better than any number of diamond rings—and I also know that if I can do my part, we'll always be financially secure." I wasn't able to buy her a larger one until I had been in practice in Houston, and by then she didn't care about a bigger diamond. When I look back, there are hundreds of things I would have done differently. I should have hocked my car to get Mary a better ring. But Dad always told me to never borrow money, no matter what.

From Dallas, we drove to Deport. My family really wanted to have a nice party. They knew I liked squirrel stew. That was about the finest thing anyone could have in Deport. It was even better than quail. Dean Oliver went hunting and brought back some nice squirrels. The party was held on the front lawn of the Dr. Kelsey house, where my Uncle Dean and Aunt Lucille lived. All the Kelseys were there. The squirrel stew was great, but Mary didn't seem very enthusiastic. Several years later she confessed that she hated that squirrel stew. She had never tasted squirrel. Squirrel was a rodent, and the idea of eating it was repulsive to her. At the time of the party I thought everything went off well. Everyone liked Mary and she seemed to like everyone. Mother had a coffee for Mary and invited all the Kelsey friends. There was one moment of tension, however. After we returned from Deport, Mary asked me what year I was born. Surprisingly, she became very upset when I told her I was born in 1912. Mary said she felt bad about marrying someone younger than she was. I told her it didn't bother me one bit. She worried about our age difference for a few days before deciding that her affection for me hadn't changed. Nevertheless, from then on she was reluctant for people to know that I am younger.

From here on out our courtship turned into a circus. Mary was entertained by many Beaumont friends. The parties were reported in detail in the Beaumont papers. The guests were listed, the menu was printed, and the decorations were described. Mary's picture with her hostesses was in the Beaumont and Houston papers day after day. Fay saved all the clippings for an album. She typed a list of twenty-eight parties, including four at Temple.

The night before the wedding, Mary's brother Waldo hosted a dinner at the Hotel Beaumont for fifty guests, including the bridal party and some out-of-town guests. After Waldo's party a special communion service was held at St. Mark's Episcopal Church, where I nearly fainted but I didn't tell anyone. Friends of the Wilson family also were entertaining out-of-town guests including Bishop and Mrs. Quin, my parents, my sister Virginia and her husband, Marvin Gibbs, as well as Mary's uncle John Wilson and Aunt Effie Wilson from Meridian, Mississippi. I should have given a bachelor party for the groomsmen. I don't remember whether I tried. Events were out of my hands. I just tagged along. It seemed to me that Beaumont stopped all business and went on an extended party to celebrate Mary's engagement and coming marriage.

The Wilsons were active in the Episcopal Church. Mr. Wilson was treasurer of the diocese. Clinton S. Quin, Bishop of the Espicopal Diocese of Texas, and his wife, Hortense, were close friends of the Wilsons. Bishop Quin agreed to officiate at our wedding. One weekend while visiting Mary, I was called into Mr. Wilson's study to meet Bishop Quin. He and Mr. Wilson asked me a lot about my career and where my family came from. Bishop Quin was born in Kentucky, like my grandmother. They teased me in a friendly way about carrying the names of two birds—Mavis, which is an English thrush, and Parrott. They got a big kick out of this. Of course I had to tell them the story of my name. Later, Bishop Quin requested Mary and I come to his house in Houston for premarital advice. They had us for dinner, and afterward he took us into his study for a serious talk about the sanctity of marriage. One thing I will always remember he said: If you are mad at your spouse, and there are times when you will be, make up before you go to sleep at night; never go to bed mad at each other. I have reminded myself of this advice many times, but not nearly as often as I should have. Bishop Quin gave us a small book, *Foundations of Happiness in Marriage,* autographed "To Mary and Mavis, C.S.Q." After offering a prayer for us, he sent us away inspired to stick to our vows.

The Wilsons were determined to make this the greatest wedding in the

Bishop Clinton S. Quinn and James Cooke Wilson, Sr.

world. Their darling Mary deserved it. They probably thought it might be her last luxury. They planned a spectacular wedding for four hundred guests in their garden. Mrs. Libby Masterson of Houston was engaged as an advisor for the event. She helped the Wilsons with hundreds of details. In the midst of all this, Mary and her mother went to the Adolphus Hotel in Dallas to stay while shopping for Mary's trousseau at Neiman Marcus. Stanley Marcus himself waited on them. For life in Rochester, Minnesota, they bought Mary a fur-trimmed winter sports suit. Neimans photographed her in this suit holding ice skates and published the picture in several Texas newspapers. Mary's trousseau was all silk—silk undies, slips, gowns, stockings—all packaged in quilted silk boxes. She also returned from Dallas with dresses and sweaters, hats and gloves, fur jackets and coats, including a fabulous shirred beaver coat.

On September 12, 1939, we obtained a marriage license at the Bell County courthouse in Belton. I selected my groomsmen, all were doctors. Fred Hammond was my best man. The other groomsmen were fellow Scott and White staff members Raleigh Curtis and Hugh DeLaurel, medical school class-mates Sam Barnes and Ralph Letteer. With Mrs Dee's help I bought leather overnight kits for the groomsmen. She also helped me select an antique pin of four garnets shaped like a clover leaf for Mary, who wore it at the wedding. Fay served as Mary's maid of honor; her sister-in-law Charlotte Wilson as matron of honor; and her good friends from Beaumont, Jane Owens, Katherine Price, and Ruby Reed as bridesmaids.

A day or two before I was to leave Temple for the wedding, I developed a fever, a rare occurrence but certainly attributable to the stress.[5] But I didn't feel too bad. Fred Hammond drove me to Beaumont where I stayed at the Hotel Beaumont, where my fever climbed to 103°, and I felt terrible. Without telling anyone I took an aspirin and went to bed for a few hours. Fortunately the fever went away, but I still think about what would have happened if I hadn't made that wedding. I can remember most of the actual wedding service. It came off on time. The weather was fine. Mary was fabulous in her wedding dress. She said I had a strange look on my face as I watched her be led by her father up the grass covered aisle to the alter. After the wedding, the bridal party was served a breakfast of quail on toast. Many guests lingered until late afternoon.

We left our families that afternoon after many hugs and kisses and good-bys and drove to the Lamar Hotel in Houston. Flowers and champagne decorated the room. That evening, we walked a couple of blocks to the Majestic Theater to see the movie *Old Maids*. Maybe we went to the movie because we were afraid of our wedding night. As we waited to buy our tickets who should join us in the line but family friends Mr. and Mrs. Harry Weiss of Houston who had attended our wedding that day in Beaumont. They were very surprised to see us and teased us a little. After the movie we walked back to the hotel. In our room Mary opened her suitcase and brought out the trousseau, pink silk, the kimono, the night gown, maybe other things. She took them to the bathroom and closed the door. I thought she would never come out. Maybe she was reading a book. I don't remember what I did but somehow I got into my pajamas. Finally Mary came out in her silk robe and gown, the prettiest, loveliest women I ever saw. We had embraced many times before, often passionately, but always fully dressed and that was as far as we got. I will summarize without being personal by saying we consummated our marriage successfully. I loved Mary even more than before. There is no way for me to express it. I have always loved Mary more than anyone else. We didn't go to a movie the next day—we never left the room.[6]

After two nights in the Lamar, Mary and I departed on our planned trip to a rustic cottage at Woodbine Lodge in Sedalia, Colorado. We were the only guests, the last ones of the season. It turned cold. The only heat was from the cottage fireplace. We took steaks up to the top of Elephant Mountain, a thousand foot climb, and grilled them. I couldn't keep up with Mary on either the

Mary and Mavis at wedding, September 17, 1939

way up or the way down. We visited a nearby fox farm, which produced hundreds of black fox furs. Fur coats were very popular then, and owning one was an aspiration of most American women. We didn't tell the lodge staff that we were on our honeymoon. We thought we acted like a long-time married couple. When we checked out a few days later, we told them that we were newlyweds. "We knew it from the day you arrived," they said. That day, we went to Denver to visit the Museum of Natural History, which has since become our favorite in Denver. I bought Mary some turquoise and silver Indian bracelets, which she wore often the rest of her life. We stayed at the Cosmopolitan Hotel and had dinner at the well-known Navare Restaurant.

Next day we drove 527 miles to Fremont, Nebraska. From North Platte, where we had lunch, to Fremont we followed the Platte River on the Lincoln Highway. Our room in the Pathfinder Hotel was on the side near the Fremont railroad yards of the Union Pacific. There must have been ninety trains going through and switching during the night. The following morning we drove to the outskirts of Humboldt, Iowa, and had a picnic lunch on the banks of the Des Moines River. Driving across the bountiful farmlands of Iowa we stopped at Belmond to visit Captain and Mrs. W. C. Tyrrell, Sr., one of Mr. Wilson's business partners. The Tyrrell's house, an imposing red brick structure, sat far back from the highway on landscaped grounds. Mrs. Tyrrell congratulated us on our marriage. She already had pictures of our wedding sent by Fay. She arranged a tour of the farm, which must have exceeded a thousand acres of corn and sugar beets harvested by Mexican farm laborers. They showed us a large spotlessly clean facility for raising hogs. Hundreds of white pigs were being raised in, of all things, air-conditioned buildings. Even the Mayo Clinic was not air conditioned! We then drove on to Minnesota, stopping at the state line to take some pictures which we still have. Mary felt like we were crossing the Rubicon. We arrived in Rochester late that afternoon to check into the Arthur Hotel, recommended by my friend Huard Hargis.

The next important stage of my life would take place in Rochester. From now on it was not just my life—but our lives. Mary wanted to start a family immediately. She wanted several children, boys and girls. Joining in her desires meant I now had two goals, a career and a family. I regret that too often I let the career take precedence over the family. Mary was the joy of my life. We had serious disagreements but always loved each other. Even when she was furious with me, she'd still brag to other people about me in the most outrageous fashion.

CHAPTER 8

The Mayo Clinic, 1939–41

When Mary and I arrived in Rochester, Minnesota, on September 27, 1939, we found a pleasant little city emerging from the depression. The entire population of twenty thousand people seemed to be employed. The business district included prosperous department stores, antique stores, china shops, garages, movies, restaurants, and banks. Notable was Lucy Wilder's bookstore, which catered to the out-of-town patients. In keeping with the surrounding farmland, a cannery had an imposing water tower shaped and painted to resemble a giant ear of corn. Nearby was a huge chicken hatchery. The Rochester Dairy claimed to manufacture the best ice cream in America; it had the most cream in it. By far the predominant institution in Rochester was the Mayo Clinic. Along with the cannery and dairy, the clinic sustained the city's economy: the dozen hotels and the hundred boarding houses, all the stores, and the majority of the work force depended on the institution.

The Mayo Clinic was the splendid tower in downtown Rochester, even though the clinic included much more. This structure is now called the Plummer Building in memory of Dr. Henry Plummer, who was most responsible for its design. It was the finest building I had ever seen. Fifteen stories tall, and covering nearly a city block, it was crowned with a bell tower of four more stories. The carillon then consisted of twenty-three bells, cast in Croydon, England. Within a day or two of our arrival in Rochester, I was coming out of the Mayo Foundation office on the fifteenth floor when I saw a small man enter the stairway to the bell tower. I introduced myself to Jimmy Drummond, the carillonneur, and inquired about the chimes Mary and I had heard several times a day. He invited us to come watch him play and enjoy the view from the tower. A few days later we climbed up in the carillon tower and saw the trees for miles around in their most beautiful fall colors. Then Jimmy rang the heavy bells manually by pulling a big lever for each bell. This required great physical effort and rhythm to produce the chimes. Jimmy retired after four thousand concerts.

The architectural style of the building was Renaissance Revival with mainly Italianate features. There were balconies, pilasters, supporting columns, round arches, gargoyles, carved stone inlays, and a heroic entrance with massive cast bronze doors. The marble halls and broad stairs led to large waiting rooms. The library reading room had a two-story ceiling. Terra cotta and carved oak fixtures abounded throughout the interior. The building was very efficient for its intended purposes. Built before the era of modern architecture, it has been criticized for its lavish embellishments. Fortunately it was not mutilated during a period when many fine buildings were. It stands today as an architectural treasure, a reminder of bygone pride and elegance and a monument to the men who built the greatest clinic in the world. Now it stands among larger buildings, but none are so fine.[1]

A flower garden and a two-story medical museum occupied a block across the street from the clinic entrance. The Kahler Hotel and Hospital, the Worrall Hospital, and the Damon Hospital were on the blocks adjoining the clinic. The Colonial Hospital was two blocks away. The Zambro Hotel was behind the clinic, occupying the same block, and connected to it by an underground tunnel, used during the sub-zero weather. A block away to the left from the clinic entrance was the Wilson Club. Often referred to as Wilson House, it was the former residence of and a gift from Louis B. Wilson, retired pathologist and Mayo Foundation director. The club served as a meeting place for the fellows where lunch was served during clinic business days. When we arrived in Rochester, we were invited to the Wilson House for a reception for new fellows, and, not knowing the Wilson Club existed, assumed we were being invited to Wilson's actual residence. We were informed he lived on a hill overlooking Rochester. Mary described the event in a letter home dated October 7:

> We went out there at eight-thirty. The hour announced was seven-thirty, but we thought any time would be good for an "at home." . . . When we arrived they were showing movies in their spacious, well furnished attic. We interrupted the movies with our arrival but didn't realize anything was wrong until afterward. It turned out that we had gone to the wrong party. The party for the new fellows was at the Wilson Club and the Wilsons were entertaining some of their friends. We had a very nice time but it was very funny . . . How is that for a debut in Rochester Society?[2]

St. Mary's Hospital, owned and operated by the Sisters of St. Francis, was ten blocks west of the clinic. The sisters came to Rochester in 1877 and pro-

Mayo Clinic, 1939

vided a hospital for William Worrall Mayo and his sons William and Charles to treat their patients. While the Mayo practice was growing into a famous clinic, St. Mary's Hospital also grew. The sisters prospered and bought a large farm west of Rochester, where they produced milk and vegetables for the hospital. I remember a huge barn on the property. Since 1939, the hospital has more than doubled in size. Two or three miles southwest of town was the Institute of Experimental Medicine, where fundamental research had been carried out for many years. Surgeons trained there on experimental animals. There were also chemistry and bacteriology facilities available at the institute to those whose research applications were approved.

Residences for staff physicians were located mostly on a slight rise on the southwest side of town. The area was called Pill Hill, because so many clinic doctors lived there, and contained some very nice, even large, houses. There were three great houses in Rochester. One was Dr. Will Mayo's former residence, which he had given to the clinic. Known as the Foundation House— it was a solid stone structure I thought was beautiful. Dr. Charles Mayo's home was in a family compound at Mayowood on a thousand acres a few miles southwest of town. His son Dr. Charles W. Mayo lived there. Several family houses and buildings were in the compound. Large Canadian geese lived there year round on a lake. Fallow deer populated a pasture on the property. Dr. Henry Plummer had a magnificent house on the bluff of Pill Hill overlooking the

Zambro Valley. A few doctors lived on farms or acreages outside the city. Many also had summer cottages on nearby lakes or in the lake country of north Minnesota.

Having grown up in a farming community, I was very interested in the Rochester countryside, where prosperous farms were scattered over the rolling landscape. Many farms were quarter section, or 160 acres in size. There were very few 1,000-acre farms. Typical was a white two-story box-shaped house, so shaped to conserve heat during the bitter winters. Most houses had a separate garage for one car. The well-kept yard was invariably planted with peonies, lilac bushes, and a shade tree or two of maple, elm, or pine. There was always a large vegetable garden and an apple orchard along with a few cherry and plum trees. Behind the house was a barn always larger than the house. Adolph Dehn, the artist laureate of Minnesota, became famous for his red barn pictures which decorated many a Christmas card. Other outbuildings included corn cribs, tool sheds, milking sheds, pig pens, creameries, poultry houses, and others sometimes totaling eight or more. Many farms had a windbreak of tall trees on the north side and a wood lot. There was always a silo or two. Larger farms had an extra house for hired help or relatives. Usually there were several cows and several work horses; dairy farms also had many cows. There were always pigs and chickens as well as sheep, geese, ducks, and turkeys. Inside the basement were dozens of jars of home-canned food, only a part of the women's work. The crops were mostly corn, but small grains, such as oats, wheat, barley, or rye, were common. A lot of English peas were grown in Olmsted County. Pheasants nested in the fields and were seen on the roadside. While at Mayo, I went pheasant hunting several times.

Everything was battened down for the winter. All livestock was brought in during the most severe snowstorms and blizzards, in which animals and people sometimes froze to death. Some farmers followed a rope from the house to the barn to avoid getting lost in a blizzard. There weren't many tractors or migrant laborers working most Minnesota fields at the time. The farm work was done by the entire family, seven days a week, from before daylight until after dark. They never caught up. A 160-acre farm was about all one family could take care of. Some of the farm boys had to find work in town, while the girls grew up to be nurses in the Rochester hospitals.

Some families had been on the land since the country was settled a hundred years before Mary and I came to Rochester. Many farmers were second or third generation Scandinavian, German, or Irish. The countryside was a beautiful sight, made so by the industry and never ending toil of the farm owners. Country stores, churches, and schools dotted the landscape. Small villages were every few miles including Byron, Kasson, Eyota, Mantorville,

Stewartville, and Oronoca in Olmsted County, and most of them had a small cheese factory. The county was densely populated. There has been a remarkable change in country life since then, with the country population diminishing while the city population increases. Rochester today is three times larger, but the Plummer Building and the Kahler Hotel remain the same.

Patients came from all over the world to the Mayo Clinic. Famous people came, such as movie stars and the King of Egypt. I saw Lou Gehrig whose amyotrophic lateral sclerosis—the disease to bear his name thereafter—was diagnosed at the clinic. When the weather was too cold to work outside, farmers from Iowa and Minnesota came to the clinic to be examined. Many had not bathed or taken off their long-handled underwear all winter. The odor was terrific when one of these farmers undressed. Poor people came and were not turned away. This was truly the golden era of medical practice. Hundreds of life saving discoveries have been made since, but the doctor-patient relationship lately has been under siege.[3]

On the day of our arrival in Rochester, Mary and I had dinner with Huard Hargis, a roommate of mine from medical school. The next morning we went to the Foundation. I found that my work as a fellow would be divided into quarters. For my first quarter, I would be assisting Alec Brown who took care of the medical side of operative cases in the Worrall Hospital, the Kahler, and the clinic. We spent the rest of the day looking at apartments. We finally found a semifurnished apartment in a fourplex with lots of space at $55.00 a month. It had a nice size living room with a big closet for a Murphy bed and another big closet in it; a dinette and kitchen equipped with an electric stove and ice box; a little hall with a linen closet and a bath off of it; and a bedroom with another big closet. Closets were rare in apartments, and this one was unusually well provided with them. The apartment was located about ten blocks from the clinic, and I planned to walk to the hospital except in the worst weather.

First thing Mary put in our new home must have been her typewriter, because a regular blizzard of letters immediately went out to family and friends. (Fortunately, Mary's mother saved practically every letter that Mary ever wrote to her. The letters, often several typewritten pages, provide a detailed account of our personal life in Rochester.) Mary soon had the apartment spotless and had talked Mrs. Reid, the owner, into painting the kitchen and getting an oriental rug for the living room. Mrs. Reid was said to be very stingy, but she was always doing something for these fourplex housewives. We were fortunate to have good couples in the fourplex too. All the men were doctors. Immediately below us lived Hugh (Red) and Mary Butt. Hugh was as red-headed as you can get, so he was called Red Butt. Red was from Norfolk,

Virginia, and had arrived in Rochester as a fellow in medicine in 1934. After his training he was taken on the staff in 1937 as one of the youngest to be accepted. He was a bright, frank spoken, mischievous man, full of wit and good humor, brimming over with enthusiasm and fresh ideas. He never knew a stranger and was completely at ease with the high and mighty. Mary Dempwolf Butt, whose disposition was calmer than her husband's, was from York, Pennsylvania, and a graduate of Smith College. Within a year or two, the Butts moved out of the Reid fourplex to a larger place for their new daughter, Lucy, who was followed by three more children. Francis and Kay McDonough moved in to take their place.[4]

Across the hall from us lived Nathan and Nancy Plimpton from Minneapolis. He was a fellow in surgery and a real gentleman. Nancy and Mary became close friends. She joined Mary in cooking our first Christmas dinner. When Nathan completed his fellowship and moved to Minneapolis, Bill and Frances Seybold moved in. Charley and Helen Kimball had the other downstairs apartment. From Seattle, Charley was a fellow in gynecology and obstetrics. They had a seven-year-old daughter, Noel. After his fellowship, Charley returned to Seattle to practice. While I was later stationed at Paine Field near Seattle in 1942, he introduced me to the Virginia Mason Clinic staff. Mary stayed with the Kimballs when she came to Seattle to see me leave for foreign duty in June 1942. We remained friends. Helen died a few years ago, and Charley died in 1997.

Only two weeks after our marriage we had gone on our honeymoon, arrived in Rochester, rented an apartment, and set up housekeeping. Mary had done more than her part, and things had worked out well. At work, I reported to the Mayo Foundation office in the clinic. Donald Balfour, the director, and Miss Elizabeth Farr, the secretary, were in charge of the three hundred fellows. They consulted with the staff, considered the fellows' requests, and assigned each fellow to a duty service each quarter. We took our complaints and requests to Balfour and Miss Farr, and they called us in for their complaints. On the first day all the new fellows, there must have been fifty, assembled in a large conference room in the Foundation office. A new group like ours entered a fellowship program quarterly during the year. Dr. Balfour introduced himself and offered a few welcoming remarks. Each fellow stood up, introduced himself, and told where he was from. Then Dr. Balfour asked a surprising question, "How many of you were married two weeks ago?" I didn't count, but it seems that about ten of us held up our hands. Dr. Balfour and everyone in the room laughed when he told us that a large number of new fellows get married and go on a two-week honeymoon before arriving for their fellowship. He enjoyed asking that question to each group of new fellows.

A fellow at the Mayo Clinic performed the same duties as a resident in other hospitals. In addition to three years of training, the Mayo fellow was expected to do a research project and write a thesis, to be approved by his advisor, the Mayo Foundation director, and a degree committee at the University of Minnesota. At the completion of training the fellow had his record reviewed and was given an oral and written examination. If the fellow passed all this, he was awarded a Master of Science degree in medicine or surgery by the University of Minnesota at the annual graduation exercises in Minneapolis. Some fellows did additional work to earn a Ph.D. Many years later the title of fellow was changed to resident and the thesis requirement was waived. Only a few residents now undertake a thesis and work for a master's degree.

My first assignment was with Dr. Alec Brown, who was in charge of internal medicine for all the hospitalized patients in dermatology, dental surgery, and proctology at Worrall Hospital and for the patients in plastic surgery at Kahler Hospital. There was no subspecialty of infectious diseases then, but Dr. Brown, a general internist, was interested in the sulfa drugs so we hit it off together right away. If a patient got a fever or any of a myriad of problems, we might be called. I performed a complete history and physical examination on every patient who entered the hospital directly without having had a previous examination at the clinic. I had not been on the Brown service a month when my previous training paid off. I was called to examine a dermatology patient who had entered directly. As part of the physical I performed a digital rectal examination, as I had been trained, and found a totally unsuspected cancer of the rectum. Dr. Brown was pleased that I had made this diagnosis. It proved the value of his service. The consulting surgeon who operated on the patient was impressed. Word circulated around some of the staff about this new fellow being so thorough and finding this unsuspected cancer.

Most skin diseases did not require hospitalization; however, we had many patients with severe problems, such as pemphigus, chronic urticaria, and psoriasis, involving most of their skin surface. Several were brought in with serious skin reactions from sulfa drugs. Some also had fever from sulfas, and a few had renal failure from sulfa crystals forming in their kidneys. A few of these patients died. On the eve of the introduction of penicillin, we were learning about the only antibiotic available. Fortunately, while I was on this service, Dr. Perrin Long, the leading authority on sulfonamides at Johns Hopkins University, was invited to speak to the entire Mayo staff.

Even though this assignment was a seven-day-a-week job, it was only a part of my training. We fellows had staff conferences in the hospital. We also attended weekly general staff meetings and countless seminars. There was a program every night, as well as a noon conference and a program every morning at seven to start the day. The clinic published a daily program listing every meeting. If you could handle it, you could attend meetings and hospital rounds straight from 7:00 A.M. until 10:00 P.M. and many visiting physicians did so. Attending physicians frequently ordered us to prepare a brief presentation for the next day about a particular disease of one of the patients. If a patient on our service died, we went to the autopsy and the subsequent clinical and pathological conference. After using up my day in meetings, I often had to go to the hospital and perform a history and physical on a patient late at night.

Meanwhile, my bride was complaining that I was never at home. Fortunately the Mayo administration realized they had to keep the fellows' wives occupied if they were to work the fellows sixteen hours a day. The clinic sponsored the Magazine Club for fellows' wives. The club brought speakers to the Foundation House, promoted volunteer work, and organized bridge clubs. Staff members' wives also entertained in their homes. From reading Mary's letters, I am reminded that on November 1, a month after our arrival, Mary attended a coffee at Mrs. Ghornley's "very attractive, large house on the hill, one block from where we live." On March 28, 1940, she went to a bridge party at Mrs. Alvarez's home, the wife of one of the most prominent men of the staff, "supposed to be the greatest gastroenterologist in the world." Mrs. Phillip W. Brown invited Mary to a luncheon. Mary reciprocated by asking Dr. and Mrs. Brown to dinner and served us a chicken dish she read about in a detective story. Mrs. Brown asked for the recipe but Mary wouldn't give it. She was ashamed to tell Mrs. Brown where she got the recipe. For years the Browns made a joke about asking Mary for her chicken recipe. They knew there was something funny about her refusal to give it. When I went to the weekly staff meeting in Plummer Hall at the main clinic, Mary often came along to read in the library. Among the medical literature were current copies of popular European magazines such as *L'Illustration, Punch,* and *Illustrated London News.* There was a browsing room with rare editions and histories.

Mary made friends rapidly and was soon going out with the wives of fellows and staff members. She also entertained Texas friends and others who came to the Mayo Clinic as patients.[5] I especially remember Lamar Cecil, a lawyer friend from Beaumont, who came to Rochester for treatment several times, often bringing his wife Mary. He was a smart, witty, fun-loving man, who liked to tell stories, particularly about uncovering fraudulent claims for physical disabilities. One day a worker wanted Lamar to sue the worker's employer for disability benefits resulting from an on-the-job back injury. The worker was carrying one end of a heavy timber when the other end was dropped causing the worker to sustain a sudden severe pain in the lower back and an equally severe pain down one leg. The pain persisted and was crippling. Lamar, a defense attorney, had never taken a plaintiff's case, but he accepted this one because the complaints seemed so genuine. I told Lamar that the man's complaints sounded like lumbar disc syndrome with sciatic pain. Lamar had never heard of it, so I took him to the Mayo library to check out some of Dr. Jim Love's articles describing the condition. Remember, I saw the first cases at Bellevue in 1936. A neurosurgeon at Mayo, Dr. Love had made a specialty of treating these patients. Lamar was very enthused. "If I win this case I will give you half of my profits," he said. A few months later Lamar came back to the clinic for additional treatment. During our visit, I wondered if he would say something about his client with a ruptured disc. Finally I asked what happened. "Oh," he said, "I owe you a drink. I won that case." He knew what he had promised me, but all I said was, "tell me about it." The case was tried before a jury in Corpus Christi. Lamar employed a well-liked local general practitioner as his expert witness and gave him the literature on ruptured discs which I had provided him in Rochester. The expert witness had never heard of ruptured discs but he soon learned. The defense had as their expert witness, G. W. N. Eggers, chief of orthopedics at the University of Texas Medical School. The defense tried to discredit Lamar's general practitioner by asking him how many bones there were in the human body. The doctor replied, "I don't know, but I'll name them and you can count them." The local doctor explained the condition to the jury, and Lamar intimated that Dr. Eggers didn't know much about a ruptured disc. The jury decided in the worker's favor, but that was not the end of the story. A few years later, Lamar and I were talking about the case. Lamar said that, as a result of his case, lawyers had caught on to the ruptured disc problem and were winning lawsuits all over Texas. Then he said, "That man whose case I won—his back is still bothering him. You know I think he really does have something wrong with his back."

Mary took cooking seriously. She collected recipes, sent some to her mother, and tried a new one on every guest, including the fellows and patients I brought home for lunch. At first, Mary cooked cheese dreams, made with cheese and mustard melted on toast, a very elementary recipe. We teased her about this, but she didn't think our comments were very funny. Mary's cuisine advanced rapidly, however. She knew what was a good menu; she only had to learn to prepare it. Her first big entertaining event was the Christmas dinner in our apartment in 1939. The Plimptons from across the hall were invited, and Nancy Plimpton contributed to the food and its preparation. Mary's six-page typewritten letter to her parents on December 27, 1939, revealed how happy and pleased she was with the event. Reading this letter deeply saddens me, because Mary is no longer with me. I know how much she would enjoy reading this letter and recounting our happy days together:

Dearest Mother,

Your many Christmas presents are grand. The book of pictures of home made me so homesick I could die but they are lovely and I am so glad to have them. The little book with its chintz covering is so attractive too. Also I was glad to have the cook book. It looks like good stuff and I am going to try some of the recipes soon. The fruit cake is plus que bon. We served it Christmas morning with eggnog and everyone enjoyed it. Those little fruit cake cookies are wonderful. The sausage is delicious. It is fun to have such delicacies from Texas on hand.

There is so much to tell you. I wrote Daddy about the parties we have attended but want to tell you about our festivities. We have a beautiful little tree—about five feet tall. We decorated it with colored icicles and big red shiny balls and it really is beautiful—the prettiest I have seen which is no doubt due to some kind of prejudice but is satisfying nonetheless—and with all the presents underneath it looked like a picture book. We decorated it Friday night. We had a wreath of balsam on the door with a big red bow and Christmas Eve night burned candles in all the windows. It was very pretty. The candles you sent are darling and such fun to have—both because they are pretty and because with their Christmas decorations I have no compunctions about burning them now. They certainly do add to the festivity of the season.

I tried to do everything just like home—and am just beginning to feel normal again. We went to the Christmas Eve service which was very nice. We were sorry to miss talking to you, Fay and Cooke and hoped you would call back but it was grand to talk to Daddy and hear from home. Christmas morning I cooked a special breakfast with sausage, hominy and pink grapefruit - also with home in mind. Mavis had to go to the hospital and make rounds before we could have our tree. This was quite a strain to keep from opening anything until he was all through but it did give me time to bathe and put on my old red dress for Christmas. Adsit's camellias came that morning. They were somewhat battered but not too much so and I had one to wear in my hair which did me lots of good. Mavis also wore a pink perfection which was beautiful. When Mavis came back, I began whipping cream for eggnog. I watched it like a hawk but, turned my back one minute, and the stuff went to butter so we had to wait for the dairy to send some more. Meanwhile we opened our presents which I will tell you about later. Nancy Plimpton and I had made arrangements to have the dinner together which made things very gay. However, she had her little baby to take care of - so, about eleven thirty - about the time fresh cream arrived - we had to start stuffing the turkey. We finally got the bird in at twelve thirty which postponed our dinner hour from three o'clock to five. While I was in Nancy's apartment with the turkey, Mavis had been stirring up the eggnog. He had brought another doctor home with him from the hospital and the Kimballs from downstairs had arrived for eggnog so between them they got it all together and it was very good. We had the Plimptons and the Butts - also from downstairs and it was lots of fun and very Christmasy.

About one thirty or so I decided to get going on my part of the dinner, have it all ready so that I'd be able to sit down and chat with our guests later. Well, I started and managed to finish just in time for the turkey. Lamar Cecil came out and had some turkey with us - also a Dr. Mildred Cariker who was in Mavis' class at medical school and who had a fellowship here in obstetrics and gynecology. We invited her for two fifteen thinking dinner would be at three and she helped me a lot in the kitchen.

The table looked lovely. Our table has three leaves so we had it stretched to full length. I used the green and white damask cloth you gave me - had a mirror belonging to Nancy in the middle of the table with grapes and fruit around it and six of your pretty Christmas candles. Nancy and I wrote out the menus in French - had individual ones and also used them for place cards. First we had, pink grapefruit, orange and red cherry cocktail with sherry in it. We get California sherry which isn't much more expensive than cococolas and seems to serve the purpose beautifully. Then we had a 12 pound turkey, stuffed with a bread and sausage dressing, surrounded with little red apples which had been cooked in cinnamon candy; giblet gravy; sweet potatoes in a casserole with marshmallows on top; Bird's-eye green peas with fresh broiled mushroom; cranberry sauce; sliced carrots, celery and olives; plum pudding (Crosse and Blackwell) on fire, hard sauce which I forgot until the very last minute but which turned out very well; coffee and chocolate mints. It really was a beautiful dinner and everything turned out marvelously well. I'll enclose a menu. We sat around for a while. Mavis had to make his evening rounds, then we went to Shicks for eggnog. Yesterday a woman came in to wash the dishes for me which was certainly a lifesaver and now things are practically back to normal. I certainly did think of you during all the activities. You would have been mightily entertained to see me scurrying around at such a rate—but it really turned out beautifully and I certainly was grateful for all the precedents of entertaining you have set for me, and I certainly did miss you every minute.

Mavis gave me a marvelous ski suit which he said he preferred for me not to use skiing but just for outdoor sports-skating. He also gave me a potted rose colored azalea which is lovely. I gave him a wine colored smoking jacket which is beautiful and which he is actually wearing which enchants me—and a lovely leather scrapbook which I am going to try and keep up.

Lots of love to you Mother dear. You certainly were sweet to send us so many grand things for Christmas and we have enjoyed and are enjoying all of them————

Write to me soon.

Sis

Winters in Rochester were tough, especially for transplanted Texans. We had the first snow in October and hard freezes by November. The first time I walked to work on such a day I was bareheaded without an overcoat. It felt pleasant when I left the house, but after a few blocks I was freezing. I thought my ears would break off if I touched them. My thighs were completely numb. It was too late to turn back. I had never heard of hypothermia, otherwise I would have broken into someone's house. I finally warmed up in the clinic. My thighs and ears were sore and swollen for several days—"chilblains," they called it. That walk was a lesson I would never forget, but I soon had another close call with freezing weather on a drive to Minneapolis. Mayo fellows were required to be licensed to practice medicine in Minnesota. On January 1, 1940, four of us drove up to Minneapolis to take the state medical boards on the following two days. We went in my Chevrolet, which was not equipped for Minnesota weather. A blizzard blew in. Snow drifted across the road, and the sky turned dark before 5:00 P.M. Ice started forming on the windshield; the car heater was totally inadequate; the windshield wiper froze. I had to drive with my head out the window to see the road. We had heard of people freezing on the road. Finally we made it into Minneapolis. Instead of studying that night, we went to a bar and lifted up our spirits. I can't remember a thing about the examination, but I passed, got my license and, as required by Mayo, joined the Minnesota Medical Association.

We saw snow fall every month of the year. Joe, the cheerful doorman at the Mayo Clinic greeted everyone who entered the clinic, even during the sub-zero weather. Once, as I waited for Mary to pick me up, he said, "If summer comes on Sunday this year I'm going to spend it in the country." Needless to say, living in Rochester improved my winter wardrobe, which included a handsome black fur cap like the ones Russians wear. I still have it today. Mary's trousseau had included all kinds of winter clothes, including three fur coats. Rochester had a public ice skating rink, created by flooding a few acres before a freeze. It stayed frozen all winter. On the ice, Mary wore her trousseau winter suit, the one she wore in the Neiman Marcus ads published in the Texas papers. She was a good skater and rarely fell, but I fell all over the rink. Other winter sports included skiing, sledding, and ice fishing. The fishermen would pitch the fish out on the ice to freeze as solid as a stick of wood. They were then stacked on a back porch to be brought in and thawed before they were cleaned and cooked.

I was fortunate to spend one or two quarters in the clinic on Dr. H. Z. Giffin's service. A fine teacher, Dr. Giffin always reviewed my histories and physical examinations carefully and treated me as if I were his professional equal. He often whistled softly while conducting examinations, a habit that startled some patients, especially women when he stared whistling while *doing a pelvic examination.* I think they wondered if he had found something amazing. We saw a general run of patients in the Giffin section. Unless referred to a certain physician, new patients were assigned on a rotation basis to the various sections of internal medicine, including hematology, cardiology, gastroenterology, metabolism (now called endocrinology), hypertension and vascular, and a general section.[6]

I was next assigned to six months of general pathology under Dr. Harold Robertson. He held weekly clinical and pathological conferences, where he was fearless and impartial in revealing the truth, even if Dr. Will Mayo himself had made a surgical mistake. He reported the results of his autopsy findings, projected slides showing the actual cause of death, then called on the clinician or surgeon for his comments. Everyone on the staff came to the conferences "to see whose head would be chopped off this time." These were the days before big malpractice suits. When I was there, it was said that the Mayo Clinic had never lost in a malpractice suit. Part of my work in the general pathology section involved assisting in these autopsies. Several fellows rotated on call at night. It may seem strange, getting up in the middle of the night to do an autopsy. The patient had died—there was nothing that could be done so why not wait until next day? The most pressing reason was that there was no morgue in the Mayo Clinic. When a patient died, the body was sent promptly to a funeral home, where the mortician insisted that the autopsy be done immediately so the body could be embalmed and shipped out to the deceased's hometown, which might be thousands of miles away.

Dr. (Robbie) Robertson was a brusque, rough old guy who scared the hell out of his fellows. I was supposed to choose a thesis subject in pathology when I got on his service. I could not think of one, so I talked to him about it. He was very blunt in telling me that I should have found a subject even before I came on the service and intimated, probably correctly, that I didn't have much imagination. I must have had some kind of mental block. Everything I thought of had been hashed over a hundred times. I went back to Robertson and told him I couldn't find a subject. He got mad and said, "I can take your pecker out for you, but I can't make you pee."

I don't know just how original the idea was with me, but while I was on Dr. Giffin's section we had talked about splenic anemia, a form of anemia which occurred when the spleen became enlarged and destroyed too many red blood cells. Some cases of enlarged spleen seemed to occur without a known cause. The splenic vein was obstructed in some cases of splenic anemia. What role did obstruction of the splenic vein play in splenic anemia? Was it cause or effect? Sir William Osler had identified the condition and coined the term splenic anemia after reporting fifteen cases in 1900. He considered the disease to be identical with Banti's syndrome. Osler's influence, through his resident Giffin, had lead to my thesis project. It was proposed that I study all cases in the autopsy files showing a diagnosis of splenic anemia, splenic and portal vein thrombosis, sclerosis, and hemangiomatous transformation, the latter thought to be the result of a previous thrombosis. There were sixty-one cases. The spleen of each case was to be studied to see if it enlarged, atrophied, or remained unchanged. Microscopic studies of the veins and spleen were to be carried out.

I turned in my request, and it was accepted for a thesis problem, allowing me to study all the tissues; cut and stain more tissues for microscopic study; review records and reports; and finally try to draw some conclusions. I had no idea it would be such a tough problem. I went to work on the project in the summer of 1940. I had hardly begun before my assignment in pathology was completed so I had to continue the work even though subsequent assignments required full-time effort. Robertson wasn't too pleased with my slow progress. He probably felt that I would never finish the study. Almost sixty years later, I obtained my confidential report grades from the Mayo Foundation. For 1940, Robertson gave me a B- in Pathology (I received As for my work in other services) and commented: "A poorly trained man who repeatedly shows lack of fundamentals. Also is rather slow mentally. Honest and a hard worker, but how did he get here?" I finished all the research before September 1941, when I was called into the Army Air Corps, but I had not completely evaluated the findings or written the thesis. I didn't get to work on it very much while in Alaska. Finally, while stationed at Wright Field, I was able to complete the thesis in 1945, five years after beginning it and just before I was released from military duty and returned to Rochester. I called on Robertson and told him I was about to present him with my thesis. He had concluded that I had forgotten the project. I could tell he was very dubious about what I would submit. When he read my thesis, however, he was surprised and very pleased. He called Drs. Giffin, Comfort, and Balfour and told them I had done an outstanding piece of research. He was all smiles with me. He treated me like a good friend and complemented me in a staff meeting. I had won his respect, and he didn't hesitate in letting me know.[7]

I most enjoyed my six months in the gastroenterology service at St. Mary's Hospital. Al Snell was the section chief. Other members of the section included good friend and fellow Texan Mandred Comfort, our former apartment neighbor Hugh Butt, Jim Weir, and Leo Morissete from Quebec. Leo, a graduate of Dalahousie Medical School, spoke French and English and was full of mischief. He and his pal, another fellow from Quebec—both Catholic—liked to tease the Catholic sister nurses and the priests who came on the floor as patients. In jest, they accused the sister in charge of our service of sleeping with the priests. She was about twenty years older than the priests and wore the full Franciscan sisters' habit, with only her face and hands showing. Leo and his friend often asked her to show them her legs. The teasing ruffled the sister a little, but she never got visibly mad. Leo was very bright and good company. I brought him home for lunch several times, and Mary liked him.

Our chief, Al Snell, was a great guy. Like most of the staff he was very sharp. He had seen so many thousands of gastroenterology, or "G.I.," patients that he could diagnose their problem before the fellow could finish citing the history. He was a good teacher. He caught mistakes and omissions before we realized it and tricked us with questions. If one of us made a far out diagnosis, he would say, "that's as rare as horse manure in a garage." He had fun with us, and often brought the patient into the fun so everyone was laughing. He didn't tolerate laxity. Snell told his young staff that when you see a patient you've got to do $500 better than the doctor he left to see you—$500 being the amount already spent by the patient getting to the clinic.

On the hospital floor I called my friend Red "Dr. Butt." He was much like Snell, but younger and more full of himself. You could get in trouble with him easily, if you expressed the wrong opinion about medicine or anything else. Red could also get himself in trouble with the senior staff. He thought certain surgeons had an inflated opinion of themselves and didn't hesitate to disagree with them. Drs. Snell and Comfort had to back him up a few times, otherwise he would have been fired. Red was very energetic: he had several research projects going at one time, and moved up rapidly in the committee system. The board of governors and the trustees had confidence in him and trained him to be chairman of the board. Red even designed his own office. But he was caught in a bitter crossfire. Red was all for developing branch clinics, and raised a gift of $50 million worth of Florida real estate for the Mayo Clinic to open an office in Florida. When some Rochester business men and doctors heard of this they were outraged. A branch clinic, they believed, would drain business away from Rochester. Red's opponents organized and voted him off of the board. They could not remove him from the trustees, however, a position he continued to hold. His recommendations for branch offices proved to be correct. A branch in Tucson, Arizona, and one in Jacksonville, Florida, are thriving today and the clinic in Rochester has lost no patients as a result. This expansionist move has put the Mayo Clinic in a good position to enter the next millennium. Red remained loyal to the clinic throughout the controversy. He has probably raised more money for the institution than any other person.

Mandred Comfort, also on the gastroenterology service at St. Mary's, became my friend and mentor. He was born in Hillsboro, Texas, and attended Austin College in Sherman, Texas, before going to the Medical Branch in Galveston, where he joined the AKK fraternity. I believe he trained at the Mayo Clinic before joining the staff in gastroenterology. He had many friends in Texas, some who recommended that I call on him. Mandred encouraged me in my training and let me join him in writing some papers on hepatic vein thrombosis and on the role of chronic gastritis in causing gastric cancer. These papers required a lot of work in studying autopsy specimens and patient records. We also did statistical analyses of the cases under the guidance of Dr. Joe Berkson, a full-time medical statistician at the clinic. The papers were presented at the staff meetings, a real honor for me, and were published in several leading medical journals. They were good solid papers, still quoted in the literature.

Mandred Comfort had built a large practice of prominent people from Texas, and, as an authority on pancreatitis, he had become a nationally famous gastroenterologist. He and his wife, Aurelia, took every Texan fellow under their wing. They hosted parties to introduce the Texas fellows to each other. Mary and I soon became close friends of the Comforts. We visited each other in our homes, but the Comforts more often entertained us. Mandred collected Texas history books and American postage stamps, renewing my stamp collecting interest. I addressed him as "Doctor" for a long time, and finally began calling him Mandred away from the clinic. I knew some of his Texas patients and he introduced me to others. While I was on the G.I. hospital service, Breckenridge Walker, a rich oil man from Fort Worth, brought his wife up to Rochester in a private train—a whole train, not just a private railroad car. Comfort assigned me to take care of the Walkers full-time, to the exclusion of all other patients. Of course, the Walkers brought their doctor, who knew Mandred. We entertained the doctor and made him feel at home.

Although most of the Mayo fellows from Texas knew each other before coming to Rochester, Dr. and Mrs. Comfort were the cohesive force in bringing the Texans together. Huard and Lucylle Hargis from San Antonio practically installed us into our apartment. Dr. Andy Rivers, a senior staff member, married Mandred's sister from Hillsboro, Texas, so he was accepted as Texan. Fellow AKK brother Jim Cain married Ida May Wirtz. Raleigh White, Jr., and his wife, Aleene, and Valter Brindley, Jr., with his wife, Cleo, came from Temple. Valter and Cleo moved into our fourplex, replacing Charlie and Helen Kimball when they left for Seattle. Frank Ashburn was a close friend of mine from the time he entered medical school in Galveston and joined AKK. His uncle Ike Ashburn had gone to Polytechnic College with my parents. When he came to the clinic for a fellowship in surgery, Frank was considered virtually to be a part of our family. He and Mary were the leaders in organizing the Texas Club, which, among its social activities, held a party each year to celebrate Texas Independence Day. Frank Ashburn and Mary's sister, Fay, became engaged briefly during World War II, but the romance faded when Frank joined the navy and fought the war in the Pacific.[8]

The most important Texas friends we had in Rochester were Bill and Frances Seybold. Bill, my future partner, belonged to Phi Alpha Sigma medical fraternity and had graduated from medical school in Galveston in 1939. He was an assistant in anatomy while I was an instructor in pathology in Galveston. Bill interned at Barnes Hospital in Saint Louis, serving under Dr. Evarts Graham, famous chest surgeon. He married Frances Rather of Austin, Texas, and came to Rochester for a fellowship in surgery in July 1941. Bill and Frances were immediately welcomed by all the Texas delegation. Of some fifty new fellows who came that quarter, I'm sure Bill and Frances had the greatest welcome. Several parties were held to welcome them. Bill had completed a two-year surgical internship in Saint Louis under the surgeon who had performed the first lung resection. Bill was poised for an outstanding fellowship in surgery at the clinic. His work was truly outstanding, and he was liked by all the surgical staff. We had a great time with the Seybolds. He and I were interested in the flora of Minnesota, plants we had never seen in Texas. We went to the woods every chance we had and learned to identify all the common trees, bushes, and wildflowers. We collected the uncommon ones and spent hours studying botany keys identifying them. But time was short. In less than three months I was called into the Army Air Corps for four years. He was later called into the navy.

Another future partner, William V. Leary, came on the gastroenterology service with me during the second quarter. A graduate of Carleton College and the University of Minnesota Medical School, Bill had served an internship at the University of Minnesota before his fellowship at Mayo. Coming from nearby Owatonna, he knew many Rochester people, medical and otherwise. We promptly became close friends, and he often came to our apartment. Bill was a popular and brilliant person, and his record was outstanding. He passed the American Board of Internal Medicine examination and became a board certified internist while on duty in World War II, even before completing his fellowship—the only person I ever knew to become board certified in a specialty before completing residency training. His military service, however, did count as practice experience. He was an original member of our Journal Club, which met weekly at one of our houses. We spent most of our time reading the clinical and pathological conferences in the *New England Journal of Medicine.* We sharpened our diagnostic acumen by guessing at the final diagnoses before we read the pathologist's findings. We also gossiped about medical personalities at the clinic. Bill Leary also liked parties, so we had much in common. Sometimes we sat up all night talking before we had to go to work the next day.

I was later assigned to the colon service at St. Mary's in July 1941 for more training in gastroenterology, my chosen specialty. The chief, J. A. Bargen, was nationally known for his work in chronic ulcerative colitis. He believed the disease resulted from an infection, the exact cause not discovered. By this time, the sulfonamides were being used with some success. We were trying sulfaguanidine, a sulfa drug which was poorly absorbed, so its effect was limited to the bowel mucosa. The staff was dedicated to teaching the fellows and spent a lot of time with us. We saw the most serious cases of ulcerative colitis. Patients lost body protein from the ulcerative lesions that had to be replaced by transfusions, blood serum, and amino acid solutions. The suffering was terrible, relieved only a little with opiates. A few died in spite of all the supportive care we could give.

Despite the hard work and long hours as a Mayo fellow, I shared Mary's great desire to start a family. Mary became pregnant soon after we came to Rochester and went to Dr. Larry Randall, who couldn't have been a finer doctor. But Mary soon miscarried. She miscarried a second time and was extremely upset. When she became pregnant for the third time, Mary received stilbestrol injections; doctors were just beginning to administer estrogens to prevent miscarriages. No one yet knew of the possible consequences. At any rate, Mary remained pregnant. She was very careful—if I hit a bump while driving she got very mad. As delivery drew near Dr. Randall did measurements and found Mary with a small pelvis. A cesarean section was ordered. Mrs. Wilson came up, and with the help of Nancy Plimpton, Mary Butt, and others, our apartment was prepared to receive another resident. On March 29, 1941, Dr. Randall performed a cesarean and delivered John Wilson Kelsey—a choice of name that had been discussed at great length. I was adamant that there would be no Rosemary. Uncle John Wilson promptly sent John a birth present of five thousand dollars. John was first photographed four hours after birth. Fay soon came to Rochester and photographed him several times a day. Since he was the first grandchild on both sides of our family, he soon became the most photographed child I have ever known.

Our son, John, came home to a well-equipped nursery and a very protective mother. Mary finally was able to visit Beaumont in late July 1941, nearly two years after we left on our honeymoon. Of course she took little John. The *Beaumont News* reported that Mrs. J. Cooke Wilson had a reception on August 1, 1941, for her daughter Mrs. Mavis P. Kelsey, who was visiting Beaumont with her baby son, John Wilson. Mary wrote from Beaumont that she was going home for two weeks only. She said she went home to relax, but she didn't have long to rest. She was in for a surprise.

The war in Europe had been going on since we first arrived in Rochester in the fall of 1939. The United States was gradually being pulled into the conflict. We were manufacturing arms and sending food and supplies to England. Canada was already in the war. Our armed forces were building up rapidly. Hitler had overrun Europe and North Africa and was planning to take the British Isles. He had made a treaty with Japan to divide the world between them. A number of doctors had been called from the Mayo Clinic. I was a reserve officer: I had accepted a commission as first lieutenant in the Medical Corps Reserve as a senior at the Medical Branch. I wrote Mary in July that I heard something big was going to happen soon at the Mayo Clinic. Still Mary and I and just about everyone else were complacent. We were looking for a house larger than our apartment. We had planned our Christmas vacation.

Something big did happen at the Mayo Clinic. In one day, I and about fifty fellows in the army reserve received telegrams ordering us to active duty in the Air Corps, beginning August 15, 1941. I called Mary to tell her the news, and she and John came back to Rochester by train. Fay came with them to help us pack and leave Rochester. While I waited for Mary to return, several of us were on the phone trying to get our orders deferred until we could finish our fellowships and get better assignments. After all, we weren't at war. Our requests for deferment was refused. Four of us who were called to duty drove together to Fort Snelling, Minnesota, for examinations. All of us passed our entrance physical and drove back to Rochester the same day.

In a few days, orders came for me to report to the army air base at Portland, Oregon. We had a mad scramble to get everything ready to leave. We shipped many things to Beaumont for storage with the rest of our wedding presents. After we left, Frank Ashburn was kind enough to express some essentials to us in Portland. After a few going away parties, we left in a state of confusion one afternoon. Our brand new Chevrolet sedan was packed with luggage, Mary, Fay, me, and little John in his cradle. When we were out about fifty miles we realized we had left John's formula and nursing bottles in Rochester. Mary called Cleo Brindley, who somehow got them to us. We were leaving Rochester to be gone for nearly four years, before returning to complete my fellowship and become a member of the staff.

CHAPTER 9

Military Service, 1941–45

We were given travel time to reach my military assignment in Portland, Oregon—about 100 to 150 miles a day. Mary and I made a sightseeing tour of our trip by stopping at various historic and scenic spots, including the Badlands of South Dakota, the Mount Rushmore Monument, and Yellowstone Park. We finally arrived at Portland Air Base, where, to my surprise, Captain Bob Blount was hospital commander. He was an AKK brother at Galveston who graduated a year before I did and went directly into the Army Air Corps for internship. He was sent to the School of Aviation Medicine at Randolph Field for flight surgeon training. He served a lifetime career in the air force. We found a nice furnished house a few miles from the air base. I was made chief of medicine at the air base hospital, since I had more training in internal medicine than any of the ten other men on the staff.

Making friends happened rapidly among soldiers who were put together during wartime or impending war. The hospital officers' mess was a pleasant place. All the nurses also ate lunch there. After lunch we played bridge. Lieutenant Jack Killins was from the Mayo Clinic. Jack's sweetheart came out and they got married. I was best man. It was our first military wedding, marching in and out under raised crossed swords. Captain James C. Barta of the Veterinary Corps took me on inspections. He was base health inspector and went to the packing houses to inspect the slaughter and processing of meat consumed by the army in the area. I learned a lot from him. Later, I had to do a lot of this kind of inspection myself in the Aleutians. Colonel Joseph Stromme, a pilot in World War I, was commanding officer (C.O.) of the base. I was required to call on the C.O. with my wife to fulfill army formalities, which were soon dropped due to the crush of new people pouring into the service. Mary was taking the Basic Army Reserve Correspondence Courses in my place. She made good grades and soon got me promoted to captain. She would have made a good infantry officer. She could read any army map, keep personnel records, do infantry maneuvers on paper, and do flag signals and Morse code. She knew company organization, field operations, rank, custom, how to set up camp, locate latrines, and sterilize water. She enjoyed the studies and taught me a great deal.

We settled down for a brief few months and listened to the news about war in Europe and the Japanese threat. We wondered what would happen to us. It didn't take long to find out. On December 7, 1941, the Japanese attacked Pearl Harbor, killing thousands of Americans. Like many, I will never forget that Sunday morning. I left Mary at home to go to the base hospital and make rounds as officer of the day (O.D.) for the hospital. I checked in with the air base O.D. The base was quiet; practically no one was there. No one was on the flight line. After rounds, I drove home, probably at about 10:30 A.M. I found Mary very excited. She had just heard the announcement on the radio that the Japanese had attacked Pearl Harbor by air. The first reports were sketchy but very ominous. We continued to listen as all other broadcasts stopped to carry news of the attack. I told Mary I had to rush back to the hospital for my duty as O.D. so I drove rapidly back to the base and found it as quiet as it was when I left not an hour before. The nurses and patients reading the Sunday papers couldn't believe what I had to say. I rushed to the base headquarters to report, and I found the base O.D. sitting comfortably at his desk also reading the Sunday paper. "Haven't you heard about the Japanese attacking Pearl Harbor?" I asked. He could hardly believe it. We turned on the local radio, and he got the news. So that is how Mary and I brought the news of the attack on Pearl Harbor to the Portland Army Air Base, which was charged with protecting our West Coast. "I've got to call the C.O." the O.D. said. "You know he had another big party at home last night for newly arrived officers and was up most of the night." Our call woke Colonel Joseph Stromme just before noon. "Haven't we heard from Army Headquarters in San Francisco?" He asked in amazement. "Get them on the phone. I'll be right out." We tried to get San Francisco headquarters. The only communication was by AT&T public phone. We had no radio communication. When Stromme arrived, he ordered the base on alert and everyone immediately called to duty.

I remained at air base headquarters and tried to locate the medical officers. Practically no one could be found. Nearly everyone was out in the country, up in mountains, fishing, or climbing Mount Hood. With fear that the Japanese would next attack the West Coast, the confusion went on for hours. Finally, our base heard from headquarters in San Francisco. Vancouver Barracks across the Columbia River was alerted, and the Engineer Corps from Vancouver moved machine gun emplacements to the entrances of our air base. Japanese Americans were growing cauliflower commercially in the middle of the base, between the barracks and the flight line: acres of Japanese American truck farming stretched between the hangers and the flight line. Indeed, after the attack, many feared the Japanese presence on the West Coast, and as a result U.S. citizens and aliens alike were placed in virtual prison camps. Many innocent people loyal to America were imprisoned. The Japanese American truck farmers were taken away, while the cauliflowers, ready for harvest, rotted in the field.

I stayed in touch with Mary at home. As the days went by, the headquarters staff organized a truck convoy to drive to Spokane. I was sent home to get what little military field clothing I had. After nightfall the convoy was called off, neither the convoy nor its false start ever explained. Was it some sort of planned retreat to the Spokane Air Base in case we were bombed out? By the time I got home that night, a blackout had been ordered over the radio. Mary had pulled every curtain in the house and had only minimal indoor lights.

After Pearl Harbor, President Roosevelt made a great speech on the radio. He told of the Japanese perfidy and the seriousness of the attack. We immediately declared all out war on Germany, Italy, and Japan and joined the Allies. A most amazing mobilization of the American population took place rapidly. Large numbers of men volunteered for service. The country rationed food, gasoline, travel, and hundreds of other privileges and items. Personal automobiles, tires, not even whiskey, were for sale. I can't remember much about our air strength at Portland Air Base but it was small; I recall a fighter squadron of P-40s, not up to full strength. They patrolled the Oregon Pacific coastline. One pilot claiming to have sunk a Japanese submarine became an instant hero. I had frequent visits with our hospital C.O., Captain Bob Blount, in his office. He and his wife, Helen, visited our house. He was quite laid back, often sitting with his feet on the office desk swatting flies while we talked. But he was no dummy: he was an AOA honor student at medical school and ran the hospital smoothly. I told him I wanted to go to the School of Aviation Medicine in San Antonio. He didn't say much, but John Barker and I soon got orders to go to the next class, beginning January 5 and ending March 28, 1942. Going to San Antonio, close to home, gave Mary and me a great lift. Things were happening fast, and many marriages took place. Bill Leary was ordered to Vancouver Barracks, an infantry post across the Columbia River from Portland. After Pearl Harbor his fiancée, Margaret "Muggs" Pierson of Minneapolis, came to Vancouver Barracks, and they were married. I was best man, and we had the wedding party at our house. Bill was allowed off the post that night but had to be on duty by noon the next day.

We left for Texas by train in December 1941. John was, by then, nine months old, a very healthy, vigorous, precocious child. Mary wrote that traveling with him was like traveling with a baby gorilla! The train was crowded with military personnel and families and a few civilians on government business. When we arrived in San Francisco there was a several hour layover. A lot of people got off at their destination, and a many were put off by the M.P.s. There was great excitement. Then it was announced on the train that a ship had just arrived in San Francisco with army and navy dependent women and children who were living in Hawaii when Pearl Harbor was attacked. Their husbands and fathers were stationed in Hawaii or other Pacific islands. Many had lost their loved ones at Pearl Harbor or had no news about those on islands taken by the Japanese. Our train was soon loaded with saddened, recently widowed mothers and their children who had been taken directly from the ship to the train, bound for whatever homes they might have across the United States.

I had on my uniform with medical insignia and was soon at work treating these distraught people. The M.P.s, conductors, and porters were extremely helpful, courteous and compassionate. I had no medications, and there were several hundred people, some with fever, diarrhea, headaches, and crying babies. Many mothers wanted to vent their tragic stories. The conductors stopped the train at various stations and telegraphed ahead to request medical supplies—aspirin, paregoric, codeine, cough medicine, and sulfa, the only antibiotic then available. I made rounds up and down the train several times a day for the next couple of days it required to reach San Antonio, where many mothers and children departed.

We got off in Beaumont. Fortunately, none of the passengers on the train became seriously ill while I was pressed into duty. We were welcomed by Mary's wonderful family in a real homecoming. I telephoned my family in Deport, who were glad to have us in Texas. This was wartime and everyone had an underlying sense of anxiety and concern about the future. Events beyond our control were happening every day. We thanked God we had been more fortunate than the poor families on that train, and we felt a deep sympathy for them. But strangely we, everyone, remained cheerful: knowing so much sorrow with friends dying in battle, we had to keep a stiff upper lip and hope the Good Lord would take care of us and our loved ones and that this war would soon end so we could resume a normal life.

Soon, I left Mary and John in Beaumont and went to San Antonio to enter the School of Aviation Medicine at Randolph Field. I found a nice little furnished house at 280 Retama Street at the corner of New Braunfels Road, across the street from the then Peacock Military Academy. Mary and John were soon with me. We were with lots of friends, San Antonians, and people stationed in the military.[1] San Antonio was a wonderful assignment; we were especially fond of the Mexican restaurants. These included La Fonda and the Original Mexican Restaurant on the riverfront. Randolph and Fort Sam Houston had wonderful officers clubs, and friends invited us to the San Antonio Country Club. Randolph Officers Club served the best enchiladas I had ever tasted. I ate them every time I could get to the club for lunch or dinner. America supported its soldiers in many ways. Movie stars volunteered their talents. One night at Fort Sam Houston we were among a thousand who were entertained in a hilarious program by Bob Hope and Bing Crosby.

During our stay in San Antonio, Ralph Letteer married Margaret Walker at the Episcopal Cathedral, and we went to their parties. Ralph was probably my best friend since we went through medical school. We were involved in another wedding at Randolph. John Barker's fiancée came down from Duluth. We helped John locate a honeymoon spot at the famous Gallagher Ranch twenty miles out of San Antonio, and I served as best man at their wedding on a Saturday night in the Randolph Field Chapel. A reception followed at the officers club. The party went on and on. Finally about midnight I asked John why he didn't take his bride to the guest ranch. "I'm afraid to go," he said. Those were the days of virtue. We literally loaded them in their car and they drove away; John had to be at roll call at Randolph 6:30 A.M. next Monday. After school at Randolph I remember seeing John and Pearl Barker off for Portland. The tread was worn off all their tires and no new ones were available, but they made it.

The course at the School of Aviation Medicine was very intense. We drove out before daylight and took strenuous group exercises before classes started. We learned aeronautics with ten hours of flying lessons, the specialty of aviation medicine, enough ophthalmology to refract and prescribe glasses, otolaryngology, neurology, psychology, psychiatry, electrocardiography, public health, and administering the regulations for examining cadets and maintaining airmen in flight. We learned to take a 45-caliber Colt pistol apart and put it back together in total darkness. We had pistol and rifle practice, and I received two marksman medals. I was proud of my diploma from the school. I soon had an assignment as a certified Air Corps flight surgeon. We wore wings like the pilots. Ours were gold with a caduceus in the center—I still have mine. Also like the pilots, we were eligible for flight pay. We had to do at least four hours of certified military flying time each month. I would later far exceed these flight hours under extremely dangerous flying conditions.

I completed the course at Randolph Field around March 28, 1942. By this time, Mary had become pregnant with our second child, Cooke, who would be born later that fall in Galveston. I left Mary and John with her parents and drove back to Portland and then to Paine Field in Everett, Washington. I wrote Mary nearly every day after I left Beaumont, and she saved virtually all my letters and telegrams.[2] I arrived at Paine Field in early April, 1942, as a flight surgeon under the command of Lieutenant Colonel McCauley and group surgeon Captain Thompson. Most of my time involved making rounds as O.D., doing physicals and eye examinations, and preparing talks on first aid, gas warfare and high-altitude flying. Here, I had my first experience witnessing a fatal plane crash. I was on the flight line waiting to take my required flight time on any plane, when a seat became available. One plane left with no available space. It took off, and I saw it crash dive from an altitude of a few hundred feet into a shrub covered slope about a mile away. I rode an ambulance out to a few yards away from the crash. The scene was shocking. The plane was totally destroyed and had created a four or five foot hole in the ground. All five bodies were badly mangled and compressed into the wreckage with varying degrees of dismemberment. I helped remove the bodies, which we brought back in the ambulance. During my term of service I saw several other fatal crashes and was later appointed as a flight surgeon medical member of a plane crash evaluation team at Wright Field. On the flight line in the Aleutians, I removed several wounded and dead crew members from planes returning from missions over Kiska.

Still unsure of my permanent orders, I spent time looking for a house and making other domestic arrangements in the possibility of Mary's arrival. After several weeks of rumors and uncertainty, I was informed on May 21 that the Fifty-fourth Fighter Squadron was ordered to foreign duty with me as their flight surgeon. My letters contain ample facts to show that I would be sent overseas, but each time I inquired of my superior officers, I was told I would stay in the Washington area for an extended time. As I review these letters, I believe I was not informed because of the secrecy of our mission. It was not announced where we were going until our ship had embarked. After the orders came, we were in a mad rush preparing our squadron for departure and arranging our personal affairs. I had little time to get acquainted with our commanding officer, Captain T. W. Jackson, and the other squadron pilots, who flew P-38s. The yellow fever and plague vaccinations we received were for the tropics, but Charlie Kimball heard we were going to Alaska.

Mary flew from Beaumont on commercial DC-3s through dangerous weather over the Rockies and arrived on May 23, just in time for us to have two nights together in an Everett hotel. Our wonderful friends from Rochester, Charlie and Helen Kimball, took care of us as though we were their own. One night they had us to dinner, the next night the Bob Kings had us. Then on the day of departure, the Kimballs took Mary to the Seattle harbor. There, a huge crowd of families looked down on the dock, where our entire squadron, except the pilots and mechanics, stood or sat waiting with all our personal gear. We waited for hours before we climbed aboard single file and waved to our loved ones from the ship's deck. The Kimballs stayed at the harbor with Mary for hours before the ship finally backed away from the dock in the late afternoon of May 25, 1942. The ship, a converted freighter, was accompanied by a destroyer escort. Mary and the Kimballs disappeared in the distance as we slowly sailed out of the harbor.

I was excited to sail into Kodiak, Alaska, early one morning for a twelve-hour layover. All aboard were allowed to go ashore. It was my first view of Alaska. Large naval vessels and sea planes filled what otherwise was a typical fishing harbor. The village extended upward from the harbor on a mountain slope. The Russian Orthodox Church stood prominently among the other town buildings. Our officers were invited to the naval officers quarters to lunch. As I went up the barrack stairs to freshen up, I was surprised to hear a funny barking and a scuttling noise behind me. I turned to find a young hair seal clambering up after me begging for a hand out. I soon learned that the officers had several pet seals that had free run of the officers barracks. We left Kodiak and sailed up the Cook Inlet to Anchorage. This proved to be our staging area for deployment to the Aleutian Islands.

Another bit of astounding information was withheld from us or was yet unknown to our commmand. As we were sailing toward Alaska, the Japanese had a huge armada off the Aleutian Islands, within a hundred miles off Dutch Harbor and six hundred miles from Kodiak. The Japanese fleet consisted of two aircraft carriers loaded with Zero fighters and bombing planes, two cruisers, three destroyers, submarines, and four transport ships carrying twenty-five thousand troops. The Japanese were on their way to destroy Dutch Harbor and occupy it as a stepping stone for conquering Northwest America. Our fighter squadron, along with various other fighter and bomber units—even a squadron of British fighters—was being rushed to Alaska to help defend it. On May 26, the day after we left Seattle, Japanese planes made a probing attack on Dutch Harbor. On June 3, they made a concerted attack with four bombers and fourteen fighter planes. Over forty Japanese planes were sighted on that day. The Japanese were very surprised when they were met by numerous U.S. Air Corps and navy bombers and fighter planes.

The Japanese were unaware that Simon Bolivar Buckner, commanding general for the Alaska Defense Command, and General Butler, commanding officer of the Eleventh Air Force, had ordered the rapid expansion of the airfield at Cold Bay and the heroic construction of a complete new air base at Umnak, all done within a few weeks. Eleventh Air Force Bomber Headquarters was moved from Anchorage to Umnak. Thus Dutch Harbor was protected by two air bases, one on either side within a hundred miles, eliminating any chance of a Pearl Harbor–type surprise. Our planes soon inflicted heavy

Arctic train rescued Mavis, 1942

damage on the Japanese planes and ships. We bombed and strafed their carriers so severely that they fled leaving many, possibly forty, Japanese planes in combat over Dutch Harbor with no place to land. Those not shot down were lost at sea.

Defeated at Dutch Harbor on June 3, the Japanese did not abandon the Aleutians, however. In June they ordered troops to Attu, where they captured ninety Aleutian natives and an American teaching couple and built fortifications. Those captured were never heard from again. Attu is only seven hundred and fifty miles from Japan. The Japanese also landed at Kiska on June 10, and feverishly built fortifications and a submarine and seaplane base and undertook building an airstrip. They even laid out streets and erected buildings. They were planning a permanent foothold in America via the Aleutians.

The real war for the Aleutians and the Northwest was joined while we were sailing from Seattle to Alaska. And we were very surprised to learn about it when we arrived. During the following months, strict censorship prevented me from telling about it in my letters to Mary. There was so much war going on all over the world that people paid little attention to the Aleutian Campaign. The planning of our Alaska generals and admirals prevented the Japanese from landing on the Alaska mainland, an event which would have quickly shifted our attention from the South Pacific.

Fort Richardson was a huge army installation in Anchorage, Alaska. The Air Corps (Eleventh Air Force) was still part of the U.S Army. There were fifty thousand troops in Fort Richardson, with hundreds of temporary wooden buildings and several hangars. The hangars were so large it could cloud up and rain inside of one; or, one could, as our farmboy pilots explained, "store a hell of a lot of hay in one." Dutch Harbor in the Aleutians was attacked from a Japanese carrier the day we landed in Anchorage, but news of it had not reached us. The Japanese had been overrunning the entire Pacific Rim, the Aleutian attack being only a part of their effort. We didn't know it at the time, but the war with Japan had suddenly turned in our favor. Immediately after the defeat of the Japanese at Dutch Harbor, the U.S. Navy defeated the Japanese Navy in the decisive Battle of Midway, June 4–6, 1942.

I was soon very busy in Anchorage running our medical station, and sharing duty in the flight surgeon's office. I was getting acquainted with the Eleventh Air Corps surgeon, Colonel Altfather; the Fighter Command surgeon; the Eleventh Fighter Command C.O., Colonel Morrell; as well as the hospital and army commanding medical officer, Colonel Moore. Our squadron pilots had flown sixteen P-38s from Paine Field, and we were all together again. It was easy to make friends with all of them. Our C.O., Captain T. W. Jackson, was regular army, a twenty-five-year-old West Point graduate and Randolph Field–trained pilot who left his wife and baby in Kansas. A wonderful man, he and I became fast friends. The second in command was Captain Frank Pope, a bright, witty, smallish young man. Most were just out of flight training and in their early twenties. I was thirty years old and, within the squadron, sort of a father figure.

Our officers were assigned quarters in the barracks. The remainder of the squadron was encamped outside of Anchorage, either due to lack of barrack space or to get accustomed to field operations. The men dug their own latrines, set up mess in a tent with field stoves and field rations, and erected tent living quarters. I was ordered to outfit and prepare for field duty. Our eight enlisted medics were fine dependable young men, but all of us were only recently trained and quite inexperienced. We had been taught to obey the chain of command. We followed it cheerfully and I believe it led to our success and very few snafus.

About June 15, 1942, most of the Fifty-fourth was jerked up from camp and loaded on a small ship in Anchorage, destination not announced. The field mess was held on the open deck, rain or shine. I ate with them. I had a stateroom but no invitation to eat with the ship's captain. This was the first time we had Spam, and we thought it was wonderful. After a few months of it, however, we would complain bitterly when it was served. Three days later we arrived at Cold Bay Harbor, a fishing village on the Alaska Peninsula. Nearby was a hastily constructed air base with a few Quonset huts, many tent quarters, and a temporary runway constructed of interlocking fenestrated iron panels. There was an infantry brigade outpost, an engineers unit, an antiaircraft unit, and a base hospital in Quonset huts. Another fighter squadron of P-40s was already stationed at the base. Captain Bob Mooney was their medical officer.

We soon had a complete squadron encampment, with everything in tents. My tentmates and I dug a four-foot deep foundation for the tent and installed a Sibley stove and chimney. We were issued lumber for a wood floor and, unlike the others, had an adequate coal allowance for our stove. We were also each issued 45-caliber Colt pistols and an M1 semi-automatic rifle, and earlier, had been given winter clothing: long underwear, woolens, a flight jacket, a big leather wool-lined coat, a fur cap, water proof parkas ("parkeys") and pants, leather boots, and pilots' fur-lined zip-up boots.

We kept our ambulance parked alongside our tent. When our pilots were flying, we kept the ambulance on the flight line. We also had a large mess tent, with separate seating for the officers. After supper was served all the tables were cleaned and the regular army mess sergeant opened his gambling hall for the enlisted men. He passed out decks of cards, ran a black jack game, and a dice game. This gambling "license" was allowed mess sergeants, and I heard that ours left Alaska with fifty thousand dollars in winnings. Meanwhile the officers played dice on a horse blanket in another tent. I usually won at dice. We also occupied ourselves playing chess and fishing for trout and salmon.

The Aleutian Islands are in a chain extending nine hundred miles westward from the Alaska Peninsula almost to Kamchatka. During World War II, significant American forces were stationed at Cold Bay Harbor and on the following islands: Unalsaka (Dutch Harbor), Umnak (Fort Mears), Adak, and Amchitka. I spent from one to three months on all the army bases. I also went on a surveillance trip to Atka Island, where we visited an evacuated Aleut Indian village. This happened to be a pretty day. We were flown in a Navy PBY rescue flying boat into the small harbor. We inflated a raft to row ashore, where we found a few vacant huts, a Russian Orthodox Church, and a cemetery with wooden grave markers. The Japanese had established bases on Kiska and Attu, only seven hundred and fifty miles from Japan.

The Aleutian Islands separate the Pacific Ocean and the Bering Sea and comprise part of the border of the Pacific basin. There are fourteen large and about fifty-five small islands with numerous islets, protruding rocks, and towering cliffs rising from the sea. Mainly volcanic, the islands contain numerous active volcanoes, such as 9,387-foot Mount Shishaldin on Unimak Island. I saw several significant eruptions and felt dozens of earthquakes during the year I was there, some severe enough to shake medicines off the dispensary shelves. When we felt severe earthquakes, we usually ran outside, but I never saw a tent or building collapse. I did see tents and their contents blown away by the strong winds. After I became command surgeon, I sailed in a supply boat to an isolated radar outpost to treat several enlisted men injured by a wind storm. The wind was so fierce it blew most of the tents and the radar out to sea. No one was lost, as all facilities were dug in. None of the men were seriously hurt, and, to their disappointment, were not relieved of duty. The sea was so rough that day, everyone got seasick including the crew. The skipper, with thirteen years experience in the Arctic, said, "The waters are so rough up here, we all get seasick."

There was almost constant wind with frequent williwaws up to ninety miles an hour, accompanied by rain and fog. The wind was so fierce, it was said, that we should be using 500-pound bombs for windsocks. There were a few sunny days in midwinter. It snowed frequently during the winter, but that snow soon melted. Often the fierce winds blew snow and dust at the same time into one's clothing or tent. The average temperature was around thirty-three degrees for winter and fifty degrees for summer—never as low as zero. The weather and terrain thus were extremely hazardous for planes and ships. We lost half the original pilots in our squadron to weather during the year we were there, as many as were shot down by the Japanese. I was living in a tent with my best friend and commanding officer, Major T. W. Jackson, when he and Lieutenant Crowe were lost when they were shot down by the Japanese over Kiska. Crowe was a favorite pilot: he had volunteered as the squadron barber and cut our hair when it became too shaggy. Lost pilots were immediately replaced by new ones. Half the original pilots survived for the entire year. The flyers described the volcanic mountains as clouds with rocks in them. Avoiding them in flight required expert navigation.

In addition to the mountainous areas, several of the larger islands had low, flat, poorly drained or swampy areas, such as we encountered when we attempted to walk across the Alaska Peninsula north of Cold Bay. There were no trees. The largest bushes were alders, some as high as six feet. The tundra, however, was populated by a great profusion of plants—coarse grasses, lupines, lilies, various asters, fireweed, cotton flower, berries, including the tasty salmon berry, and mosses, even orchids, all intermingled. Animal life included hundreds of bird species, especially ducks, geese, and swans. Bald eagles frequently sat on rocks around our camps observing us. Ptarmigans were common. Porcupines wandered into camp without fear. There were various marmots. Alaska brown bears were common on the peninsula.

My most vivid memory of this time concerned a transport plane crash in July, killing four officers and eight enlisted men from our squadron. With Majors Jackson and Bissel and Lieutenant Karlstrom, a medical officer, I started off on July 7 on an expedition for some bodies and wreckage that had been seen by plane on a beach about twenty miles off. It was the most arduous experience of my life. We stumbled through miles of hip-high tussocks of tundra in the constant cold, rain, and fog. Our boots and clothes were soaked.

We were often threatened by Alaska brown bears and had virtually no sleep for three days. Sadly we failed to reach our goal.

During the third night we were stumbling half lost, back toward camp over higher dryer ground. We found some caterpillar tracks, which we followed. We knew there were infantry outposts in this area so we started shooting our rifles to attract help. By this time, one of our group was actually crawling on the ground. Finally, about midnight, we recognized the sound of a caterpillar pulling a tracked wagon coming through the fog and darkness toward our rifle shots. Soon we saw their lights and heard their calls. The tractor arrived with three or four infantrymen. You can imagine our relief. They had to lift Karlstrom into the wagon. On the way back to camp, the soldiers told us that people had been searching for us, because the weather had been too bad for our pilots to follow us from the air during the last day. Our infantry friends took us into their camp a couple of miles away, arriving well after midnight. Everyone was up to welcome us. They cooked a big meal and gave us warm clothes and boots. Our feet were black and blue; another day and we would have lost parts from trench foot. They put us to bed in their pup tents, which had been dug into the ground to avoid enemy fire. For a week I couldn't wear shoes or boots because my feet were so painfully swollen. In a letter to Mary dated July 11, 1942, I described the exhausting search:

> We left by boat and went as far as possible, then started walking about 2:30 A.M. We walked until ten o'clock next night and never could get to the plane due to swift rivers, swamps and other obstructions. We saw many bears. They were extremely large, many weighing over a 1000 lbs easily. Some must have weighed about 1500 lb. Many had two cubs with them. They varied in color from almost black, brown to almost white. They were very curious, stood on their hind legs and looked at us. Apparently they couldn't see well. They could smell well. As soon as they got wind of us they would turn and gallop off. We always approached them upwind & tried not to surprise them. Just before we made camp we were skirting the sea with a hugh swamp to the side. A large almost white bear & two cubs were playing on the beach. We waded about 100 yards out to sea to avoid them and get upwind but she started toward us with the cubs following. We fired over her head but she kept coming. We all drew bead on her. She got so close to us we could see the whites of her eyes, probably about 50–75 ft and coming faster. She picked out the most isolated member of our party and made a bee line. As she went toward him she got wind of us and turned and ran. We had army rifles, but they say that they won't stop these huge bears and once you shoot them they go wild and kill everything in

sight. So we were in a dilemma. Another time during the day there were several bears around us and some of our planes came over and chased them away. At one time one flyer counted twenty five bears within a five mile radius of us. . . . The terrain was so rough with hills, mud flats, swamps etc. that we become almost completely exhausted. We tried to wade across a bay and the tide came in when we were about 1-1/2 miles from land so we had to scamper back. We got in water and mud up to our waists. It was chilling cold too. We built a fire the second night and tried to sleep but had trouble keeping warm. It started raining about 3:00 A.M. just as we had dried out, so we had to start moving again. Just as we were stretching our muscles a bit we looked up and a huge brown bear about 50 ft. away was coming right for us. We scampered up a slight hill with our rifles and as soon as he smelled us he was off in a gallop. We got on our way and tried to cross a bay but the tide was up so we finally got a fire going right in a rain and sat around until noon. Then we walked until after midnight, it raining and the wind blowing up to 50 MPH the whole time. Eventually we reached an outpost. They had hot coffee, fried chicken and warm sleeping bags. We slept until noon next day and then had the largest breakfast I ever ate. Then we drove into camp in a Jeep. I have never seen such a traveling machine. It actually climbed hills and went through mud holes that looked completely impassable. We were all extremely happy to get home. Although this is a hole with no conveniences at all it looked like a city to us. I have been resting since then.

After our rescue mission failed a boat was sent around the west end of the peninsula and back along the north shore on the Bering Sea. The party located the plane wreckage and retrieved some of the bodies of our missing squadron staff.

On September 11, 1942, the Fifty-fourth Fighter Squadron moved to Adak Island, where troops and naval personnel were concentrated to ward off a Japanese advance up the Aleutian Isles. A temporary runway made of interlocking fenestrated steel panels had been constructed. I arrived in a DC-3 with our medical team. The Fifty-fourth, which had been patrolling Adak from Umnak a couple hundred miles away, was welcomed with great celebration, since the Japanese had been bombing the base at night and strafing during the day with their planes based at Kiska. Our fighter planes flew cover for us, and we were the first planes to land on the Adak air strip. Transport planes and bombers always had fighter plane cover in this area. I was in a plane only once when a Japanese plane was encountered.

The Air Corps heavy bomber squadrons soon were bombing Kiska and

Attu from Adak. We promptly set up a first aid station on the flight line and dug several foxholes nearby. Other units failed to dig fox holes. A few days later, when a Japanese plane made a strafing raid down our flight line, we all rushed for the foxholes, which were so packed with other personnel that arms and legs were sticking out. We could not get in. After that attack many foxholes were dug on that flight line.

In this move our ambulance had failed to arrive, in spite of the fact that I saw it loaded on the ship before we left Umnak—a real mystery. I was given a Jeep to make out. One day, a medic and I were driving our Jeep back from the harbor when we passed our ambulance, which we identified by the number. We turned around quickly and caught up. The ambulance was being driven by two enlisted infantry men when we stopped it. They had been hauling coal in our beloved vehicle and were going back to the harbor for another load. We left the soldiers on the road complaining that they'd have to walk five miles back to their unit. We cleaned up our ambulance and guarded it carefully. Stealing other people's equipment was known in the service as a "flashlight" requisition.

We had begun to lose our pilots. Some disappeared in the terrible weather, some were shot down by the Japanese. Pilots had to fly by seat-of-the-pants navigation, without radar, for fear the Japanese would home in on us. One could fly only east or west along the Aleutian Chain. There was nowhere to land north or south, just the open Bering Sea or Pacific Ocean. More than once, as I flew up and down the Aleutians—eight round trips during the year—we were lost; when we'd finally land, we'd kiss the earth and thank God for saving us. Our pilots flew fighter planes, P-38s, P-40s, and P-39s. The medium bombers were B-26s and B-36s and the heavy bombers, B17s and B24s. I rode in all the bombers many times, as I hitchhiked rides from island to island performing my duties. I also went by boat to several outlying radar stations in the Fighter Command.

Vic Walton was the most interesting of the fighter pilots in the Fifty-fourth. He won the Distinguished Flying Cross for flying the longest fighter mission in history and made more trips over enemy territory than any other fighter pilot in Alaska. The P-38s were very popular with the pilots; they had twin engines and could fly on one and take a lot of flak. In spite of their size they were quite maneuverable. By installing wing tanks, the P-38 could fly longer missions than any other fighter plane. Kiska was eight hundred miles west of our base. I well remember meeting Vic on the flight line when he returned from the first mission. He was tired but excited. He had strafed the Kiska installation several times and destroyed several float planes while receiving much flak from Japanese antiaircraft guns. Numerous bullet holes pockmarked his plane, any one of which could have been fatal. I routinely met these pilots on the flight line when they returned. After several missions, during which we lost some pilots and planes, Vic got out of his plane and said, "Doc, I'm like the bad penny, I always come back, the Japanese can't get rid of me."[3]

I examined and kept detailed records on our P-38 pilots who flew eight-hour missions to strafe the Japanese on Kiska, eventually publishing important findings on flyer fatigue. Going down at sea was another life-and-death hazard our pilots confronted from being shot down, having engine trouble, or running out of fuel. The pilots were forced to parachute out or land their plane in the water. Few men could survive more than an hour in the icy conditions. I treated and interviewed fifty airmen who had been rescued from the freezing water and later published the results. In a letter to Mary, dated July 24, 1942, I described the experiences of one exposure victim: "Yesterday Krenytzky, a fishing pal, had a forced landing into the bay and floated in his safety belt for 1 1/2 hours. He was unconscious from exposure when a boat finally reached him. He almost died. Today he is in the hospital cussing like a sailor because he can't get out."

Krenytzky had a narrow escape. But there were many other hardships that airmen and ground crew had to suffer. A few broke down and had to be evacuated. Two men in our command committed suicide by zipping themselves up in their sleeping bags and shooting themselves with their own Colt pistols. The vast majority, however, were tough young men who rarely got sick. I don't even remember a case of appendicitis.[4]

Adak rapidly became a huge installation, scattered over many square miles and hosting large infantry, artillery, signal corps, antiaircraft, and engineer forces—everything but cavalry. The navy brought extensive units in the harbor, including various sea planes, patrol boats, destroyers, submarines, cruisers, carriers, and main line battleships. I think the entire Pacific Fleet was there at one time. This was the build up to drive the Japanese out of the Aleutians. Tokyo Rose broadcast every night for hours telling us to leave before it was too late. Japanese propaganda leaflets were also dropped. Once, I invited myself out to a navy airplane tender vessel to visit the flight surgeon. I found the crew, officers and all, living in comparative luxury with nicely starched uniforms, while our unbathed squadron lived in tents with dirt floors. My letters to Mary were filled with comments about the inadequacies of sponge baths and the frustrations of laundering clothes, drying them, and discovering them just as dusty and dirty as they were before! I was also invited for lunch and ate at a table with tablecloth and cloth napkins, something I hadn't seen in months.

In late September I was promoted to major and group surgeon of the 343rd Fighter Group, of which the Fifty-fourth was a part, although the promotion meant I'd be leaving my beloved unit. The commanding officer was Colonel Jack Chenault, son of the famous General Claire Chenault, head of Chiang Kai-shek's air force in China. I returned to Umnak, where, fortunately, our group medical department was assigned a Quonset hut for a dispensary—a great improvement over the sixteen-by-sixteen foot canvas tent dispensaries. We had enough room in the Quonset hut to set up a twenty foot eye lane for doing refractions and prescribing glasses. Soon, it seemed as if every soldier at Umnak wanted glasses. I could have been busy full-time prescribing glasses. We sent the prescriptions by ATS (Air Transport Service) to Anchorage. A private oculist ground the lens and sent new glasses back in six weeks. In the Quonset hut we were able to do limited physiotherapy. Ultraviolet light treatments were in demand, because there was so little sunlight. Compared to the tent dispensaries, however, the Quonset huts did have one disadvantage. If they collapsed during one of the frequent earthquakes the occupants could get hurt. No one worried about tents collapsing. Many times the medicines fell off the shelves and everyone ran outside during an earthquake, while those in a tent stayed inside rocking comfortably. Fortunately no huts or tents collapsed. Dr. Geiss who took my place as the Fifty-fourth's squadron surgeon followed the regulations to the limit and had soon grounded some of our best pilots for insignificant health problems. The squadron C.O. called me raising hell. I had to teach Geiss in a hurry that field conditions were totally different from the rules and regulations. He caught on quickly and became a popular doctor.[5]

During this time, I was concerned about the outcome of Mary's pregnancy—whether it was a boy or a girl, what the little rascal was named, and how Mary was doing. Finally, after weeks of waiting and not hearing anything, I received a telegram in Anchorage on October 26, sent by Mrs. Wilson from St. Mary's Hospital, Galveston, on October 16, the day of my son's birth. It stated simply: "Son born, Family well, All send love." I was greatly relieved but did not hear anything more for about a month—I didn't even know his name—when a letter said he was named Cooke Randolph Kelsey. For at least three months I considered that to be his name. Finally I heard that it was Cooke Wilson Kelsey.[6]

When I got word of Cooke's birth I wrote Mary from Anchorage:

> Don't think I haven't been proud around here. I've met one helluva lot of people here, so I go up to them & give them a cigar and they say "Congratulations on your promotion." I say, "Promotion Hell, I just had word of another son." The only catch is I usually have to end up by giving two cigars. . . . We all went to town Saturday night and hung on a good one,

ending up in the city jail for driving without lights, refusing to stop at an officer's beckoning and having to be chased down. We got to the police station, ridiculed the cops so that they got raging mad but finally let us go about daylight, so we came home, woke up the whole barracks and had more trouble.[7]

December 1942 saw another promotion for me, this time to surgeon of the XI Fighter Command. "This cinches my station for the duration," I wrote Mary, "I'm not having any dreams of tropical isles or Texas flying fields." In fact, on Christmas Eve I saw a spectacular winter scene which I related to her: "Today I made a trip of several miles to get to a patient who was burned. There was a pretty white snow and we passed within several hundred feet of two herds of reindeer. I thought it was quite appropriate for Xmas." I spent that Christmas on Umnak in Capt. Gillsdorf's dispensary. There were several of us. I brought goodies from Anchorage, and Gillsdorf had saved a quart of Four Roses medical whiskey. The bottle appeared full. We poured out the first drink, and a cigarette butt floated out. We figured Sergeant McNulty, a known alcoholic, had been in it and accidentally dropped the butt in. He didn't deny it. We feared we might get nicotine poison from drinking the whiskey, so we took small sips and awaited results. As we kept sipping, nothing happened so we drank the whole bottle, which I suspect McNulty had diluted.

Censorship prevented me from mentioning my activities on Amchitka Island. This duty was in the latter part of my stay in the Aleutians. The U.S. Navy and engineers had landed on Amchitka, only eighty miles from Kiska, and quickly built a runway. The infantry moved troops in, and the Air Corps operated out of the airfield, launching a relentless air attack on Kiska and Attu. Colonel Morrell sent me down to Amchitka to look after the pilots and other personnel of the XI Fighter Command. I remember visiting the hastily constructed field hospital in two tents with a mud floor. I spent most of my time on the flight line. The Japanese air force virtually had become eliminated. As I recall, only one Japanese plane made a strafing pass over the Amchitka airfield before it was shot down. There was still antiaircraft fire over Kiska. Captain Tawlk had taken the radio equipment out of a P-38, making just enough room for a person to crawl in behind the pilot and ride as a passenger. The pilots were taking enlisted mechanics up for a ride to show them what they had been working for and how their planes performed. I gladly accepted a ride with Tawlk, and we flew over Kiska. I got a good look at Kiska Harbor and the Japanese installations. The scene resembled the intelligence photos I had seen many times in the photo laboratory late at night. The intelligence officers developed and studied the aerial photos taken on each day's flight,

Major Mavis Parrott Kelsey, MC, USAF, XI Fighter Command, on duty, Adak, Alaska, 1943

and the pilots used them to plan their targets for the next day's mission. Needless to say, I was really anxious to get away from Kiska Harbor, but Tawlk didn't seem to be a bit concerned.

Our bomber and fighter planes bombed and strafed Kiska and Attu unceasingly, destroying virtually all of the Japanese installations. Our naval vessels surrounded these islands preventing Japanese reinforcements, while our forces prepared a landing on Kiska and Attu. When we landed on Attu we destroyed the Japanese but lost hundreds of soldiers to enemy fire and exposure. I went on an army hospital evacuation ship to see hundreds of soldiers with trench foot. Some would lose their feet. Unknown to us, the Japanese were able to evade our naval and air forces during a storm and get ships into Kiska Harbor and evacuated the entire base. In July 1943, soon after I left Alaska, the Americans landed on Kiska to find that every Japanese soldier had gone.

In early June, 1943, I finally heard rumors that I might soon return to the States as an overage. Three weeks later, on June 21, I sent Mary the following telegram: WILL BE IN TEXAS SOON WITH FIFTEEN DAYS LEAVE DON'T KNOW NEXT STATION. MAVIS KELSEY. I got my things together and took an Air Transport DC-3 from Anchorage. The weather was perfect. We saw the Alaskan glaciers and snow-covered peaks and Mount Ranier before landing at a large aircraft factory near Seattle. Mary met me in Dallas on about June 23, and we went to the Adolphus Hotel. My brother John, who was attending medical school in Dallas, and our friend James Grant from Deport came up to our room for a visit. It didn't take long to thank them for coming and then dismiss them! They brought me a new Chevrolet sedan from the Kelsey Motor Company. At that time a new auto was very difficult to obtain. The next day, we went to Deport for a couple of days, where our family welcomed us with open arms, and then on to Beaumont. I remember walking in to see our sons, John and Cooke, neither of whom obviously knew who I was.

Mary and I had a wonderful reunion. It was like falling in love again. After all, we had not seen each other for a year. We spent many hours talking and planning and playing with John and Cooke. John was jealous of this man who was occupying his mother's time. Cooke was too young to be concerned. A few months were required for me to be taken back into the family. I called several friends who were also fortunate enough to be returning from foreign duty. Fellow AKK brothers Sam Barnes and Jim Little had been through all the battles of Guadalcanal as medical officers in the marines. I could not imagine a worse experience of seeing American soldiers slaughtered. We exchanged experiences; I said I was glad I wasn't on Guadalcanal, and Jim replied he was glad he wasn't in the Aleutians.

When my leave expired in mid-July, Mary and I drove to San Francisco where I was to report for temporary duty and wait for permanent assignment. We were assigned a room in the Mark Hopkins Hotel paid for by our housing allowance. The personnel officer at headquarters even asked me where I wanted to be assigned. I requested a large air base in Texas with a hospital where I could see patients again. Personnel agreed to apply for one in El Paso. Meanwhile, my friend Pete Pearson was chief of medicine at a large air base near Omaha, Nebraska, and wanted to get me assigned there.

I reported day after day, waiting for my assignment to arrive. We had nothing to do but loaf around San Francisco, go to movies, restaurants, and museums. The Army Corps Headquarters tried to find work for us while we waited. Examination facilities were set up at headquarters for women applying to the Women's Army Corps (WAC). I was put to work doing entrance examinations on these young women. Having women in the service was a great departure for a male army. Other officers thought we had been assigned a rare privilege to examine these young women, but I saw it as a job that kept me away from vacationing and sightseeing. On about August 5 my orders came to report to Sheppard Field, Wichita Falls, Texas, on August 18, 1943. On the way back to Texas, we drove across the Mojave Desert during the night to avoid the heat. The next day in the Arizona desert we had a flat tire. I left Mary at an isolated filling station while I hitchhiked in my uniform to a town to find another tire. While I was gone, the filling station owner entertained Mary. Looking for a wife, he gave her a written list of his glowing qualifications that included the nice filling station all paid for. He asked Mary to help him locate a good woman when she got back to where people lived.

I considered the assignment at Sheppard Field to be temporary, believing that I would be transferred to Nebraska. Wichita Falls, like Alaska, was not considered a desirable assignment. People kept asking, "What did you do wrong to be sent here?" We arrived during a heat wave. Cadets were falling out on the drill field, thus being disqualified for pilot training. Attic fans were the only form of air conditioning. The winters weren't fun either. Northers blew in from the North Pole. The only heat was by risky gas-fired room heaters. Housing was virtually impossible to locate in this small city with an air base of fifty thousand men. We stayed in the Kemp Hotel, then in a motel, until finally we located a nice house at 1663 Dayton. It had a large enclosed backyard, with a sandpile for the boys.

As I soon found out, however, the real reason I was sent to Sheppard was because the Air Corps was processing thousands of air cadet applicants, and I was an experienced flight surgeon and internist. Soon I was on the assembly line for cadet applicants.[8] We lined up twenty-five to fifty or so boys while several doctors went down the line. A cardiologist listened to their hearts for murmurs, checked for hypertension, and did exercise tests. Another doctor checked the genitals ("short arms inspection") and tested for hernias. Others examined the body for any deformity or musculo-skeletal problem. In another room visual and hearing tests were performed. Normal color vision, 20/20 vision without glasses, and good hearing were required for all cadets. The requirement for a college degree was dropped, as the demand for airmen increased. One month, we worked eighteen-hour shifts processing ten thousand applicants to fill the quotas for flying schools. When we finished these examinations we had selected the finest young men in America, and the war killed many of them.

Sheppard Field was a highly efficient operation. It was put together rapidly, requiring team work and a rigid chain of command. We enjoyed an active social life among the doctors' families. Collie Smith, an AKK brother from Mart, Texas, was there with his wife Mary. Jim Little's brother, a prominent general practitioner in Wichita Falls, entertained us. I had friends at the Wichita Falls State Hospital who remembered me from when I externed there as a medical student. We drove to Throckmorton to visit relatives. We went history hopping to Fort Griffin and Fort Sill. John and Cooke were growing, and, as she wished, Mary was soon pregnant with what she hoped would be a girl.

I had about decided that we would be at Sheppard Field for the duration. One night in February 1944, however, a phone call came from our friend Colonel Randy Lovelace, chief of the Aeromedical Research Laboratory in Dayton, Ohio. He told me that they were starting an air force medical journal and asked if I would like to come to Dayton and run it. "I sure would," was my reply. He told me that I would be sent orders to travel to Washington, D.C., for an interview with the air surgeon, Major General David N. W. Grant, then I would come to Dayton and look over the job. My C.O. didn't like it, and said he might stop the order, but when the order came from the air surgeon general he had no choice. Anyway, he was nice about it and wished me well.

In Washington I went to the Pentagon to see General Grant. He told me that the papers I had submitted on pilots exposed to Arctic waters and pilot fatigue in long-range flight had brought me to their attention. I also met Colonel Weigand, medical director of Eli Lilly Company, who was doing his military duty in the air surgeon's office and would be my advisor in Washington. Then I flew to Wright-Patterson Field, Dayton, Ohio, where Randy interviewed me. I would be in charge of the service liaison section, a position calling for the rank of lieutenant colonel. My principal duty would be to disseminate aeromedical information to each medical department officer of the Army Air Corps worldwide, to other appropriate branches of military services and Allied Nations, and to individuals directly engaged in aeromedical activities that contributed to the war effort. Randy planned to use art in the medical journal to increase readership. Wright and Patterson Fields had called to duty a staff of fine commercial artists, who had helped aeronautical engineers illustrate various manuals, and they were available to do illustrations for the *Air Surgeon's Bulletin*. One issue of the bulletin was already published, and my articles submitted from the Aleutians were planned for future issues.[9]

I met my staff-to-be, some eight fine people. The group included a copy editor named Katherine Drusilla Young and another editor, Lieutenant Helen Loeb. The art director was D. W. Pierce, who came from Saint Louis, where he did the famous flower arrangement books for Coca-Cola. Frank Johnson was a make-up man from Time-Life, and J. F. Donahue was a production manager. After I arrived, I arranged for Sergeant James Groshong, my secretary in Alaska, to be transferred in as my secretary. Besides producing the *Air Surgeon's Bulletin,* we had other liaison functions directed by Major Harvey Savely, an aviation physiologist. I would spend nearly two enlightening years among the scientists and engineers at Wright Field, where many of the U.S. Air Corps planes and equipment were designed and tested.

An important part of producing the *Air Surgeon's Bulletin* was locating important material for publication. I wrote command surgeons all over the world, and numerous articles poured in. I traveled to various installations, including the School of Aviation Medicine in San Antonio, the Naval Aeromedical Laboratory in Pensacola, the Tropical Medicine Center in Orlando, and the Mayo Clinic. The Mayo Clinic carried out aeromedical research projects under E. J. Baldes. Each month I took the print-ready manuscripts of the *Bulletin* to Donnelly Printing Company in Chicago and watched the magazine being made up, and I returned to Washington, D.C., with the proof copies for final approval. We could hardly wait to see each final magazine and cringe at the typographical errors that we, and every publisher, invariably overlooked.

Much of our material was sent to us from the air surgeon's office, which each month composed for publication a letter signed by General Grant. The aeromedical laboratory also sent us much material. We published the first information about many discoveries, such as parachute-opening shock, which Randy Lovelace experienced when he bailed out at thirty-five thousand feet. Other new subjects included the demand oxygen mask, explosive decompression, G-suits, heated suits and gloves, aptitude tests for flying ability, bends in flight, hyperventilation, decompression sickness, pressure breathing, aeroembolism from flight, aerodontalgia, positive acceleration, and pilot ejection seats. We were proud of the art work, graphs, and diagrams by the artists at Patterson Field. After all, they were the leading commercial artists in the United States. Our greatest triumph, however, was being among the first to publish color photographs of disease, including some of tropical fungus diseases of the skin. Mary thought they were awful and could never understand why I would print such a horrible thing!

Our journal went all over the world. The Army Air Corps was fighting the war on every continent. When I entered the service in 1941 there were four hundred thousand personnel in the Air Corps, with only eight hundred medical officers, including four hundred aviation medical examiners. Two years later, when I arrived at Dayton there were ten thousand medical officers including thirty-nine hundred aviation medical examiners, probably half of whom were rated flight surgeons. The Army Air Corps had become the United States Air Force or USAF, with two million men and women.

There was little housing to be found in Dayton. Eventually I found a fine house at 86 Grafton Avenue, owned by a Mrs. Radcliffe who was a buyer for a large department store in Dayton. An irascible character, she moved in with her sister to make the house available to us. In a few months the sister said she'd had enough of her, so Mrs. Radcliffe planned to come back to her house and live with us. She had the legal right to do this in wartime. We were later fortunate to find a fine house in a good residential area. Mary was tough. She never complained about these moves. Actually Mary never complained. My mother arrived by train to take care of the children while Mary delivered our third son, Thomas Randolph Kelsey. While there, John started saying "goddamn it." This upset my mother. There were some noisy couples living across the street and Mother heard them yelling. She told Mary, "Now I know where John learned those bad words. He heard them from those awful people across the street." Mary agreed. One day, Cooke mashed off a fingernail and fell out of a swing on his head. Then he and John opened a bottle of Tabasco sauce and got it in their eyes. That also happened to be the day Mrs. Radcliffe called saying her sister was kicking her out and she planned to move back with us. All in all, it was a tough day for Mary who had just come home with a new baby after a cesarean delivery.[10]

Our new house at 715 Oakwood was located in a fine neighborhood. We were close to an Episcopal Church and a kindergarten. Orville Wright, one of the brothers who flew the first airplane, lived in his mansion two blocks away. Our back yard extended to another street. Across this street was a very large estate. It belonged to the family who owned the National Cash Register Company, the largest industry in Dayton. The property had been turned over to the government for the duration of the war. We were given one of the garden plots on the property and grew fresh vegetables, highly appreciated then because few were obtainable elsewhere. Millions of families raised vegetables in Victory Gardens during the war. During the winter, our children rode their sleds down a hill on the property. Directly across the street from our backyard was a huge private recreation building on this estate, said to include a tennis court, swimming pool, and movie house. All this was enclosed and constantly guarded. We thought the guards were there just to protect the property, but we were in for a surprise. When the atomic bomb exploded over Hiroshima, I learned that several people I knew at Wright Field worked on the Manhattan Project. One was a nuclear physicist who had been at our house. Some of the research for the atomic bomb was being carried out in the recreation hall behind our house!

Frank Ashburn, our great friend, came from Washington, D.C., to visit when Tom was born. We saw each other often. He was stationed at the U.S.

Mavis and Mary with John (left) and Cooke. Mavis's mother, Bonita, holding
newborn Thomas. Dayton, Ohio, July 1944

Naval Hospital as a chest surgeon, and I travelled to Washington each month
to get the *Air Surgeon's Bulletin* approved for publication. Frank knew all the
chefs in the fine Washington restaurants. He was one of the few nonchefs claiming membership in a club of chefs who, once a month, took turns hosting
dinners at their respective restaurants. Frank always took me—and Mary when

she joined me on those trips—to a fine restaurant. While in Washington, I usually managed to visit a museum and go to a rare book store. I bought for a few dollars books and maps that eventually became worth hundreds of dollars. I had the same experience in Chicago where I bought books in Brentano's and Marshall Field's rare book departments. In Chicago, I went to Wright Howe's apartment, where he had his famous rare book store. Among dozens of books I purchased from him through the years was a first edition of the *Lewis and Clark Expedition.* At Brentanos I bought a first edition of Joutel's *Voyage—de la Salle.* The Field Museum and the Chicago Art Museum were my favorites in Chicago. I ate my first pizza during one of these trips to the city. I was told that it was the first and only pizza restaurant in Chicago. Mary and I learned to make pizzas, sort of, and people ate pizzas at our house for the first time. Food in America underwent great diversification when the boys came home from World War II.

The largest part of our social life in Dayton revolved around our friends at the aeromedical laboratory. We already knew Randy and Mary Lovelace, George and Marion Hallenbeck, and the John Lillys from Rochester. Pharo and Eddie Gagge lived near us and became lifetime friends. They had three adopted children a little older than ours. Colonel Pharo Gagge, a native of Richmond, Virginia, went into the service as a biophysicist from the Yale faculty. He remained in the air force for several years after World War II then returned to the Pierce Laboratory at Yale. We visited each other every year or two until it became too difficult for us to travel. Pharo died about 1993.[11]

Several important family events also occurred during this time. In October 1944, Mary took the children down to Beaumont so that Mr. Wilson could see them, especially Tom whom he had never seen. Mary's father died later that month of prostate cancer. I went down for the funeral. The service was held at St. Mark's Episcopal Church in the morning. The same afternoon we took Tom to the same church to be christened. Bishop Quin held both services. A few months later, my brother John married Mary Margaret "Mickey" Wier on March 2, 1945. Instead of being drafted during World War II, he attended Baylor University Medical College as a service man. John met Mickey when Baylor moved from Dallas to Houston. I was able to schedule one of my official trips to Texas so that I could serve as John's best man. He graduated from medical school in June and went to Baltimore City Hospital for internship.

Within a few months after arrival in Dayton, I was promoted to lieutenant colonel as chief of the section. The section was sort of a catchall. In addition to the *Air Surgeon's Bulletin,* it included several equipment development projects, the most important of which was the development of litter supports for airplanes to carry the sick and wounded from battle areas. I played no role in the project. Major Doyce Clark from Lubbock, Texas, was in charge of the program. He designed supports to place litters in bombers and small planes, but his big project was to develop litters for transport planes. We had little idea how successful this program would be. Thousands of lives were saved by aerial evacuation of the wounded. I remember going on a troop ship in the Aleutians that held about two hundred exposure victims from the Battle of Attu. These poor men, stacked in bunks in the hold of a converted freighter, had black swollen feet, almost gangrenous. They would endure several days of rough seas before reaching a hospital to get much needed treatment. Some would lose limbs or die before the ship arrived. With aerial evacuation, however, these casualties could have been in a stateside hospital within hours. Before we had published the last issue of the *Air Surgeon's Bulletin*, two years later, over a million patients had been evacuated by air.[12]

Other duties included coordinating the visits of those who came to the aeromedical laboratory on business. As part of this duty I witnessed a tragic event, the death of Lieutenant Colonel M. W. Boynton, chief of the medical safety division. I spent some time with Colonel Boynton, as he prepared for a free-fall parachute jump from forty-two thousand to five thousand feet. I wished him well on August 19, 1944, when he boarded a high altitude B-17 bomber for the jump. Major Herman Wigodsky from the Air Surgeon's Office and I took an ambulance to the field where Boynton was supposed to land. The weather was perfect, and about fifty official people were on hand. The bomber crew announced by radio when Boynton jumped. We knew exactly how long it would take for him to drop thirty-seven thousand feet, at which time his parachute would open automatically and he would float to earth safely. He also had another parachute if the automatic release failed. We were horrified to see Boynton hurtling through the air with no open parachute, showing no signs of life. He crashed into a cornfield a few hundred feet away. We rushed over to the site to find his body badly mangled. Dr. Wigodsky and I took his body to the hospital and immediately performed an autopsy. If his death occurred before the crash, we could find no explanation for it. This was before the days of forensic medicine in the air force.

As a flight surgeon I was required to report at least four hours of flying time in military aircraft each month to receive flight pay. Some of the daredevil test pilots at Wright Field scared the hell out of me doing stalls, dives, loops, testing positive and negative G forces. I was the doctor on hand during parachute test jumps. No one could get me to do a parachute jump, however. After surviving Alaska, I swore not to take any more chances unless I was ordered to do so. Many of the officers and enlisted men at the aeromedical laboratory also volunteered as subjects for their own experiments and those of their fellow researchers. I volunteered for testing clothing, adjustable seats, and a ventilated suit while in a one-hundred-sixty-degree room; I took part in altitude chamber experiments, flight experiments, and others. There was one instrument I refused to volunteer for—the human centrifuge, or accelerator. They could court martial me, but they couldn't get me on that machine. The centrifuge was in a circular room. The subject took a seat on the end of a large metal arm that spun round and round; the subject would ride for as long as he could tolerate the pull of gravity. Talk about a torture device! My friends George Hallenbeck and George Maison operated this diabolical machine. They made some important discoveries about how much the human body could and could not tolerate. No one ever thought of having the subject sign a waiver for these volunteer experiments.

While we were in Dayton, the war was being won all over the world. The Germans had been pushed out of Africa, Italy fell, France was liberated. Hitler had to pull out of Russia. I can remember D-Day when our troops landed on Normandy. I was at the air force's School of Applied Tactics at Orlando, Florida. We listened to the news on the radio in the officers club. Some of my pilot friends from the Aleutian Islands were there being trained for duty in the tropics. We celebrated D-Day and being united again.

I also vividly remember V-E Day. Everyone at Wright Field came to work in a car pool, and I was with Pharo Gagge when the news broke. When V-E Day occurred we celebrated, but the celebration was short-lived. The armed forces were being reduced. Men were being released. I had more seniority points, considering foreign duty, than most people I knew. Nearly everyone wanted out, but there was still a war going on. General Eisenhower started sending a half million soldiers from Europe to the Pacific in preparation for a landing in Japan. Many of these men had been on foreign duty for two or three years without seeing their families. Landing in Japan would be a blood bath for American soldiers. Everyone was so sad about this. These men deserved to come home. They had destroyed Mussolini's and Hitler's armies at great sacrifice and had helped liberate Europe. Japan declared that they would fight to the last man and not surrender and were still killing hundreds by Kamikaze attacks nearly every day.

Then on August 6, 1945, the United States dropped an atom bomb on Hiroshima. The Japanese refused to surrender. Three days later on August 9, another bomb was dropped on Nagasaki, forcing Japan's surrender. On V-J Day, the town of Dayton went wild. No more Americans would be killed. Our boys would come home. We celebrated at the Gagges. Horns and whistles blew, and people ran up and down the streets hugging and kissing friends and strangers. We were toasting our victory with neat vodka, Swedish style, as Pharo liked to do, he being half Swede. I don't remember ever going to bed. I remember the event as one of universal joy, excitement, and thanksgiving.

At Wright Field, people were allowed to drive in without a pass, and some public celebrations were held on the base. I remember one such event in a large hanger, where the base showed off some of its research. They let the public walk past some captured German and Japanese aircraft. There was a television set on exhibit, the first I ever saw. The screen was about eight inches square, and it showed surrounding scenes in the hangar. People crowded around to see it. Meanwhile the Wright Field personnel office began screening people in preparation for discharge. I was fully eligible for release. Randy Lovelace offered me a trip to Japan, however, to review the Japanese aviation medical system. I was also to bring back what I could about their aeromedical research. Randy knew I had adequate points for discharge, so he didn't order me to go. I was enthused about the trip, but I turned it down because I was afraid I might get stuck in Japan or ordered to Washington, D.C., or no telling where. As long as you were on duty, you could be ordered anywhere.

On September 1, 1945, my dismissal came. By this time, Mary had become tired of waiting and was in Beaumont with the children. We had planned a trip when I was released, so she came back without them. We packed and shipped our household goods to Rochester and started an auto trip. First we drove to Rochester, visited friends, and looked for a house. Then we drove through New England and up into Canada, staying in Montreal and Quebec City. On our return trip we made stops in New York, Baltimore, and Meridian, Mississippi, to visit friends and relatives.

Eventually we reached Texas, stopping at Deport for a day or two before going on to Beaumont. Our family thought we were crazy doing all that driving. It must have been some form of release. We stayed in Beaumont a few days, and I suffered a brief but real depression. I missed the sheltered life of the military. I missed not working. I also must have been afraid of the future. I actually cried. I wouldn't come out of the bedroom to see visitors. I've only experienced such depression one other time in my life, when our son Cooke was killed.

CHAPTER 10

Return to the Mayo Clinic, 1946–47, and Staff, 1947–49

We spent Christmas 1945 in Beaumont, a family once again. Soon after, I drove up to Rochester to resume my work at the Mayo Clinic on January 1, 1946. Mary stayed in Beaumont until after Fay and Jamie Griffith were married on March 2. Fay had been halfway engaged to Frank Ashburn and then to Ed Edson of Beaumont. She never accepted a ring. In 1945 she went with family friend Mrs. Cecil Easley to Mexico on a pleasure trip. Here she met an eligible bachelor from Houston named James P. S. Griffith, who was also on a pleasure trip following his World War II service. Jamie loved the good life, and so did Fay.

Their wedding was a huge affair, done in grand style. I went down for the occasion. By this time, Mary was pregnant with our fourth child, hoping for a girl. Before returning to Rochester, I went over to Louisiana and persuaded Annie Mickens to come to Minnesota with us. Annie had worked for the Wilson family helping take care of the children, and Mary needed Annie in Rochester to look after our three boys while she was pregnant. Annie was a wonderful person, innocent of the world and devoted only to her job as housekeeper, good cook, and children's nurse. Annie found very few other blacks in Rochester, however, and was soon homesick. Mary went with her to the Baptist Church, since Annie missed that aspect of her life. In spite of being so homesick, Annie stuck it out for more than a year.

A few months earlier, Mary and I had purchased a house at 630 Fifth Street, eight blocks from the clinic. This was a typical Minnesota house—a box-shaped, white wooden structure, with two floors, a full basement, and an attic. The main floor had a large living room, a dining room, and kitchen. Upstairs was a large bedroom, two small ones, and one bath. The yard was small, large enough only for the children's sand pile. The Balfours who lived across the street invited our children to their playground. Mrs. Balfour was a daughter of Dr. William Mayo.[1] The Balfours also invited us on several occasions to their dairy farm, where a large Norman stone house, covered with English ivy, sat high on a hill with views of the corn fields and a winding river.

After arriving in Rochester with the children and Annie, Mary noticed that our pantry had been stocked by Mary Lovelace. That was the kind of friends we had. The Lovelaces and the Hallenbecks had been released from duty at Wright Field at the same time as we and lived close by in Rochester. Many other friends had returned from the service with four years of war experiences and two or three more children to talk about. The Seybolds and the Butts had served in the navy and the Cains in the army. Bill Leary had been with the army in England. Lefty (Bradley) Brownson had been in the Air Corps. Frank Ashburn came back from the war with his wife, Ida Norman, a beautiful young woman from Natchez, Mississippi, whom he met in Washington, D.C. Ida joined in the activities of our friends. The Ashburns soon had a son, Frank, Jr., and named Mary his godmother.[2] Other returnees were the John Thomases, Jack Grindlays, Burgess Sealys, Raleigh Whites, and the Oliver Gooches.

Back together again, we revived the Texas Club, and I was elected president. We held our annual meeting at the Arthur Hotel, and thirty people were present. As usual, we tried to drink all the alcohol in town. Bill Seybold was master of ceremonies. He called on me to speak. I got up and tried to talk but couldn't say a word. I just stood there with a vapid grin, until someone helped me sit down. Andy Rivers was there, because his wife was a Texan. He stood up and made a remark about Texas, considered by some to be derogatory, and prompting Bill Seybold to strike Andy a hard blow. After some sharp words were spoken, the party went on as if nothing had happened. The Texas Club was good for promoting the Mayo Clinic in Texas. Texans didn't need any promotion in Rochester, but the event, minus the Rivers-Seybold encounter, was reported in the Rochester newspaper.

Other Rochester traditions returned. Mary was soon entertaining a steady stream of visitors who were patients at the clinic. Patients frequently had meals with us, and those who were close friends ate with us every day. There were conspicuous changes in lifestyle immediately following the war, however. Virtually everything was in short supply—most notably toilet paper. We had no toilet paper for two weeks. Mary's family shipped us soap, toilet paper, and other supplies from the Hotel Beaumont. One time her mother sent us some blue toilet paper. Mary said it was too fancy to use and promised to keep it until her parents came to visit. We couldn't buy a tricycle for Cooke, because of a metal shortage. Meat was scarce in the shops, so we bought a steer at nineteen cents a pound from a local farmer, had it butchered, and put in a frozen food locker. Wonderful steaks and roasts! Morey's Restaurant, the favorite eating place in Rochester, served the biggest, fattest steaks in town. Customers would devour a one pound porterhouse.

In July 1946, a severe poliomyelitis epidemic spread across the country and was especially severe in Rochester. Since Mary was about to deliver, Mrs. Wilson rented a cottage for two months at Blakes By the Lakes, a well-known resort in Minnesota, to take care of our children away from the polio outbreak, and give Mary some time to rest in Rochester before the birth. Mavis, Jr., was born July 16, 1946, Mary's fourth boy and fourth cesarean section. Dr. Larry Randall, who had delivered John, was her doctor. Mary wrote that the baby was a "darling with nice features, long head and golden hair. His face is fat but the rest of him is scrawny."

Resuming my fellowship, my first assignment was in the clinic on Herman Moersch's chest section, along with staff members Art Olsen, Herb Schmidt, and Corwin Hinshaw. Tuberculosis was still a common disease. Patients were treated at state and private sanitariums, where the only known treatments besides surgery were isolation, rest, good nutrition, and sometimes pneumothorax. Dr. Hinshaw was becoming famous treating patients with streptomycin, the first antibiotic to be used for tuberculosis. Isoniazid or similar synthetic antibacterials were also being tested. The development of antituberculosis drugs has almost eradicated the disease today and has led to the closing of American sanitariums. The patients who came to the Mayo Clinic with chest problems requiring hospitalization were sent to the Colonial Hospital. The hospital chest service was a desirable assignment for fellows, because it provided the opportunity to learn endoscopy of the lungs and upper gastrointestinal tract. The procedures of rigid bronchoscopy, contrast bronchograms, rigid esophagoscopy, flexible gastroscopy, and esophageal dilatation were performed every day. Bill Leary was assigned to the service. His performance was outstanding. As a result, he was taken on the staff as a member of the chest section in 1947.

Moersch was a cheerful perfectionist and an expert technician. He was also a disciplinarian. I learned about this when I applied for leave to go to Beaumont for Fay and Jamie's wedding and to bring my family back to Rochester. His answer was, "No." I was older than most of the fellows. I had just spent four years in wartime military service and had achieved some authority as a command surgeon and department chief. I politely told Moersch I was going on the trip. He said I could leave his service. By the time I returned from Beaumont, however, he had relented and accepted me back in good humor. He was pleased with my work, but I made another mistake that incurred his wrath. Late one afternoon, soon after I had gone on the hospital service, a child was brought in from another town who had inhaled a foreign object, possibly a peanut. The patient did not seem to be in distress. Somehow, I treated the patient as a routine admission and did not call a staff member. Before many hours had passed, Moersch learned about the patient. He came to the hospital promptly and told me in no uncertain terms that a foreign object in the lung was an emergency of the highest order. By midnight, he had called out the operating room staff and performed a bronchoscopy on the child, removing the peanut.

I also spent time on the neurology and psychiatry service. Even in 1946 the two specialties were still combined in one service. For such a large clinic, the psychiatry half of the service was very small. Psychiatry had not yet come into its own. I remember only one floor on one wing of St. Mary's Hospital devoted to psychiatric patients. In those days most patients received little psychiatric care or were sent to a state insane asylum. The neurology half of the service was different. We were taught to do a complete one-hour neurological examination on every patient, even if the complaint was as localized as carpal tunnel syndrome. Not only this, a patient was required to have a general examination on a medical service before he could be referred to neurology. These exhaustive examinations led to many delays. Neurology had a two-month backlog of appointments. For example, if a patient came a thousand miles with a major neurological problem, he had to undergo a three-day general examination, often not related in any way to his chief complaint. Afterward, the patient was referred to neurology where there were no appointments available for two months or more. The patient had to go home and return two months later for the neurological consultation. Even so, the Mayo neurological section was among the finest in the world, its doctors noted for diagnosing the rarest of neurological problems. Once, after diagnosing a very rare disease, the attending doctor jokingly told us to forget it because we would never see another as long as we lived.

I went on the neurology hospital service on July 1, 1946. Soon thereafter, the two sons of Randy and Mary Lovelace were brought in with poliomyelitis. As a fellow, I examined these sons of our best friends. The older boy had some trouble swallowing. He had bulbar polio, a condition which was just being understood. There were no respirators at the Mayo Clinic or virtually anywhere else. The boy died within a few days. The younger son died several weeks later at Warm Springs, Georgia, the leading center for polio research, popularized by President Roosevelt—himself crippled by poliomyelitis.[3] This was years before the cause and epidemiology of polio had been discovered. Edward Rosenow, Sr., then past retirement age, was driving his car around Rochester with exposed culture plates trying to capture a microbe causing polio. He believed there was a different microbe for each nerve muscle group attacked by polio. For example, the microbe which caused leg paralysis was different from the one which attacked the shoulder girdle. When this epidemic started, polio patients in the hospital were not isolated. Cases were so scattered that personal contact was not considered a mode of transmission. The epidemic was still raging long after we came to Houston in 1949. Our son, Cooke, had nonparalytic polio while we were vacationing in Cuernavaca, Mexico, in 1952. Only after the polio virus was isolated and a vaccine produced did we get relief from this dread disease.

On October 1, 1946, I was assigned to a six-month service at St. Mary's in the metabolic, or endocrine, section. The chief of service was Dr. Sam Haines. Other staff members were Randall Sprague, Eddie Rynearson, Raymond Keating, and Larry Underdahl. At this time, endocrinology was about the hottest thing going in internal medicine, and the Mayo Clinic was leading the pack. Radioiodine had just been produced, leading to rapid advances in thyroid physiology and treatment. We were beginning to understand and treat disturbances of the body electrolytes. The adrenal hormones were being isolated and an extract of the adrenal cortex was being used to treat Addison's disease. Dr. Edward Kendall at the Mayo Clinic had isolated cortisone. A few years earlier, Eddie Rynearson had proved that a tumor of islet cells of the pancreas produced excess insulin and caused hypoglycemia. I was fortunate to be on this service and observe and take part in these advances.

I wondered where I would eventually practice medicine. Since I never entertained the idea of being invited on the staff of the Mayo Clinic, I made trips, wrote letters, and searched around Texas for a place to practice. Mary complained that, since I was always trying to decide where to go, she couldn't make any plans. She wanted to settle in Texas, in or near Beaumont. As it turned out, I was presented with several choices. Before I went in the service, I had written a number of medical papers edited by the Mayo Clinic; this led me to become acquainted with Richard Hewitt, head of the editorial section. Later, while I was in the service, I asked for his help as editor of the *Air Surgeon's Bulletin.* When I went on the staff, Dr. Hewitt chose me as his personal doctor. During late 1946, he invited me to his office and offered me a position in the editorial section. He was nearing retirement and wanted to phase me into his job as chief of the section. It was an unexpected and flattering offer. I had written a lot, but my grammar and composition were terrible. Other people had to edit my papers before they were suitable for publication. Although I was titled editor of the *Air Surgeon's Bulletin,* I had two professionals who did the copy editing. I only directed the department. I talked to my friend and mentor, Dr. Comfort. He recommended that I decline Dr. Hewitt's offer and wait a while. He thought I should be a practicing physician, not a medical editor. He felt that I would be offered a staff position in internal medicine and that he would like to have me in the Snell section with him, if there was an opening. So I declined Hewitt's offer.

Soon after this, in early November 1946, I got a call to see Dr. Sam Haines, chairman of the board of governors and chief of the metabolic section. He offered me a staff position in the metabolic section. It was difficult to change course. I had spent a great deal of time and effort in the previous five years exploring possibilities in Texas. John Hart and I, for example, were discussing opening a clinic in a building across the street from the Baptist Hospital in Beaumont. John, a general surgeon, was a close family friend but much older than I. There were several other possibilities, including Lee Clark's invitation to come to Houston as chief of medicine at the new M. D. Anderson Hospital. Mary was very excited about the honor of Dr. Haines's fine offer, concealing her strong desire to move to Texas. She must have thought the decision was mine to make. Finally, I decided to accept the offer to join the Mayo Clinic staff. I would go on the payroll as a staff physician on January 1, 1947, but would be allowed to complete my fellowship. As a fellow, I was paid $75.00 a month; as a staff physician, I would receive $1000 a month. I had been trained as a gastroenterologist, but would be assigned to treat metabolic problems after training only six months in the specialty.

I was very excited to receive an offer to be on the staff of the greatest clinic in the world. Although I preferred gastroenterology, at the time endocrinology was the most exciting specialty of internal medicine. Over fifty years later, however, after reading for the first time one of Mary's letters to her family, dated November 16, 1946, I realized how disappointed she was in not going to Texas:

> I have big news for you—Mavis has decided to stay here on the staff which I am sure will not surprise you very much. He goes on the first of January which is the first time I ever heard of anyone being taken before finishing the fellowship. He also gets a month's vacation yearly, a month's study trips and all expenses paid for a junket like his present one to Cleveland. My disappointment is thinking of being so far away from the family but I hope with some degree of cooperation that this might work out well also. If you all will come to see us, and often, the children can grow up knowing each other in two states instead of one. . . . You will have to count on a few white Christmases with us.

Joining the Mayo Clinic was one of the momentous events of my life. I was thirty-four years old and had finally completed my education and training. I was entering my career in the private practice of medicine. I would treat my own patients without supervision. I would have fellows to assist me. For such a major event in my life, however, it was ushered in rather uneventfully. I never had a day off. There was no party, no ceremony, and no champagne. Some of my friends congratulated me as they passed by in the halls.

After completing six months of service at St. Mary's in the metabolic section, I was transferred to the Mayo Clinic building, where we saw new ambulatory patients of all kinds and endocrine patients who were referred directly to the section. I was assigned an examining room and shared a secretary with two other staff men. I examined new patients after a fellow had done the original history and physical examination. For each patient, the fellow and I made a preliminary diagnosis and decided what laboratory work, X rays, and consultations should be performed. After the tests the patient came back to be told the diagnosis; I'd discuss the problem with the patient and prescribe treatment. Sometimes we diagnosed a serious disease that required surgery. I scheduled an appointment for the appropriate surgeon and would meet with him when he came to see the patient. Some surgeons came alone and handled the consultation in a simple, efficient manner. Other surgeons preferred to arrive with a retinue of nurses, fellows, and visiting firemen. They created a great ceremony with introductions all around, thus impressing the patient with their importance.

Patients referred to our section had every endocrine problem known to man. Of the rare diseases, the Mayo Clinic saw more than any other medical center in the world. The common diseases were diabetes and goiters of every type. Less common were pituitary tumors, acromegaly, various types of dwarfism, gigantism, insulinomas, parathyroid adenomas, pheochromocytomas, diabetes insipidus, Addison's disease, Cushing's syndrome, and many more. I saw at least a few of each of these diseases. We saw all the complications of diabetes. Our staff believed in strict control of blood sugar in diabetics, a view I have always held. New types of insulin were just coming on the market, making diabetes much easier to control. We held group classes to educate diabetics. Each diabetic was sent to the diet kitchen to learn proper diet. I gave many lectures there. With longer acting insulins, we were able to increase the carbohydrates and decrease the fats in the diabetic diet. Diabetic acidosis was being treated more effectively with the newer knowledge of electrolytes.

Of all endocrine problems, the Mayo Clinic was most famous for treating thyroid disease. The clinic was in the Goiter Belt, those states around the Great Lakes where there was an iodine deficiency. Before iodine was put in table salt, nearly everyone in this area had a goiter. Thyroxin, the active hormone of the thyroid, was discovered at the Mayo Clinic by Edward Kendall. Dr. Henry Plummer was a world authority on goiter. He discovered the difference between diffuse toxic goiter and toxic nodular goiter, a distinction which would prove to be of everyday clinical importance. Dr. Plummer died before I arrived but his brother Will was still practicing actively at the metabolic section.

Dr. John deJ. Pemberton at the clinic had the reputation of performing more thyroidectomies—fifty thousand as I recall—than any other surgeon in the world. I will never forget the time he chastised me. The event unfolded when Dr. Pemberton met me in the hall and told me that a patient I sent him had severe bleeding in the operative wound when he did a thyroidectomy. He asked me if I had any idea why this happened. I thought a minute and remembered that this patient had rheumatoid arthritis and was being treated with large doses of aspirin. The medical profession had just learned that aspirin often caused intestinal bleeding, and, furthermore, the bleeding was caused by aspirin's interference with blood clotting. This was new information that very few people knew, even at the Mayo Clinic. I had learned it only recently. It flashed through my mind that our patient may have bled at the operative site because she had been taking large doses of aspirin. No one before had even proposed that patients taking aspirin would be prone to bleed at surgery. I told Dr. Pemberton that the patient had been on aspirin and it may have caused the bleeding. I thought I was very smart thinking up the possible cause of surgical bleeding. Dr. Pemberton was furious, wondering why had I let this happen. He never forgave me.[4]

Dr. Samuel Haines, my chief, was a native of Rochester and had worked as a youth doing various jobs in the clinic for Drs. Will and Charles Mayo. He graduated from Harvard Medical College and trained in Boston, where he met his wife, Emily. Then he returned to spend his career and serve as chairman of the board of governors at the Mayo Clinic. He was a warm, friendly person, a modest, yet powerful man, who detested pretense. He was a serious student of the thyroid and became president of the American Goiter Society, later to be known as the American Thyroid Association. Like many of the staff doctors, he was very helpful to the younger staff and fellows. Sam made me his assistant. When he went out of town I handled his mail and patient referrals. I even handled his mail in the board chairman's office. His younger daughter, Olivia, worked in the clinic, as did many relatives of the staff. I was very fond of her.[5]

Ray Keating was the intellectual whiz in the metabolic section, however. He earned his bachelor's degree in biology at Cornell University by working his way through as an ornithologist. Although he had only recently joined the staff, Ray had established himself as an authority in thyroidology. When radioactive isotopes became available, Ray saw the opportunity to study the thyroid with tracer doses of radioiodine. The biophysics department and others, such as I, volunteered to help Ray, and we were soon experimenting on ourselves. We learned how iodine was taken from the blood stream by the thyroid to make thyroxin, the active hormone of the thyroid. While studying the physiology of the thyroid, we were also learning how to use radioiodine for diagnosing and treating thyroid diseases.[6]

By today's standards, our equipment was very crude, and we had not learned of the harmful effects of radiation to which we were subjecting ourselves. Each of us must have taken a thousand microcuries of radioiodine 131 during these experiments. We carried bottles around to collect our urine, much as I did as a freshman in medical school. We lay under crude Geiger counters for hours, measuring thyroid uptake of radioiodine. Recently, the media have reported about government agencies experimenting on humans with dangerous doses of radioactive isotopes during the late 1940s and early 1950s, the reports suggesting that the agencies knew they were poisoning innocent volunteers. I think few if any people in these agencies knowingly gave dangerous doses of radioisotopes. During that period, I knew many thyroidologists who were giving radioiodine to themselves as experimental subjects, just as we were. We thought our doses were perfectly safe. Fifteen or twenty years later we learned that even very small amounts of radioactivity may be harmful. Forty years later, I developed hypothyroidism which must have been the result of this self-experimentation.

Our experiments, and those of others, however, proved the diagnostic value of radioiodine tracers. We also developed the use of radioiodine for the treatment of hyperthyroidism and certain types of thyroid cancer. Physicians in our section published many papers on these subjects, and my name was on several of them as principal author or co-author. I became licensed by the Atomic Energy Commission to administer radioiodine and radiophosphorus. In the early days radioiodine was the only significant isotope used in clinical medicine. Today there are hundreds of useful radioactive isotopes, beyond our wildest imagination in the 1940s.

There were other exciting breakthroughs in endocrinology. Although I took no active part in it, I watched Dr. Phillip Hench use cortisone in treating the first patients with rheumatoid arthritis. He was using cortical extract, isolated and produced in Dr. Kendall's laboratory. The patients were in the metabolic unit of St. Mary's. Endocrinologists in our section assisted. The signs and symptoms of rheumatoid arthritis responded amazingly to cortisone, which was soon produced synthetically. Pain, swelling, increased sedimentation rates— all parameters of the disease—improved promptly. Unfortunately, the rheumatic symptoms returned when cortisone was discontinued and adverse reactions occurred from cortisone when it was continued. Nonetheless this was a dramatic event in medicine, an important breakthrough which benefited millions of people. For this discovery, Drs. Hench and Kendall received the Nobel Prize. I knew both of them. Phil Hench had a cleft palate, severely affecting his speech, but this didn't slow him down. He was a dynamic, outgoing man. Dr. Kendall, typical for a successful researcher, was highly intelligent and determined, a quiet, modest, almost retiring man. He chose me as his personal physician when I went on the staff of the clinic.[7]

Staff members at the Mayo Clinic were expected to do clinical research, present their experiences at medical meetings, and publish the results in leading medical journals. We were also expected to join and take an active part in the medical societies of our specialty. One time, Dr. Balfour called me in his office to tell me that he had arranged for me to speak at the American College of Surgeons annual meeting in Cleveland. I was encouraged to join the American Goiter Society, the American Endocrine Society, and the American Diabetes Association. Drs. Will Mayo and Henry Plummer were original members of the Goiter Society. Sam Haines made a special effort to have me elected to the Goiter Society and Sigma Xi, the honor research society. I went to Minneapolis in May 1947 for an oral examination to complete the requirements for a master's degree in medicine. Later, Mary and I went to an outdoor graduation ceremony at the University of Minnesota, where I was one of thousands who lined up to receive a diploma. During this time, I was studying for and obtained board certification in internal medicine and fellowship in the American College of Physicians.

Meanwhile, my personal practice at the clinic thrived. Dr. Comfort continued to send me his overflow from Texas. I tried to know every one of the three hundred doctors on the Mayo staff. I was invited to join a luncheon club of Mayo staff doctors who met daily in a private dining room of the Kahler Hotel. Soon I was being called in consultation by Mayo staff doctors. Out of town doctors, pleased with the care I had given their patients, began referring patients directly to me. People in Texas began referring their friends. On October 27, 1947, Mary wrote her mother that, "Helen Anderson is here from Houston and she is Mavis' patient—Mavis has been flooded lately with special patients—one from Houston came by private plane tonight and he has another pair coming by private plane next Monday also from Houston." In those days healthy people, as well as the sick, came to Rochester for a general examination just to be sure they were in good health.

One of the more famous patients to pass through the clinic was Lyndon Johnson. One day, John Thomas called to invite me to Mandred Comfort's house for a stag talk session with Lyndon Johnson, then a U.S. Congressman.

John Thomas, Jim Cain, Bill Seybold, and I gathered with Mandred to listen to Lyndon until 2:00 A.M. Lyndon told us much Washington inside information concerning the war. Most of all, Lyndon talked about his relationship with President Roosevelt, whom he first met in Texas when he was a young assistant to Congressman Kleberg. Roosevelt was very fond of Lyndon, often calling him in to visit. During one visit to the Oval Office, Roosevelt asked Lyndon to sit in the president's chair and, as I recall, said, "Son, some day I expect you to sit in this chair." We had a big laugh about this, since Lyndon at that time was only a young congressman. A year later, Lyndon came to Rochester with a kidney stone. As an endocrinologist, I was called to the hospital to see him to rule out a parathyroid adenoma, which can be a cause of kidney stones. On this visit, Lyndon was running for the U.S. Senate. He asked me to help him in Northeast Texas, where I was from. Obviously I couldn't do much, but I took it as a compliment. I saw Lyndon several times in the following years.

Our family life was busy and hectic. Tom swallowed a safety pin, crushed a finger in a door, and ate pills from my medical bag. Cooke fell out of a tree and broke his jaw in July 1948. His jaw was wired for three weeks. There was never a dull moment! I was also busy with research and writing papers. There were many out-of-town visitors and visits from family members. In April 1947, my brother John and his wife, Mickey, came for an interview for a fellowship in medicine, to begin July 1, 1948. He was accepted and we were together in Rochester for several months, before Mary and I returned to Texas.

By this time, however, we had also outgrown our small house. Mary and I and our four children shared one bathroom. She entertained visitors in ever increasing numbers—I do not know how she did it. We had planned to buy a beautiful wooded tract near Rochester, when Dr. Giffin's house became available. We were talking about buying the property for $25,000, but the Mayo Properties Association wanted the land for their long-term plans. They bought the house and rented it to us at $125.00 a month. Mary fell in love with the large yard and gardens. There were several flower gardens, a large back lawn, an apple tree, and several oaks. The house was a prefabricated structure, sold by Sears and Roebuck after World War I, with several bedrooms and a full attic that made a wonderful playroom for the children during the winter. After Annie Mickens went home about late 1947, we employed Jo Anne Schatz, a twenty-year-old woman, as a live-in full-time maid, cook, nurse, and general assistant for Mary.

I was very enthusiastic about my career on the Mayo staff. Endocrinology with all its new advances was an exciting specialty. I became involved in several research projects. My practice was expanding. We had moved into a large, comfortable house, and settled down for a life in Rochester. On the surface, everything was going smoothly in our lives. The idea of going back to Texas began to crop up with more frequency, however, driven largely by two powerful forces. The first concerned an idea that I had been formulating for a long time—that of organizing my own clinic. Even as a schoolboy, I had heard of the famous Mayo Clinic. In Deport, if someone developed a serious medical problem that Dr. Grant could not handle, the patient was sent to the Scott and White Clinic in Temple. It had a fine reputation as the largest clinic in Texas. These early influences remained with me. Scott and White had provided my first experience in a private practice general clinic. It seemed to me that Scott and White delivered the best medical care in Texas. My later training at the Mayo Clinic—an institution at the forefront of the clinical practice of medicine—made me even more determined to practice in a clinic. My friends and I talked about it in our journal club. Then, the future was very nebulous to us. We also talked about other kinds of practice; solo, specialty group, university appointment, military, public health, even foreign missionary practice. The friends I remember talking with most were Frank Ashburn, Bill Leary, Jim Cain, and Pete Pearson. Bill Seybold did not arrive in Rochester until July 1, 1941, three months before I entered the service, but I did tell him about our discussions, and he was interested.

Our training and our plans had been interrupted by World War II. Then, we were scattered to the four corners of the earth. During the war, I corresponded with several friends, mostly Texans since we shared a goal to practice in Texas. I was in touch mostly with Frank Ashburn, Jim Little, Ralph Letteer, Huard Hargis, Ross Margraves, and Bill Seybold. When I was released from the military in 1945, and before returning for my fellowship, I made several visits in Texas to talk about practice. One was to the McCuistion Clinic in Paris. My brother John, after completing his Mayo training, did join that group in Paris and practiced for two years before joining our clinic in Houston. I visited my classmate, Choice Matthews, who was an internist in Kerrville. He was enthusiastic about joining me and starting a clinic in Kerrville. In Beaumont, John Hart and I discussed renting a building across the street from Baptist Hospital.

After accepting the position at Mayo, plans for organizing a clinic appeared to have collapsed. My friends in Rochester were also offered attractive positions at clinics: Bill Seybold, Jim Cain, Larry Underdahl, and Bill Leary were all taken on the Mayo staff. Pete Pearson went to the Virginia Mason Clinic in Seattle. Frank Ashburn joined a surgical group in Washington, D.C. My patients and others who came to Rochester from Texas who enthusiastically embraced the idea of me organizing a clinic were a second motivating force.

Dr. Ernst W. Bertner, 1949

The most spectacular of my patients were Wesley and Neva West of Houston. They came in their private DC-3, the finest private plane then available. The Wests enjoyed their wealth and gave thoughtful and generous gifts to their friends as well as to the needy. They soon made friends with our circle and made frequent trips to Rochester. Wesley liked the Rochester Dairy ice cream and took gallons back to his friends in Houston. He wanted me to come to Houston and practice medicine. He even offered to build me a clinic on a tract of land near the new medical center.[8]

Other Houstonians included Mr. and Mrs. Horace Wilkins. Mr. Wilkins was one of the three trustees of the M. D. Anderson Foundation. We entertained the Wilkins during their several visits to the Mayo Clinic. Mr. Wilkins told glowing stories about the new Texas Medical Center in Houston. He invited me to come to Houston so he could show me the center and meet some of the leaders. Dr. E. W. Bertner, president of the Texas Medical Center, was the most enthusiastic of our visitors from Houston, however. He and Dr. Comfort were great friends and fellow AKKs. I had known Dr. Bertner since he rescued the AKK fraternity from bankruptcy while I was in medical school. Dr. and Mrs. Bertner came to the Mayo Clinic as patients of Dr. Comfort. The Comforts invited us to their house to see them. Dr. Bertner invited us to come to Texas; he even invited me to office with him until I got an office of my own.[9]

While the medical pastures were beginning to look greener in Houston, there were personal pressures that wouldn't go away. Mary enjoyed Rochester and had made many lovely friends, but her heart was in Texas. She worried about her widowed mother. Since Mr. Wilson died and Fay married, none of the family was coming to see Mary in Rochester. As fifth generation Texans, Mary and I also had sentimental reasons for wanting to return.[10] We wanted our sons to be Texans, and felt they would have a better future there. As a result of these pressures I made a list of the reasons why we should return to Texas. I also made some crude calculations of fixed expenses and projected annual income for each year through 1955. I have saved these lists for fifty years.

1948

1. Money—need to make about $25,000/yr to support family and build house, educate boys & start some reserve.
2. Be near family & friends, for our sake & their desire.
3. To take care of financial interests in Texas.
4. To learn of better opportunities for investment.
5. Build better future for children
    a. Better education (more money)
    b. Better opportunity in business & social life.
    c. Better heritage (can turn over practice to any who care to enter medicine).
6. Texas patriotism & Texas hobbies.
7. Opportunity to organize my own clinic.
8. Public participation & self discipline.

My salary at the Mayo Clinic was $12,000 a year. I projected an annual income for 1955 of $21,000 at the Mayo Clinic and $30,000 for private practice in Houston.

FIXED EXPENSES

Rent	*$150*
Insurance	*200*
(Retirement, auto, etc.)	
Income Tax	*300*
Domestic Help	*125*
Utilities	*50*
Auto	*70*
Church	*10*
Milk	*30*
Medical Books,	
Dues, etc.	*20*
Other Books	*10*
Furniture,	
etc.	*100*
Clothes	*100*
Entertainment	*35*
Groceries	*150*
Family Trips	*50*
Monthly Expenses	*1,675*
	x 12
Annual Living Expenses	*$20,000*

I again inquired about practice opportunities in Houston. I revived conversations with Bill Seybold and Bill Leary about moving to Houston to develop a practice together and start a clinic of our own. We envisioned a general clinic with specialists. The Texas Medical Center was growing, surrounded by great enthusiasm, and the doctors were busy. Several new hospitals were to be built. This was an opportunity to take part in the growth of a great center. There would be ready access to facilities, which at first, we would not be large enough to provide. The center had fine laboratories and X-ray departments and specialists in all fields of medicine. There were fine hospitals. All these things we were accustomed to at the Mayo Clinic. I went to Houston in the fall of 1948 and called on several doctors—Bertner, Lee Clark, and Paul Ledbetter. I called on some of my medical school friends, as well as some older AKK brothers. George Waldron was a Mayo-trained surgeon and had the largest practice in Houston, said to be $300,000 a year. He encouraged me and told me I could practice in his office until mine was ready.

In Houston, I found that the medical center was expanding rapidly. The

Hermann estate had almost completed construction of the Hermann Professional Building across the street from Hermann Hospital. A large addition, actually a complete new Hermann Hospital was being built adjacent to the original Hermann Hospital. I was advised to rent space in the Hermann Professional Building right away, before all the space was taken. I went to the architect's office and selected a 750 square foot office. Mary and I were staying with Fay and Jamie. Mrs. Wilson came over from Beaumont, and the ladies started looking for a house. They chose the Jack Flaitz house at 2136 Brentwood. The price was $50,000. We were in deep. I had to make one of those decisions which changed our lives forever. Mary was for it, so we plunged in together on a new adventure with an unknown future and a very expensive commitment. I talked to Dad again. He would lend me the money to get started, and Mrs. Wilson would lend Mary the money to buy the house. Meanwhile, Bill Seybold, Bill Leary, and I had many conversations. When I left Rochester, there was a confidential and tacit understanding that if all worked out as planned, they would come to Houston and decide whether they would resign their Mayo positions and join me in forming a clinic.

It was September 1948 when I went—with great reluctance—to see Sam Haines and tell him of my decision to move to Houston. Very few doctors had resigned from the Mayo staff. He was surprised and didn't believe I was really serious, until I told him in detail what Mary and I had done. He was disappointed after all he had done for me, promoted me, and practically made me a member of his family. He was very kind and continued his friendship with me as long as he lived. We left many other dear friends in Rochester, including Hugh and Mary Butt, Mandred and Aurelia Comfort, George and Marion Hallenbeck, Ray and Marion Keating, and Jim and Ida May Cain. I left Rochester at age thirty-six with a wife and four sons. Mary and I were returning to our native state to begin a new life and a new career. I was going to start a clinic. This was the last move we would ever make.

Part 3

Medicine in Postwar America, 1949 to the Present

CHAPTER II

Settling in Houston, 1949

We left Rochester on January 8, 1949. Mary, the children, and Jo Anne Schatz boarded the Katy Rocket at Owatonna—a passenger train that ran between Minneapolis and Houston—while I drove down in the car, passing through a terrible ice storm in Iowa. Since Rochester had been our home for several years, we had accumulated furniture, books, toys, and impedimenta, enough to fill a large moving van. We didn't give up stuff we might need again some day, such as a snow shovel, ice skates, sleds, and snow suits and fur caps—some of which are still around the house today.

When we arrived in Houston our son John was seven years old, Cooke was six, Tom was four, and Mavis was two. John and Cooke were sent to the River Oaks Elementary School. Mary soon got to know the teachers. One of the best was Mrs. Grainger. Tom was sent to kindergarten, soon to be followed by Mavis. We sent the boys to Sunday school at St. John's Episcopal Church. Jo Ann Schatz who came to Houston with us had been Mary's maid, baby sitter, and assistant for a year in Rochester. She stayed two years with us in Houston. Jo Ann was great with the boys, and they were a handful to manage. She was a fine person. She later returned to Minnesota to marry and raise a family of her own.

Our home at 2136 Brentwood was in River Oaks, the most desirable residential area of Houston and a ten-minute drive to the Texas Medical Center or to the downtown hotels, where I made night calls. The house was a white Greek revival in the southern style, with two-story columns on the front porch. We had a window air conditioner in the master bedroom and a big attic fan. There was very little central air-conditioning in those days, but we did have a gas-fired central heater in the small basement. The first floor had a foyer, powder room, large living and play room, dining and breakfast rooms, kitchen and pantry, and a screened veranda. Four bedrooms and two baths were upstairs. There was a two-car garage, servant quarters, and a very comfortable back yard.

Kelseys' first house in Houston, 2136 Brentwood, 1949–57

We were fortunate to have good neighbors. The first neighbor to call on us was seven-year-old Nelson Smith, who came to our back door immediately on our arrival. He brought a gift and welcomed us to the neighborhood. He was the son of Dr. Ed and Bernice Smith. Ed was an orthopedist and chief of staff at Hermann Hospital. Nelson had a brother Taylor who became an orthopedist. One cute sister, Martha, was very mischievous. One night our boys and some neighborhood boys, including Nelson, were camped out in our back yard. Martha slipped over and turned on the lawn sprinklers, drenching the boys and their gear and breaking up the party. It was many months, maybe years, before the boys learned who drowned them out. Next door to us was Colonel William Bates and his family. He was a partner in the law firm of Fulbright, Cooker, Freeman and Bates, and also a trustee of the M. D. Anderson Foundation and a director of the Texas Medical Center. Also next door was the Meredith family, including Mrs. Meredith's mother, Mrs. Wilkins.[1]

Wesley and Neva West had entertained us as house guests in 1948, when we were considering moving from Rochester to Houston. During this visit, they gave a party and introduced us to a number of people, including Harmon Whittington, Fisher Reynolds, and Hugh Potter, who became patients. I especially remember meeting Milton Underwood, who became a patient and a good friend. After we moved to Houston, the Wests invited us to several parties. They gave me a membership in the Houston Club. They also gave us our first television set in 1949. It had a screen about ten inches wide, one of the really early ones. There was one T.V. station in Houston at the time. Senator Lyndon Johnson was a friend of the Wests. We saw Lyndon with the Wests several times, especially at the West ranch, which was near the LBJ Ranch. Mary's closest lifetime friend, Justa Cartwright, had come to Houston and married Shirley Helm, a prominent lawyer. They gave us an introductory party and invited us to many other social gatherings.[2]

Dr. E. W. Bertner and his wife Julia also went to great lengths to help us get established. Soon after we arrived, the Bertners invited Mary and me to go to the Assembly Ball, an exclusive gathering. Dr. Bertner was suffering from cancer and was not able to go to the ball but insisted that Mary and I go. When he became disabled he gave me his formal clothes—tails, tux, and white dress jacket—which fit perfectly. Eventually, I gave these clothes to the archival collection at the Houston Academy of Medicine. Among the Bertners' friends were the Oschners of New Orleans, the Herbert Hayes, Paul Ledbetters, Allen McMurrays, John Walls, and the General R. C. Kuldells. Among the Wilsons' best friends in Houston was Bishop Quin. One night we took Bishop Quin and his wife to Maxim's Restaurant, which was downtown then. We had cherries jubilee. Camille Berman, Maxim's owner, was so thrilled at having Bishop Quin in his restaurant that he never forgot it as long as he lived.[3]

Governor Will Hobby had a newspaper in Beaumont during the Spindletop oil boom and knew Mary's mother, Mary Bradley Randolph, before she married. Governor Hobby told me that he had once proposed to Mary Randolph but she turned him down for Cooke Wilson. By the time we moved to Houston, Will Hobby had been governor of Texas, married Oveta Culp, and was raising a family in Houston. He owned the *Houston Post*. The Hobbys were very cordial to Mary and me and had us to numerous parties. I especially remember a party the Hobbys had that spring of 1949, during the opening festivities for the Shamrock Hotel. Many movie stars and public figures were at the Hobby party. I talked to Eddie Rickenbacker, who recently had survived a plane crash in the Pacific Ocean. The Hobby family became my patients. Dr. and Mrs. Jimmy Hill also invited us to dinner at the Shamrock festivities, hosted by his brother-in-law, Gus Wortham. There were several parties in private dining rooms, and movie stars circulated in and out. When Jack Benny came to our party he talked about how big and rich Texas was. He joked that he went to a poker game the night before and Galveston changed hands three times while he was there.

All told, settling down in Houston was an exhilarating experience. We were well received except for one time. One day our son John came home from school crying. He said the kids were calling him a Yankee.

The city itself was an exciting place to be. In 1949 Houston's population was nine hundred thousand, three times its size when I was in medical school. The Rice Hotel was the social and commercial center of the city. Kelly's Oyster Bar was directly across the street. The Lamar Hotel was the most distinguished address. The Gulf and the Mellie Esperson Buildings were the tallest in town. A few of the fine old houses were still standing on and near South Main where skyscrapers stand today. Swayze's Barbecue was between South Main and Fannin, easy to remember because it advertised "The Best Barbecue in the World or Anywhere Else." The College Inn was on Main across from the Rice campus. Prince's Drive-In Hamburgers was at Main and Old Spanish Trail. There was a restaurant called Old Mexico near M. D. Anderson Hospital, which was then in temporary quarters on Baldwin. I have fond memories of this restaurant. While employed at M. D. Anderson, I walked over there with two or more staff doctors, often including Lee Clark, Cliff Howe, Ed White, John Wall, or C. C. Shullenberger. We had a genuine Tex-Mex lunch and an hour of pleasant gossip. Cliff Howe frequently touted us on investing in one of the Mitchell brothers oil wells. I had forgotten who owned the restaurant, until I read the obituary of Emiti Cerecedo Knorbin, age ninety-three, on May 2, 1994. She and her husband had built the restaurant in the 1930s and had headed the first fund benefit to support the M. D. Anderson Hospital.

Herbert Fletcher still had his rare book store in Houston. I had shopped there while I was in medical school. Mary and I resumed collecting Texana with a vengeance at Fletcher's and in Austin, San Antonio, and Dallas—whenever we could. Harris Masterson called on us in our new house. His mother had directed our wedding. Harris was on duty in San Antonio while we were there in World War II. After the war, he opened an antique store on Westheimer near our house. He was very knowledgeable about furniture and fine art, about which he advised Mary. Later, he married Carrol Sterling Winston, another family the Wilsons knew in Beaumont during the Spindletop oil boom. Harris and Carrol were among the greatest collectors of furniture and fine art in Houston. Many years later Carrol's grandson Cliffe Reckling IV married our niece Margaret Wilson. Miss Ima Hogg was a friend and contemporary of Mary's parents. She still lived at Bayou Bend, when she first invited us to dinner. She showed us a mark on the wall where the Buffalo Bayou flood of 1935 had come into the house. Miss Ima also took us to the Varner Plantation, where Governor Will Hogg once lived. We went down with Fay and Jamie Griffith and had lunch at the Griffith ranch across the Brazos River from the Varner Plantation, which is now a state park.[4]

There were nine hundred doctors in Houston when I arrived in 1949, and well over half of them were general practitioners. Many did general practice but tended to specialize in another field, such as surgery or medicine. Only seven board certified surgeons practiced in Houston immediately after World War II. Soon, however, many certified specialists came into the city. Newly organized specialty societies were growing rapidly. The Academy of General Practice was organized about this time. I joined the Houston Society of Internal Medicine immediately after I arrived. One of the members or a guest speaker presented an informative scientific paper at each meeting. I was invited as a guest to surgical, gynecological, and other specialty society meetings. The general practitioners were becoming worried about losing patients to the incoming specialists. Their hospital privileges were being threatened. None of us realized that the medical profession was about to enter a profound revolution. My old colleagues often remind me that we lived and practiced in the golden era of medicine.

The Texas Medical Center was getting underway, but some doctors said it was too far out of town. Many of the older doctors still had their offices in downtown Houston, only a short drive from the residential areas and close to Memorial, St. Joseph, and Methodist Hospitals. They thought they would stick it out downtown. In spite of their concerns, an air of optimism and excitement pervaded the city's medical community. Physicians occupied offices in the Hermann Professional Building as soon as they were completed. A large new Hermann Hospital was just being completed. Baylor University College of Medicine was in full operation in the Center. Plans for constructing a new University of Texas Dental College, the M. D. Anderson Cancer Hospital, a new Methodist Hospital, as well as an entirely new St. Luke's Episcopal Hospital and Texas Children's Hospital were all in the pipeline. Many believed that the Texas Medical Center represented the future in American medicine.

The Texas Medical Center, today the largest medical complex in the United States, with forty-two member institutions encompassing some 900 acres, had its roots in the vision of several individuals and the financial backing of the M. D. Anderson Foundation. Indeed, a motivating force behind the Center came from the generosity of a man who would never see it: Monroe Dunaway Anderson, born June 29, 1873, in Jackson, Madison County, Tennessee, one of eight children. Like most southern families, the Andersons suffered from the Civil War, but his father's death soon after the conflict, when Monroe was only five years old, meant a difficult period of financial recovery. Monroe and his brothers went to work when they were boys and learned the value of money and hard work. They attended public schools and regional colleges, but got most of their education on the job. Monroe's older brother Frank Anderson

Hermann Professional Building, 1949

learned banking but saw a great future in the merchandising of cotton. He moved to Oklahoma City in 1900, and was highly successful in his business. He married Burdine Clayton in Jackson, Tennessee, and had six sons.[5]

Monroe Anderson left his job at a Tennessee bank to join Frank in the cotton business in Oklahoma City. They were soon joined by Mrs. Frank Anderson's brothers, Will and Ben Clayton. This partnership of young men, the Anderson and Clayton Company, was amazingly successful. Monroe Anderson moved to Houston in 1907 to open a branch office. Later, the entire company eventually moved there to become one of the largest cotton businesses in the world. When Frank died in 1924, Monroe became trustee to Tommy Anderson, one of Frank Anderson's six sons. Tommy moved to Houston with his mother and brothers about 1928, and "Uncle Mon," as family members called

Monroe, came to visit them often in Houston. Uncle Mon loved a free meal of home cooked food and always picked a flower to take to a lady friend. A bachelor, he lived in various Houston hotels and was very frugal, teaching Tommy to be careful with his money.

As a partner of Anderson Clayton, Uncle Mon became very wealthy. He needed to form a foundation which could take over his interest in the Anderson Clayton partnership, otherwise the other partners would have the burden of buying his share when he died. Tommy Anderson told me several times that Uncle Mon had an additional motive. He didn't want to see any of his money go into estate taxes, which "that liberal president, Franklin D. Roosevelt would squander away." Monroe Anderson's close friends Colonel William Bates and Judge John Freeman helped organize the foundation in June 1936 and joined him as trustees.

Monroe died on August 6, 1939. The foundation came into ownership of most of M. D. Anderson's estate of $20 million. Horace Wilkins, whom I met while he was a patient at the Mayo Clinic, replaced M. D. Anderson as the third trustee of the foundation. The foundation's goals included "improvement of working conditions among workers generally; establishment, support and maintenance of hospitals and other institutions for care of the sick, the young and the aged, the incompetent and helpless; improvement of people's living conditions; and promotion of health, science, education and diffusion of knowledge and understanding among people." At first, some rather minor

Texas Medical Center, ca. 1952

gifts were made by the M. D. Anderson Foundation. Soon, however, the foundation acted on an opportunity which changed Houston forever and created the Texas Medical Center, the largest industry in the city today.[6]

In 1941, the Texas legislature appropriated $500,000 to establish a cancer research hospital, triggering the Anderson Foundation's move toward establishment of a medical center. The funds had been entrusted to the University of Texas board of regents, and the bill had also authorized acceptance of other gifts for development of the research hospital. The M. D. Anderson Foundation trustees, with advice from E. W. Bertner, promptly invited John Spies, president of the University of Texas Medical Branch at Galveston; Dr. Homer Rainey, University of Texas president; and Dan Harrison, University of Texas regent and prominent Houstonian, to meet with them at Colonel Bates's home. The trustees decided that if the cancer hospital was located in Houston it would be named for M. D. Anderson. The M. D. Anderson Foundation matched the legislative appropriation with a $500,000 grant and secured temporary quarters—and, later, a permanent site—for the hospital.

About one year later, the University of Texas board of regents approved the proposal for the M. D. Anderson Hospital for Cancer Research, and E. W. Bertner was named acting director. The M. D. Anderson Foundation purchased 134 acres from the City of Houston near the Hermann Hospital for use as a medical center. This land was once part of a dairy farm operated by the Abercrombie family, originally from Huntsville, Texas, which delivered milk to Houston households. Mike Hogg bought the land in 1925, when there was an effort to move the University of Texas Medical School to Houston. When this failed, he sold the land to the city. Land in the medical center tract was soon allocated to the Arabia Temple Crippled Children's Hospital, Baylor University College of Medicine, M. D. Anderson Hospital, University of Texas Dental College, Methodist Hospital, and St. Luke's–Texas Children's Hospital. Donations of $500,000 were given by M. D. Anderson Foundation to each of these hospitals for their building fund. Mr. & Mrs. Roy Cullen also made gifts of $1 million each to several Houston hospitals. Hermann Hospital which adjoined the center soon joined to become an institution of the medical center.[7]

In 1942, the M. D. Anderson Hospital for Cancer Research opened its doors in temporary quarters while awaiting the construction of a new hospital in the Texas Medical Center. The Anderson Foundation had purchased a Frank Lloyd Wright house, The Oaks at 2310 Baldwin, from Rice University for $68,000. Located on a six-acre tract near downtown Houston, the house had been a gift to Rice from the estate of Captain James Baker. In addition to his many other duties, E. W. Bertner was acting director of the hospital. Beginning in 1942 he recruited a staff of the leading doctors of Houston. Chauncey Leake, dean of the Medical School in Galveston, provided some equipment and personnel. John Musgrove from Galveston became the business manager of the temporary hospital and the new one being built in the Texas Medical Center. Dr. Roy Heflebower from Galveston came as assistant director and Zuma Krum as a secretary. Miss Anna Hanselman was chief of nurses. These resourceful people were still in charge when I arrived, and I worked with them for years until they retired.

Twelve army surplus temporary buildings were moved to Baldwin Street from Camp Wallace and served as hospital wards for sixty-six patients, as well as doctors offices, X-ray rooms, and laboratories. The Baker house was used for administrative offices and headquarters for the Texas division of the American Cancer Society, with J. Louis Neff as executive director. The stables and servant quarters were converted into research laboratories. We constructed our first diagnostic Geiger counter and treated patients with radioactive isotopes there. The temporary hospital opened to patients on February 17, 1944. The Cancer Hospital had twenty-two surgical beds leased at Hermann Hospital. Dr. Lee Clark was employed as the first full-time director in 1946. Dr. Bertner found Lee by contacting Dr. Claude Dixon, a surgeon at the Mayo Clinic. Dixon referred his former protégé, Lee Clark. By the time I arrived, Lee was well installed in a spacious office in the Baker house. The walls were lined with his many diplomas. Lee gave me a part-time job as soon as I arrived.

Dr. Bertner continued to play an important part in establishing a medical center in Houston. For a few years the medical center operated on an informal basis, but on November 1, 1945, his dreams came to fruition when the M. D. Anderson Foundation trustees incorporated the Texas Medical Center. The board was composed of the Anderson Foundation trustees and representatives from each of the medical center institutions. Dr. Bertner was elected president of the Texas Medical Center, a position he held until his death in July 1950; John Freeman, vice president; Dr. Frederick C. Elliott, secretary; and Colonel James Anderson (no relation to the M. D. Anderson family), treasurer. Other members included Hines H. Baker, Horace Wilkins, Bishop Quin, and Leland Anderson. Dr. Bertner became the main source of my information about the center after I arrived in Houston. I was one of his doctors and saw him every day for months. He referred me many patients. He always talked about the medical center. There was no doubt about E. W. Bertner being in charge of the Texas Medical Center. He was so fired up and dedicated to the center that he had little patience with people who delayed its progress. He guided the center through its birth and early development and enjoyed tremendous respect from the business leaders of Houston.[8]

There were many other individuals, both physicians and business leaders, who supported the Texas Medical Center. It is my belief that Fred Elliott had the original concept of a medical center in Houston. He came to Houston in July 1932, from the University of Tennessee College of Dentistry at Memphis to assume the deanship of the Texas Dental College. Fred Elliott was the head of the only institution in Houston awarding degrees in the field of health care. From the time of his arrival, he deeply influenced the Houston medical community. Among his many activities was the promotion of public health, accomplished in part by his chairship of the Public Health Committee of the chamber of commerce.[9] In the early 1940s, the Harris County Medical Society and chamber of commerce urged the University of Texas to take over the Texas Dental College. In 1943, when the M. D. Anderson Foundation offered to give the school a permanent site in the new medical center and a grant of $500,000 toward a new building, the Texas legislature and University of Texas Board of Regents agreed. Eventually, in May 1952, the University of Texas Dental Branch broke ground for a new facility in the Texas Medical Center.

Initially, Fred Elliott conceived the Houston Medical Center as a public multistory building with offices for doctors and dentists and space for research. Dr. Bertner was more ambitious, however. He called the proposed center the Texas Medical Center. After all, one of the first institutions to be built was a statewide facility, the University of Texas M. D. Anderson Cancer Hospital. Fred had sketches drawn of the tower, which I have seen. He built a model on a table in the basement of the old dental college on Blodgett Street. He trained dental students to make miniature models of the center with dental ceramic. These models were given to civic leaders, women's groups, the chamber of commerce, and other organizations. Soon, Drs. Bertner and Elliott joined their efforts to create a medical center. But even Bertner could not have put it over without the help of many physicians and business leaders. The physicians included Ed Smith, Marvin Graves, M. D. Levy, Fred Lummis, Paul Ledbetter, Herman Johnson, Robert Johnston, Frank Barnes, Herbert Poyner, C. C. Cody, Jr., Weems Turner, Herbert Hayes, Lyle Logue, E. L. Goar, James Greenwood, Sr., Judson Taylor, and James H. Park. Business leaders instrumental in developing the medical center were J. S. Abercrombie, Roy Cullen, Ray Dudley, Wesley West, W. P. Hobby, F. M. Law, Judge Jim Elkins, Earl Hankamer, Tom Monroe, Mayor Oscar Holcombe, Dee Simpson, Warren Bellows, and Bishops Frank Smith and Clinton S. Quin. There were many more.

I arrived in Houston well after the medical center started, but even then only two institutions—Baylor and Hermann—stood in the spacious wooded acres, often flooded by a little creek that ran across the property. Except for the new Shamrock Hotel, the surrounding property was vacant or occupied

Dr. Fred Elliott, who conceived idea for Medical Center

by used car lots, restaurants, a dance hall, residences, small shops, and a filling station. Within the next few years there was feverish activity.

Early in the planning, the Anderson trustees and Dr. Bertner saw the need for a medical school in the center. There had been an unsuccessful effort to get the University of Texas Medical Branch in Galveston moved to Houston. In the meantime, Baylor University Medical College in Dallas and the Southwest Medical Foundation had a bruising disagreement. In the early 1940s the Southwestern Medical Foundation of Dallas announced plans to build a medical center, and its trustees invited the Baylor medical school to become a part of the proposed center. The Baylor University trustees approved a contract with the foundation on June 23, 1942. As the academic year progressed,

Baylor Medical College, 1948

however, it became apparent that the Southwestern Medical Foundation construed the contract to have given them total control of the college. The situation reached crisis proportions when the foundation announced that no college under the control of a religious denomination—Baylor is a Baptist school—could use Parkland Hospital as a teaching facility. The contract was canceled on April 27, 1943.[10]

After the debacle, the Baylor University president and trustees considered closing the medical school. Instead, they asked the M. D. Anderson Foundation trustees if they would be interested in the college's move to Houston. The foundation welcomed the idea and proposed giving the college an adequate site in the new Texas Medical Center, as well as $1 million for construction and $1 million, payable in annual amounts of $100,000, for research. The final agreement, signed May 7, 1943, also made clear that the foundation had no desire to participate in the management or control of the medical school. Plans were promptly considered to move the college to Houston by the end of the 1942–43 session.

When Baylor decided to move to Houston, many of its faculty and medical students were persuaded to stay in Dallas and join the hastily organized Southwestern Medical College. Baylor held its last Dallas graduation in May 1943. Dr. Bertner gave the commencement address entitled, "A New Era in Medicine." Out of this conflict emerged two medical schools—both disorganized and in serious financial straits—hardly able to keep their doors open. Dallas citizens and the University of Texas saved Southwestern while the M. D. Anderson Foundation, the Houston Chamber of Commerce, Roy Cullen, Roy Hankamer, and many Houstonians saved Baylor. My brother John told me the school was financially strapped. The story was that Dr. Bertner kept the school from going under by persuading the chamber of commerce and the Anderson Foundation to give a $100,000 a year for ten years to run the medical school. Today, Baylor and Southwestern are among the finest medical schools in America.

The Harris County Medical Society appointed a committee to offer helpful advice and assistance in organizing a clinical faculty for Houston's new medical college. The society promoted cooperative relationships between the staffs of the city's hospitals and Baylor University College of Medicine in its education programs. The board of managers of Jefferson Davis Hospital, a city institution, promptly promised its cooperation as a teaching hospital. Similar assurances were received from Memorial, Methodist, and St. Joseph's Hospitals. Several buildings were inspected for the school to use temporarily while a structure in the Texas Medical Center was being built. The decision was made to use space formerly occupied by Sears, Roebuck & Company on Buffalo Drive (now Allen Parkway) and Lincoln Street. This location was advantageous, in that it was quite near the Jefferson Davis Hospital.

Moving vans began to arrive at the Houston site in early June 1943. On July 13, 1943, the opening of Baylor University College of Medicine in Houston was celebrated at a banquet in the Rice Hotel. Some sixty-seven days had lapsed between the agreement to move Baylor University Medical College from Dallas and its opening in rented quarters in Houston—a phenomenal feat. My brother John was a sophomore at Baylor. He was one of thirty-eight in his class who chose to move to Houston. The students pitched in and helped load and unload the vans and install the medical school in the Sears warehouse. The entire move was completed in thirty days. John said eighteen full-time faculty members came from Dallas. Houston doctors rapidly became volunteer medical school professors. Four years later, on October 26, 1947, the school opened classes in the new Roy and Lillie Cullen Building, the first new building to be completed within the Texas Medical Center.[11]

Aside from Baylor University College of Medicine, Hermann Hospital was the only other institution—and the only hospital—in the medical center when I arrived in 1949. It was the product of the generosity of George Hermann, a frugal old bachelor who had made a huge fortune in Texas real estate. He left most of his fortune to support a park and a hospital for charity patients, both of which bear his name. The original hospital was built in 1925 on property that would adjoin the medical center property. The hospital also accepted private pay patients. A charity out-clinic was maintained from the first. There was a well-organized internship and residency program at Hermann. When I arrived, a fine new 375-bed facility was just being completed as a nearby separate structure. It opened in March 1949, about the same time my office was completed in the Hermann Professional Building across the street on Fannin.

Several other well-established hospitals and medical institutions were located in the city. St. Joseph's was the oldest hospital in Houston. It opened in 1887 as St. Joseph's Infirmary, run by the Sisters of Charity of Incarnate Word. A fire destroyed the original hospital in 1894, but a new 100-bed facility opened two years later. The sisters at St. Joseph's were very kind to me and took me on staff immediately. The hospital had a large psychiatric section where I sent several alcoholic patients who were willing to go. Once, I sent one who was not willing to go. The patient's wife and children persuaded first me, then Dr. Rockaway, the staff psychiatrist, to commit the patient. Armed with commitment papers, the police hauled the father to the lockup at St. Joseph's. Everyone felt relieved. The next day, I received a telephone call from the patient's lawyer. The patient was sober as a judge and the lawyer threatened serious legal action against Rockaway and me if we didn't release the patient at once. I told the lawyer, "Yes, he can go immediately!" Rockaway and I agreed that it was the first and last time we would ever commit a patient. The patient and his family continued to see me as their doctor.

St. Joseph's Infirmary was the first hospital in Houston to offer charity care to the area's sick and indigent. In 1919, the Houston Municipal Hospital was established at Camp Logan, and those patients were transferred from St. Joseph's. Operated jointly by the city and county, Jefferson Davis Hospital, with 150 beds, was opened in 1924 at Elder and Gerard streets in downtown Houston. In January 1938, the Jefferson Davis Hospital moved into a $2,500,000 facility with 500 beds, located on Buffalo Drive. Baylor University College of Medicine took over the hospital staff after the move to Houston in 1943. The hospital was staffed mainly by volunteer faculty. I served on the staff.

The Jefferson Davis Hospital published a popular little pharmacy handbook, or pharmacopoeia. It was passed out to medical students in Galveston. I used a copy of it for years, even at the Mayo Clinic. During the poliomyelitis epidemic of the 1940s and 1950s, a respiratory center was established at Jefferson Davis Hospital. Its main purpose was to provide respirators (iron lungs) for polio patients. I remember treating two patients there; one a member of the Lawler family who originated in Deport. She survived to live for years in a respirator. She learned to paint by holding a paint brush in her mouth.

Another patient was a young man named Chubb, of the Chubb insurance family. He came down with polio while visiting Houston. He died after a valiant struggle.

The Memorial Hospital and Nursing School, which had originated in 1905 as the Ida Rudisill Sanitarium, was another established institution. The Baptists bought it in 1907 and renamed it the Baptist Sanitarium. The hospital went through several expansions and adopted the name Memorial Hospital in 1932. In 1948, the $2 million Cullen Nurses Building was constructed across Lamar Avenue with funds provided by Mr. and Mrs. Hugh Roy Cullen. Shortly after I reached Houston in 1949, the bed capacity of Memorial Baptist had grown to 485, and four years later the 15-story Medical and Professional Building expanded Memorial to cover two city blocks.[12]

New facilities within the developing medical center were being built everywhere one turned, however. The Methodist Hospital was still located downtown in 1949, but four years earlier, Mr. and Mrs. Hugh Roy Cullen had announced a $1 million contribution for a new facility. Ground was broken for a 300-bed hospital in the Texas Medical Center on December 12, 1949. I remember the occasion well. Bertner had told me the date of the ground breaking ceremony, but I did not go. When I called on him in his room that night, he asked how the ground breaking came off. I made the lame excuse that I was too busy to go. Dr. Bertner was mad. Mrs. Bertner came to my defense, arguing that I couldn't leave my patients to attend a ground breaking. Methodist Hospital signed a very important affiliation agreement with the Baylor medical school in 1950. The agreement gave Baylor considerable control over hospital beds used for the admission of private patients by the Baylor faculty. Michael DeBakey, chief of surgery, assumed full control of the surgical program: beds, operating rooms, teaching program, the whole works. His leadership catapulted Methodist Hospital into one of the greatest hospitals in America.[13]

Like Methodist, St. Luke's Hospital was not yet built in 1949, but its future presence in the Texas Medical Center was assured thanks to Bishop Quin. He was very proud of his role. He told Mary and me the well-known story of how he raised $1 million from the Cullens for the hospital. The Cullens had given $1 million each to Memorial, Methodist, and St. Joseph's Hospitals. Bishop Quin thought that if the Cullens were giving the Baptists, Methodists, and Catholics each a million, they should certainly do the same for the Episcopalians. He went to Mrs. and Mrs. Cullen and told them the Episcopalians also needed a hospital. The Cullens gave him a million. The M. D. Anderson Foundation gave $500,000 and gift of a site in the new Texas Medical Center. The hospital received its charter in 1945. On February 20, 1951,

Bishop Quin conducted the ground breaking ceremony. The dignitaries were seated on a platform at least six feet high. Bishop Quin saw me in the audience and called me to come up, and I sat on the stage by him. The Texas Children's Hospital was built to connect with St. Luke's Hospital, the two sharing many facilities in common. Both hospitals opened in 1954.[14]

Other construction projects included the Veterans Administration Hospital of Houston that began in 1946 as a 1000-bed U.S. Navy Hospital. The hospital was transferred to the Veterans Administration on January 21, 1949, and soon became affiliated with the Baylor medical school. The Arabia Temple Crippled Children's Hospital, or the Shrine Hospital, was first housed in the Children's Building of the old Methodist Hospital. It was moved to adjoin Hermann Hospital in 1949. In 1952, a new Arabia Temple Crippled Children's Building was constructed in the medical center. The medical center also became home to the Houston Academy of Medicine Library—a longtime dream of the Harris County Medical Society—and one realized three years after my move to Houston. The Harris County Medical Society had established the Houston Academy of Medicine in 1915. From the beginning, the academy's primary goal had been the collection of medical books to create a library serving primarily the physicians of Houston. In 1926, the library occupied the sixteenth floor of the Medical Arts Professional Building. The Houston Dental Society joined with the medical society to make the library a shared project in 1931. With the announcement of the Texas Medical Center, the doctors agreed that a single library should exist in that center to service the entire medical community. The M. D. Anderson Foundation assured the new library a site of 3.42 acres.

In the year I arrived, the medical library moved to temporary housing within the Baylor University College of Medicine. By 1952, sufficient funds had been raised to break ground for the new building. Julia Bertner, Dr. Bertner's widow, was among those who turned the soil at the ground breaking ceremony on October 15, 1953. Mr. and Mrs. Jesse H. Jones, through Houston Endowment Inc., had donated $600,000, and the Anderson Foundation had added $300,000. The Jesse H. Jones Library Building was completed in July 1954 at a cost of $1,250,000. For years it housed the library as well as the offices of the Texas Medical Center and Harris County Medical Society, the Doctors Club, and meeting rooms.

This then was the medical community in Houston that I had decided to become a part of. The excitement and anticipation that went hand-in-hand with the evolving medical center was contagious. Opening a private practice in this fertile medical ground was thus both exhilarating and daunting. There were increasing pressures, since in the immediate postwar period thousands of doctors had been released from the armed forces and were looking for career opportunities. There were only a few clinic groups in the country at that time. Some young doctors entered solo practice after they had become known in the community while serving as assistants to doctors already established. Only a few were taken into partnership by the senior doctors, since the majority of practitioners still maintained an individual practice, even if they shared offices. Opportunities existed in country towns, but specialty oriented doctors declined these in preference to city practice.

After spending huge amounts of money and many years in study and training, a young specialist was still in for a period of near starvation while building his practice. He also had to furnish his office and buy another car for his wife and children. The American Medical Association's code of ethics was very strict about advertising in any form. In Harris County, a doctor could not place an announcement in the newspaper; he could not erect a sign larger than the proverbial shingle; he could not solicit practice; and he could not mention his specialty in the telephone directory. If he was lucky like I was, he could get his arrival written up in a gossip column in the newspapers. Basically, when setting up a private practice as a solo practitioner, there was little choice but to wait for patients to come. I could not have made it without the help of our families and professional friends, many I will never be able to repay.

CHAPTER 12

Solo Practice, 1949–50

Entering private solo practice was the most challenging experience of my life. The strong support I had from family and friends was no guarantee that I would succeed. If I failed, there would be a huge mess and a lot of disappointed people. Thousands of young doctors were in exactly the same situation, probably a hundred in Houston alone, beginning a solo practice. Since my office in the Hermann Professional Building was not yet completed, Dr. Bertner invited me to see my patients in his office in the mornings while he was at surgery in the hospital. He admitted my patients to his service at Hermann Hospital while I was awaiting staff privileges. George Waldron invited me to see patients in his office during the afternoons while he was at surgery. He also admitted my hospital patients on his service. Both doctors' entire office staffs were at my disposal. They handled my appointments and prepared my patients for examination. My very slim practice was no burden for them, but it was a lifesaver for me. Neither Dr. Bertner nor George would accept any rent from me. Dr. Bertner had a cattle ranch at Monaville, in Waller County. An Aggie classmate of mine, Edgar Hudgins, was a member of the family who owned a ranch at Hungerford, which was famous for Brahman cattle. Edgar selected a fine registered Brahman heifer, which I bought as a gift for Dr. Bertner. He was pleased—the heifer became a fine cow and had many calves. I kept up with her for years. I have forgotten what I gave to George Waldron as a gift. I also gave small presents to their office personnel.[1]

Before my office opened I employed a part-time secretary in my home and ordered supplies and equipment. I applied for staff privileges at several hospitals and a faculty appointment at Baylor medical school. I prepared announcements and wrote every doctor I knew who might send me a patient. Lee Clark immediately gave me a part-time job at M. D. Anderson Hospital on Baldwin Street and put me to work developing the isotope department. And then I mailed my first announcement:

Mavis P. Kelsey, M.D.
announces the opening of his office
Hermann Professional Building,
6410 Fannin Street
Houston, Texas

| *Practice Limited to* | *Keystone 3-4948* |
| *Internal Medicine* | *Keystone 3-5304* |

I moved into my office in 1201 Hermann Professional Building on March 15, 1949. I had 750 square feet of space. I sat up past midnight many times, drawing and re-drawing plans and ultimately was able to crowd into this limited space a waiting room with seating for six people. There was an office for the receptionist-secretary, with an open counter to the waiting room. The receptionist said it was so small she had to back out to turn around. A hall passed from the waiting room to an examining room, an X-ray room, an office, and a treatment room, each about eight by ten square feet. There was a cubbyhole laboratory and an X-ray development room. There was no toilet in the office but public toilets were available on the twelfth floor. Patients took their enemas at home before coming to the office for a proctoscopic examination. I was proud of the office, and it served me well.

I ordered a Mayo examining table from Rochester. That table is still in use today in the Kelsey-Seybold Clinic. A carpenter built a combination basal metabolism–proctoscopy table-chest of many drawers, which I admired. My future partners would find it too cumbersome and, with much derision, would vote it out of the office. It serves today as part work table, part catch-all cabinet, in my tool room. Another relic in that tool room is a tall white enamel metal storage cabinet, also banned from the office. I store brooms and mops and long-handled tools in it today, and the latches still work perfectly.

I wanted an original painting of a Texas scene for the waiting room. We received the *Humble Way,* a magazine published for Humble Oil Company stockholders. Many issues were illustrated with Texas scenes, the work of E. M. Schiwetz. I took a chance and looked him up in the Houston telephone directory. A telephone call to Edward (Buck) Muegge Schiwetz led to a lifetime friendship with this lovable man who was probably the most popular artist Texas ever had. On that first call I told Buck I wanted a painting of a Texas ranch house with Brahman cattle grazing in front of the house and an oil well off to one side. Buck said he could do that for $500. He brought a large portfolio of his artwork, with fifty or more pieces beginning with sketches

Original St. Luke's, opened 1954

he made when he was a boy, followed by others he made while an architecture student at Texas A&M, and finally many pictures of Texas scenes. His painting for my office was a great success, and after retirement was still treasured by us at home.[2] In 1998 the painting was given to A&M to be hung in the Mavis and Mary Kelsey Reading Room of the Cushing Library.

Carl Herzog designed and printed my first stationery. I had corresponded with and collected books printed by Carl at the Texas Western Press in El Paso. He was a leading typographer and bookmaker whose works today are collectors' items. I also opened an account for the exclusive use of the practice in the First National Bank. That remained our main bank account continuously for many years, providing proof of uninterrupted business since 1949 of what is now called the Kelsey-Seybold Clinic.

There was a great view from my office window on the southwest corner of the Hermann Building. From here I watched the Shamrock Hotel in its final completion. The Rice Stadium at Rice University was under construction by Brown and Root Company, which built it at cost in record time. As popular legend has it, the football coach asked George Brown if he could have the stadium open for the first game of the season. George Brown replied, "I think so. Is it an afternoon game or a night game?" Within a year after I arrived, the Prudential Building was under construction. And in the medical center itself, Methodist, St. Luke's, Texas Children's, and M. D. Anderson Hospitals were soon to be built.

My office was next door to Dr. Bertner's. He continued to play an important role in my professional career, although his health had deteriorated. Indeed, he and his wife took us in almost as members of their family. They invited my family to their ranch at Monaville several times. They introduced us to their friends, many who became our friends and patients. Many of their friends were doctors who sent me patients. Dr. Bertner also arranged for me to take night calls for the Jones's hotels, which included the Lamar where Mary and I had spent our first two honeymoon nights in 1939. The hotel was a ten minute drive from our house in River Oaks. Many of the calls were from the hotel personnel, who occasionally wanted me to give a noisy drunk something to put him to sleep so that the other guests could get some rest. While I was at Bellevue Hospital and the Wichita Falls State Hospital I learned to administer intravenous amytal to maniacal patients. At the Lamar, the housekeepers and porters would hold the patients down while I put them to sleep. I can remember chasing a screaming naked woman down the hall while other guests were sticking their heads out of the door to see the commotion. I treated others at the hotel who had fever, chest pain, or food poisoning, and some of them required hospitalization.

Dr. Bertner suffered from a coronary occlusion a few months after we arrived in Houston. As his doctor, I put him in Hermann Hospital. The responsibility was so great that I told Dr. Bertner I wanted a consultation. He agreed to calling Dr. M. D. Levy, who was one of the most highly regarded internists in Houston and, at the time, chief of medicine at Hermann. Thereafter, Dr. Levy and I attended Dr. Bertner together. He soon developed a pain in one leg and was found to have an osteogenic sarcoma. I believe Ed Smith was the one who did a total amputation of the thigh and leg. Dr. Bertner was undaunted and exhibited tremendous determination. He was soon walking on crutches and going everywhere, including a cocktail party at our house. He eventually developed metastasis to the lungs. I called on him at the hotel every day. I remember visiting him with Lee Clark. Knowing his plight, Dr. Bertner volunteered himself for any treatment that might help others. At that time there were no known cancer drugs. The specialty of oncology had not been developed. Dr. Bertner went to the Oschner Clinic for a partial lung resection to remove a tumor. He was found to have an additional malignancy, a rhabdomyosarcoma. He was taken around in a wheelchair, but eventually became bedfast. Secretaries came in while he continued to run the Texas Medical Center and his own business until he became unconscious.

By July 1950, Dr. Bertner was on oxygen full time and his lungs were spotted with metastasis. While he was terminally ill, an isotope specialist came from the National Institute of Health and injected a dose of radioactive gallium. Several nationally known specialists took part in his treatment. For three nights before his death Ed Smith, Dudley Oldham, and I sat up with him.

On the morning of July 28, 1950, Dr. Bertner's family called to tell me he had died. I remember going to his apartment in the Rice Hotel. His three nieces and their husbands were there with Mrs. Bertner, who was distressed but relieved that his suffering had ended. I gave her a barbiturate. Soon many people were coming to the apartment to offer condolences. I watched Bill Russell, chief of pathology at M. D. Anderson, perform an autopsy on the body. He later sent me a copy of the protocol, a three-hundred-page book with illustrations of gross and microscopic sections.[3]

I felt my practice in Houston started off slowly. Mary and I did know quite a few people who were extremely helpful, but to open an office in a city of nearly a million people and wait for patients to come walking in required great patience, especially when I had borrowed many thousands of dollars. When I arrived in Houston, Dr. Bertner had two patients waiting for me in Hermann Hospital. Seeing them on that first day was a great psychological boost. I would go for days without seeing a new patient, however. That first patient, Mrs. George Stevenson, was a thirty-five-year-old cousin of my brother-in-law Jamie Griffith. I had seen her a few months before at the Mayo Clinic, where she underwent treatment for severe brittle diabetes. When I saw her in Houston, the diabetes was out of control and required several days to correct. She and her family continued to be patients for years. The other patient, Mrs. Juliette Kendall, was an obese, cheerful sixty-two-year-old widow who was fond of alcohol. Her complaint was jaundice. I thought it was caused by alcoholic cirrhosis. The jaundice cleared in a month, and a few months later she had perfectly normal liver function. Obviously her jaundice was caused by infectious hepatitis, not alcohol.[4]

Although starting a practice was a challenging task that required enormous patience, I did have plenty of self-confidence. I was well trained and had a variety of experiences behind me. My parents had taught me to be polite and reserved, but I decided to become aggressive and forward. I walked right up and introduced myself to prominent people who had never heard of me. I frequently stood up in medical staff meetings and talked. I publicized that I had been on the Mayo staff. I let everyone know how smart I was. I was a real bore. I went to every meeting and social function to which I was invited. When I did get patients, I would call them at home later to see how he or she was doing.

I know that more than a few doctors didn't like my aggressiveness, but, bad as it was, it—along with hard work and long hours—paid off. In a few months, I became fairly well-known in my part of Houston. I was still quite naïve about solo practice, however. At first, I let people come to our house to be treated at night or on Sunday, the only times I was at home. Some patients wouldn't leave, however. I soon learned not to have people call on me at home except friends or family members. I had a frantic call from a man whose wife often came to my house on Sunday mornings for treatment; she should have been seeing a psychiatrist. He insisted that I come to their house at once. When I arrived, I found his nude wife in the bathtub, covered in blood. She had committed suicide while her husband had been out of the house briefly. In those days it was very difficult to convince a patient to seek psychiatric help; usually, the patient had to be hallucinating before the family would accept a psychiatrist.

I held office hours from eight to five—or later if I had patients—five days a week, and from eight to twelve o'clock on Saturday. For years there were no afternoons off, until finally many doctors started taking off on Thursday afternoons. When I had more partners, we covered for each other and rotated an afternoon and Saturday morning off. Before going to the office I made hospital rounds, usually starting before seven o'clock in the morning. When I had patients in two or more hospitals, I raced to see them all. The usual hospital rounds began at Memorial, then St. Joseph's, then Hermann Hospital. When Methodist and St. Luke's opened after Bill Leary and Bill Seybold joined, we had to cover them also, but we rotated coverage. After office hours, I also made afternoon rounds on hospital patients, thus seeing each patient twice a day. If I was tied up in the office all day I performed consultations or physical examinations on new hospital patients after office hours. I saw patients at the Heights Hospital at night. I saw hospital patients seven days a week.

House calls had to be taken care of either in early morning, at noon, or at night. I bought a pistol grip spotlight so that I could read house numbers from my car during these nighttime calls, of which there were plenty. At first, house calls were a high percentage of my practice. Many, including those hotel calls, occurred at night. I'd call twice a day on patients sick at home. I gained some of my practice by seeing patients at home when the patient's regular doctor refused or failed to come. I called on some chronically ill patients as often as once daily or possibly once a week on Saturday afternoon or Sunday morning. These calls consumed a lot of time and gasoline. I drove about two thousand miles a month. I made house calls as far away as Alief, Channelview, Missouri City, and Katy. I remember one patient who I knew didn't need a house call. I argued with the patient over the phone, but she insisted I see her. I got out of bed and made the call. Still mad at her, I asked, "Why in the devil did you call me? You didn't need me." She replied, "Well, I just wanted to see you." Another time I was called to see a patient. I hadn't been there long when Dr. Fred Lummis, Sr., came in with his medical bag. The patient had called both of us. Dr. Lummis said, "You got here first, you take care of her," and he left.

Although I was trained as an endocrinologist at Mayo, I would have starved if I had limited my practice to endocrinology. I had to start making a living in Houston before I could concentrate on my specialty. I had been exposed to general practice by Dr. Steve Grant and to psychiatry at the Wichita Falls State Hospital. I had served a mixed medical and surgical internship at Bellevue and had broad training in internal medicine and neurology at Mayo, as well as diverse experiences at the School of Aviation Medicine and four years as a flight surgeon in the Air Corps. I had done a little of everything except major work in orthopedics, surgery, and obstetrics. I was a half-way decent general practitioner. So I treated everything that I could do well, just to make a living. In dermatology I treated psoriasis, ichthyosis, alopecia, herpes zoster, decubitus, and pediculous. Salicylic acid ointment would cure practically any fungus infection. I missed a case of scabies on my son John, however. Mary got tired of my treatment and took John to Everett Seale, our dermatologist, who diagnosed it. He was delighted to tell me that I shouldn't be doing dermatology and teased me about it for years. I coagulated various warts, lanced boils, and sewed minor lacerations. Lee Clark warned me not to mess around with pigmented nevi—I might overlook a malignant melanoma.

I had fitted hundreds of eyeglasses in the Aleutians, but I passed this on to ophthalmologists Elizabeth Crawford, Maury Campbell, and Ed Griffey. I opened eustachian tubes, even lanced an ear drum and drained the maxillary sinuses and inspected the vocal cords, things I had done routinely in Alaska. I did thoracenteses and paracenteses, drained hydrococles and hydrarthroses, and later injected cortisone in joints. I did my own spinal taps—something I first learned while at the Wichita Falls State Hospital. I did office gynecology, cauterized cervices, dilated urethras, drained Bartholin cysts, treated gonorrhea and syphilis, including neurosyphilis. I did prostocopics, snared rectal polyps, and lanced hemorrhoidal clots. I diagnosed and treated a tape worm and hookworms. I diagnosed a gastric trichobezoar in an elderly woman. I treated coronary occlusions in the home, taking my trusty string galvanometer electrocardiograph machine to the patient's house. In those days it was considered too risky to move the patient to a hospital. There wasn't much to do in the hospital anyway. I drew blood for prothrombin times for treatment with coumarin. Gastric analysis was a popular form of medical torture, which I performed in the office. I also did basal metabolic rates in the office, which was soon replaced by radioiodine tests and protein bound iodine blood tests.

An unexpected part of my practice was treating snake bites. One of my patients came in with a snake bite on her ankle. She didn't have the snake, but her description of it fitted that of a copperhead. I called Mr. Stimson. Stimson, a surveyor in town whose employees had sustained snake bites while surveying, had studied snake bites and their treatment and notified the Harris County Medical Society office that he could identify the snake by the puncture mark of its bite. He also had learned the present knowledge of treatment and knew about the available snake antitoxins. He had left his telephone number and was willing to advise doctors who had snake bite patients. He came to the hospital promptly and identified the bite as that of a copperhead. I put a tourniquet on the leg, made a cruciate incision over the bite, and applied a suction cup. I also administered antitoxin. The patient got well without permanent damage. In retrospect, she might have done just as well without my treatment. Stimson and I became friends. He helped me treat another snake bite and started referring me patients, when other doctors didn't want to treat them. One night, Wesley West called me. His father-in-law had been bitten by a snake in his home town of Welch, Louisiana. Wesley flew me over to Welch that night, and I treated the patient. In all, I must have treated four or five snake bites within a one- to two-year period—a lot for a city internist.

I had been trained for years to do a thorough complete history and physical examination on every patient who came to me. I'd perform and charge for a complete examinations on people who complained only of a sore throat or minor indigestion, costing me some patients. At least these examinations gave me a reputation for being thorough and thus enhanced my reputation. Some people came because they wanted a thorough examination, even if they had no complaints. In today's medical world such examinations may be considered wasteful of a "caregiver's" time and a patient is lucky to get such an examination. I think everyone should have a thorough periodic examination just like an airplane gets a thousand-hour check, whether anything seems wrong or not. Many otherwise fatal diseases can be cured, if discovered early enough.

At that time, doctors charged some very low fees in Houston. Many doctors charged $3.00 for an office visit and $5.00 for a house call. Very few did a complete examination, so there was no standard fee for such a visit. I was ambitious. I planned to charge more than the local doctors. I concluded that my time was worth $20.00 an hour. If I worked full time ten hours a day for five-and-a-half days a week I could book $1,000 a week. If I took off two weeks for vacation and two weeks for medical meetings, as I had at the Mayo Clinic, I could book $48,000 a year. With 30-percent overhead and a 90-percent collection rate, I could earn a net profit of $32,000 a year, more than twice what I would earn at Mayo. Of course it was completely impossible to have my schedule full. And this left no time for charity work, which I was soon assigned at Jeff Davis Hospital. I solved that problem by working fourteen hours a day and extra hours on Saturdays and Sundays doing house calls and hospital visits. I also planned to make some extra money in the laboratory and X-ray department.

Accordingly, I charged $25.00 for a complete one-hour history and physical examination plus a fifteen-minute follow-up visit. Quite a few patients complained about this exorbitant fee. Hospital fees were $5.00 per visit. House calls ranged from $5.00 to $15.00. Ministers and their families, doctors and families, employees, and relatives were seen free. I also had discounts for the poor. I charged $5.00 for a complete blood count and did many myself. A complete $3.00 urinalysis required boiling the urine in a test tube to determine the presence of sugar. A proctoscopic examination was $15.00—it didn't take long and was a real moneymaker. Patients complained about the examination, not the fee. An electrocardiogram was $10.00, or $15.00 with a step test. I could perform a few blood chemistries in the office, such as a blood sugar and a blood urea nitrogen, as well as a bilirubin and congo red liver function test for $5.00 each. I performed blood smears for streptococci, staphylococci, gonococci, syphilis, and tuberculosis. I collected cultures to be sent to an outside laboratory. A one-plate X ray of the chest, abdomen, spine or a bone was $5.00 to $10.00. A basal metabolic rate, at that time the only test available for thyroid function, was $15.00. I was specializing in thyroid diseases and was soon sending the patients to the isotope laboratory, which I had helped set up at M. D. Anderson Hospital.

The word soon spread that I was a high-priced doctor who spent a whole hour giving a thorough examination. Wealthy patients could afford me, although some complained and tried to get me to reduce my fees. I employed Doris Durden as a full-time office nurse, secretary, bookkeeper, and receptionist for $150 a month. She was quite competent and took medical shorthand, but I was too demanding and let her go after the first year. She went away crying. I admit I was a mean son of a bitch and have always regretted this action. Thereafter, I rarely fired anyone, even though I should have. I used a dictaphone that recorded on a wax cylinder. The cylinder was later replaced by a plastic roll. I employed Annette Hill, a Rice graduate, who was certified both as a laboratory and X-ray technician, and paid her $175 a month. Her hours were from eight to five or to whenever I finished seeing patients, whichever came last. She stayed with me for three or four years but was hired away by St. Luke's Hospital, where she spent the remainder of her career. I saw her there often.

I looked for other ways to build up my practice. Ross Margraves referred the personnel director of Foley's department store to me as a patient. The director said that the executives at Foley's had gone through a period of great stress opening the new store, and he wanted all of them to have a physical examination. Of the sixteen executives, four had duodenal ulcer from stress. Foley's became the Kelsey-Seybold Clinic's first company account, which has continued to this day. I also did life insurance examinations. They didn't pay much, but when other patients were scarce, the $7.50 insurance examination was welcome. Preemployment examinations weren't done very often then, but I did a few—anything to make a buck. An organization in New York City called Executive Health Examiners did company examinations in their New York office, but soon branched out to contract with local doctors to examine employees of nationwide companies. I got on their panel. The fees were very low, however, and only worthwhile if you had spare time. I also examined a number of patients in preparation for foreign travel.

A certified FAA examiner, I conducted complete Class I FAA examinations in the office, especially for Delta and Texas (later Continental) Airlines pilots. I taught several FAA courses and was a visiting lecturer at the School of Aviation Medicine, Randolph Field, Texas. On one occasion, I went out to see the U.S. Air Force base at Ellington Field, south of town on the old Galveston highway. I was nostalgic for the Air Corps, where I had spent four years during World War II. I asked the hospital commander if there was anything I could do. He was a regular air force flight surgeon running a fairly large hospital with several young resident-level medical officers serving their military requirements. They had no internist and were shipping patients to Brooke Hospital in San Antonio for consultation. He asked if I would be a consultant in medicine and make rounds with the staff on a weekly basis. The standard consultant fee was $50.00. I accepted and went to the Ellington Field hospital every Thursday afternoon. As time went on I rotated consultations with Melville Cody in gynecology and possibly other specialists until I eventually could not find time to go.

When I had no office appointments or house calls—and I wasn't nearly as busy as the above description of my schedule might suggest—I did hospital work. In addition to Jefferson Davis, a fine charity hospital, Hermann Hospital ran a charity service where I served. I also had my part-time staff position at M. D. Anderson, working with Lee Clark who was also interested in thyroid disease. As early as 1946, when Lee became director of M. D. Anderson Hospital, he wrote me at the Mayo Clinic, inviting me to join the Anderson staff. Lee and I had been good friends since we were together in the Aeromedical Laboratory at Dayton, Ohio, during World War II. Mary and I had been with Lee and his wife Bert several times in Dayton. When we arrived in Houston we had dinner with them at Mad Tony's on Montrose Avenue. That night, Bert was in good form with her earthy language, and she tried to shock Mary. The two became good friends.

In 1949 the M.D. Anderson Hospital was still operating in temporary quarters while their new pink marble building was under construction in the Texas

Medical Center. They had $1,250,000 to build the hospital. Before it was completed Lee had raised enough money to build a $10,000,000 hospital. Gossip around Austin was that the Texas legislature would give Lee Clark anything he asked for. Lee was a person of vision, imagination, and enthusiasm. He once told me, "I only accomplish about 10 percent of my ideas." He was always interested in hearing people's ideas. His willingness to try innovations contributed to his success in building the M. D. Anderson Hospital into a famous institution.[5]

Lee wanted me to do four things. I was to develop the clinical isotope program, since I had the first license in Houston from the Atomic Energy Commission to administer radioisotopes; help edit a new publication, the *Cancer Bulletin,* under Russ Curmley, chief of publications; see patients in M. D. Anderson's department of internal medicine under Cliff Howe, chief of medicine; and start an endocrine clinic and see endocrine consults.

To begin a clinical isotope program, we mounted the Geiger counter for counting thyroid uptake of radioiodine on an old X-ray tube stand, and it worked perfectly. We immediately began using radioiodine for diagnosing and treating hyperthyroidism and thyroid cancer. We gave the first dose of radioiodine to a patient in Houston in 1949. I talked at various medical meetings about it, and patients began coming in by referral. As the years went on, M. D. Anderson Hospital accumulated one of the largest series of thyroid cancer cases in the country. Several papers on treatment of thyroid cancer were published with my name as one of the authors. As for my editorial work, within a year or two Russ and Lee were publishing the *Heart Bulletin* and the *Psychiatric Bulletin* as part of the Medical Arts Publishing Foundation, with me as an editor for each publication. Russ used art illustrations like the ones we had used in the *Air Surgeon's Bulletin.* For M. D. Anderson's endocrine clinic, I helped recruit full-time endocrinologists, including Ray Rose, Tom Haynie, and Stratton Hill.

During this time, many other fine physicians joined the staff at M. D. Anderson. I had trained with C. C. Shullenberger at the Mayo Clinic. One day he appeared in my office, planning to practice in Houston. I called Lee Clark, who immediately gave him a job as the first trained hematologist at Anderson Hospital. Alando J. Ballantyne trained as a head and neck surgeon at Mayo while I was there and came to Anderson for his career. He married Maria Mitchell from Galveston, the younger sister of George, Johnny, and Christy Mitchell. I met her when she was twelve years old helping her uncle run the College Inn Restaurant, where we medical students ate, drank beer, and played pitch. When I returned to the Mayo Clinic after World War II, Mary and I went to a reception for new and returning fellows. Suddenly a beautiful woman rushed up and hugged and kissed me profusely. "Mavis, you remember me!" I drew a blank. "I'm Maria who served you beer at the College Inn." Maria frequently reminds me of how she surprised me in Rochester. Today, her son-in-law Gilchrist Jackson is a prominent surgeon at the Kelsey-Seybold Clinic.

Leonard Grimmett, a radiation physicist from Hammersmith Hospital in London, came to set up the Cobalt 60 machine. He and his wife were nearly killed during the Nazi bombing raids over London. Mrs. Grimmett claimed to have seen an unidentified flying object. This was during the time when people all over the country were seeing hundreds of these objects. Everyone knew someone who had seen one. I had a patient who had seen one. She described it in detail and received a lot of attention from her friends and neighbors. Many observers were written up in the newspapers, especially when their object landed near them and little green men got out. I quizzed Mrs. Grimmett. I was curious to learn what her flying object looked like. It didn't come very close, however, so she could give no details.

Ben Wells came to M. D. Anderson about the same time as I. We got acquainted at Scott and White, where we were residents, and also were at the Mayo Clinic together. He had a research fellowship in biochemistry and had worked for Edward Kendall. Dr. Kendall told me that Ben had done some very important research in adrenal steroids. Ben came directly from Mayo to the M. D. Anderson Hospital. Bill Derrick was in charge of anesthesia. Bill McComb came from Memorial Hospital as a head and neck surgeon. Bob Nelson came as chief of gastroenterology. Seaborn Dale was an oncologist. Allen Chamberlain was a part time head and neck surgeon who trained at Memorial Hospital. Dick Martin was a young surgeon who eventually became chief. Felix Rutledge and John Wall were both doing gynecology, Felix finally becoming full-time for the remainder of his career.[6]

The staff at Anderson faced cancer every day. Many of the patients had advanced cancer when they were admitted and died within months. Since 1949, they have witnessed the remission and cure of many cancers, which formerly were fatal. These dedicated people have developed a spirit of hope and compassion. I was always inspired when I visited Anderson Hospital. One morning, a dying patient impressed me in a way I will never forget. I was in a foul mood, mad at the world and feeling sorry for myself, when I walked into an examining room to see a patient in the Anderson out-clinic. This patient had widespread cancer and knew he didn't have long to live. As I walked in the patient struggled to his feet, all smiles, and said, "Doc, thank God I'm still here!" Here was I in good health, nothing really wrong, in a foul mood. I was ashamed of myself. I braced myself, forced a smile, and congratulated the patient on being alive. Sometimes when I'm about to feel mistreated I think of that patient and his smile.

My professional career also continued to develop. Soon after my arrival in Houston, Dr. Bertner got me appointed to the board of the Harris County Unit of the American Cancer Society. Mary Lou King was the executive director. The volunteer board of directors was organized to have a triangle of leadership: the president, a physician, provided medical advice; a leading business person provided financial advice; and a prominent civic figure headed the annual fund drive. Dr. Culver Griswold was president when I joined. He, John Wall, and Everett Lewis were among those who served several years. Among the active board members I remember were Mrs. Lamar Fleming, Mrs. W. Aubrey Smith, Mrs. Gus Wortham, Mrs. Oveta Hobby, C. P. Simpson, Frank Smith, Harris McAshan, J. P. Bryan, James Anderson and Vernon Frost. Among the early achievements of the Harris County Cancer Society was organizing the many women's clubs in support of the society. Another was the educational program. Doctors volunteered to talk to numerous groups about the seven danger signs of cancer and the seven cancer facts. One fact proved incorrect. We used to reassure people that cancer was not hereditary. Now we know of many types of cancer that are, at least in part, hereditary. Every year the society publicized a different prevention program. These programs included breast self-examination (this was years before mammograms); Pap (Papanicolaou) smears for uterine cancer (Dr. Papanicolaou was still alive and came to Houston for a visit); and smoking cessation (many people denied that smoking caused lung cancer). I stayed on the board for many years and served various offices. Bill Seybold was also very active in the cancer society and served as president of both the Harris County Unit and Texas Division.[7]

I also tried to attend as many medical meetings as possible, including the Harris County Medical Society, the Ninth District Medical Society, and the Texas State Medical Association. I presented papers at these meetings. The Houston Society of Internal Medicine had been recently organized. I thoroughly enjoyed these monthly dinner meetings and scientific presentations. A few osteopaths practiced in Houston and operated a small hospital. I became acquainted with the osteopaths when I saw some patients they had referred to M. D. Anderson Hospital for consultation and treatment. In those days osteopaths were not accepted in the county medical society, even though they were required to pass the same state licensing board examinations as the medical doctors. Other professional societies included the Texas Chapter of the American College of Physicians and the Texas Society of Internal Medicine. I have been a fellow of the American College of Physicians since my Mayo Clinic days. There has been a Texas Diabetes Society meeting ever since I came to Texas, usually held in conjunction with the state medical meeting.[8]

The national medical meeting I was most anxious to attend was that of the American Goiter Society, later called the American Thyroid Society. I had been elected to the society before I left Mayo. The first meeting I attended was in Madison, Wisconsin, in July 1949. Wesley West sent me and Mary up in his DC-3. When the meeting was over he sent his plane back and flew us to Rochester, Minnesota, to visit Bill Seybold and Bill Leary, their families, as well as other friends at the Mayo Clinic. At the Madison meeting we met Selwyn Taylor, a leading thyroid surgeon from London. He was in America on a Rockefeller fellowship to attend the goiter meeting and study at leading American medical centers. The Mayo Clinic was part of his itinerary, so we invited him to ride with us to Rochester in Wesley's plane. Selwyn and his wife, Ruth, became good friends. I was active in the Goiter Society for years, including serving as chair of the membership committee for many years and as vice president. I was offered the position of president in return for serving as secretary for a year, but I thought I was too busy building a clinic to take on those duties.

When I came to Houston in the late 1940s, internal medicine was at the cutting edge of medical practice. Most doctors did not realize, however, that they were entering a profound revolution in medical knowledge and in the way medicine would be practiced—a revolution which is still going on. Very likely, we are only in its beginning. During the fifty years that I practiced, from 1936 to 1986, medical knowledge has doubled or tripled. The practitioners of allopathic medicine—my brand of medicine—have been responsible for 99 percent of these advances, saving millions of lives. Amazingly the prestige of the medical profession has declined. It seems that the more that is done to save lives, the greater the criticism. People now want instant cures for everything. I have just read that 57 percent of the public resorts to alternative medicine. Much alternative medicine is without scientific proof but people accept it blindly. Most worthwhile treatments regardless of source have been accepted and utilized by today's established medical profession. Finally, to confront this trend in the use of alternative medicine, medical research institutes with grants from the National Institute of Health test these alternative methods for actual proof of effectiveness. The colonic irrigation parlors I found in Houston fifty years ago are enjoying a revival. M. D. Anderson Hospital gave acupuncture a serious trial for several years. They abandoned it when they could discern no benefit in pain relief or cure for cancer sufferers.

Reading articles written fifty years ago is like reading about the Middle Ages. Most articles are of historical value only. Medical indices before the 1950s are so obsolete they are no longer available on the computer, where medical researchers now go to find references.

There were real breakthroughs in medicine in my first years of practice. I can think of a number of small victories I enjoyed as a result of these advances. Mrs. Bracci was a nice Italian lady who had Addison's disease, or failure of the adrenal cortex. She was referred by the Mayo Clinic. I was treating her with the terribly expensive aqueous adrenal extract. She nearly died in an adrenal crisis before we could obtain cortisone, which was very scarce. Cortisone had not yet been completely synthesized but was being produced in limited quantities from Mexican yams. After synthetic cortisone treatments, Mrs. Bracci became a new person, healthy and vigorous and lived for years. President Kennedy had Addison's disease, diagnosed by Boston endocrinologists—acquaintances of mine. We endocrinologists knew his secret diagnosis long before the general public. Kennedy was treated successfully with cortisone and lived a vigorous life before he was assassinated.

Everyone wanted to try cortisone. My patients tried to get it. I gave it to some advanced cancer patients at M. D. Anderson Hospital. It made them feel better but didn't stop the disease. Some doctors said it allowed the patient to walk to the autopsy table. We immediately found it useful for allergic reactions. Dr. Robert Johnson had such severe hay fever he had to leave town during the season. Cortisone made it possible for him to stay in Houston. Some doctors tried it as a tonic. They were not yet aware of the side effects of large doses of cortisone.

Penicillin, streptomycin, and aureomycin—the new antibiotics—were miracle drugs. Before their advent, 50 percent of all deaths were from infections such as pneumonia, peritonitis, septicemia, tuberculous, and syphilis. While visiting a hospital in Boston, I was told it had closed down two-thirds of the ear, nose, and throat beds, because they had no more acute mastoiditis, tonsillar abscesses, or patients with suppurative sinusitis. We were learning more about the antibiotics. For a while, surgeons were giving prophylactic injections of penicillin to prevent possible post-operative infections. One patient I saw in consultation lost her life from a prophylactic injection of penicillin given her before a routine hysterectomy for fibroids. The operation went fine, but the patient developed exfoliative dermatitis from penicillin. She lingered for many weeks in the hospital before she died.

The use of radioiodine in treating hyperthyroidism and thyroid cancer had proved successful. Radioiodine and blood iodine studies made it possible to better diagnose hyper- and hypothyroidism. I found the captain of a big passenger plane to have myxedema or total thyroid failure. His reflexes were extremely slow. Thyroid replacement medication put him back on flying status in six weeks. Before we had medium- and long-acting insulins, pregnant diabetics rarely carried their pregnancy to term. In fact, Dr. Russell Wilder once said that pregnancy was so devastating to diabetic women that they should be sterilized. After we had the new insulins, we carried most diabetic women to term.

We were not yet so successful with heart attacks. Diets were high in animal fats, and the cholesterol level was considered normal up to 300 milligrams. We didn't know about unsaturated fats. The mortality rate from coronary artery disease was very high, making it a dreaded disease like cancer. Anticoagulants were just becoming useful and saved many, but it was years before coronary artery bypass surgery. The heart pump had not been invented. Except for sewing up stab wounds and ligating a ductus arteriosus, the only heart surgery I recall was inserting a knife into the heart and cutting open a stenosed mitral valve.

I have vivid memories of my first two years in Houston. I can remember many doctors with whom I shared patients. It was always a pleasant surprise when another doctor called for the first time and referred a patient to me. I took a sudden liking to that doctor and tried to reciprocate. I had many AKK brothers in Houston: Holman Taylor, Jr., dermatologist; Fred Bloom, orthopedist; Denton Cooley and Grady Hallman, cardiac surgeons; and Claude Pollard, neurosurgeon. Ross Margraves, fellow Aggie and AKK brother, died on the operating table of a ruptured aorta while Everett Lewis was trying to save him. Luke Able was the first pediatric surgeon in Houston. He became chief of surgery at Texas Children's Hospital and remains a friend today. Tom and Donald Gready, Phillip Bellegie, and Al and David Braden were other AKKs. Among the older friends who were AKKs were Herbert Hayes, Dr. Weems Turner, W. B. Thorning, and Alvis Greer, each of whom developed a large practice with associates. Dr. Allen Kyle was a striking figure with white hair and trimmed goatee. Kyle Field at A&M was named for him. Tom Cronin was a Mayo-trained plastic surgeon who pioneered breast implants. The group he organized is still active. One of his partners, Tom Biggs, did a face lift on Mary. Dan Jenkins was an AKK who became chief of the pulmonary section of internal medicine at Baylor. AKK brother Maury Campbell from Nacogdoches became an ophthalmologist and developed a fine practice in Houston, before he gave it up to marry a very wealthy rancher from around Edna. This upset Maury's mother, who was my patient. She said, "That woman married the most expensive yard man in Texas."[9]

Among my closest friends were some AKKs in San Antonio. Ralph Letteer was my best friend for many years. Al Hartman was a surgeon. Huard Hargis was an internist who died during the polio epidemic in 1950. Carl Goeth was a general practitioner-surgeon. Other medical school friends not in AKK included Frank Parrish, an orthopedist who joined his uncle, Joe Foster. Frank became chief of orthopedics at M.D. Anderson Hospital. He perpetuated his uncle's practice with a group of partners, including Mike Donovan. Frank and Mike died while still in active practice, but the group continues today. Seale Johnson was the oldest member of our class, so we called him Pop. He did general practice in Houston, as did Bert Estes, Juan Ruiz, and Max Diamond. Fred Aves became a surgeon. Isadore Peters became a psychiatrist and practiced in Houston. Other psychiatrists were Harlan Crank, Alvin Bayer, and Henry Little. Henry joined our clinic for a few years before moving to Galveston as part of the UTMB faculty.[10]

Galveston graduates included my great friend J. T. Armstrong, who became a leading gynecologist-obstetrician and president of the Houston Academy of Medicine. Don Paton was instructor in obstetrics in Galveston, before he entered practice in Houston. John Wall was a Bertner protégé. We became friends in Galveston, and he and his wife, Millicent, were our close friends in Houston. My son Tom married his cousin Ann Heinzerling. The Arnold brothers, Hugh and Hiram, were friends in Galveston. Their younger brother Tommy came later and joined the Lummis and Reece group, which eventually became the Diagnostic Clinic, with Tommy as chief. Herman Gardner came as an obstetrician and gynecologist. He became chief of his department at St. Luke's Hospital. Herman was a successful business man. He was a pioneer in breeding Brangus cattle and introducing coastal bermuda grass to Texas. He developed a large show place ranch in Washington County. C. M. Ashmore was another gynecologist and a Bertner protégé.

I knew Everett Lewis in Galveston and at the Mayo Clinic. He and his chief, Waltman Walters, wrote a definitive book on cancer of the stomach. Gossip was that Everett wrote the entire book. He became a leading surgeon in Houston, president of the Hermann staff, the Harris County Cancer Society, and the County Medical Society. Like a surprising number of my colleagues, he died young. Abe Hauser taught me neurology in medical school and was practicing neurology and psychiatry when I came to Houston. He had three sons who became neurologists or psychiatrists. His son Harris trained at the Mayo Clinic and for a while was on our clinic staff.

Among the Mayo-trained doctors in Houston, I have already mentioned George Waldron, Tom Cronin, Everett Lewis, Oliver Gooch, Luke Vaughn, C. C. Shullenburger, Ben Wells, and Tom Van Zandt. Others were Hartman Kilgore, Fred Braasted, Louis Daily, Jeff Fatheree, Don Butler, and O. A. Fly. George Ehni trained in neurosurgery at the Mayo Clinic while I was there. He joined the Scott and White Clinic for a year, before coming to Houston in 1950. He eventually became chief of neurosurgery at M. D. Anderson, Methodist Hospital, and Baylor medical school, all at the same time. He was soon joined in practice by Milo Leavens, also Mayo-trained. Later came Herbert, Bill Seybold's brother, as a urologist, and Bob Moreton as a radiologist. Herman Shultz came as a dermatologist. Cowgill Usher, trained as a surgeon, practiced in Houston for a few years. Sam Haigler also trained in surgery, was a member of our journal club at Mayo before coming to Wharton to practice in the Rugeley Blassingame Clinic. He later moved to Denver. Highly regarded gynecologist E. D. Straussman trained at the Mayo Clinic before World War I. My classmate Mildred Cariker was on the gynecology staff at the Mayo Clinic, before coming to Houston to practice a few years, then moving to another location in East Texas. Luke Vaughn came to Houston to be chief of radiology at Hermann Hospital.

Medical friends other than Galveston graduates and Mayo alumni included Jack Staub. I met him during the war at the U.S. Naval Hospital in Washington, D.C., where he was a young naval officer and surgery resident under Frank Ashburn. Jack was the son of John Staub, the famous architect who designed the Cooke Wilson house in Beaumont. Jack was at our house often. He was a free spirit, deeply interested in tropical horticulture and Mexican folk culture, especially Mexican bands and music. Jack spent a great deal of time in the Mexican and Central American tropics collecting plants for cultivation in Houston. Jack was a board-certified general surgeon who became a member of the Magregor Clinic. He died rather suddenly of an overwhelming infection while fairly young.

There was the Daily family in ophthalmology, as well as Dick Leigh, Conrad Moore, Guy Knolle, Tom Royce, Ed Griffey, Tom Cloud, and R. M. Johnson from Paris, Texas. Dr. Everett L. Goar was the dean of ophthalmology, a nationally known leader in that field. Some of the old surgeons were still around: Drs. Flynn, Adam Boyd, John T. Moore, Herbert Poyner, and Hugh Welch. Other surgeons included Jim Pittman, a great friend who trained in Saint Louis and was surgical assistant to Evarts Graham in the first successful pneumonectomy in history. Jim Pittman was a leading surgeon at Hermann Hospital. A wonderful man, he took my brother John and me under his wing and helped us get established. Howard Barkley and Jed Daly were partners in chest surgery, Howard being chief of chest surgery at M. D. Anderson. Joe Gandy was chief of surgery at Southern Pacific Hospital. Dewey Tuttle did surgery at Methodist Hospital. Bromley Freeman was a plastic surgeon active at St. Luke's. Wade Harris was a competent proctologist and colon surgeon. Cecil Crigler had the largest urology practice at Hermann Hospital. He was famous for urethral dilation in female patients. His wife became a patient of mine. Cecil sent me many patients. Other urologists included Tobe Shearer, Max Goodloe, Mike O'Heeron, Ty Robinson and Abel Leader.[11]

Among the Houston orthopedists I became close friends with was F. O. McGehee. He was very active in fund raising and as chief of orthopedics at St. Luke's. Duncan McKeever, another orthopedist, had a huge practice doing spinal fusions. This procedure fell into disrepute, although it is being revived for selected cases. Duncan's life ended tragically. He was driving home from the hospital one night, when his car went dead on Allen Parkway. He got out to check and was struck by another car. Bruce Cameron happened by at the time and found him in extremis, his abdomen ruptured and his bowels extruded. He died before anything could be done. Other orthopedists were Arthur Glassman, Bill Burdeaux, Kenneth Duff, Alex Brodsky, and Ben Kitchen.

Kenneth Von Pohle and Al Calhoun were among the Houston gynecologists and obstetricians. Denton Kerr was the first chief of gynecology at St. Luke's. Art Faris, Jimmy Clapp, Stanley Rogers, and Ruth Heartgraves were other gynecologist-obstetricians. Herman Johnson had just retired from practice with Robert Johnston to spend full-time as department chief at Baylor. Seward Wills followed Herman Johnson at Baylor. I remember driving to Baytown one night with Seward and Jim Greenwood and Bill Palm to address a staff meeting. Seward, a graduate of Tulane medical school, told the story of the assassination of Louisiana governor Huey Long. Some members of the medical profession in New Orleans had developed a great animosity for Governor Long. Long had diverted support from the Tulane medical school to one of his pet projects, the new Louisiana State University medical school in Baton Rouge. A conspiracy to assassinate Governor Long developed among several doctors. They drew straws to see who would do the job. Carl Weiss drew the fatal straw and, in carrying out his mission, was killed on the spot by the governor's bodyguards.

Dan McNamara came as chief cardiologist at Texas Children's Hospital. He and Earl Beard organized the cardiac catheterization laboratory at Texas Children's Hospital. Laura Bickel was a fine pediatrician who treated our children. We were friends of her brother Bill, an orthopedist at Mayo. She was active in the new Texas Children's Hospital. Other pediatricians were Byron York, Ed Fitch, Layne Mitchell, Allan Bloxsom, George Salmon, and Frank Glenn. Fred Taylor taught pediatrics at Baylor and joined the Kelsey-Seybold Clinic for a time. Russell Blattner was chief of Texas Children's Hospital for years before retiring. Other pediatricians I knew and liked were Martha and Ellard Yow, Jack Hild, M. D. Burnett, Frank Windrow, and Bob Gardner. I spent a lot of time with George Clayton, chief of endocrinology at Texas

Children's. George trained under Lawson Wilkins at Johns Hopkins. Wilkins led George to a false belief that boys and girls were identical in growth and behavior until puberty, when hormones developed their different features and behavior. We argued this. I maintained that boys and girls behaved differently from the day they were born. To my way of thinking, pediatricians are the finest people in the medical profession. Obstetricians come next.

Among the Houston general practitioners I knew and who referred patients to me was Cecil Jorns, an outstanding man, who became president of the Academy of General Practice and of the Harris County Medical Society. Lynn Zarr and Lynn Bourden at the Heights Hospital also referred patients. John Mecom's brother-in-law Henry Withers was another general practitioner. I took care of several in the Mecom family. Jack Brannon was a friend. He and Ed Smith were doctors for the Rice football team. Jack was active in the Foreign Counseler Corps. Other general practitioners were George Gatura, Lucian Bukowski, Irving Meisler, George Merriman, John Nichols, and the Sammons brothers from Baytown. James Sammons became executive vice president of the American Medical Association.

I soon knew most of the internists in Houston. As one, I'm admittedly biased when I say the Houston internists were an outstanding group who practiced by the highest professional and ethical standards. Since Houston was booming with plenty of patients to share, we had no bitter competition. There were several small practice groups of internists. I have already described the group headed by Paul and Abbe Ledbetter. M. D. Levy, his son Moise, Jr., and sons-in-law Leonard Robbins and Dr. Malawitz had a very active practice. Fred Lummis and Charles Reece were practicing in a group, which became the Diagnostic Clinic. Alvis Greer and Gomoets had a small clinic. Ralph Bowen had a practice in allergy. His assistant, John McGovern, developed the practice into a major allergy clinic. John was a great scholar of Sir William Osler. I invited him to join our clinic, but he had greater goals of his own and became a very wealthy man, making large contributions to several medical institutions. Another group of internists grew into the Medical Clinic of Houston, which included E. L. Wagner, Rugeley Livesay, Bill Baird, and Charley Armburst.

Ben Smith was one of the most interesting internists in the city. He must have been sixty-five years old when I arrived and was especially interested in treating diabetic and heart patients. He was very thorough and meticulous. He imparted the same self-discipline to his diabetics: one should live an orderly life and measure one's food carefully, adjust one's insulin dosage, and keep one's urine sugar-free. Such a program goes a long way in preventing complications. Dr. Smith must have had the first electrocardiogram machine in Houston. It was a string galvanometer type, a huge affair in a well-polished mahogany box occupying most of a small room. He handled it with tender loving care, and it produced exquisite tracings. Oddly, he was killed one night when he must have fallen asleep while driving down to West Columbia.[12]

Some of the out-of-town doctors who favored me with referrals while I was in solo practice were: Bing Blassingame, Jim Little, Vernon Black and Sam Haigler from the Rugeley Blassingame Clinic in Wharton, Walt Haskall and his father, Dr. Haskall, Dr. Shoenvogel and Dr. Giddings from a practice that became the Brenham Clinic, and Beaumont doctors John Hart, Jay Crager, Bob Stevens, H. B. Barr, Peel Allison, M. E. Suehs, and Lamar Bevil. Old-time AKK brother S. D. Coleman sent patients from Navasota. Hamlin K. McWilliams of Waller and Dr. Walker of Hempstead sent patients. Later, Bill Seybold performed surgery in the Hempstead hospital on a regular basis. Hamlin and his wife, Byrnne, became friends and patients and were very nice to our boys. Bob Kimbrough, a Galveston collegemate, sent patients from Cleburne and eventually started his own clinic. Sam Barnes sent numerous patients from Trinity. C. H. Dolph, an otolaryngologist at Baytown, sent patients. Harold High of Cuero sent patients and became a great friends with members of our clinic, especially with John Kelsey, Jim McMurrey, and Don Pranke, who hunted quail with him in Cuero.

Mike DeBakey came to Houston a few months before I did. We were friends and sent patients to each other. When he operated on a patient of mine he always called and told me what was done. That was when he was building his practice. We went to his house a few times. Soon after I came to Houston, Denton Cooley came to town to enter practice as an associate of Mike DeBakey. Dr. Bertner, who was a family friend of the Cooleys, introduced me to Denton. Denton's rise was meteoric. He and Mike soon fell out, and Denton moved from Methodist to St. Luke's Hospital.[13] Denton sent his mother to me as a patient. I had a good relationship with Denton and our clinic sent him hundreds of patients. Early in Denton's practice I sent him a patient for an abdominal operation. The patient was originally referred to me by Ted Hannon, the gynecologist. When Ted heard about it, he called and questioned me about sending his former patient to a young untried surgeon who claimed to be a cardiovascular surgeon. Denton had told me he was a general as well as a cardiovascular surgeon. I reassured Ted. Denton's operation was successful. I'm sure Denton would have been just as great a doctor, if he had chosen general surgery to the exclusion of heart surgery—a field in which he stands as a pioneer.

Many of my early patients referred by Dr. Bertner remained patients of the clinic. Several are still patients. One even later married into my family: John and Margaret Heinzerling became patients, and their daughter Ann married my son Tom. Judge and Mrs. Freeman and their family became friends and patients. Judge Freeman served as principal lawyer for the Kelsey and Wilson families as well as the Kelsey, Seybold and Leary partnership. He and his firm continued for many years as lawyers for our clinic. He told me that the Fulbright, Crooker, Freeman and Bates law firm went for years without a written partnership agreement. He gave us advice for many months yet sent no bills. When I inquired, he said our partners had done so much for the Medical Center that he would not charge us. In later years we were charged regular fees.

Mary and I spent much time with Bishop Quin and his wife, Hortense. Clinton S. Quin came to Houston in 1917 from Paducah, Kentucky. At one time he was a professional baseball player. The Quins were my patients until I retired. They had three married children and several grandchildren. One day I walked out to the waiting room to find four generations of Quins; Hortense Quin with daughter Derby along with grandson Quin, who came with his children, not knowing Mrs. Quin and Derby would be there.

Bishop Quin was a tall, hale and hearty man who could be quite brusque. Once, an Episcopal priest in East Texas called and asked the bishop if he could bury a Baptist. "Bury all you can!" was the bishop's reply. He called Catholics "Romans." "All Christians are catholics" he said. Every day that Bishop Quin was in town he called on patients in the hospitals. I frequently saw him on his rounds and persuaded him to call on some of my patients and offer a prayer. One patient was a country preacher. He didn't like Bishop Quin's prayer. "It wasn't devout enough." The bishop was devout but not obsequious to the Lord or anybody else. The bishop referred several Episcopal priests and their families to me. He retired to a cottage in Richmond, Texas, where he died from throat cancer. After his death, John Hines became bishop of the Texas diocese in 1955. I knew his brother Ed on the staff of the Mayo Clinic. I soon became friends of the new bishop and doctor to some of his family. In 1964, John Hines became the presiding bishop of the Episcopal Church in America.

Our friends the Wests also became patients. Wesley introduced me to his brother Jim "Silver Dollar" West, a very likeable person and one of the most eccentric people I've ever met. A graduate of the University of Texas School of Law, he spent much of his time on his numerous hobbies. He carried pockets full of silver dollars which he threw out for children to scramble over. Once he threw about forty in his swimming pool for our boys to dive for. They recovered all of them and took them home. His Chupadero ranch house near Carrizo Springs on the Rio Grande had one dollar slot machines for guests to play. Jim provided the dollars. The machines were set for the players to win. On the ranch were many blue quail, which we hunted. Jim West had a mild diabetes I treated for many months. I put him in Hermann Hospital. He installed an aerial on the hospital roof so he could communicate by radio from his hospital room. He liked the hospital and kept a room there for years, or long after I was no longer his doctor. He employed Aggie Greer as a full time nurse. Aggie later became my office nurse. After his death, a truck load of silver dollars was removed from his basement.

Jack Grindlay at the Mayo Clinic referred Noble Means from East Bernard, Texas. Noble and his wife, Maxine, became close friends. Bill Leary and I and our sons hunted doves, ducks, and geese on the Means's several farms and ranches. We often stayed overnight at their house in order to be up and in the field hunting before daylight. Noble had suffered a stroke, which affected his speech and walking, but he could drive a car on their ranch roads while we sat in the back seat and shot doves on the barbed wire fences—an illegal activity done only when no game wardens were in sight. After Noble died, Maxine became a trustee of the Kelsey-Leary Foundation, later the Kelsey-Seybold Foundation. She was very generous and also raised money for the Foundation. She owned a Chevrolet agency where I bought a Corvette. I heard that she ran East Bernard's bank and also its Methodist Church, which was next door to her house. I also remember Frank Buck who captured wild animals all over the world for zoos. He wrote *Bringing Em Back Alive* and gave our boys a copy. Buck would not be very popular today, considering the animal rights movement and the realization that many species are becoming endangered or extinct.

Our family life was hectic in 1949 and 1950. Although Mary had help, she still had four little boys to take care of. John, Cooke, and Tom were delivered to and from River Oaks Elementary every school day. Mavis, Jr., was taken to kindergarten. Helping the kids with their homework wasn't as difficult as keeping them on the books. Mary got the boys dressed and to Sunday School, but church going didn't take. Mischief rises geometrically with the number of boys you have. We gave the boys a chemistry set for them to learn some elementary chemistry. They were soon making explosives. The neighborhood druggist called me and asked why the boys were buying all that saltpeter. I got to them in time to avert a major pipe bomb explosion. Colonel William Bates and his wife, Mary, and their two daughters were our next door neighbors. They were very kind to us, and we became good friends. Our friendship with the Bates family was tested, however, when someone broke out about thirty small window panes in their garage. Mrs. Bates thought the breakage occurred on a certain date. Mary and I were greatly relieved because our family was down at the beach at that time. A little research however proved that the mischief was done on another day by the Kelsey boys. They fessed up and apologized to the Bates. We replaced the lights, and the Bates continued to remain warm friends. We had a slide and a trampoline in the back yard. In April 1950, Mavis, Jr., fell off the slide and broke his arm. Fortunately, it healed with no deformity or disability. A lot of other things went on I never heard about.

During the next few years, we sent the boys to summer camps: Camp Arrowhead in East Texas, Camp Rio Vista in the Hill Country, a camp in Wisconsin, a camp in New Mexico, and one in Colorado. LeCaprice, the beach house at Caplen on Bolivar Peninsula, was a godsend. Mary spent a month to six weeks there with the children each summer. I tried to get down on weekends. The boys learned to swim, fish in the surf, and go crabbing in Trinity Bay. We built a platform and put it in the surf in front of the house for them to fish from. The boys seined for crabs and shrimp and trout. Everyone liked to collect shells. Over time, hundreds of fine shells were accumulated and placed on every table in the house, and we had a glass case to exhibit the very rare specimens. The beach was virtually abandoned during the winter. We started going to the beach house during the Christmas holidays and had a great time. The beach was loaded with beautiful shells that had washed up and accumulated while the beachcombers were gone for the winter. The commercial fishermen provided fat oysters during the winter. A breakfast of a dozen fried oysters was hard to beat.

The children slept under many blankets in the swinging beds on the porches. Leona made deviled crab—one of the best dishes I have ever eaten. Almost as good was the gumbo, which was full of oysters, shrimp, and crabmeat. We often ate the shrimp and crabs out of the shell, smearing our hands, face, and laps with gumbo. For a few summers, Mary's mother kept a motorboat in a nearby slip on the intracoastal canal. It slept a few people. We could sail it into the bay to fish, crab, and flounder. Mary's brother Waldo had a house of his own on the grounds. LeCaprice was a meeting place for all the family. I remember many happy days there.

We have always been big on family parties at Thanksgiving and Christmas. After returning to Texas we were able to join our families in Beaumont or Deport, or they came to Houston. Another annual family event was the gathering in Deport for the opening of the dove hunting season. My brother-in-law Marvin Gibbs was a great hunter. We had our own fields to hunt, but Marvin also located maize fields, goat weed patches, and water holes all over Lamar and Red River Counties. We hunted several locations each season and always got our limit. We plucked the birds while we sat under a shade tree waiting for more to fly into range. At night we feasted on fried doves with hot homemade biscuits and cream gravy. Marvin's son Kelsey, John's sons John and Bob, and our boys learned to be good hunters.

Our life became fairly well established during these first two years: school, Cub Scouts, neighborhood friends, boys' pranks, summer at Bolivar Peninsula, family gatherings, boys at summer camp, and church. Mary spent her time as a mother directing all these events, keeping house, and developing our social life in Houston. She was an unsung heroine—she ran the family and made it a true family. Mary could have had a fine business career. She was financially able to have a life of play and self-indulgence. Mary chose to marry and spend her life devoted to a family. She made our home.

CHAPTER 13

Kelsey, Seybold, and Leary Partnership, 1950–53

Much of my practice was neither exciting nor challenging. Many people had minor complaints or uninteresting problems such as irritable bowel, constipation, flatulence, gaseous eructations or belching, insomnia, minor headaches, bad colds, body odor, sun burn, flat feet, halitosis, snoring, wet dreams, crabs, hot flashes, vaginal discharge, penile discharge, bad grades in school, marital infidelity, backaches, bursitis, and drinking problems. Practicing medicine required a lot of patience and compassion.

My practice was growing, albeit slowly. My correspondence with future partners Bill Seybold and Bill Leary in Rochester shows that establishing a practice was a roller-coaster ride. On February 4, 1949, I wrote that I had not collected a penny since arriving. In those days, no respectable doctor would demand payment when seeing a patient. It was indiscreet to tell a patient how much an examination would cost. Some patients considered it an insult. "Send me a bill," they said. I soon learned that many would never pay. Very few patients offered to pay cash. After I moved into my own office on March 15, 1949, monthly bookings gradually increased, but I still had plenty of time to watch the construction of the Rice stadium from my twelfth floor office window.[1]

In May of that year, I collected $2,200 from practice and from the M. D. Anderson Hospital salary. My part-time job at M. D. Anderson paid $600 a month. In a few months I reduced my hours and was paid $400 a month. I was discouraged. I had spent $25,000 and was $15,000 in debt, not counting the note on our house. I had spent our meager savings. By the end of July, 30 percent of my patients were from out of town. I had a fair number of thyroid patients coming in as a result of my connection with M. D. Anderson and the radioiodine laboratory. I called it the radioiodine laboratory instead of the nuclear medicine laboratory, because radioiodine was virtually the only radioisotope in clinical use. I was also a consultant at Ellington Field to bring in a little additional money. On October 22, 1949, however, I wrote that practice was going well. At the end of my first year I had seen six hundred new patients. On January 6, 1950, I reported in correspondence that I was occupied full time with the practice. I was very busy at M. D. Anderson and had more than I could handle in my office. I was looking for an assistant and needed more office space. I thought I would be making a profit from then on. But we owed $75,000, including the house note, and my practice for 1949 showed a net loss of $19,000.

In early March 1950, I wrote of tentative plans to organize a diagnostic group. I was eager to establish a larger practice to provide surgery referrals to Bill Seybold when he arrived. While I worked part time at Anderson on Baldwin Street, Cleon Shullenberger, Cliff Howe, and I often had lunch at the nearby Old Mexico Restaurant. We had several enthusiastic discussions about forming a diagnostic group. Shully, working part time at Anderson, had developed some private practice. Cliff would resign as chief of medicine at Anderson to join. All of us hoped to continue part time at M. D. Anderson. Shully had an office in the Hermann Professional Building with Jeff Fatheree. We trained with Jeff at the Mayo Clinic. Jeff would do our gastroenterologic radiology and consults. There were two or three other doctors we intended to invite into the group. Although I had been so busy the previous three months that I needed an assistant, when I next wrote Bill Seybold I reported that practice was slow. As the size of my practice fluctuated, so too did my plans. If I hadn't committed myself so deeply to Seybold and Leary I might have given up our goal. About this time, Lee Clark asked me to become chief of medicine at Anderson. I considered the offer, but Cliff was my friend, and we were talking about forming a clinic. I also thought Cliff was taking too big a risk giving up his job as chief to enter private practice, and I didn't want to leave my practice. We cooled off promoting the diagnostic group.

In April 1950, I booked $2,800 and was away for about ten days at meetings. I reported bookings for May of $3,400 plus $400 in salary and was away three days for the state medical society meeting. I decided to stay close by my practice for the rest of the year. I reduced my fees and worked hard to bring in more patients, even if a $3.00 office visit called for a general examination. One lady complained when I sent her a bill for $10.00 for an hour-and-a-half examination. She wrote that she had never paid more than $5.00 for an examination. I called her to explain that she had received a thorough and lengthy examination. She hadn't thought about it that way, but insisted that $5.00

was enough to pay for seeing a doctor, never mind what he did. Anyway, she was pleased with my explanation and continued as my patient.[2]

My practice was good in June 1950, by which time I had seen more than a thousand new patients. Patients would come after two or three friends recommended me. I began to realize the importance of becoming well-known. For that month I collected $3,647.18 plus $400 for work at Anderson and Ellington Field. I had greatly reduced my time at Anderson. Overhead for June was $1500, leaving more than $2,000 profit, my best month in practice to that point—and better than most internists were doing. Now, this might be around $6,000, a paltry sum for today's internists.

By mid-August, I was complaining again about how slow practice was, as were all my friends who said this was a seasonal slump. But things picked up. August bookings totaled $4,319.80, of which only $128.50 was cash—illustrating how very few patients paid cash. Receipts for the month were $2,920.20 and I had registered 1,190 patients. I had patient appointments filled for several days ahead. I had ten very sick patients in the hospital and several sick at home. Next time I wrote to Bill, I predicted that I soon wouldn't have anything to do and would be complaining about how poor practice was. At the end of my second year, my total receipts were over $47,000, and my income from practice was around $20,000.

A few months earlier, in the spring of 1950, Bill Seybold and Bill Leary had visited Houston, and, possibly as a result of my enthusiasm, had made the final decision to resign from the Mayo Clinic and join me in practice. We had been discussing future practice together on and off since the summer of 1941, after Seybold arrived in Rochester, Minnesota, to begin his fellowship at the Mayo Clinic. We would now dedicate our efforts to develop a general clinic. From then on, until the time they arrived, I made a point of telling my patients about my partners-to-be. I talked about them in glowing terms. I was not exaggerating; they were two of the finest doctors I knew or ever would know.

William Dempsey Seybold was born in Temple, Texas, on February 15, 1915. His father was a banker who died before I had a chance to meet him. Bill's mother, Lillian, was a fine lady who became our friend. Bill studied premedical subjects at the University of Texas at Austin for two years before entering the University of Texas Medical School in Galveston. He was awarded a Bachelor of Science Degree in Medicine from the University in 1936. He obtained his M.D. degree in 1938 and was inducted into Alpha Omega Alpha (AOA), the honor medical fraternity. His fellowship at the Mayo Clinic was interrupted by the war, and he served in the navy from October 1944 to July 1946. He was appointed to the surgical staff at Mayo in 1947 as instructor in sur-

Dr. William D. Seybold, 1954

gery. After three years on the Mayo staff he resigned to enter private practice with me and Bill Leary in Houston, Texas.

Besides his desire to enter private practice, Bill Seybold was influenced by his wife, Frances, who had developed multiple sclerosis and wanted to be with her family in Texas. Warm weather was supposed to lessen the ravages of multiple sclerosis, and Bill would not hesitate to sacrifice his career for Frances's betterment. Frances was a cultivated, beautiful, brilliant woman.[3] Bill and Frances had three children: William Rather, Randolph Cochran, and Frances Rather. I was named godfather to little Francie. After the war, when Bill and I returned to complete our Mayo fellowships, our families became close.

William Vincent Leary was born June 13, 1913, in Owatonna, Minnesota, the son of Vincent P. and Eleanor Gunhilde Leary. His parents were of Irish and Scandinavian descent, as were many Minnesotans. Bill was born with a good sense of humor. He worked in his father's men's clothing store and learned how to dress well. He went to Carleton College and learned how to write and speak well. He graduated AOA from the University of Minnesota Medical School, one of the best in America and interned at Anker Hospital, an affiliate of Minnesota University. He entered a fellowship in medicine at the Mayo Clinic in 1939. Bill was a man-about-town in Rochester. He and I soon became friends and with several other fellows joined to form a journal club. We met each week to sharpen our diagnostic skills by studying the clinical and pathologic case reports published weekly in the *New England Journal of Medicine*. Bill and I tended to drink too much when we'd get together at night to discuss medicine. On more than one occasion, we talked all night and went to work the next day without any sleep. Bill saw wartime duty in Cirencester,

Dr. William V. Leary, 1954

England, at a U.S. Army hospital. He had married Margaret (Muggs) Pierson in Portland, Oregon, just after the Japanese attacked Pearl Harbor.[4] Bill and Muggs had four children: Michael William, Jean Margaret (for whom I was named godfather), Stephen P., and Margaret Wells.

Bill Leary and Bill Seybold had a close professional relationship. Both were interested in chest diseases and served together on the same hospital services, including Herman Moersch's service, where they learned endoscopy. Seybold trained as a general surgeon and specialized in chest surgery. Leary trained as an internist, with a subspecialty in diseases of the chest.

As my practice was growing the prospects for starting a clinic increased. I inquired of many people, including Drs. Bertner, Clark, and others about whether different specialists who depended on doctor referrals could join together without losing a lot of referrals. They approved, but several surgeons said they would not send us patients if we had a surgeon, because they depended on referrals from internists to whom they referred patients. Internists also would not be sending Seybold referrals, since he could not reciprocate, because his partners were internists. When Seybold, Leary, and I joined practice, we would have to depend on referrals from patients and friends, from out-of-town doctors with whom we didn't compete, and from some general practitioners.

In spite of this obstacle, we believed we could build a practice. I went back to Rochester once or twice and we discussed our project at great length. The Seybolds and Learys came down to Houston in March 1950 to review the situation. I remember well when they came. The Wesley Wests entertained us and encouraged us, and Seybold and Leary interviewed some people in Houston. We talked and talked until our guests almost missed their plane back to Rochester. Only in the last few minutes did both Bills commit themselves to moving. They submitted their resignations from the Mayo Clinic as soon as they got back to Rochester.

During this planning stage, we three carried on an extensive correspondence involving long discussions about income distribution while our practice was building. Bill Seybold offered a formula by which a certain base income would always be shared equally while the remainder would be based on production. The Kelsey-Seybold Clinic used this basic formula for many years. As we accepted younger doctors and turned some of our own practice over to them, we added a seniority benefit based on the number of years a doctor had been at the clinic. During the many years I was in the clinic, the pay distribution committee had a difficult job of making everyone happy. There has never been a perfect way for partners to share their joint profits. The greatest variant is the human element: no one ever feels he gets what he deserves. Some are more insistent in their demands than others.

As I read the correspondence with Leary and Seybold written nearly fifty years ago, I am impressed by the risks we took. Each gave up a comfortable job, leaving a secure position in Rochester for a risky undertaking in Houston. Seybold's fabulous appointment to the Mayo surgical staff was the envy of nearly every surgeon in America. Leary was highly regarded by his Mayo colleagues. Periods of exhilarating enthusiasm alternated with periods of painful uncertainty. I like to think we had great courage, but there were moments of great doubt.

Francie Seybold and Jean Leary were born during this period. We missed our annual Thanksgiving and Christmas parties together. Our letters from this time discuss our friends and those we left behind in Rochester—the Comforts, Hallenbecks, Haines, Keatings, Clagetts, Coventrys, Cains, Logans, and Donaghues—to mention a few. We mentioned the support of our Texas friends and families, particularly Tommy and Helen Anderson, Neva and Wesley West, Dr. and Mrs. E. W. Bertner, Mrs. Florence Rather, and Fay and Jamie Griffith. We sought the advice of Mr. Harry Harwick, the business manager of the Mayo Clinic, as well as Drs. "Tack" Harrington, Herb Schmidt, Larry Randall, Al Goode, Phil Hench, and Benjamin Spock. Meanwhile in Houston, Drs. E. W. Bertner, Mike DeBakey, Val Baird, Lee Clark, and many others were providing us much advice. We also discussed prospective partners for our clinic-to-be, including Tom Dry, Oliver Gooch, Pete Pierson, Jim Cain, Bill Dodge, Bruce Cameron, C. C. Shullenberger, Cliff Howe, and Lee Clark. We decided to follow Mr. Harwick's advice not to take additional partners until we were well established. We followed Wesley West's advice not to commit ourselves to a building. He told us to rent space, because half of all new partnerships did not work out. He also pointed out that we didn't have the money to finance a building.

We became entangled in the red tape of medical practice requirements, obtaining medical licenses, as well as membership in the county medical society and appointments to hospital staffs and the Baylor faculty. We corresponded extensively on several other issues, ranging from the purchase of instruments and office supplies, to appropriate stationary, letterheads, and announcements. We discussed insurance agents, accountants, lawyers, partnership agreements, and pay distribution. In the middle of our efforts to join in practice, however, the Korean War was getting underway. There was much talk about a doctor draft, of calling up doctors who had experience in World War II or were in the inactive reserve. This created quite a bit of apprehension at a vulnerable time for us. I was in debt up to my neck. My practice and finances would be wrecked if I were called into service. I had the right to resign from the Medical Corps Reserve, but my requests had brought no response from Washington. I called Senator Lyndon Johnson, whom I had met several times through the Wesley Wests. I asked him if he could help me resign my commission. A few days later I received a telegram from Lyndon saying that my resignation had been accepted. This was a lucky stroke. Soon after, I received a telephone call from the air surgeon's office and was told to come back on duty to edit a medical journal like the one I had edited in World War II. My orders would be forthcoming. I said I was no longer a reserve officer. The air surgeon's office had not learned of my resignation. I told them to look it up. I never heard from them again.

After years of planning, discussions, false starts, and some doubts, we finally joined in a partnership practice in Houston. Seybold joined me on October 1, 1950, Leary three months later on January 1, 1951. When Bill and Frances Seybold moved to Houston they were welcomed by their numerous friends, especially the University of Texas and Austin crowd, spearheaded by the Tommy Andersons. Many parties were given for the couple after their arrival. They bought a house in Royden Oaks, on Wickersham. Many Texas doctors already knew Bill. Frances was a college beauty and was invited to Hollywood as a starlet but had fled from there within a few days when she saw the life she'd have to lead. Bill and Frances were soon introducing us to their friends.

In mid-October 1950, three weeks after Seybold had left Rochester for Houston, Leary wrote, "I am eagerly awaiting with bated breath the report of any progress that you two are making." Seybold replied that things were lining up well at M. D. Anderson with Lee Clark, and he listed several major operations he had performed. Seybold's letter of November 3 told Leary about performing more major surgery and his favorable reaction to the Houston Tuberculosis Hospital and the Veterans Administration Hospital. Some people down here were just as smart as those at Mayo. There had been a blue norther through Houston, with everyone shivering at 45 degrees. I was late coming in and Bill was going to reprimand me!

The Learys arrived during the Christmas holidays. They stayed at our house a few days awaiting their household goods. The Seybolds and Kelseys took them to Christmas parties where they were introduced to most of our friends. The Griffiths and others soon befriended them. The Learys were delighted with southern hospitality and impressed with Texas brags and how big everything in Texas was. One morning we were at the breakfast table when our sons' box turtle came waddling into the room. "What's this, a Texas cockroach!" exclaimed Muggs. It would not do to tell what Bill said when he took a large bite from his first jalapeno. Bill and Muggs both had a lot of wit. Bill and Muggs were soon installed in their house at 3208 Locke Lane, which was in our neighborhood. They sent their children to River Oaks Elementary School with the Seybold and Kelsey children and later to St. John's Episcopal.

Leary had a close relationship with me as a fellow internist and a close relationship with Seybold as a fellow pulmonary specialist. In addition to his knowledge of pulmonary problems Leary was a fine cardiologist. I had been trained in gastroenterology and endocrinology including gynecologic endocrinology. For an internist, I had more than the usual training and experience in neurology and psychiatry. Seybold was a good general doctor as well as a surgeon. We were able to treat a wide variety of patients. We felt free to treat anything we knew to treat. Specialization had not yet become so restrictive that you had to send a right-thumb problem to a right-thumb specialist.

Lee Clark gave Seybold and Leary part-time jobs at M. D. Anderson. Both Bills were soon accepted on Houston hospital staffs. I had two fine partners. Both were among the top in their class at medical school. They received the finest training. They were certified by the American Boards in their specialty. They were mature and experienced and had already developed good reputations. They were fair, scrupulously honest, and totally without deceit. They were kind and compassionate. Seybold was smoother in handling patients, while Leary compensated with his wit. Both were totally dedicated to the practice of medicine and stayed abreast of new developments. They got along well with their colleagues. They were industrious and unselfish and willingly shared in our work load.

We did have our differences. Seybold was more conservative than I, less impulsive, not such a promoter. He gave things more thought before acting. He was more modest. When we had differences, he was more often right. I had more ideas, both right and wrong. Leary was more amiable, less determined to have his way. His frank honesty cost him some patients, but many were undyingly supportive; they loved him for his sincerity, compassion, and wit. The three of us had faults. I often failed to see mine.

While Seybold was admired for his remarkable surgical talent and general knowledge of medicine, his admirers were not very eager to send him patients. After all, he was in partnership with two internists and was not likely to refer his patients to other internists. Surgeons were reluctant to send patients to Leary and me, because we sent our patients to our partner, Bill Seybold. This made practice slow. We expected this.

A medical practice is not only oriented to the money that could be made by referring patients back and forth. Doctors must work together with their patients. Reputable doctors do not refer patients to specialists they do not consider to be capable. Doctors want their patients well cared for when they are referred. Bad referrals can damage a doctor's reputation. The patient's welfare is the goal of any reputable doctor. If the patient has a problem that can be cured by a certain specialist, the good doctor will refer him to that specialist regardless of whether he will get referrals in return. General practitioners depend on referrals from patients and friends, not doctors. They feel free to refer patients to specialists regardless of their associations. For this reason our partnership received many referrals from general practitioners.

During our partnership we held various part-time jobs, some with pay, some volunteer. All three of us were on the faculty of the Post Graduate School of Medicine of the University of Texas. We participated in its programs for years. From 1951 to 1954, I was acting dean of the school on two different occasions. The school was a noble effort which never fully achieved its original goals, however. In January 1947 the University of Texas committed itself to a preceptorial training center that was to operate a postgraduate school of medicine. The school came to be called the Post Graduate School of Medicine of the University of Texas. Since M. D. Anderson Hospital and the Dental College ran statewide programs, the Post Graduate School of Medicine was also to become statewide for undergraduate, graduate, and postgraduate medical education.

Faculty members were chosen from the Texas Medical Center. Lee Clark was appointed acting dean and professor of surgery. A full-time director was authorized on September 16, 1949, and M. D. Anderson was designated as a teaching hospital for the school. This provided much-needed faculty appointments for the Anderson staff. They served as professors in many of the postgraduate school programs, which included courses, symposia, and seminars pertaining to oncology and other areas of medical study. For years, the Post Graduate School was the principal teaching facility at M. D. Anderson.

Since I was a staff member of M. D. Anderson Hospital, I was appointed an associate professor in internal medicine as part of the original faculty. The board of regents appointed Dr. Jack Ewalt the first full-time dean of the Post Graduate School of Medicine. Before becoming dean, Jack was on the faculty in the department of psychiatry at the Medical Branch in Galveston. He moved to Houston with his secretary, Miss Jacqueline McCord. Jacky spent the remainder of her career with the school even after it was converted, years later, to the School of Biomedical Science. Jack Ewalt was a very effective person. He quickly organized the school and appointed a functioning faculty. He engaged the faculty in a number of postgraduate teaching programs at M. D. Anderson and other hospitals and in county and district medical societies. During this time the Academy of Family Practice was getting established statewide and the Post Graduate School of Medicine provided numerous refresher courses to these doctors.

On November 30, 1951, Jack Ewalt resigned to become health commissioner for the State of Massachusetts. That month, I attended a meeting of the University of Texas board of regents. Chancellor Hart recommended my name to the board as acting dean of the school, starting in December. The regents approved my appointment. I was assigned Ewalt's task of coordinating postgraduate efforts between the medical units of the university.

Most of the early planners of the Texas Medical Center and the Post Graduate School of Medicine had been to the Mayo Clinic as patients. They wanted something similar to the Mayo Clinic—multiple operations combined as a single unit, possibly with the Texas Medical Center Trustees overseeing the whole. They had no idea how improbable it would be to meld all these into one unit. These deans were to meet once a year and coordinate their postgraduate programs (which meant their residency programs). An affiliation and exchange program and a record keeping program were to be organized. Residents in all units would be required to register through the Post Graduate School of Medicine. To me this looked like red tape on top of red tape. I did manage to establish the framework of coordinating deans, all of whom I already knew as friends. They accepted the rulings of the regents reluctantly. We even tried to get Baylor's medical school involved. Baylor was willing if the Texas legislature was going to appropriate large sums for the program. Fortunately, this elaborate program never got underway.

A good thing did happen with the program of teaching practicing doctors. They welcomed our efforts. During the two terms I served as acting dean, divisions were established in Corpus Christi, Tyler, Lubbock, Amarillo, San Angelo, El Paso, and Temple (at Scott and White). St. Joseph's, Memorial, and Southern Pacific Hospitals became affiliated in Houston. We also instituted a teaching program and a free cancer consultation program at the two Houston hospitals for African Americans. Contracts were let with Lackland Field Air Force Base and Randolph Field Air Force Base. Otis Benson, a friend from the war, was commanding officer of the School of Aviation Medicine at Randolph Field. He flew me to Randolph to give lectures at the school.

I was among those who appeared before the Legislative Appropriations Committee in Austin to appeal for funds to develop the Post Graduate School. The efforts to take over graduate medical education in the state had created much opposition, and most legislators wanted to close the school. Finally, they made a small appropriation which would get us off their backs while starving us out. The M. D. Anderson Foundation again came to the aid of the Post Graduate School and kept it going.

The university hired a full-time dean in 1952, but he proved to be a disappointment. Jacky McCord, the executive secretary, actually ran the school until

I was called again and accepted an appointment as acting dean on a part-time basis, starting June 1, 1953. She was a competent, dedicated, and loyal employee, without whom the Post Graduate School would have collapsed during those lean times. Eventually she was rewarded by promotion from secretary to administrative assistant. Jacky became my patient and good friend.[5] When I resumed, the school was still struggling in spite of a program that was enthusiastically received by the practicing doctors and strongly supported by the university and its board of regents. The school stayed alive by a measly $25,000 "revolving fund" from the state legislature; $50,000 a year from the M. D. Anderson Foundation; and $100,000 in tuition fees paid by doctors. In September 1953, the office was moved from the Hermann Professional Building to surplus space in the new Shriners Children's Hospital. Rent was $75.00 a month. Later we moved to the new Academy of Medicine (Jesse Jones Library) Building.

The Post Graduate School took me away from home and practice. I made numerous trips, on the weekends when I could arrange it, to Amarillo, Lubbock, Tyler, San Angelo, Austin, Corpus Christi, Temple, and El Paso, where we were organizing divisions. I often gave medical talks on these trips. I was also required to attend regents meetings every month. It was a privilege to attend these meetings. I'm sure I was looked upon as an upstart dean when compared to the seasoned people surrounding me, such as Chauncey Leake, who represented the medical school in Galveston. I must have been unbearably cocky, a real bore. Nevertheless, Chancellor James Hart became my lifetime friend.

The university was searching for a full-time dean. I heard that Grant Taylor had returned to Duke University after five years in Japan as director of the Atomic Bomb Casualty Commission. I wrote Taylor a letter telling him about the opportunities with the University of Texas in the Texas Medical Center. He soon interviewed with Lee Clark. He accepted, effective January 15, 1954, a joint appointment as dean and professor of pediatrics at the Post Graduate School of Medicine and chief of pediatrics at M. D. Anderson Hospital. My last act as dean was to accompany Grant Taylor to Temple and introduce him to the Scott and White staff. I remained on as voluntary assistant dean and clinical professor of medicine. I gradually reduced my activities there as my practice responsibilities became greater.

Grant and I became friends. He was a man of many talents—an administrator, a pediatrician, an oncologist, and a scholar. He was a kind and gentle person. Grant made many children happy while they spent their remaining days at Anderson Hospital. He organized many programs for the Post Graduate School and the School for Continuing Medical Education, which replaced the Post Graduate School. Grant stayed on the university staff as emeritus director until he was about ninety years old. Despite Grant's leadership, the Post Graduate School floundered. The state legislature made virtually no contributions to its running. In 1950–51, 366 doctors attended courses. The number increased each year. In 1955, the last year for which I have data, there were 2,600 attendees—36 from out of state for 32 different courses. The school was eventually converted to an education program for M. D. Anderson Hospital and renamed the University of Texas Graduate School of Biomedical Sciences, with a Division of Continuing Medical Education.[6]

Our 750 square feet of office space was adequate for the first two years of practice. When Seybold joined me in October 1950 there was still room. At least one of us was often out of the office in the hospital or on house calls. When Leary joined us in January 1951, however, we needed additional space. We obtained two rooms that adjoined from Bertner's office. These rooms became available after his death. Then, the Bills moved to available space on the third floor, a terribly unsatisfactory arrangement. We had poor communications, which I think played some part in Seybold's resignation from our partnership two years later. There were not yet sufficient surgical referrals for Seybold and he naturally became restless. As we had expected some internists told Bill they couldn't afford to send him patients.

In spite of local referral problems, our practice grew. Houston was booming. We were making a living—enough to support our families—from the time the Bills joined me in practice. We didn't turn anything down. Although we were trained as specialists, we did general practice, gynecology, insurance examinations, house calls, preschool exams, company medicine, minor surgery, major surgery, part-time work at M. D. Anderson Hospital, consultant work at Ellington Air Base Hospital, teaching at the Post Graduate School of Medicine—anything to make an honest dollar. Even though much of this practice seemed trivial, it lead to more practice and more referrals from patients. Referrals from out-of-town doctors gradually built up. Our Mayo friends sent us patients. We were seeing more and more specialty consultations and general examinations. Both Bills were doing more and more bronchoscopies and gastroscopies. We were reading our own chest X rays. Seybold's name was on more and more operating room schedules.

The majority of our patients received treatment in the fine new Hermann Hospital, which was across the street from our office. Most of the medical center property was still wooded, while the center hospitals were under construction. During 1951 and 1952, buildings were going up everywhere, including M. D. Anderson, Methodist, Texas Children's, St. Luke's and Shriners Children's Hospitals, and the Jesse Jones Library. Both Bills were very active in the Houston Tuberculosis Hospital and at the Veterans Hospital. We had occasional patients in each of the large Houston hospitals. All three of us were seeing patients at M. D. Anderson's temporary quarters on Baldwin Street. Patients still expected us to make house calls. We would go out and swab a throat, give a little bismuth and paregoric, rub on a little calamine, or wrap an ankle. We also had some dire emergencies, such as acute heart failure, exsanguinating hemorrhage, stroke, strangulated hernia, ruptured appendix—conditions often brought on by failure to see a doctor in time.

Seybold operated on just about every major problem. There was no 911 emergency phone number, and it was difficult to find an ambulance. Some funeral homes had ambulances, which were converted hearses. There was very little ambulance chasing. Ethical doctors, lawyers, and dentists did not advertise. The *Houston Post* was running full page ads by chiropractors. I complained to Governor Hobby about it, and he stopped printing the ads. Today, we are the guilty ones. I now see Kelsey-Seybold television and billboard advertisements regularly. Drs. Bertner and Steve Grant would turn over in their graves if they could see these changes. Home treatments of hemorrhoids, constipation, athletes foot, and female trouble were limited to one inch notices in the classifieds and were not found on prime-time television.

We had two groups of social friends—those in the medical profession and those who weren't. The majority of our medical friends were from M. D. Anderson.[7] Some of our patients and neighbors and people from church also became friends. Houston was a friendly town, without snobbishness among the old established families, even though people did like to brag about their Texas heritage. We mainly entertained in our homes with dinners and cocktail parties. Dinner parties were more formal then; the ladies got out all the silver and fine linens and served several courses.

We joined the Forest Club, where we spent a lot of time with our children in the swimming pool. We also entertained guests there. A few years later we joined the Houston Country Club. Mary played golf, but I had given up trying to play years ago. There were several dance clubs. The Caduces Club was a medical dance group we belonged to for a while. We were invited to join The Hundred Club, Terpsichore, and the Racket Club, where most of our friends belonged. Life was pleasant for the whole family. We did not foresee the tragedy that would befall us with the loss of our son Cooke in an auto accident.

In late 1952 Bill Seybold decided that it was best for him to go on his own. Being in practice with internists had greatly curtailed his referrals. We were planning to move out of the Hermann Professional Building to a building of our own on Travis Street. The move, Bill felt, might restrict his practice even more. He joined John Overstreet in an office in the Hermann Professional Building. Seybold's leaving was a disappointment, but Leary and I understood fully, and we had no hard feelings about it. We sent patients to Bill Seybold in his new office, and he sent patients to us.

CHAPTER 14

Kelsey-Leary Clinic Years, 1953–61

When Bill Seybold left, I had just completed my fourth year of practice in Houston. Leary's and my practice of internal medicine was thriving. We leased out the original office, and I moved down to the third floor with Leary. During this period our Mayo friend Cleon Shullenberger was on the staff at M. D. Anderson but had outside consulting privileges. We called on him frequently for hematology consults. Across the hall from our office was Jeff Fatheree, who had his own X-ray equipment, including a fluoroscope for gastrointestinal studies. He was soon performing our gastrointestinal X rays.

Leary and I were determined to start a clinic. To present such an image, we named our group The Kelsey Leary Clinic. On our staff were Mavis Kelsey and William Leary, with C. C. Shullenberger and Jefferson Fatheree as consultants. Dugan Drugs printed free prescription pads for "Kelsey and Leary Clinic." The simple name change worked. Patients congratulated us on starting a clinic and promised to refer others.

The office at 311 Hermann Professional Building served us as we continued to grow. Betty Zeigler joined us on January 15, 1954, as a receptionist-trainee but soon became office manager. Betty stayed with us until she retired and nursed us through many crises. I consider her one of my best friends and one of the most important persons in developing our clinic. Manager meant doing everything from cleaning examining rooms to ordering supplies. She and many other dedicated employees supported the doctors and kept the office open through internal storms, such as doctor disagreements, and external storms, such as Hurricane Carla in 1962.

Soon Leary and I were ready to take another internist. We had invited my brother John to join us even before he finished his training as a gastroenterologist at the Mayo Clinic. I think John believed that our practice in Houston

Dr. John R. Kelsey

was pretty shaky and that prospects seemed better in our home county at Paris, Texas. He entered the practice of internal medicine there in July 1951. He became part of the group that practiced at the Paris Sanitarium, although I think he and his wife, Mickey, were attracted to Houston, Mickey's hometown.

We arranged an interview with Belton Griffin from the Lahey Clinic in Houston in April 1953. The weekend before Belton came, I attended a Texas Mayo reunion at a guest ranch near Bandera. John was there, and I told him that we were to interview Belton Griffin the next day. We wanted John but he had to decide immediately or we would offer the job to Belton. John called me the night he returned to Paris from the Mayo reunion: he and Mickey had decided to join us in Houston. The next day, Leary and I met Griffin and told him that my brother had accepted and recommended that he apply at the Lummis and Reece partnership (today, the Diagnostic Clinic). Belton promptly accepted a position there. John joined us for the remainder of his career. He immediately bought a one-third interest in the partnership, paying part in cash and the remainder out of his pay distribution. John assumed his share of the work load and began bringing new patients to our fledgling clinic. He had been training himself in gastrointestinal fluoroscopy and took on this duty. He also performed all the proctoscopies. He worked at the V.A. Hospital to supplement our income. After he arrived, all three of us rotated taking care of our hospital service at Hermann.

We did not have a partnership agreement when John came. Since he had helped develop one for the medical group in Paris, he assumed a leading role in creating our first formal partnership agreement. It called for a waiting period of two years on the staff before a doctor became eligible for partnership if approved by all the partners. Judge John Freeman, our patient and friend, wrote our first partnership agreement in 1956.

My brother was born in Deport, on May 20, 1922. After graduating from Deport High School, he attended the University of Texas for his premedical training. John entered Baylor Medical College in Dallas, in September 1942, and was one of the students who moved from Dallas to Houston when Baylor relocated. In 1943, John was taken into the Army Specialized Training Program. This was a crash program, and John went to school seven days a week until he graduated from medical school, first in his class, in June 1945, two years and nine months after he began. While in medical school, in 1943 John met Margaret (Mickey) Wier, the daughter of Thomas and Eleanor Jones Wier. They married in March 1945. I was John's best man in their wedding. John and Mickey had four children: John Roger III (born October 8, 1947); Margaret Ann (March 18, 1949); Robert Wier (November 28, 1952); and Virginia Wier (August 30, 1960).

John interned at Baltimore City Hospital while still in the army. At his request, he was transferred to the U.S. Public Health Service. They sent him to the U.S. Marine Hospital in Saint Louis, Missouri. This old hospital was built during the Civil War and had been converted to a quarantine hospital for treating patients for venereal diseases. When John was there, the facility was a trial center for testing penicillin, then a relatively new drug with undetermined dosage. After a few months under quarantine, John was transferred to the U.S.P.H.S. Kirkwood General Hospital, where he served as an intern on the internal medicine sections for a year and a half. He then entered the Mayo Clinic as a fellow in internal medicine in July 1948. John and I were together in Rochester for six months, before I left for Houston in January 1949. When John completed his training at Mayo in July 1952, he immediately entered practice in Paris, Texas. John also served as a consultant in medicine at the Veterans Administration Hospital in Bonham, Texas. Later, he was certified in internal medicine and gastroenterology.[1]

We continued to expand. During 1953, Albert Owers decided to leave the

Menninger Clinic. After several visits, we offered him space to practice in our office with the goal of joining our partnership as a psychiatrist and psychoanalyst. I had first met Albert and his wife, Nell, at the Scott and White Clinic, where we both served on the junior staff in internal medicine. Albert was a graduate of Tulane University Medical College. He was called into the Army Air Corps during World War II and was in my class at the School of Aviation Medicine. Albert was sent to England as a flight surgeon and did psychiatric counseling with pilots during the European campaign. After World War II, he went to the Menninger Clinic in Topeka, Kansas, for a residency in psychiatry. He was on the Menninger staff, when he moved to Houston. Al became fully occupied immediately. Several patients followed Al from Menninger. As a psychoanalyst, he only wanted to see thirty regular patients. Thirty patients undergoing psychoanalysis would occupy Al full time for a couple of years, if they stayed with him to complete their treatment. Al managed to crowd in psychiatric consultations for our clinic patients. He didn't plan to be psychiatrist to the Kelsey Leary Clinic, but soon he became psychiatric consultant for our doctors and staff. It was said that Al spent half his time taking care of the psychiatric problems within the clinic and keeping the group together. He certainly helped me hold together.

We soon became crowded in the Hermann Professional Building. Since we had become a clinic, small as we were, we thought we should be in a building of our own. There was vacant land near the medical center on Travis Street, between Dryden and Southmore. The Hannah family owned this land. John and Mickey knew the Hannah brothers, John and David, so John did most of the negotiating. The Hannahs agreed to build and lease us an office with an adjoining parking area. For architects, we chose the firm of Wilson, Morris and Crain, which was noted for a modern style of architecture, then popular. The firm assigned Ralph Anderson, a Rice graduate, to the project. Mickey had graduated from high school with Ralph. All members of this architectural firm were our social friends.

We were very pleased with the final building, so much so that Ralph Anderson would continue to design the next five buildings for our clinic. We moved into our new facility on December 5, 1954. It was located within an easy two-block walk from the new Methodist, St. Luke's, and Texas Children's Hospitals. Doctors and patients had ample parking at our new building. A sketch of the building was published in the Houston papers. Our first announcement of the Kelsey Leary Clinic listed as staff Mavis P. Kelsey, William V. Leary, John Roger Kelsey, Jr., and Albert Owers, with C. C. Shullenberger as consultant.

By this time, our practice was generating a large volume of diagnostic radiology. Before we employed a full time radiologist, Luther Vaughan and

Kelsey-Leary Clinic, 1954

William Owsley—two radiologists at Herman Hospital—were our consultants. They read all our films, except for chest X rays. A chest physician, Leary said he could read chest X rays better than any radiologist. Luke Vaughan trained at the Mayo Clinic with Leary and me and became a longtime friend. We installed a clinical laboratory under the direction of Annette Hill and hired additional technicians. Insisting on quality, we received laboratory reports as accurate, and often times more accurate, than those in the hospital. Shullenberger spent some scheduled time in the new clinic directing hematology in our laboratory and seeing consultations. Shully considered joining our clinic full time, but he was destined for a fruitful career at M. D. Anderson Hospital, where he became chief of medicine after Cliff Howe died. He served once as president of the Harris County Medical Society. After retiring from M. D. Anderson, he became full-time director for the Houston Blood Bank for a few years. Shully always had a joke for me, but the only ones I remember are not printable. We still have lunch together occasionally to reminisce about the early days at M. D. Anderson.

We decided that the next member of our group should be a cardiologist. Mayo-oriented, we looked to Rochester first for a new partner. Hugh Butt recommended Earl Beard, with whom John had trained as a Mayo fellow. Earl had already achieved remarkable success as a pioneer in cardiac catheterization. He had graduated from Northwestern University Medical School in 1948. He spent three years on active duty during a leave of absence from the Mayo Clinic to serve in the department of physiology and cardiology at the U.S. Air Force School of Aviation Medicine in San Antonio. While there, he set up the cardiac catheterization laboratory at the Brooke Field Hospital (later, Brooke General). After completing his fellowship in cardiology at the Mayo Clinic, he entered the practice of internal medicine in his hometown of Peoria, Illinois, but found Peoria had little need for cardiac catheterization. Earl and his wife, Lovey, drove down to Texas in their old Chevy for an interview. Earl accepted and reported for work just as we were moving into our new building. His salary was $1,000 a month with a promise of a $200 monthly raise the next year, and, if all went well, partnership in two years.

Coming to Houston provided Earl with a rare opportunity to use his special talent. Our friend Dan McNamara was the chief of Cardiology at the new Texas Children's Hospital. A cardiac catheterization laboratory was planned for the hospital. In those days, most cardiac catheterizations were done on children with congenital heart defects. This was years before coronary artery bypass operations had become frequent. Earl arrived just at the right time to join Dan in doing much of the original work in setting up the laboratory. Dan and Earl performed the first cardiac catheterization at St. Luke's and at Texas Children's Hospital in 1954. From this humble beginning have evolved the largest catheterization laboratories in the world. Denton Cooley developed the Texas Heart Institute as a major unit of St. Luke's Hospital. Earl Beard has continued to do cardiac catheterization at Texas Children's and at the Texas Heart Institute. He has done thousands while chief of cardiology of our clinic and has contributed significantly to the knowledge of cardiology.

Our practice continued to thrive. Our next partner-to-be was Alfred E. Leiser, the first internist not from the Mayo Clinic. We learned about Al from Pen Skillern, who trained in endocrinology with me at Mayo. Pen, in practice at the Cleveland Clinic, told me that Al Leiser was the finest young man they had ever trained. I remember very well the day the Leisers moved into town. We had them for dinner at our house with their three boys and our four boys. I was in the cooking mode at that time. I cooked eggplant with shrimp stuffing, one of my few successes in cooking for company. The Leisers were a warm and friendly family, with such bright children. Al and Marge were from Wisconsin. His father was a Swiss immigrant cheesemaker. Al said he didn't learn English until he was seven years old. He was an air force flight surgeon during the Korean War, attaining the rank of major. He flew missions over Korea with his squadron and often returned in a flak-scarred plane. He was lucky to survive the Korean War.

Al's practice grew rapidly. He was the hardest working doctor I have ever known, in the hospital before seven every morning and the last to leave every day. Al developed a large practice from Mexico. For years he had a three-month waiting list for appointments. Al was often mistaken for a Jew, especially by Jewish patients who wanted to get their daughters married to Al's sons. An Episcopalian, Al said he didn't try to correct the situation when the Jewish parents were rich. Either Al's patients wouldn't leave him or he wouldn't share them with other doctors, causing him to work eighteen-hour days. His living habits were good, otherwise he wouldn't have survived. He was brisk and cheerful and had a sincere compassion for all patients. Al was very active in his profession and he won awards as the best teacher at Baylor. He always had a group of admiring medical students or residents in tow. He became a clinical professor of medicine at Baylor and chief of endocrinology at St. Luke's. Al was widely known in endocrine circles, participating in many meetings and conferences worldwide. Al's nurse, almost from the beginning, was Beatrice (Bea) Davilla. She was one of the people who made the clinic.[2]

In the meantime, Albert Owers referred overflow patients to several psychiatrists. We particularly liked Chester Cochran, who handled patients well. In 1957, we offered Chester a full-time position, which he gladly accepted. Chester was an easy going fellow. He met his wife, Jamie, while they were medical students in the class of 1951 at University of Texas Medical Branch in Galveston. The Cochrans had a whole bunch of boys, and Jamie stayed home to raise them. After the boys grew up, Jamie trained as a psychiatrist and entered practice. She shared a practice with Chester when he retired from the clinic. Raising all those boys on a psychiatrist's income was quite a strain for the Cochrans, however. Chester kept his old car in the doctor's parking lot. I thought this car was a bad reflection on the clinic, and Owers and I recommended that he at least keep it clean. Chester and Jamie were lovable people, very family oriented. Like many psychiatrists, they knew there was more to life than striving for riches. They found their riches in other ways, as in a small tract of land in the piney woods of East Texas. Chester established lengthy relationships with his patients and worried about their problems.

James W. Kemper was the next doctor to join our clinic. In 1956, John was in Rochester looking around for another internist, when he was introduced to Jim, who was completing a fellowship in rheumatology. He trained under Nobel Prize winner Phillip Hench. When Jim joined us in May 1957, he accepted a part-time job at Baylor Medical College and was the only formally trained rheumatologist in town. He was chief of rheumatology for several years, until Baylor recruited a full-time rheumatologist. Jim turned his Baylor salary in to the clinic, as we all did. His beginning salary at the clinic was $1,000 a month. Our salary for all the new doctors who came to the clinic continued for years to be $1,000 a month, or $12,000 a year. This included time off, two weeks for vacation, and two weeks for study or medical meetings paid by the clinic. As I recall, the second year salary was $14,400 a year. After turning partner, the doctor shared in the net income of the clinic based on an ever-changing formula and was required to buy an equal share of the clinic assets. This purchase price was paid off by monthly withdrawal from his paycheck.

Jim was a calm and sensible person who avoided some of the serious controversies I often participated in. He was highly respected by the partners and became chief of the clinic, a position he held for ten years. Jim was very modest. He never showed the least sign of pomp or arrogance as chief.

Before Kemper joined, we had outgrown our first office on Travis at Dryden.

In 1956–57, the Hannahs built a much larger clinic exclusively for us on the corner of Southgate and Travis. We were given complete control in designing this building. Ralph Anderson was the architect, with the Ellerbe architectural firm, which had designed the Mayo Clinic, as consultant. We used many of the methods for patient flow which had been developed and used successfully at the Mayo Clinic. The formal opening and dedication of the new Kelsey Leary Clinic on March 6, 1957 was officiated by Reverends Arthur Knapp and Ralph Miller of Trinity Episcopal Church. The architect, the builder, the landlord, the entire staff, and some family members and patients attended. It was a solemn yet exciting event for all of us.

This dedication occurred only eight years after I had entered solo practice. In a short time, we had assembled a group of seven full-time physicians, and several part-time consultants. We were still recruiting for other specialists. We had a staff of some twenty-five or thirty people including X-ray, isotope, and clinical laboratory technicians, nurses, secretaries, clerks, receptionists, and patient assistants. We employed our friend Margery Mallett to keep books, but the volume of work soon overwhelmed her. The growth of our clinic would have ceased at this stage, if we had not employed a manager and other key personnel. Although they were not partners and did not invest money, many individuals invested their lives, their careers, their very hearts and souls in the clinic. These faithful employees "owned" the clinic as much as did any physician partner.

Several individuals stand out. A key person was Betty Zeigler, who began work in the clinic as a receptionist-trainee in January 1954. Warm and personable, she would undertake any task she was assigned. She answered the phone, ran the reception desk, made appointments, and performed the original interviews with patients. Although not a nurse, she prepared patients and assisted in examinations including proctoscopies. She did electrocardiograms and BMRs, applied dressings and hot soaks, made friends with patients and allayed their anxieties, as she did for employees and doctors when they needed help.

In our search for a clinic manager, we found Alice M. (Jackie) Greer in 1956. Jackie's husband was killed during World War II and she never remarried. Jackie had worked for the City National Bank (later, the First National Bank), before joining us. She had been an assistant cashier at the City National Bank under Judge J. A. Elkins, who was the bank's president and chairman. Jackie was sincere, bright, knowledgeable, and completely dedicated to her job. She readily joined us in our goal to build a high quality clinic.[3]

Soon after Jackie arrived we employed William A. (Bill) Stovall as accountant. A CPA, he also had a law degree. In addition to being comptroller, Bill served the clinic admirably as an assistant administrator. He was a friendly, conscientious, honest man. When Jackie left us in 1963, he served as acting manager, until we employed Jim Bakken. Bill later left the clinic to become a private lawyer and accountant. Joyce Burch came to the clinic as a receptionist about 1956. At seventeen, Joyce had become a professional ice skater and made world tours. As telephone operator–chief receptionist, she knew every patient who entered the clinic and every doctor and employee who made a phone call. Joyce was the nerve center of the clinic.

Another important person was Dorothy Teall. She had started as Bill Seybold's secretary in 1957, while he was in solo practice, and came to the clinic when Bill returned in 1961. In 1964, she became supervisor of secretaries. Very interested in the clinic's history, Dorothy accumulated the early letters of the first partners, as well as photographs of the early Texas Medical Center. Mildred Coyle came as an assistant in the X-ray department in 1956 and has been with the clinic longer than any other employee. I knew every employee when she came. I hired her personally, as I did all employees then. Mildred used to borrow money from me and pay me back regularly as agreed. Of course, I never charged interest. Mildred was a capable, dependable employee.

Almost from the beginning, we employed Lloyd Jard of Peat, Marwick and Mitchell, as an outside accountant. Lloyd became well acquainted with our doctors and served us for years with much important tax advice. The maximum tax was 70 percent in the 1950s. There were many tax loopholes—the promoters of which usually drained the money off the taxpayer and the government at the same time. Lloyd made several safe recommendations to Mary and me, however.

One other person from those early years was my office nurse, Aggie Greer, although she did not come to the clinic until 1964. With the exception of my brother, Aggie Greer was the most important person in my thirty-seven years at the clinic. Born Agnes Fallwell in Palestine, Texas, on July 23, 1923, Aggie attended Incarnate Word College in San Antonio in 1940 and 1941. She had no intention of becoming a nurse, until an army nurse recruiter persuaded her to enter the Santa Rosa Hospital Nursing School. She graduated in 1944 and entered the army service at Fort Sam Houston. She served in France and Germany in the Army of Occupation for two years. Aggie had returned to nurse in Texas, when the Texas City explosion occurred on April 15, 1947, killing several hundred people. Aggie joined the Red Cross and spent the summer in Texas City nursing victims of the explosion. She took the last victim of the explosion out on a train to Pennsylvania. In 1948 she married Boyd (Jing) Greer, a World War II pilot who had his own insurance business. Aggie resumed private nursing in 1951. She nursed Jim West, Wesley West's brother, for four-and-a-half years. I had admitted Jim into Hermann Hospital in 1953,

Aggie Greer, Mavis's office nurse for twenty-seven years

and he kept a room there for all of that time. Aggie was paid whether Jim was in the hospital or not.

In 1959, Aggie was called to nurse my patient, Governor Hobby, in his home. I met her the first day she nursed him, and I count that as the first time Aggie nursed for me. Governor Hobby died in 1964. Within a month Aggie was in the clinic as my office nurse, a position she held until I retired in 1986. Before retiring, Aggie stayed in the clinic for six more months to get my patients assigned to other doctors. Aggie soon knew every patient I had, and they loved her. Some would have left me if it weren't for Aggie. Some preferred her telephone advice to mine. She kept me on schedule and arranged care for many patients while I was gone. Aggie had clout. She could get patients in the hospital when I couldn't. She received many presents from our patients, some-times making me a little jealous. Two patients left their estates to Aggie.[4]

By 1960, our clinic was composed of internists and psychiatrists, but we had not given up our goal of a general clinic. We had long-range plans for an in-house radiologist, an orthopedist, and an otolaryngologist. Since we had developed a significant number of private patients in our clinic needing radioiodine diagnostic studies and treatments, we also decided to develop our own isotope laboratory. There was still very little standard equipment, so we built our own stand for the Geiger counter. The thyroid uptake study rapidly replaced the unreliable BMR test. Within a few years, protein-bound iodine determinations, TSH levels, and other blood tests replaced many of the origi-nal radioiodine diagnostic studies. We treated hyperthyroidism with radio-iodine in the clinic, but sent those patients with thyroid cancer who could not be treated by surgery to M. D. Anderson. For the first few years before a full-time nuclear medicine specialist was employed at M. D. Anderson Hos-pital, I treated all the inoperable thyroid cancers that took up radioiodine. Over the years the M. D. Anderson Cancer Center accumulated a very large number of thyroid cancers. Our own radioisotope laboratory proved to be very successful, and it has continued until today as the Nuclear Medicine Laboratory. Many new radioactive isotopes, tests, and treatments have been developed for every system of the body. Every physician in today's clinic uses the laboratory. Al Leiser and I operated the laboratory until David Mouton joined the clinic as a specialist in nuclear medicine. Later, Ralph Gorten also joined the department. Mouton brought in Bob Millis, who has served for years as a very competent chief technician.

We developed a large practice of office gynecology, a result of our belief that every general examination of female patients should include an examina-tion of the pelvic organs. We knew several fine gynecologists, but had devel-oped the closest relationship with Robert A. Johnston ("Dr. Robert") and his younger partner, Melville Cody. Dr. Robert was a leading gynecologist-obste-trician in Houston and professor of gynecology and obstetrics at Baylor. We had referred many patients to each other. Dr. Robert delivered Bill Leary's daughter Maggie and some of the Griffith children. He wanted to reduce his practice and turn it over to Mel Cody. After much discussion and negotia-tion, Dr. Robert and Mel joined our clinic.

Dr. Robert was a highly competent, charming, old-fashioned doctor. I had known Melville since he was a sophomore at the Medical Branch in Galveston and I was instructor in pathology. Dr. Robert and I had numerous patients in common, more than a few being referred to me by him. Soon after joining the clinic, however, he found the young doctors lacking in respect and not duly grateful for referrals, a judgement many senior doctors have shared. He also felt that the pay distribution system did not reward him for the patients he brought in. Unfortunately, Dr. Robert resigned on May 17, 1962, feeling that I had let him down. He had been very helpful in getting me started in practice, and our families had become close friends. I was disappointed about the whole affair. Melville Cody remained in the clinic as a partner. He was highly supportive of our institution and brought many fine people into the clinic as patients.[5]

We decided that our next internist should be a specialist in hypertension, because we had noticed many patients with this condition. One of the medical sections for the Mayo Clinic specialized in hypertension and peripheral vascular diseases, and it was here that we found our man, Gene E. Burke. In addition to medicine, Gene had studied finance as a minor subject at the University of Texas. He contributed his knowledge to the business affairs of our rapidly expanding clinic, and in 1974 he opened and operated our second branch office in downtown Houston.

Essential hypertension, or high blood pressure, has always been a prevalent disease responsible for many deaths. No effective treatment had been devised, until the 1950s, when drugs were being developed which could directly lower blood pressure. The first of these drugs was from a plant product called Indian (East Indian) snake root, with the botanical name of rauwolfia serpentina. In the early 1950s, an American drug company started producing and promoting this medication in pill form. The active ingredient was reserpine—the trade name was Rauwaloid. George Maison, my former colleague at the aeromedical laboratory in Dayton, Ohio, had become medical director of this company. Before Rauwaloid was put on the market, George sent me hundreds of the pills and asked me to try them. I tested more than a dozen patients and, finding the pills effective, sent him regular reports. My cases were some of the original ones tested and reported. I remember telling some of my friends at the Houston Internist Society meetings about it. They thought Indian snake root was pure quackery. It was two or three years before reserpine was accepted as a legitimate treatment. Reserpine had some side effects, and more effective drugs soon followed.

As the clinic's internal structure took shape, we also looked for other ways to develop the general practice. While at the Mayo Clinic, I had observed that many large companies, such as General Motors, sent their executives for an annual physical examination. In 1949, we had obtained the account of Foley's Department Store. We also enjoyed a friendly relationship with the First National Bank, where Judge Freeman was on the board. Horace Wilkins, a bank officer, referred several First National employees to us. Carroll Simmons was there as financial officer of the M. D. Anderson Foundation. We knew Perk Butler, who had been president of the Beaumont National Bank—the Wilsons's bank—before he moved to Houston to become president of First National. Jackie Greer was the bank's personnel director. Mr. Butler called one day and invited us to come to the bank and discuss a program of annual physical examinations for the bank officers. Bill Leary, John, and I ambled in a few minutes late for the appointment. We were shocked to walk into a board-room full of irate bank officers who had been waiting fifteen minutes for our arrival. We managed to regain our composure and describe the merits of an annual physical examination to be paid for by the bank. After a few friendly digs about having to wait for doctors they accepted our proposal. This account lasted many years, and we gained family members of the bank officers as patients and friends.

The experience with Foley's and First National encouraged us to develop this type of "company medicine" practice, as we called it. In subsequent years we won several competitive contracts to provide medical services to NASA.[6] Soon we were providing services for more than a hundred companies. Before I retired we had served more than five hundred companies. These examinations kept us busy and brought income. Most important, they generated practice for our specialists and promoted the growth of our clinic. One of our early accounts was the Dialog Company, an oil well service company. Leary brought the account through his friendship with company president Billy McNulty, who also became a contributor to the Kelsey Leary Foundation. Billy had a ranch in Colorado to which he'd fly his own plane on weekends. One weekend at the ranch, his son was riding horseback, and the horse ran away. The boy fell out of the saddle, but his leg caught the stirrup and he was dragged to death. Billy picked up his son, put him in the plane, and flew back to Houston. I had just lost my son Cooke and I knew the pain he suffered. I went to see Bill and offered him my condolences and support, and we shared our grief.

The Pennzoil account, which resulted from a house call, became one of my most gratifying relationships during my practice. One night, Bill Liedtke, vice president of Pennzoil, who had just moved to Houston from Midland, Texas, called me. He had a fever and felt terrible. Bill and his wife, Bessie, had just returned from a guest resort in California, where they had met Mary's brother Cooke and his wife, Betty, who were also guests. Cooke had told Bill if they needed a doctor in Houston to call me. They lived in a house only a few blocks away. I went to see Bill, treated his fever, and we became friends. It was probably the most important house call I ever made. This experience illustrated the value of personal relationships in medicine. Today, Bill Liedtke would be directed by a switchboard operator to report to an emergency room for treatment by a total stranger. Fat chance for a clinic to be chosen as a company doctor!

Bill Liedtke and his brother Hugh were in the process of moving to Houston and bringing the headquarters of Pennzoil Company with them. The two brothers had started their careers in the oil business in their home town of Tulsa, Oklahoma. They moved to Midland during the great Permian Basin oil boom after World War II. Many well-educated enterprising young men had moved there to seek their fortune—George Bush among them. He became a partner of the Liedtke brothers in another company, which also moved to Houston. We soon met Hugh and Bettie Liedtke and started seeing officers and employees of the Pennzoil Company. One day Hugh Liedtke, the CEO, called me to come to his office, where he and Bill Liedtke told me they wanted the Kelsey Leary Clinic to be the Pennzoil doctors. They wanted us to do annual physical examinations on the officers, treat employee's families, advise the company nurse, and take care of any medical problems that arose. These men were used to doing business on a handshake. I accepted. We didn't even discuss fees. We had a deal in fifteen minutes, one that has lasted more than thirty years.

As the clinic grew, our mode of practice and handling patients became routine. We developed a health questionnaire for patients to fill out, alerting us to important symptoms and saving time. The original sheet had a hundred numbered questions. My friend and patient Jake Hershey asked me, "Why should it take exactly one hundred questions to know one's health status?" We omitted the numbers next time we printed the questionnaire. Our clinic personnel registered, interviewed, and recorded a preliminary history from each patient. Every new patient was to have a complete history and physical examination, usually taking about forty-five minutes. After the physical examination, the clinic staff put the patient through all the X rays, laboratory tests, and consultations, which sometimes lasted three or more days. The patient came back for a fifteen- to thirty-minute visit with the doctor for reports, diagnosis, and treatment. This complete examination was subject to many variations, such as consultations with an outside doctor, a return for new tests, a referral to the surgeon for an operation, admission to the hospital, even referral to the Mayo Clinic. If the patient had been sent by an outside doctor a complete report and recommendations were dictated for the referring doctor.

We scheduled thirty minutes for an annual examination of a return patient. Office visits for minor complaints took fifteen minutes. The appointment clerk, knowing the time required for each type of examination, could schedule the doctors' appointments for days in advance. Doctors' fees in those days were very reasonable, so that people with modest incomes could afford good medical care, even if they had to pay the bill in a few monthly install-ments. Health care costs paid by the federal government were only a small percentage of what they are today. We encouraged annual physical examina-tions to detect and treat diseases early. When fees were modest, this method of care was cost effective. We proved this by doing several research studies of our case records, which revealed that we had diagnosed and treated many early malignancies, as well as cases of diabetes, hypertension, and other chronic diseases. A regular health program reduced smoking, drinking, and overeat-ing. I still believe in annual or periodic examinations instead of waiting until the patient gets in trouble. This is very effective preventive medicine. We also helped many patients get through their emotional problems. We were grati-fied to solve some difficult problem cases that other doctors had referred to us. We treated many serious illnesses. Unfortunately there were patients we could not save, and sometimes we missed a diagnosis. I can remember several humiliating instances when I missed an obvious diagnosis. This was before the days of frequent malpractice suits, and doctors were given the benefit of exercising reasonable judgment. Fortunately, I was never sued for malpractice.

I never let my appointment schedule get ahead more than two weeks. I referred the overflow to the younger doctors who needed the practice to be-come established. The new doctors also helped care for my hospital practice. Aggie Greer helped handle the phone calls. I often got forty phone calls a day. I interrupted seeing patients for emergency calls and some VIP patients, but I learned never to answer a phone call in the presence of a patient. I made phone call replies every day in the office or from home, sometimes in the middle of the night. Some patients could tie me up on the phone for thirty minutes several nights a week. I continued to make house calls and night calls.

Most of our group knew or learned how to handle patients, how to make them feel at home and be relaxed, how to impart confidence, how to show sympathy and be compassionate, respectful, polite, and gentle, and when and how to give bad news to a patient or family. We also learned how to judge people. Some patients wanted their doctor to order them around, even scold them. They thought that was what a doctor should do. If you were not an authoritarian, they lost confidence in you. I knew doctors who were brusque, frank, and superior and had huge practices. Other patients needed gentle coaxing. Others were highly suspicious of doctors and challenged their every remark, especially if they were kept waiting or were sent a bill they didn't like.

Some patients, male and female, were very shy and practically jumped off the table during a rectal or pelvic exam. Others threw off the sheet after the exam and walked completely naked over to their clothes and got dressed in the doctor's presence, often embarrassing the doctor unintentionally. I also remember some women who practically pulled you on the table with them. I never, never, conceded, in spite of the temptation, although I heard of some doctors who did. I politely kept my distance, but I believed that, even if I had responded in kind, many of these women would have gotten mad and pushed me away. I think they were only interested in teasing the doctor. In those days we didn't have professional sex therapists who specialized in this line of work. I had several patients I could have referred to them.

There were many other occupational hazards. Patients often misquoted doctors. I have had many patients come up and tell me something I allegedly said—remarks I never would have made—which they had repeated to their friends. Others wrote pages of symptoms and questions and were disappointed if I didn't answer them in detail. I often told them that I would answer their questions when I was relaxed and had time to study them. Surprisingly, many patients would forget the list, but they usually brought in a new one. Some patients would talk for an hour unless you changed the subject by starting the physical examination. Others were convinced they had a life-threatening disease such as cancer and continually returned to ask for additional tests.

I heard the most amazing stories from my patients. Some felt they could tell me everything about their personal life, details I would consider innermost secrets. Without any coaxing from me, patients have revealed their private finances, from how much they owned to what they made in business—things I'm sure they would never tell another person. New patients have confessed to me their infidelities or a hidden unfulfilled love for another's spouse. I have often wondered why these patients tell all to their doctor. There was a time when people held doctors in the highest regard; perhaps people who tell their doctors everything have such an attitude. I have never divulged my patients' intimate revelations; in fact, I was very reluctant to hear these stories—they made me feel as if I was intruding in their lives.

We had lots of jokes and stories about patients' foibles. My medical school classmate Steve Williams, for example, proved that when a couple walked into your office you could tell immediately which was the patient. If the woman held her husband's hat, then he was the patient; if the husband held his wife's purse, then she was. When a patient came in the office for an insignificant complaint, then prolonged the interview, he or she was holding back the reason for coming. One patient kept delaying his departure, until he finally said, "Oh yes, my wife told me to tell you I've been drinking too much." I sat him down again and we discussed his real reason for coming. Finally he said, "I told my wife I wasn't going to drink anymore." "Good," I said. "But I also told her I wasn't going to drink any less." The patient was very pleased with this wisecrack.

Some patients were very demanding and wanted you to stop everything to see them. I'm guilty of this, myself. Others were so retiring, they often got overlooked or neglected. I've also had patients, for whom I haven't done a great deal, shower me with gifts. It was very embarrassing. One patient dedicated several rooms to me in St. Luke's Hospital and repeatedly sent me gifts. It was hard not to have a guilty feeling that the gifts were not deserved—and easy to see how doctors who are charlatans take advantage of vulnerable people. Some patients walked uninvited down the doctors' private halls and into offices as if they owned the place. One such patient was Governor Hobby, but he was so charming and friendly that he could get away with it. We felt honored when he walked in unannounced.

There were other patients I will never forget. One we all remember was Mrs. McCaughan, a very wealthy elderly woman. We called her the Purple Lady. She drove to the clinic in a purple Cadillac. Her hair was purple, as were her fingernails, toenails, numerous large jewels, dress, shoes, stockings, even her undies. She said all the furnishings in her house were purple. She was always in a good humor and liked to be kidded about her love of purple.[7]

Our clinic had many famous and wealthy patients: nobility from oil-rich Middle Eastern countries; Madam Chiang Kai-shek and members of her extended family; important Latin Americans by the score; locally and nationally prominent politicians and judges; well-known business leaders; and several movie stars. The first one I saw was Roy Rogers. For several years he was a guest star at the Houston Livestock Show and Rodeo, and while in Houston he came to the clinic for an annual physical examination. He and other stars, such as Rock Hudson, always created quite a commotion around the clinic. We were never specially organized to handle the VIPs and we charged them our regular fees. The famous were treated like everyone else, except for the personal attention given by Betty Zeigler, who took it upon herself to see that no hang-ups occurred during their visits. It became fashionable for the wealthy and famous to undergo a thorough annual examination at our clinic. Meanwhile, many of our patients were of very modest means—those in financial distress or unable to work were charged low fees or their charges were totally dismissed.

The downside of affordable medical care was that it was sometimes not very effective. Except for antibiotics, none of the really great highly expensive technical advances had been invented. Medical costs rose meteorically when procedures like CAT Scans, MRIs, coronary bypasses, renal dialyses, and organ transplants became available. A consensus developed that everyone deserved the benefits of these advances, regardless of whether they could afford it. At first people bought reasonably priced health insurance. Health insurance became perquisites for employees, but the cost of insurance soon skyrocketed to meet the costly benefits of high technology. Medical care became a multibillion dollar industry. Hospitals quickly joined the rush for riches. A half-cent aspirin, formerly given free in a twenty-dollar hospital room, soon cost $1.50 in a $500 room. Interns and residents who had worked long hours for a pittance, as I had, struck for a forty-hour week and a $20,000 salary. Many practicing physicians decided that money was more important than service and increased their fees by a multiple of ten. A cardiac catheterization or a gastroscopy increased from $150 to $1,500. Specialization and subspecialization often resulted in several expensive consultations for a problem that good general practitioners like Sam Barnes could handle with a $10 office examination. The golden era of medicine was nearing an end. My contemporaries and I watched it happen and contributed to it.

Like our practice, the Texas Medical Center was expanding at a phenomenal rate. During the 1950s and early 1960s, new streets were built and seven hospitals, a dental college, a library, a rehabilitation facility, an institute of religion, and two schools of nursing had gone up at the same time. The M. D. Anderson Hospital had vacated its temporary Baldwin Street address and occupied the pink marble edifice in the medical center. Since our office on Travis Street was in easy walking distance from the new Methodist Hospital and St. Luke's–Texas Children's Hospitals, we began using these facilities and gradually drifted away from Hermann Hospital. Methodist Hospital had moved into the center as a teaching hospital affiliated with Baylor. John, a Methodist and a Baylor alumnus, was very active at Methodist. Mickey's father, Tom Wier, was a life member of the Methodist Hospital board. An Episcopalian and friend of Bishop Quin, I became more active at St. Luke's and served for many years on the executive committee as an original member. I served on the original laboratory and bylaws committee and, along with Ed Doak, wrote the original staff bylaws. Clyde Warner was the original chairman of the executive Committee. The first department chiefs on the staff I remember were Paul Ledbetter, internal medicine; Weems Turner, urology; Jack Ehlers, surgery; and Herman Gardner, gynecology.[8]

Our clinic was very active at St. Luke's Hospital from the day it opened. Maynard Martin, who became my patient, was the first executive director of St. Luke's and Texas Children's Hospitals. These hospitals had separate professional staff structures, while the management of their physical facilities was under one organization. Many years later, probably in the late 1970s, Texas Children's became separately managed, although many of the same services were provided to both hospitals. A favorite friend at St. Luke's was Opal Benage, who came as chief of nurses for St. Luke's and Texas Children's in 1959. She became an important administrator and was in charge of admissions for a long time. It paid to be Opal's friend if you wanted to get your patients admitted.

From the time it opened, I was a consultant at Texas Children's Hospital. I saw very few patients there, but I enjoyed the endocrine conferences with George Clayton and Leon Librick. One day, as I walked through a hall in Texas Children's, I saw smoke coming out of a patient's room. The fire alarm went off. Almost instantly the hall was full of smoke, and everyone was racing around screaming. People crawled out of windows onto the ledges that surround the building on each floor. A nurse had the presence of mind to rush in with a fire extinguisher and put out a blaze in a bed and remove the child who, amazingly, was not burned. The fire was caused by a mother smoking in the room while the child was in an oxygen tent. She had disobeyed strict orders not to smoke while oxygen was being administered. The fire department arrived within a very few minutes, but the fire could have spread within seconds. In those days, nearly everyone smoked in hospital rooms. There were ashtrays in every room. Smoking was prohibited only in patient rooms, where oxygen was being administered. Doctors and nurses made rounds smoking. Medical conferences were held in smoke-filled rooms. In homes, hostesses offered cigarettes to guests. People smoked in airplanes, while stewardesses passed out small packages of free cigarettes.

The Jones Library was completed in 1954. The library building also housed Texas Medical Center and the Harris County Medical Society offices, a large meeting hall, meeting rooms, and a fine club for doctors, dentists, and other professionals. Another new facility, the Institute of Religion, opened in the medical center in 1956. It was first housed in the Jessie Jones building, while its new brick structure was being built next to Methodist Hospital in 1960. A few years later, my wife Mary took a lead role with the Houston Garden Club in establishing a beautiful garden on the institute grounds. The University of Texas Dental College was designed by McKie and Kamrath in the same modern architectural style as M. D. Anderson Hospital, next door. The Dental College, also clad in Georgia pink marble, presented a beautiful scene. The new building opened in 1956. Forty years later, it still maintains its architectural integrity, while most of the original M. D. Anderson Hospital building has been surrounded by massive expansions.

Members of our clinic volunteered a tremendous amount of time to the Baylor teaching program. We worked in the hospitals and the medical college and accepted hundreds of medical students and interns and residents in our clinic offices. All of our early members, except for me, attained the rank of clinical professor. On retirement I was named emeritus professor, as were several hundred others. I was flattered, although I must admit my contribution was rather limited. The huge new Ben Taub Hospital was opened in 1963 next door to Baylor. I was assigned to the medicine out-clinics of both the Jefferson Davis and Ben Taub Hospitals, a very onerous task because of the way the academics had set it up. Charity patients sat for hours waiting to be seen for ten minutes for an inadequate examination and limited laboratory testing. The patient had to come back another day and wait long hours to get the tests, then wait several days to come back for another long wait to get the results from another doctor who had to start over, and on and on. I was an internist trained to do thorough examinations and could not adjust. I had more patients than I could see waiting for appointments in my office.[9]

The clinic partners also were members of their respective specialty societies. The clinic promoted attendance at medical meetings by paying the expenses. We were paying ourselves out of our own money, but if we didn't attend we didn't receive the benefits we paid for. We always tried to combine vacation with study and enjoyed some wonderful trips. We saw our out-of-town colleagues and became acquainted with many medical leaders.

I was on the executive committee of the Harris County Medical Society in 1954 and was treasurer for a year or two. I attended the Texas State Medical Association meetings for years and was on the Scientific Council. I prepared a talk nearly every year for the medical society or for an affiliated society, such as the Texas Diabetes Society. The American College of Physicians meetings were very helpful. I focused on the American Goiter Society (later, the American Thyroid Association) and was chairman of the membership committee for years. The American Thyroid Association joined with other national thyroid societies in England, France, Italy, Germany, Japan, and other countries to produce an International Thyroid Congress every four years. The dates and locations were arranged so that we could attend other international meetings on the same trip. The International Thyroid meeting in London in 1954 was the most enjoyable meeting I ever attended. On trips to thyroid, endocrine, and diabetes society meetings held in places such as Copenhagen, Stockholm, Leningrad, Vienna, Rome, Madrid, Berne, Paris, Southampton, and The Hague, Mary and I always visited the art museums, opera houses, and rare bookstores.

Many advances in medicine occurred in the 1950s. Polio, or infantile paralysis, had been endemic for centuries. After World War II, the disease became a worldwide protracted epidemic, attacking the rich and poor, adults and children, alike. While I was treating patients with polio in Houston, the disease struck one of my best friends, William Huard Hargis, Jr., of San Antonio, a classmate from medical school. The disease killed him in August of 1954. His twin sisters and their families had vacationed at a church encampment near San Antonio. After returning home, most members of the families came down with polio. Huard treated them and contracted the disease. Within a couple of weeks four members of the families were dead, including Huard, and others were left paralyzed. I flew to San Antonio the day of Huard's death to offer his wife, Lucylle, what comfort I could. Ralph Letteer and I were pallbearers at his funeral. Mary stayed at home with our children. In those days, everyone stayed in as much as they could to avoid the disease.

Since 1909, polio had been transmitted from monkey to monkey in the laboratory. No bacteria had been isolated, so the disease was assumed to be caused by a virus. Viruses could not be seen and could live only in living tissue. They were called filterable viruses, because they could pass through a Berkfeld filter, while bacteria could not. Only in 1948 was the virus isolated and cultured in the laboratory and finally seen under the newly developed electron microscope. Many children had survived a mild polio infection diagnosed as a sore throat and, as a result, gained permanent immunity to polio, explaining the strange distribution of the disease. My brother John developed symptoms in his fifties that suggested he had polio that went undiagnosed when he was a child. Many patients contracted the disease, but in only a few did the virus reach the brain and spinal cord to create paralysis. When the virus breaks the blood brain bearer, the patient develops headaches and a stiff neck. The spinal fluid reveals increased white blood cells and protein. The polio epidemic after World War II was characterized by many cases of bulbar palsy and respiratory failure. There was a great rush to build respirators to assist patients through this acute phase, after which some recovered their respiratory function. Without the respirator, many died, sometimes within a couple of days. Some survived to require a respirator for the remainder of their lives.

The polio virus was found to inhabit the gastrointestinal tract and be transmitted by fecal-oral transmission, often by unwashed hands. Paralytic polio was not common in some poor sections, because most babies had been exposed to it and developed immunity before they were three years old. Thus, the virus could be widespread, and yet few people would develop paralysis. We didn't know these epidemiological facts when we heard there was no polio in Mexico, so we rented a house in Cuernavaca and moved our family there in the summer of 1952. Soon after arrival, all four boys had sore throats and fever, probably the result of polio which we thought was not present in Mexico. Only Cooke developed clinical, or cerebrospinal, polio. He had high fever, a splitting headache, and a stiff neck. The local doctor and I did a spinal tap at the house and found the tell tale signs of polio in his spinal fluid. Fortunately, Cooke recovered at our house in Cuernavaca with no paralysis.

About 1955 the polio vaccine was developed by Jonas Salk. There was a nationwide rush to vaccinate everyone, especially the children. The Harris County Medical Society undertook this task, with Dr. E. L. Goar in charge. Houston was among the first mass test centers to determine the effectiveness of the oral vaccine. All the Houston doctors and nurses volunteered, as well as many public-spirited citizens. On two weekends we volunteered to give vaccine to most of the populace at stations throughout Houston. The incidence of polio rapidly fell to almost zero. The introduction of a successful polio vaccine was one of the greatest medical achievements of the twentieth century.[10]

Tuberculosis was also coming under control as a result of streptomycin. Sanitoria for treating tuberculosis were closing down, resulting in less thoracic surgery and other work for chest physicians. Doctors, nevertheless, were pleased to see the dreaded disease come under control. We recommended annual chest X rays and the Tuberculosis Society had mobile facilities for screening. X-ray vans parked in downtown Houston offered $1.00 chest films for early diagnosis of tuberculosis. Jeff Davis Hospital was to become a tuberculosis hospital after Ben Taub was opened. But not enough patients appeared. The Houston Tuberculosis Hospital also closed. Separate facilities for treating tuberculosis were no longer needed. Unfortunately, tuberculosis is still widespread in undeveloped nations and is appearing among patients with AIDS.

Vascular surgery really took off on October 12, 1954, when DeBakey, Cooley, and Creech performed an operation telecast nationwide. They replaced a diseased aorta with a section of preserved aorta from another person. Artificial arteries were replacing diseased ones all over the body. The heart bypass pump was developed, making it possible to continue the circulation of blood while a diseased or malformed heart was being surgically repaired. I believe the development of open heart surgery was the most important medical advance in the twentieth century. DeBakey and Cooley were world leaders, each with their teams doing more heart surgery than anyone else.

Organ transplants got underway, slowly but surely, hampered by the body's rejection of transplanted tissue. The specialty of oncology was evolving. Memorial Hospital in New York City, Roswell Park in Buffalo, New York, and the M. D. Anderson Hospital were the only cancer hospitals in America. M. D. Anderson had general surgeons who specialized in treating cancer but there were no internists who were designated as, or could be qualified as, medical oncologists. At the time there were not enough treatment modalities available to justify a separate specialty. Many Texas doctors opposed M. D. Anderson, claiming they could treat cancers as well as anyone at a cancer hospital. There was some truth in their claim.

One of the first medical treatments for cancer was hormone therapy. Some prostate cancers could be suppressed by estrogen, and some breast cancers by androgens, or male hormones. I treated a number of these patients with hormones. I have mentioned treatment of thyroid cancer with radioiodine. This was one of the innovations in cancer therapy. But it was useful in only a few cancers. The isotopes came into their own with Cobalt 60 radiation, which was introduced in 1958 at M. D. Anderson. The specialty of oncology didn't take off until drugs were invented that had the same effects on the cancer cell as did radiation. Nitrogen mustard was the first I can remember. Then came dozens of new drugs, the use of which was called cancer chemotherapy, a complicated and dangerous procedure which not just any doctor could do. Doctors were glad to refer their cancer patients to the new specialist, the oncologist. I knew C. L. Spurr, who used the first chemotherapeutic agents at M. D. Anderson. He left in a year or two and Cliff Howe, a general internist and chief of medicine, took charge of the program, becoming the first oncologist at M. D. Anderson. He was one of the first full-time cancer specialists in America. Another important advance in medicine, developed mainly in Houston, was the mammogram for detecting breast cancer. The original research was done in 1956 at St. Joseph's and M. D. Anderson Hospitals.[11]

By the early 1960s, the Kelsey Leary Clinic was profitable, and we doctors were finally making big money, in the $40,000 annual range. Mary's income, based on trusts and inheritances, was also growing. Mary and I finally could invest, but our experience suggests that doctors are very poor investors. They are suckers for every kind of venture a slick operator can invent. Business training is not part of a medical education, and doctors are too busy to evaluate investments. We ran our clinic in a business-like manner, because we spent a lot of time managing it. But outside investments were a different matter.

The first investments I remember were oil leases. Virtually everyone in Texas invested in oil. I joined Cliff Howe and other M. D. Anderson doctors in buying "whispering interests" in the Mitchell brothers' wildcat drilling projects. George Mitchell, the managing partner, was a very dynamic young man, and operating on a shoestring, he sold interests to our group. Some of their wells were strippers at Blue Ridge. We dabbled with them a few years but dropped out before George made a big discovery in Wise County that led him to riches. Another oil venture was with Ray Southworth, on the recommendation of Jamie Griffith. We did have a little production. The first big loss I suffered was with Bradco Oil, $35,000 as I recall. Unbelievably, I kept dropping money in these deals all the way into the 1980s. I also bought stock in small oil companies, but few paid off. I never knew when to sell. There were real estate investments, too. One $20,000 investment in a real estate development on Lake

Kelsey house at #2 Longbow Lane, 1958

Tetesquitengo, about fifty miles south of Cuernavaca, Mexico, provided my family many times the price in fun and friendship, but no profit. The lake was large and beautiful, with a romantic history, and we visited it on many vacation trips. The developer, Al Pullen, and his family often entertained us. They and many of their friends became patients in the clinic.

As our boys got older we tried to find a larger house so each son could have a room of his own. New houses in Houston were being centrally air conditioned and had more bathrooms and storage space. The Houston residential area was extending westward. Our housing problem was finally solved in 1956, when Roy Rather persuaded Billy and Victor Carter to develop the woods adjoining their homes in Sherwood Forest, where streets were named after stories in *The Adventures of Robin Hood.* We selected Lot Number Two on Longbow Lane; it had romance, giant trees, 600 feet on the Buffalo Bayou, and 4.03 acres in all. The lot cost $28,000. There were dozens of tall pines and the largest white oak and magnolia tree in Harris County.

We interviewed several architects including Don Barthelme and Ralph Anderson. We selected Ralph, who had previously designed two clinic buildings for us. He had become noted for his clean designs in the modern style. Ralph was very responsive to our desires. We wanted a simple modern one-story brick house with a concealing front and a full-glass exposure to the woods and Buffalo Bayou in the back. Our Mexican travels convinced us to have a patio. We wanted large living and dining areas that were partially separated by a large bookshelf. There were large bookshelves in the study and in the boys' wing—enough for several thousand books in all. We placed an attached large deck and a swimming pool off to one side, so as not to distract from our view of the woods. As amateur architects, Mary and I often sat up past midnight with ruler and drawing paper designing every detail. Not only was Ralph competent, he was patient. We became good friends and invited him to our Thanksgiving and Christmas dinners. I also studied our clinic plans in great detail. The architectural firm awarded me an elaborate certificate designating me as an amateur architect. The wording of the certificate politely intimated that I had wasted a lot of their time.

Jake Koenig was our builder, and he did a superb job. One example proves his craftsmanship. The facade of the eaves facing the woods is 118 feet long. It was perfectly straight, not a fraction of an inch off, its entire length. Jake was proud of this perfect craftsmanship and showed it to contractors or prospective clients. While writing this autobiography I went outside and got up on the deck where I could view this facade again. It is still as straight as it was forty years ago, when Jake built it. Jake also became our friend. He built many fine houses in Houston and hired our boys in the summer. We went on numerous hunts together. For a gift, Jake made Mary and me a large walnut trestle table. I am writing on it now. It will last for centuries.

Mary, who loved gardening, gave talks to garden clubs. She enjoyed developing our property and consulted landscape architects Pat Fleming and Ralph Gunn. One result was a patio filled with tropical plants and highlighted by a fountain with a bronze replica of *September Morn.* Outside, there was a combination drip fountain–bird bath, with a Japanese-style gravel walk, bordered by azaleas, leading to a large goldfish pond. Mary moved about thirty large camellia plants and some statuary from the Wilson house in Beaumont to our garden. From Cooke Wilson, Jr.'s woods in the Big Thicket we transplanted some young American beech, bay magnolia, and silver bell trees. Forty years later most of these are now large. Mary's mother, who was also a great gardener, helped us develop our garden. She invited me to accompany the Beaumont Garden Club on a one week trip to the grand gardens of southern Louisiana, Mississippi, and Alabama. I met the bus one morning before daylight. There was a large crowd of men and women at the bus station. When it came time to leave, forty-five women got on the bus, including Mrs. Wilson and Cooke, Jr.'s wife, Betty. I was alarmed to learn that I was the only man on the bus except the driver. The driver and I managed to get together alone occasionally for a cigarette and a cup of coffee. Nevertheless, it was a great trip to places such as Avery Island, private gardens in New Orleans, and the Bellingrath Gardens near Mobile. I learned enough to argue with Mary about plants.[12]

Our family loved to travel. Once on a medical trip to Monterrey we stayed at the Gran Ancira Hotel. My host was to pick me up at 8:00 P.M. for the lecture. He finally arrived at 10:00. I was very concerned that I had missed the lecture. We drove to the medical school where a few people were waiting. By 10:30 there were about thirty doctors. I read my talk in Spanish, but I learned that the guests all spoke English. After the talk, the entire group gathered at a large bar, where we sang and drank until 2:00 A.M. I left town at 8:00 A.M. with a terrible hangover. Our first trip to Europe was in 1954, when I attended several medical meetings, the most important one being the International Thyroid Meeting in London. The Selwyn Taylors gave us a party in their home and invited us to a dinner in the Lord Mayor's House. The Taylors must have given us their seats at the dinner, because we sat at the head table across from the Lord Mayor and the Queen's Physician. Our son John was with us on this trip, and we spent a month touring Europe in a Volkswagen. We brought the Volkswagen, one of the first, back to Houston, where Volks drivers waved at each other when they passed on the street. On another trip to London, I talked to the staff at Hammersmith Hospital and received a five pound note, which was the standard honorarium for a guest speaker.[13]

An important part of our social life at this time revolved around our activities in the Cooking Club. Following World War II, cooking had become a hobby for men. Except for barbecue cooks and famous male chefs, cooking had been a woman's domain. While I was stationed in the Aleutians, some of the officers cooked game and fish outdoors. In Anchorage we tried to cook some like-home dinners in the officers' quarters. The first cooking I remember doing as a husband in our household was making pizzas while stationed in Dayton, Ohio, in 1943. I wasn't the only man who cooked at home. My friends Tommy Anderson and Billy Rubey had been cooking, even bragged about it. On November 25, 1951, Tommy invited Billy and me, with our wives, to a complete dinner that he prepared. The menu included smoked oysters on beaten biscuits, Virginia ham Mornay, served with salad and toasted french bread with garlic butter, and Baked Alaska for dessert. On December 9, 1951, Billy Rubey had us to dinner. He prepared a chafing dish of Crab Suzette and a main course of a rare beef tenderloin with a brown sauce and large fresh mushrooms broiled in butter. For dessert he had an orange mousse. Bill had a staff of several assistants for this dinner. I must have had the next dinner, but I have no record of it. Tommy Anderson proposed that we have a cooking club. Billy and I agreed and elected Tommy as president. Once a year, each member would prepare a complete dinner. Originally, we planned a joint husband and wife effort. The wives rebelled after the first dinner, when they discovered their role would be running errands and washing dishes.

In 1952, Tommy entertained our new cooking club by serving Oysters College Inn, named for Houston's favorite restaurant on South Main Street. Tommy also served Crabmeat Ponchartrain, named for the famous hotel and restaurant in New Orleans. For dessert, he served Baked Alaska again. Since I had been to Mexico several times, I prepared for the club a Mexican dinner of chilies rellenos with walnut sauce, enchiladas with mole, and enselada guacamole. We were cooking the favorite Houston foods. Houston is in an enviable location, where several cuisines converge. Southern food was the original cuisine of Houston. When we arrived in 1949, the cuisine had been enhanced by the creole dishes from New Orleans. This was twenty five years before the spicy food of the Cajuns became so popular. Barbecue was popular, the kind cooked in South and East Texas, before West Texas style barbecue had spread its smokey mesquite aroma across the state. There were a few Tex-Mex restaurants in Houston and one at Richmond, but very few Anglos cooked Mexican food at home. The traditional foods of Mexico, such as chilies rellenos and mole, had not yet become popular in Texas.

In 1953, we invited Billy Carter to become a member. The cooking club was never given a specific name, and we had no charter or bylaws. But the club was a serious endeavor, not a party affair to which we'd invite a lot of friends. Only occasionally did we have guests—close family members or friends who happened to be here from out of town. Billy Carter made several important contributions to the club. He provided the foods of deep East Texas, where the Carter Lumber Company held thousands of acres of timber lands. The Carter men had hunted and cooked quail, ducks, and other game. Billy understood the soul food of East Texas African Americans. Billy was the only patient I ever treated who was injured by a falling goose. Billy shot the goose at Eagle Lake, and it fell hitting Billy in the chest and knocking him breathless and to the ground. He was left with painful bruises, but he recovered completely. Billy, on his own, became the official secretary of the cooking club. He recorded the menus and some recipes of our meetings in a strong three-quarter leather-bound ledger. His first dinner in 1953 included barbecued fresh pork ham and East Texas–style fried corn. Tommy Anderson served Oysters Ellis, and Beef Bourguignon. I served for my dinner, oysters in a chafing dish with Sauce Kelsey (sautéed onions, mushrooms, and celery with Worcestershire and Tabasco sauce); and squab with Virginia ham on toast.

As time went on we sought cuisines outside of the region and, even though we had little experience cooking, undertook complicated famous dishes. Our dinners were held on Sunday nights, so that we could spend the weekend experimenting. Several times we had to discard our failures and start over; sometimes we gave up and changed the menu. Tommy Anderson once attempted Chicken Hawaiian. The recipe called for chopping off the top of a coconut, leaving the meat in. The coconut was stuffed with chicken, cooked with bacon, onions, peppers, fresh corn, tomatoes, bay leaf, and white wine. A stuffed coconut for each guest was to be cooked in the hollows of a muffin pan. Something didn't work. This dish was not reported in Billy Carter's register of menus. One night Billy Rubey invited Marian's two elderly aunts and Mary's mother. All went well, until Billy made crepe Suzettes. When he poured brandy in the chafing dish flames raced into the bottle spewing brandy all over the table and down on the floor. The flames spread over the table, ran down the table leg and across the floor. The women screamed. Before we could do anything the flames burned out, leaving us safe but half-scared to death.

There was one memorable meeting of the Cooking Club in New Orleans, and one also in Copenhagen at the Tivoli Gardens while attending a medical conference with our families. On January 22, 1961, I reached the climax of my cooking career by serving a roast suckling pig. Fat seeped out of the piglet and ran out of the oven onto the floor. Mary helped by placing false eyelashes on the pig and a red cinnamon spiced apple in its mouth. She prepared the menu in French with appropriate quotations, and I signed it. The Cooking Club provided us friendship and conviviality and an education. We learned much about food and wine, enhancing our enjoyment of travel. Mary and I collected a couple hundred cookbooks. My new knowledge of nutrition helped me in prescribing diets for my patients. I recommend cooking clubs such as ours.

Mary and I were also very active in Houston social life, so active that it interfered with our family life. Social life and a busy practice distanced me from my boys. Sending them away to summer camp was not the right answer, even though they benefited from the camps. Our boys grew so fast and were learning things that I didn't know until I went to college. There was no work in the city as there was on the farm and in Dad's hardware store and garage. We tried to make work. I gave them jobs in the clinic and later at the ranch we purchased. Perhaps I was so strict the boys would not confide in me. John and Cooke were withholding information about things Mary and I would not approve. The boys were ahead of me in many ways and behind me in others. Nevertheless, they did well, and were highly motivated. I did take the boys hunting and fishing, as my father had taken me. I can remember some very happy trips with them—to Deport to hunt dove and to Cuero and Muldoon to hunt deer. I especially remember a trip to the post oak woods near Bryan with Bill Seybold and his sons. We stationed John at a spot about a quarter mile from the hunter's shack. In less than an hour, we heard two quick shots. John had killed one nice buck and said that he had hit another.

Kelsey family, 1958. *Standing left to right*: Mavis Parrott Kelsey, Sr., John Wilson Kelsey, and Mary Wilson Kelsey. *Sitting left to right:* Thomas Randolph Kelsey, Mavis Parrott Kelsey, Jr., and Cooke Wilson Kelsey

Sure enough, there was a fresh blood trail. I can't remember if we found the deer. This was John's first kill. He became one of the best hunters I know.

Mary took the lead role in educating our boys. She made the decisions, and I always agreed. After John finished River Oaks Elementary, he went to Lanier Junior High School for a year and was admitted to St. John's Episcopal School, where he graduated with honors in May 1959. He went to Harvard that fall, and roomed with his friend Albert Maher. Cooke went to St. John's when he finished River Oaks. Tom went to St. John's when he was in the fifth grade, and Mavis went when he was in the third grade. St. John's Episcopal School, now St. John's School, then only a few years old, was closely affiliated with St. John's Episcopal Church, where we were members. The school was adjacent to the church, where students attended daily chapel services. From its beginning, the school has maintained very high scholastic standards. Alan Lake Chidsey had been with the school as headmaster since its beginning. Then, the school was small, and we came to know the entire faculty as well as the other parents and made many friends.

I knew that our boys and some of their friends were a little wild and got into various minor problems. I had been so restricted when I was a boy that I went wild at college. I thought it was better for the boys to sow their wild oats, as Mother said, while they were still at home under parental surveillance. But they were wilder than I thought. Yet they were such nice boys, so friendly and well liked, so handsome, so promising. Nothing could go wrong. Our boys were fond of girls. They always had a sweetheart. Tom and Ann Heinzerling fell in love when they were twelve years old. They were still being carried to parties and being taken home by their parents. One night I went to the Vernon Frost house to pick up Tom. I opened the front door to the foyer and found Tom and Ann in an embrace. They have been in love ever since, and we still have laughs about that childhood tryst.

Everything seemed to be going famously for the Kelseys—the clinic, my professional career, and our family life. In early August 1959, our world fell apart. Mary and the boys had the beach house for that month. As usual I went down on weekends. John and Cooke seemed to prefer staying in Houston to be with their friends. Our younger sons Tom and Mavis were still happy staying at the beach. John had his own car and, being eighteen years old, was in Houston coming and going as he pleased. Cooke, aged sixteen, was in town doing pretty much as he pleased, too. On Thursday night, August 6, Fay and Jamie Griffith invited Cooke and me to supper. We had a happy evening talking and laughed about how Cooke would be the top dog in our household when John went off to college. Cooke and I drove home that night chuckling about the conversations. That entire evening is deeply imprinted in my memory. The next day, we were to go to the beach. I left the office early and went home to pack and pick up Cooke. Cooke had changed his mind and didn't want to go. He wanted to stay in Houston and go out with friends. I tried to persuade him in a friendly way. He insisted he would be okay. I started to demand that he go with me but I thought to myself that I should trust Cooke, that I shouldn't be so authoritarian. I didn't think about staying in Houston to look after him. It was a selfish misjudgment. I drove to the beach alone. Mary was a little upset with Cooke for not coming with me. Actually, she had been more lenient with the boys than I. But I was the one who made the mistake.

Mrs. Wilson was visiting Mary and the children at the beach that weekend. We went to bed. I remember reading late, a book by the Houston author David Westheimer. There was no phone at the house. About 3:30 A.M., Saturday, August 8, the deputy sheriff drove up to the beach house. He also ran the Caplen grocery and filling station about a mile away, where the summer residents went to make phone calls. The deputy said I had a call, he would take me to the store and bring me back. It was a strange remark. He knew I had my own car and didn't need to be carried. He would give no details. I immediately sensed that I would be receiving tragic news, and I thought about John and Cooke. When we got to the phone there was a call from John. He told me that Cooke had been killed in an automobile accident on South Post Oak. He was with three boys who were not seriously injured. I can't describe the reaction of sorrow that overcame me and gripped me for many weeks before it lessened, yet never disappeared.

I dreaded telling Mary. As I went up the stairs I had angina pectoris, the only time of my life. I thought, "I can't die now." The pain disappeared when I got up the stairs. There is no way to tell of Mary's shock and sorrow, and that of Mrs. Wilson, Tom, and Mavis when I woke them to break the sad news. It was daylight before we had packed our station wagon. We were all in tears. Someone drove Mrs. Wilson to Beaumont. We had to wait for the Galveston ferry. Every event surrounding this tragedy is permanently imprinted in my memory. I even remember the roadside flowers.

Friends and family were waiting for us in Houston. They were deeply saddened and sympathetic. There is no sorrow greater than losing one's child. I have learned this from many others who have lost a son or daughter. Mary and I realized how deeply we had loved Cooke and all our children. Cooke was buried at the Memorial Cemetery on Katy Road. We were amazed at the support we received from so many friends and family. The Seybolds were vacationing in the home of Frank Smith in Colorado Springs, Colorado. Bill came down for Cooke's funeral. Frank and Tweed Smith invited us to join the Seybolds in Colorado Springs. Everyone insisted that we go and get away from the scene of our tragedy. John Maher flew us to Colorado Springs and back. We stayed there several days. The trip was a life saver.

Cooke's death was a painful way for me to learn what goes on in every family when a young member is suddenly taken away. The emotional reaction to Cooke's death reverberated in our family for months, even years. I have been ridden by guilt and denial for the rest of my life. I became irascible. It affected my ability to practice medicine and my relationship with my partners. At my worst, I projected my guilt on other people, even on my dear Mary who could not have been more innocent. For years, all of the family had varying degrees of emotional problems that were related in part to Cooke's death.

In spite of the sorrow we still cherish fond memories of Cooke. We laugh, half crying, when we recount his antics and remember his cheerful grin. It would have been so much fun to have him grow up with his brothers and have a career. Like them, he would have brought us cheer and tears. In Cooke's memory, an athletic award was established at St. John's School. Mary, Waldo, Cooke, and Fay Griffith installed the Cooke Wilson Kelsey Memorial Language Laboratory at St. John's School. In 1993 Mary and I refurbished the laboratory and brought it up to date.[14]

Bill Seybold had an open invitation from all our partners to rejoin the group. As time passed, while not knowing whether Bill Seybold would return, we began to look elsewhere for a general surgeon. From 1959 to 1961, we considered inviting several Houston surgeons to join us. Each of these men were highly qualified and interested in joining our group. Meanwhile, Bill Seybold's solo practice continued to grow. He had a desire to return to the group and work toward our goal of developing a general clinic. Naturally, he was concerned about losing referrals and whether our group had grown enough to provide him an adequate number of patients. Finally, in 1961, Bill accepted our invitation to return, and he merged his practice with ours on January 26. On February 1, 1961, the executive committee changed our name to the Kelsey Leary Seybold Clinic. Bill moved in three months later on May 1, bringing to the clinic the practice he had developed while on his own. He was given seniority credits as if he had remained at the clinic. The three of us were back together again.

CHAPTER 15

Kelsey Leary Seybold Clinic, 1961–65

When Bill Seybold returned, we could rightfully call ourselves a clinic. My understanding of a real clinic, in American terms, is a group of doctors, representing both medical and surgical specialties, joined together in a single business entity. Bill fit right into our growing clinic. He sent letters to his patients and professional colleagues announcing he was rejoining as a partner. He brought patients to us, and his practice increased. When the clinic gained Bill, it also gained his secretary, Dorothy Teall. Our clinic went through a period of rapid expansion. We had to do a lot of recruiting to meet our growth. When we needed a new person in another specialty we wanted only the best qualified. We also looked for people already in practice who could bring practice to the clinic without being a financial burden.

Irving H. Schweppe joined us in July 1961. I first knew of Irving through his parents, who were friends and patients. He was a native Texan who graduated from the University of Texas at Austin and then from the Medical Branch in Galveston in 1954. Irving gained much of his graduate training in Boston. One of his mentors was John Hickam, who served with me at the aeromedical laboratory in Dayton, Ohio, and later joined Harvard's medical school faculty. Irving returned to Galveston to complete his training as a chest specialist. After coming to the clinic, Irving soon fell in love with Laura Randall, the daughter of our Galveston friends Edward and Katharine Randall, Jr. Irving and Laura married and had three daughters.[1]

Next came Phillip S. Bentlif, a gastroenterologist who had trained at the University of London and Johns Hopkins. By this time, our clinic had generated enough ophthalmology referrals to support a full-time ophthalmologist. This was an opportunity to broaden our service, another step toward a general clinic. We invited Frank G. Anderson, Jr., for an interview. He was completing his training in ophthalmology at the Mayo Clinic. Frank was a native of College Station and took his premedical training at Texas A&M. He was, and still is, an excellent ophthalmologist, just the perfectionist needed to do precise eye work. We had met with James D. McMurrey and offered him a position as surgeon in the clinic before Bill Seybold returned in 1961. Bill knew that Jim McMurrey would be a great addition to our staff and invited him into the clinic. Jim McMurrey joined in September of that year. A native Texan and son of a successful oil refiner in East Texas, he received his bachelor's and medical degrees from Harvard University. Jim then came to Baylor Medical College to join the surgical staff of Mike DeBakey, but he was not completely happy there and joined us.[2]

These new appointments completed our staff in 1961. Our clinical laboratory was staffed with registered technicians, our laboratory approved by the State Board of Pathologists. Ours was the only laboratory in town measuring urinary steroids. Our X-ray and Isotope Departments were staffed by registered technicians. Edward Singleton, chief of radiology at St. Luke's Hospital, was our consultant in radiology. The clinic was well organized, and our overhead was very low, about 35 percent. We had a proven partnership agreement and a plan for new doctors to become partners after two years on salary. Partners owned a separate corporation, which held the physical assets, and the leasehold on the Hannah property. The executive committee met each Monday morning at seven, and our entire staff met each quarter. We were members of the staffs of hospitals in the Texas Medical Center and held courtesy privileges in the other large city hospitals. Every doctor was board certified or eligible for certification in his specialty. All the members were on the Baylor faculty. Most of us had paying positions in the medical center institutions, where we also took an active part in administrative committees and teaching students and house staff.

Our three-year-old office building was overly crowded by this time. We had outgrown two offices in the Hermann Professional Building and two buildings on Travis Street. When the walls pulsated from crowds inside, we made the most profit. Our administrative offices had been moved to a vacant house, across the street from our clinic. And, because we had made commitments to add departments of otolaryngology and pediatrics, we were forced to enlarge our space for the fourth time in the twelve years since I had come to Houston. Our good landlord, the Hannah group, responded to our needs again. On July 13, 1961, we met with John and David Hannah to tell them we needed a larger clinic that could be further expanded, on the 65,000 square foot tract opposite the hospitals. There was a used car lot on the property. The brothers agreed on a forty-year lease at a fixed price, with lease renewal

Kelsey Leary Seybold Clinic, 1963

rights every ten years at a negotiated price. We arranged all of the financing with John Dunn to build a 30,000 square foot structure.

We employed, as consultants, the architectural firm of Ellerbe and Company of Minneapolis, which had designed several of the Mayo Clinic buildings. We went to Mayo to study a new clinic building then under construction. Our chief architect Ralph Anderson, who had designed our two previous buildings, had learned our needs. He designed a beautiful building, with white marble embellishments, a reflection of the quality of practice we were determined to deliver. The building had style, inside and out. It won several architectural awards, including the American Association of Medical Clinics' first award for a clinic building. We have built several structures since, but they have lacked the elegance of this building. On September 13, 1962, we awarded the contract to Bellows Construction Company. The building, at 6624 Fannin Street, had two stories and a full basement, with 11,000 square feet of space on each floor. The foundation was built to support an additional four floors.

We were pleased with our new building and its conveniences when we moved there in July 1963. Three or four doctors practiced from each nursing station, supplied and staffed for the doctor's specialty. Signals at each room identified which doctor should see the patient and whether the room was occupied. A well-organized patient record with an order sheet attached was placed in a slot outside the examining room. There was also a receptacle for the X rays. Each doctor had a call number for the speaker system. This efficient system was, in part, responsible for our success. We continually upgraded our methods, and ideas from our nurses, receptionists, and administrators also contributed to our success.

Our recruiting now continued with added vigor. We provided a large space for the X-ray department and employed our first full-time radiologist, Tom Harle. We also approached J. Charles Dickson, a leading otolaryngologist who treated many prominent Houstonians. Born in Lampasas, Texas, in 1903, he graduated from the University of Nebraska Medical School and interned at Jefferson Davis Hospital in Houston. Charlie developed his own solo private practice in Houston. He had argyria, or silver gray pigmentation of the skin, from using silver nitrite and Argerol during his early practice. Charlie had only a few hairs on his head, and he clipped them short. He was conscientious, affable, and very patient. Before we had a commitment from Charlie Dickson, however, I had also sought out James L. Smith, another otolaryngologist who was serving his military duty as base flight surgeon at Ellington Field, where I was a consultant in medicine. He received his bachelor's degree in 1949, his master's in 1951, and his medical degree in 1955, all from the University of Texas. He bled U.T. orange. He interned at Brooke Army Hospital, before being assigned to Ellington Field. I was afraid I'd be in trouble accepting two otolaryngologists at once, but otolaryngologists were scarce as hen's teeth, and we would never get another chance. I didn't know how Jim and Charlie would accept each other, who would want to be chief, and whether they thought there was enough practice for both. It was with some apprehension that I met with both Jim and Charlie on August 22, 1961. The two came together like hand-in-glove, Charlie, who was the senior of the two, accepted being the chief, and the three of us left the meeting happy.[3]

Dickson and Smith both joined the clinic several months before we had completed the Fannin Building. They continued to practice in the Hermann Professional Building, until the new building was ready. They had designed their own department. For months, Dickson worked with the architect and contractor, designing a sound-proof room for hearing tests. It was very expensive. When the clinic was completed, Charlie proudly put a patient in his sound-proof room. But he heard cars honking and trucks passing on the street outside! Oh well. He had to use his imperfect room.

I could write a book about Earl Johnson Brewer, pediatrician and the next addition to our clinic in 1962. He was a distinguished member of our institution, as a result of his work with juvenile arthritis. After his military service Earl, a Texan, graduated from Texas Christian University in Fort Worth. He worked at night as a technician in the Terrell Laboratory under the direction of Dr. May Owen. He earned his medical degree at Baylor medical school in

1954. Earl became an AKK. After two years of internship and a residency in pediatrics at Baylor, Earl spent two years at the Children's Hospital, Harvard University, in Boston. In 1957, he returned to Houston and served as chief resident at Texas Children's Hospital for two years. Earl took a part-time job in the Rugely Blassingame Clinic in Wharton and commuted part time to Texas Children's Hospital developing a department of rheumatology.

We had heard about this smart young resident at Texas Children's who had specialized in pediatric rheumatology, the first doctor to do so in Houston. Earl Brewer and I had friends in common in Fort Worth and Wharton who belonged to AKK. I invited Earl to our house with a few partners to offer him a job at the clinic. Earl accepted. He planned to develop a department of pediatrics at the clinic while continuing on the staff at Texas Children's Hospital, developing his section of rheumatology. He would be successful in both of these goals. Earl soon had a thriving practice in pediatrics at the clinic, and, with so many new patients, it wasn't long before we had to recruit for more pediatricians. To me, pediatrics has always been the most satisfying department in the clinic. There is a certain kindness and gentleness found among pediatricians and their staff.[4]

Earl, always a good natured, cheerful person, was something of a romantic and a visionary, often seen in people of achievement. Earl ended up getting me personally and the clinic sued for alienation of affections, something I couldn't do regardless of how hard I tried. When I came to Houston, one didn't hear of many malpractice suits against doctors. I subscribed to a $2,500 malpractice insurance policy issued by a company that claimed it had never lost a case. At the time, to be sued for malpractice was very humiliating, because only a genuine offense would lead to a lawsuit. Of course, since then, many frivolous claims have been filed, and many plaintiffs have collected outrageously high settlements. Malpractice insurance has become very expensive, another significant factor in rising health costs. I was never sued or named in a lawsuit for malpractice. But the one lawsuit that named me as the defendant gained national recognition.

The lawsuit was the result of Earl Brewer's marital problems while a partner at the clinic. The suit was based on the legal theory that, as chief of the clinic, I was responsible for the acts of an employee. In 1967, Earl had been separated from his first wife, and the two were in process of getting a divorce. He met Maria (Ria) Winterbotham Maclay, when she was a volunteer at Texas Children's Hospital. Her marriage was also on the rocks, with divorce proceedings in progress. Earl and Ria fell in love, a romance that originated in the hospital, not in the Kelsey-Seybold Clinic. Ria's estranged husband claimed Earl had seduced his wife while acting as her doctor and sued him for alienation of affections. The clinic and I also were named in the suit, which alleged that we had not controlled our doctor's behavior. The lawsuit was a total surprise. At that time, I had never laid eyes on Ria and was being sued for alienation of affections. In a way I was flattered to think that I was being represented as a lothario.

The lawsuit gained nationwide publicity, because it was one of the first to claim that a partnership should be liable for the independent and personal conduct of one of its partners. The *Houston Post,* dubbing it the "'Love' Case," on April 29, 1971, reported: "The Texas Supreme Court in a split decision held Wednesday that a Houston medical clinic must stand trial along with one of its partners on charges of alienating the affections of a female patient from her husband. . . . Maclay charged that Brewer's actions occurred while he was acting as a medical doctor for the family and that Dr. Mavis Kelsey, one of the senior partners of the clinic, 'had knowledge of Dr. Brewer's actions . . . and that the partnership approved of, consented to, and ratified and condoned such conduct of his partner, Brewer, and refused to come to the aid of your plaintiff or in any way attempt to halt or disapprove the actions of Brewer. . . .'" Associate Justices Joe Greenhill and Sears McGee dissented, saying they were "unable to agree that the partners of Dr. Brewer or the Kelsey Clinic are even potentially liable."

The case did not go to trial, because the plaintiff's lawyer asked to settle the $500,000 suit out of court for $10,000 to cover his expenses. We were relieved to settle. An interesting thing about this case was that the families involved seemed to remain friends. Some were among my patients. I went to a party at the Bayou Club as a guest of one family member and was surprised to see the principals and other family members together and having a great time, as if nothing had happened. Both Earl and Ria had children from their first marriages. They got their respective divorces and married in May 1970 to raise another family and are happily married today.

For several years I held a rush party at our home for the Alpha Kappa Kappa medical fraternity. I met Wilson Fraser at one of these parties. Wilson graduated from the University of Texas Medical Branch and trained as a dermatologist. He was a native Houstonian and entered practice in Houston. The clinic was sending a large number of dermatology cases to several dermatologists, including him. His practice was also growing. About a year after Wilson entered practice we invited him to join us. He came in 1963. Wilson was a very attractive young man with an equally attractive family. He was active in the Baylor teaching program and soon developed a thriving practice at the clinic. Several members of his family became my patients. Wilson stayed for many years.

We continued to search for a urologist. Among the urologists we were sending patients to was Donald W. Pranke, who was in a successful partnership with Tobe Shearer. But we took a chance and asked Don if he was interested in joining. He accepted and moved in with us on May 1, 1964. A highly trained surgeon from the University of Illinois in his home state, he came to Houston after World War II. He was fortunate in having a fine family. His wife, Pat, was active in volunteer work and promoted friendship and social activities among the clinic wives. They had two daughters. Don was a practical, straightforward doctor, especially well liked by his men patients.

In 1963 we had added a dentist. I had pushed for one, because the dental service was so successful at Mayo. There was quite a bit of opposition, because dentists occupied so much office space. Dentists were very anxious to join our clinic. John Olsen, dean of the University of Texas School of Dentistry, and Fred Elliott passed the word around, and we soon had applicants. Our first, James Orr, was an excellent dentist. He taught in the dental college and held dental work shops for practicing dentists. He became well known in England, where spent a great deal of time in dental conferences and teaching workshops. After a few years with the clinic, he moved to Austin to organize a group of dentists.

Before he left, Orr located another great dentist as his replacement. Bill Gray had just retired from the army, where he was dentist for the Pentagon and the White House. President Truman was among his patients. Bill came in 1964. He was a great believer in dental hygiene and prevention. Mary and I became good friends of Bill and his wife, Millie. He started collecting clocks in the military, while stationed in Germany. Most of his clocks were wall clocks with various chimes and moving parts. Some were very amusing cuckoo clocks. He kept some thirty-five on display and all running.[5]

From 1961 to mid-1965—the years of the Kelsey Leary Seybold Clinic—these additions made up a full-time staff of twenty-eight doctors. We also had several consultants. We filled our new building at 6624 Fannin and continued to recruit doctors. Mary was a tremendous help in my practice. She spent many nights helping me entertain prospective and visiting doctors. Many of our friends from Rochester, the military, and medical school came through town and visited. Mary was not alone in entertaining. Other doctors' wives were just as busy entertaining visitors, contributing a great deal to the success of the clinic. Many wives were active in the medical auxiliary or served as volunteers in charitable, religious, and political organizations. The wives social club met regularly at different homes. They compiled information for the members, such as names of children, their hobbies and other activities, and circulated a newsletter. This went on for a number of years.

On the administrative side, manager Jackie Greer and comptroller Bill

Stovall were doing a fine job running the clinic, when Bill Seybold returned in 1961. With Jackie's departure to the Fannin Bank in 1962, however, Bill Stovall reluctantly assumed the additional duty as manager. We quickly began a nationwide search for a qualified clinic manager. We recruited through our acquaintances in the American Association of Medical Clinics, an organization that had been in existence only a few years. Clinics weren't very numerous, and there were about forty member clinics when we joined. I was delegate for our clinic and attended every annual meeting for years and served on some committees. We learned that the Bowman Gray College of Medicine in Winston-Salem, North Carolina, had a training program for clinic managers, about the only one in the country. Here, we located James A. Bakken, who became our administrator in May 1963.

Jim stayed with us until 1983. For his first few years, I spent more time with him than any other person in the clinic. Jim was very competent, easy to work with, an honest guy, and well liked by doctors and employees. For years, he managed to get along with all the doctors, even when they numbered a hundred, a feat very few clinic managers ever achieve. Eventually, his departure resulted from a few disgruntled doctors who claimed Jim used some clinic property to his own benefit. I assured everyone that Jim never misused anything belonging to the clinic. He did have some trouble with some clinic employee politics, but who wouldn't? Jim was very popular with clinic managers nationwide and became president of the American Medical Group Management Association. I have had a few pleasant visits with Jim after he left and worked elsewhere in medical administration.

Among other outstanding employees, Nell Barnette was an executive secretary and administrative assistant. Billy Jo Farris Reiske was another. Ruth Jordan came as an untrained receptionist and worked her way up to become a capable administrator. She became certified as a clinic manager and eventually left to manage a growing out-of-state clinic.

In the early days, the clinic doctors were assigned registered nurses as assistants in charge of handling their patients in the examining room and on the phone. When a doctor's practice became large enough he was assigned a nurse full time. Before Aggie Greer came in 1965, two fine nurses, Pat Slavens and Doris Evans, served me at different times. Jean Perkins was a highly qualified nurse assistant. One fine secretary was Cora Lynn Pollard. She left when she married Leon Librick, an endocrinologist at Texas Children's Hospital. Another secretary who spent her career with the clinic was Pat Lamb. Jean Fatheree, the cousin of Jeff Fatheree, also spent many years with us as a secretary. She had a pleasant English accent and a fine knowledge of the English language.[6] I got along well with the nondoctor employees.

In these years, the Kelsey Leary Seybold Clinic became a prototype for the large general clinic of the future. It was a proving ground for developing our own methods of operation and patient care. As at Mayo, our clinic stressed quality as the important consideration in all of our ventures. If a prospective doctor was not good enough to treat our family member's most serious problems, he or she would not be offered a position. Quality meant recruiting physicians with exceptional credentials, those who graduated at or near the top of their medical classes and were either board certified or eligible. We also strived for quality service and convenience for the patient. Most of our doctors were members of AOA, the honorary medical fraternity.

Physicians, then, considered themselves superior to all others in the healing profession. We believed we knew more about the body than any podiatrist, physical therapist, dietitian, optometrist, dentist, psychologist, nurse, osteopath, or other registered medical caregiver, all put together. We ignored that these people knew something about their profession that medical doctors didn't know, and we viewed chiropractors with special disdain. When I was at the Mayo Clinic, chiropractors were not to be called "Doctor" by the staff. Midwives had no standing whatsoever. Acupuncturists, hypnotists, and naturopaths were dismissed as quacks. Doctors are not so exalted today. We are still, by far, the best educated of the medical professionals, but we have come to realize that others have knowledge in their special fields that medical doctors do not have. Many clinic and hospital staffs today include midwives, optometrists, osteopaths, dietitians, nurse practitioners, podiatrists, physician assistants, and others whose services are accepted and appreciated.

Specialization was the order of the day. All doctors at our clinic were specialists. We planned to add other specialists to cover the major medical specialties. To meet our goal of providing our patients with total care among a group of specialists, we encouraged each patient to select one doctor as a personal physician. This doctor would coordinate the patient's care, making referrals to other specialists, and ordering laboratory, X-ray, and other diagnostic studies as needed. Even Charlie Dickson, an otolaryngologist, brought several hundred patients with him when he joined the clinic, and most of his patients continued to consider Charlie to be their personal physician. When Bill Seybold returned he also brought many patients who considered him to be their personal physician. With one personal doctor and one medical record, duplicate studies were eliminated and the high-quality, cost-effective care was provided. Care took precedence over costs. But we carried medical specialization entirely too far. We should have employed more general internists and general practitioners.

As the clinic expanded, we developed several other small corporations. The use of computers was just beginning, and the Mayo Clinic was trying to computerize its entire operation. IBM even built a factory in Rochester and developed numerous computer functions for the Mayo Clinic, although they eventually gave up on computerizing patient records. Record keeping, bookkeeping, billing, and management was causing us all kinds of headaches, so we organized the Medical Computer Company. IBM installed a computer in our basement that occupied the space of two examining rooms. The machine required special air conditioning, otherwise it would break down. IBM service men frequently were down in the basement, coaxing the computer to work. Large round metal containers held hundreds of tapes. We were able to keep this monster in operation and thought we might make some money providing computer services such as doing billings for other doctors. We did get a few customers. We didn't realize it, but in Dallas there was a young man named Ross Perot who started at about the same time providing computer services. I wish we had hired him. Our computer company didn't set the world on fire, and we finally sold it to a firm in Dallas (not Perot's) at a neat profit.

Like other clinics, we kept adding computer facilities to our operations and stayed relatively up to date. Even today, however, our patient records are not yet fully computerized. The clinic now has a building exclusively for the 1,300,000 patient records. We have eight vans in continuous circulation delivering records to thirty locations in Houston. Another little company was Clinic Business Forms. It operated in a rented building outside the clinic.

We appointed new committees for each new problem. Different committees addressed payroll, budget, professional, building, personnel, X-ray, isotope, laboratory, pharmacy, recruiting, branch-office, contract, and pension problems. I was spread too thin, as chief of the partnership, chief of the executive committee, chief of staff, chief of medicine, chief of everything, and president of all these little companies. I was micromanaging everything and had too many ideas I was trying to institute. In 1964, I bought a ranch and tried to micromanage that. The ranch did direct my attention away from the details of the clinic. I was trying to micromanage my family in spite of ongoing rebellion. I must have been a terrible bore. I was working or socializing up to eighteen hours a day. I was having fun seeing the clinic grow, but it probably would have grown faster if I had let others do more. My compulsion for detail did bear a little fruit, however. I designed the doctors' order sheet, which, with various alterations, has been used to this day. I designed schedules for fees and examinations that were printed in a handbook for company accounts. I also wrote a health questionnaire we used for years.

As our practice grew the source of our patients struck a balance that held for years: 30 percent of patients were referred by other doctors, and 30 percent of patients were from outside Houston. By 1963 we had reached an annual gross income of $1,000,000. Our doctors' income ranged from $12,000 to $50,000 a year. This was great for the time, but the days of big income for doctors had already begun. Some orthopedists and surgeons were netting $100,000, while a very few were carrying home more than $300,000.

A prestigious event for our doctors was to be called out of town for a consultation. I remember calls to Huntsville, Brenham, Beaumont, East Bernard, and Wharton. Jim Little called me to Wharton to see a patient in 1963. I was always apprehensive when Jim called. Jim, like Sam Barnes, was a smarter doctor than I. This patient, a young woman, had unexplained jaundice. She wasn't very sick, and I couldn't find much wrong. On checking her medications I found that she had been taking thorazine, a drug recently put on the market for treating mental problems. The thorazine was discontinued and the jaundice went away.

At M. D. Anderson Hospital and in private practice I had quite a few patients with tetany, resulting from destruction of the parathyroid glands. The glands were accidentally or unavoidably destroyed during surgical removal of the thyroid gland for various types of goiters including cancer. Tetany has always been a difficult problem to treat. Organ transplants were being discussed. There had been successful corneal transplants, even kidney transplants. At the time there was little to prevent tissue rejection by the host or recipient of the transplant. I talked about doing a parathyroid transplant with George Jordan, professor of surgery at Baylor who had trained at the Mayo Clinic. George decided to transplant the parathyroid glands from a deceased infant. Our patient with severe tetany stayed on alert for weeks before Jordan could obtain fresh parathyroid tissue from the body of an infant. He transplanted the baby's parathyroid tissue into a vascular area of the patient's neck. The patient was soon almost completely relieved of tetany and stayed so for a few years before it gradually returned. We never reported this case in the literature. I wonder if anyone has repeated this procedure on a number of patients.

After several renal transplants had become successful and Christian Barnard in South Africa had performed the first successful human heart transplant in 1967, there was a great flurry to promote organ transplants. Many were talking about replacing organs as they wore out, so people could live forever. Mrs. Floyd Karstens of Houston organized the Living Bank and encouraged people to will their organs to those in need. Next of kin were encouraged to donate the organs of their loved ones. The Living Bank opened an office in a mobile home on Fannin Street near the Clinic. I was on the original board. I thought we should be recruiting a transplant surgeon. Bill Seybold rightfully thought we weren't quite ready for it. Since, hematologists and allergists have developed methods to reduce tissue rejection. Across the street in Methodist and St. Luke's Hospitals, heart transplants would soon be performed by DeBakey and Cooley. A complete new field of medicine evolved, but not so fast as I thought it would, when I thought all we had to do was employ a transplant surgeon.

I remained active in the thyroid clinic at M. D. Anderson Hospital. On July 15, 1964, I was reappointed clinical associate internist on a one-sixth time basis at $1,800 a year. It was a labor of love. Ray Rose had become full time in the thyroid and endocrine sections. We published several articles together before he left and was replaced by Tom Haynie, who was also chief of nuclear medicine. Bob Moreton had joined the staff to be in charge of patient care. We were fellows together at the Mayo Clinic. He practiced radiology in Fort Worth before coming to Anderson. Bob played an important role in developing the feeling of caring and compassion that Anderson Hospital is noted for. Bob died while he was still contributing to Anderson's fine reputation. He left many friends among the patients he had served.

I became close to many patients whom I admired. I've mentioned Governor Hobby. Unfortunately, I was in New York City when he died. I read about it in a New York newspaper. Milton and Catherine Underwood bought Rosedown Plantation in Louisiana. They built a house of their own there and restored the old antebellum home for tourists to visit. We were their guests during the extensive restoration process. Milton later had a coronary occlusion while he and Catherine were at Rosedown and was treated at home by a local physician. I was flown over to see him. He had an uneventful recovery. I had a similar experience with Ernie Cockrell. He had a coronary occlusion on his boat off Nassau in July 1965, and I was flown to see him in a local hospital. He also made an uneventful recovery. The Fields family in Baytown were patients. I watched their son Jack grow up and graduate from Baylor. I was very surprised when he came in one day and said he was going to run for Congress against well-entrenched Bob Eckhardt, whom I also knew. Sure enough, Jack won the election and served several terms before retiring voluntarily. Bob Casey and his family were patients. He was a popular county judge when he decided to run for the United States Congress. He won and served several terms. Congressman and Mrs. Albert Thomas were patients. As were Congressman Charles Wilson of Lufkin, Governor Allen Shivers and some of his family, and Senator Lloyd Bentsen. Governor John Connelly was a patient for years. I well remember the day President John Kennedy was assassinated in Dallas in 1963, and Connelly was severely wounded by the same assassin. The next time he came for an annual physical, I was surprised to see the extensive scars on his chest resulting from the assassin's bullet or bullets. I was surprised that he survived.

I had some colorful Texans as patients. There was Mrs. Caperton, a wealthy old ranch woman from Shamrock, Texas. Once, after subjecting her to an unpleasant test, she said, "If you do that to me again I'm going to ship you." Any cattle rancher will know what she meant. We were already seeing many patients from Mexico and other Latin American countries. Many patients were generous. They gave us presents and invited us on trips and to their ranches. They gave money to various causes in our honor. That was how the Kelsey-Seybold Foundation got its start. For years my life revolved around my patients. Only a few were wealthy; I was close with many others. I still have dozens of modest presents from patients I will always remember. Some have sent me Christmas cards for fifty years. I do take pride in the number of prominent and wealthy people treated by our clinic. Many came great distances to see us. Having such patients was a mark of quality, since they could afford the best doctors and chose us. I also take pride in having treated all patients, rich and poor alike, with the same concern.

My parents were growing old in Deport. We celebrated their fiftieth wedding anniversary in 1961, with every Kelsey in Texas present. The family gave them a silver tea set with which Mother could entertain her church and club friends. Mary's mother lived alone in the Wilson house in Beaumont. She remained active until she had a stroke about 1960. Mary made many extended trips to Beaumont to be with her mother during this long illness. She died in November 1961. Mary's sister, Fay, and her husband, Jamie Griffith, lived in Houston near us. Their four children were in Houston schools. Our families were close. Mary saw Fay several times a week. Jamie and I made several trips together to Mexico sightseeing. Mary's brother Cooke, Jr. and his wife, Betty, moved from Beaumont to Houston in 1961. They also had four small children in a house near us. The Kelseys and Wilsons all lived close to each other in southwest Houston. All of us belonged to the Houston Country Club. John and Mickey Kelsey had a house near Brenham. The Griffiths had a ranch on the Brazos River at East Columbia. Mary and I bought a ranch near Katy. These facilities and the beach house on Bolivar Peninsula provided many opportunities for family gatherings.

The Kelsey and Wilson grandchildren were growing up together. Ours were the oldest grandchildren in the family. John had graduated with honors from St. John's School and had gone to Harvard for a year or two. He married Elizabeth Rice Winston of Houston on July 27, 1962, and continued his education at Vanderbilt University. John and Elizabeth divorced in 1964. After graduating from Vanderbilt, John earned a law degree at the University of Texas Law School. Our son Tom graduated from St. John's School in Houston and attended Washington and Lee University in Lynchburg, Virginia, graduating in 1966. Mavis, Jr., completed his high school education at Westminster School in Simsbury, Connecticut, then also attended Washington and Lee.

Hurricane Carla struck in September 1961. Weather predictions were not nearly so accurate then. There were no satellites, and storms and hurricanes were monitored from airplanes flying above the clouds. People did not know how severe a hurricane would be, until it was over and the damage was assessed. We knew Carla was coming and it was big and probably would hit the Gulf Coast below Freeport. I was on a "white-wing" dove hunt in the Rio Grande valley. The weather there was calm but we were advised to leave. I rode back to Houston in the Tenneco Plane, said to be the last one into the Houston airport before the weather closed in. We taped our floor-to-ceiling glass windows, bought batteries, groceries, and dry ice for our deep freeze, and stored water in the bath tubs.

That night the storm began. The house rocked. No one slept. The full fury of the hurricane came after daylight the next day. We could see limbs flying through the air. Giant pine trees bent like a celluloid ruler. Some large elm and oak trees fell. I watched one large oak in our yard. It fell over so fast that no one could have gotten out of the way. The crash shook the whole house. Huge limbs broke and punched into the ground several feet. The yard was full of storm litter two or three feet deep. Trees had fallen across the streets, making it impossible to get in or out. We lost electricity for several days. High water blocked the Galveston freeway. The clinic was closed, but Jackie Greer and Bill Seybold managed to get there. Bill sewed up some wounds of patients hurt in the storm. It took weeks to get over the hurricane. Our greatest loss was the Wilson beach house, Le Caprice, on Bolivar Peninsula. The large two story house that could sleep twenty people was gone. Only a spoon engraved "Le Caprice" was found on the lot.

For relaxation, I went on hunting and fishing trips with my sons and many other ventures with friends. Once, Bobby Kuldell organized a fishing trip out of Freeport. A busload of Bobby's friends left Houston one night. A waiter served drinks from an open bar on the bus. We were in good shape when we arrived at a motel in Freeport and continued to celebrate past midnight. We were up at five in the morning to board the chartered fishing boat and get out in the Gulf by sunup. A persistent rain and high wind blew in. We didn't see the sun all day. I had a terrible hangover and was soon deathly seasick. I was not alone. I had heard of people being so seasick they had nausea, vomiting, and diarrhea at the same time. It happened to me that day. We caught very few fish.

Another annual event was a duck hunt at Alfred Glassell's family camp in the Louisiana swamps near Lake Arthur. Like everything else the Glassells did, this was deluxe. The "camp," accessible only by a several-mile boat ride, was a large converted two-story dormitory, formerly used for oil field crews. There were other quarters for the Cajun guides and servants, as well as docks and kennels. The compound was on a small artificial island in a vast swamp, with no neighbors for miles. Before daylight each guide with his Labrador retriever took a guest hunter out in an airboat. The guide zoomed through long narrow canals surrounded by tall swamp grass, until he reached his blind. He stationed the hunter in the blind, put out the decoys, got in the blind and started calling ducks. I went on many trips, and the ducks always came. When I was lucky enough to shoot one, the dog never failed to retrieve it. We zoomed back to camp about noon for a Louisiana seafood lunch. My favorite was duck gizzard gumbo. At night we played poker and told stories. Alfred's father, Alfred Glassell, Sr., or Pops, was usually there. One day while all the hunters were out in their blinds, the hunting lodge caught fire and rapidly burned up. The hunters watched the fire from a distance. They could do nothing but come back to a pile of ashes. Pops Glassell later moved some mobile homes in to replace the destroyed buildings, and the hunts resumed.[7]

On another trip, I was guest of Bill Liedtke and the Pennzoil Company. As Pennzoil medical director, I knew the executives and board members as friends and patients. Bing Crosby was a guest. We hunted the McAllen ranch. Another annual trip was a white-wing dove hunt in the Rio Grande valley. For most white-wing hunts I was the guest of Russ Birdwell, owner of the Monte Christo Drilling Company. Russ was a patient and the uncle of Hal Boylston, a psychiatrist in our clinic. As I recall, the white-wing hunting season opened on September 15, two weeks after the Labor Day dove hunt in Deport. We hunted mourning doves around Deport. Many of these doves were in fall migration to the south from the grain fields of Kansas and Oklahoma. The white-wing dove is slightly larger than the mourning dove. It has several white feathers on each wing, easily discernible while the bird is in flight. Its habitat is limited to both sides of the lower Rio Grande and northern Mexico. Before they were badly depleted by hunters, there were literally millions of white-wing doves in the lower Rio Grande Valley. Due to strict hunting restrictions, the doves have made a comeback in recent years.

Hundreds, maybe thousands, of hunters converged on the Rio Grande Valley for the white-wing event. The McAllen airport was crowded with private and company planes. Company CEOs flew their top management personnel and guests down to hunt in the afternoons and celebrate at night in the bars and restaurants of Reynosa. Hundreds of prostitutes from all over Mexico came to the Mexican border towns to participate in the celebrations. We hunted on either side of the Rio Grande on large ranches, where our party had been invited. I hunted on the Bentsen ranch several times. The hunts were elaborate affairs. There were often a dozen guest hunters in a party and a dozen Mexican youths on hand to serve cold drinks and pick up birds. When darkness came, all of us were dusty, sweaty, and thirsty. We usually returned to the McAllen Country Club Inn, which Russ Birdwell owned. We showered and dressed and gathered for a party sometimes at Russ's house. Then the younger members often went to Boys' Town to see the performances, drink margaritas, and tip the girls.

The game limit was twenty birds. When the birds flew in by the thousands we sometimes lost count and exceeded our limits. The valley was swarming with game wardens. Fines up to $100 for each bird that exceeded the limit and a possible jail sentence made us very careful. On the Mexican side there were few game wardens. I remember one trip to the Mexican side, hosted by Russ Birdwell, when we lost count of birds. After dark the boys cleaned the birds, shook them in a large paper sack with flour, salt and, black pepper, then deep-fried them in a big pot of hot oil. After a feast of white-wing doves and a few drinks, we drove back across the Rio Grande to Texas. Each of our cars was stopped by customs officers and game wardens. They asked if we had anything to declare or any game birds in the car. The driver of our car, honestly unaware of any birds in the car, said no, and we were allowed to proceed without being searched. When we got to the motel, we opened the trunk to remove our gear and were shocked to find the trunk filled with white-wing doves we had shot. Apparently, the Mexican boys had picked up the birds in the field and pitched them in the trunk of the car. There must have been 150 birds. We would have been in much trouble had we been caught. Russ was stuck with the birds. He called out some help who spent the rest of the night cleaning birds and putting them in the freezer.

In October 1963, I was invited, along with Dorman David and John Jenkins, to a bird hunt on the Guerra Ranch in Mexico, fifty miles south of Reynosa. Mr. Guerra was another rare book collector. Each of us were served a roasted goat head, eyes and all. We talked rare books and hunted doves, rock pigeons, and quail. Mr. Guerra was a bilingual international citizen of Texas and Mexico, a descendant of people who owned the land on both sides of the Rio Grande since Spanish colonial days, long before Texas won its independence from Mexico. When we were ready to return home from the Guerra Ranch, Mr. Guerra drove us to his large modern house in Reynosa. He put our game in Mrs. Guerra's car, and she drove across the border to their Texas residence, waving to the customs officials who knew her. She took the birds to our waiting plane. A half-hour later, Mr. Guerra drove us across the border in his station wagon. We had our hunting gear but no game. The officials stopped us and searched our car thoroughly, and, remembering that Mrs. Guerra had driven across a few minutes before, exclaimed, "You have fooled us again. Mrs. Guerra has the birds!" We acted surprised, but after we crossed the border we raced to our plane and took off for Houston before the Texas wardens could reach us, in case they had been alerted.[8]

These years saw another transition for the clinic, with the departure of Bill Leary from the practice in 1965. Bill was a great partner. He provided many useful ideas. More a supporter than a leader, he shared our vision of a general clinic. He often counseled against an aggressive approach, even though he was all for expansion. He, like Bill Seybold, was willing to share his patients and carry his load. Bill Leary was a kind and sensitive person who never had a malicious thought. Rough and tumble competition was hard on him. He worried about his patients, because some did not understand his blunt humor. On the other hand many patients were dedicated to Bill and would do anything for him. Bill resigned from the clinic in June 1965 and accepted a full-time position at M. D. Anderson, becoming chief of the pulmonary medicine department, a position he held for several years. He continued on the Kelsey-Leary Foundation board and served as chairman of the grants committee.

Bill and Margaret were divorced in 1969. He later married Elizabeth, his secretary at M. D. Anderson. After retiring from M. D. Anderson Hospital, Bill worked for the Veterans Administration in Kirksville, Missouri, and Beaumont, Texas. He eventually retired to San Antonio. He developed severe arthritis, eventually had a stroke, and died about 1994. I attended his funeral at St. John's Episcopal Church in Houston. Today, Margaret Leary lives in Austin, near her daughter Jean Works.

CHAPTER 16

Kelsey-Seybold Clinic, 1965–86

We had become a real general clinic, even though we had only thirty-one full-time physicians and a few part-time consultants. Our new building was completely filled and we were planning to enlarge it. The Kelsey-Leary Foundation was a modest operation, which depended solely on unsolicited gifts from grateful patients. The clinic employed a full-time administrator, accountant, and a staff of a hundred people. We had a well-functioning clinical laboratory, radiology department, and nuclear medicine laboratory. Several auxiliary services included a dietician, a physical therapist, and psychologists.

The entire staff was energetic and enthusiastic. We had fine nurses, receptionists, secretaries, and technicians. Our partnership agreement was fair and popular. An executive committee, elected by the partners, directed our efforts. I considered every doctor my friend and I believe everyone else had the same feeling.

Doctors rotated on hospital and night call. Schedules were organized to provide round-the-clock service to our patients. We made house calls. We weren't getting rich, but many doctors, then, didn't think about getting rich; they were motivated more by a desire to render service and increase their knowledge. We attended frequent staff meetings. We were on the Baylor faculty and took an active part in teaching medical students and house staff. A newsletter, the *K-S Review,* kept doctors and employees up to date. Several important events were on the immediate horizon, including winning a contract to provide medical services at the Johnson Space Center and opening our first branch clinic. Changes began with the enlargement of the clinic building, the fifth expansion since 1949. We planned to add four floors of 11,000 square feet each to the 1963 building, which had two floors and a full basement. With the addition, we would have a total of 77,000 square feet of useable space. On

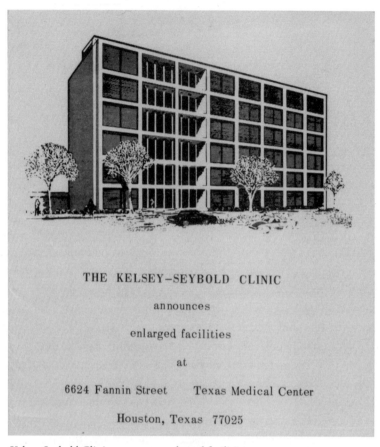

THE KELSEY–SEYBOLD CLINIC

announces

enlarged facilities

at

6624 Fannin Street   Texas Medical Center

Houston, Texas 77025

Kelsey-Seybold Clinic announces enlarged facilities

November 23, 1965, brother John and I met with our landlord, John Hannah of University Realty Company, and Ralph Anderson, our architect. By mid-December 1966, we had signed a new lease purchase agreement. American General Life Insurance Company financed us. The contractor did a superb job making the external structure a continuation of the 1963 building. There were marble-clad pilasters extending to the top of the building and large recessed floor-to-ceiling glass walls for the waiting rooms on each floor.

We occupied the new space in 1967. The extension also contained a library and meeting rooms with movable partitions. A small kitchen adjoined the large meeting hall on the sixth floor. A catered buffet lunch was served each of the five working days. By this time, we were staying open only five days a week, instead of the five-and-a-half to six days we worked in 1949 at the

Hermann Building. All of the professional and house staff and assigned medical students and visiting doctors ate lunch together and discussed medicine and anything else they could think of. Medical presentations were made each week. Staff meetings and dinners were held on a regular schedule. These lunches and meetings were a great success. I still meet doctors who tell me they learned a lot at the lunches while they were medical students.

The building was efficient and convenient. Ralph Anderson deserved high praise for such a successful, award-winning structure. The building entrances were above flood level. We thought we were waterproof until June 15, 1976, when a flood filled every medical center basement with water. The water got into our basement through a city conduit for water and gas pipes. Water had filled the basement of the Medical Tower building and was being forced through the common conduit into our otherwise waterproof basement. Six inches of water accumulated before we could plug the hole. Three years later, in April 1979, a huge flood filled the medical center basements again but we remained dry. After that the medical center developed a major flood prevention plan. The system is yet to be tested with another flood like those of 1976 and 1979.[1]

By 1973 we had outgrown our facility again and had rented space upstairs in the Corrigan shopping center across the street and in the Medical Tower next door. In May 1974, we built a five-level parking garage for 300 cars. The first floor of this structure was built as office space, containing 8500 square feet for administrative offices. The garage could be enlarged for 700 cars. A large space was left between the garage and the clinic for a future high rise building. The partners held long discussions about constructing the high rise. About $4 million was needed, which would not be easy to get. The clinic considered buying the Medical Tower building, but it had asbestos problems. Furthermore, St. Luke's owned, or had a lien on, the land, a previous gift from the Bertner Foundation. We were advised not to buy it. Meanwhile, an out-of-town investor bought the building. We continued to rent from him. Among my patients was Abdullah Aleriza from Saudi Arabia. Extremely wealthy, he made some investments in some medium rise buildings in Houston. In early November 1981, I went to lunch at the Warwick Hotel with Abdullah and his secretary, Anne Marie Anders. He told me he would build us a high rise clinic at 6624 Fannin, but it would be strictly business. I met with the clinic executive committee, and they declined the offer, not wishing to do business with an investor whom they knew little about. Abdullah asked me about it later including the last time I saw him in London in 1987.

Eventually times got hard, the clinic couldn't raise the money, and St. Luke's bought our lease from the Hannahs. In the early 1980s, St. Luke's bought our clinic building, dismantled it, and built St. Luke's Medical Tower. While the

St. Luke's Tower was in construction, the clinic was moved to temporary quarters in the Doctors Building on Fannin. Large remodeling expenses were again incurred. Several floors of St. Luke's Tower were outfitted for the clinic. The clinic moved back to its original site in the new tower after I had retired.[2]

Jim Bakken and Ron Rushing, the clinic administrators, accomplished much during this period. The two men got along well in handling the complexities of clinic administration. Jim, with help from Ron, recruited and organized a personnel staff of several hundred people with many different talents, ranging from cleaning women to chemists. They put together an efficient management team, handled wages, work schedules, a newsletter, government regulations, taxes, insurance, and pensions. All supplies and equipment were bought by them, from paper towels to the CAT scanner. Jim and Ron assembled a happy and loyal group who worked together and generated very few problems. The joyous annual employee picnic and Christmas parties were evidence of their success. Ron, with help from Jim, handled the bookkeeping. They collected the accounts. In one month in 1978, they sent out 22,000 statements. The collection rate was more than 95 percent. They operated the clinic with a low overhead of some 40 percent for several years. Ron prepared an annual budget, which always hit the target within 1 or 2 percent, and did trial run after trial run on doctors' pay distribution each month. He spent many hours explaining the results to individuals and to the pay distribution committee, which frequently changed the formulas. These were handwritten figures taken from an adding machine before the days of computers.

The management team prepared programs for several partner retreats and exhibited the patience of Job with some of our prima donna doctors. They took patients' complaints. They represented the clinic in many business and civic affairs. Jim became president of the American Group Practice Association, and Ron published a book on clinic management. As the years went on Jim Bakken was promoted from manager to executive director. Often he had to implement decisions of the executive committee, displeasing some of the partners, which was not hard to do, since most decisions seemed to displease at least someone. In spite of his numerous capabilities and accomplishments, Jim fell into disfavor with several doctors and was forced to leave in May 1983, after twenty years at the clinic. After he resigned, the clinic was left without an administrator. Ron Rushing became acting director and guided the clinic through a difficult period. He was a modest man of great patience.

At that time, clinic directors were in short supply. We finally found Robert A. Payne at the Honolulu Medical Group. He came in June 1983 as executive director and stayed for two years. By the time Bob Payne left, the clinic had grown so large that it needed a director with advanced business qualifications. The practice of medicine had become a big business, beyond the realm of most practicing physicians. Our doctors and administrative staff could run the practice of medicine, but we had to employ a business leader. By this time I was out of the partnership and practiced as a consultant. I had no role in the search for the next director, but I recall that the partners sought the advice of Bill Harvin, who was president of the Kelsey-Seybold Foundation. The search ended with the employment of Breaux Castleman. Breaux came from Midland, Texas, where his father was in the oil business. He had graduated from Yale and worked for a leading management consulting company. He stayed with the clinic until 1994.[3]

Most of our nonphysician employees were women, and many of the feminine traits I admire most pervaded the atmosphere. There was a sense of warmth and welcome. Many of the women were cheerful when times were bad and provided compassionate support to patients who had received bad news. Not infrequently, our nurses and receptionists voluntarily visited our sick patients in the hospitals or nursing homes. These women had a high sense of moral and ethical values. Anyone, patient or doctor, who skirted the fringes of right or wrong or mistreated someone soon felt the displeasure of the women. These employees supported their doctors with a fierce loyalty, sometimes too fierce, when they covered his tardiness and testiness. Of course some jealousies developed. Jealousy is a trait falsely attributed to women more than men. There was plenty of professional jealousy among the men. But the employees' strong support for each other far outweighed any jealousies. Many employees joined together in social life outside the Clinic. Jim Bakken promoted social events, which have lasted: the choir, the softball team, the annual Thanksgiving and Christmas parties, and the annual picnic.

I was fortunate to have Virginia Smith as my secretary for ten or more years, longer than any other. Virginia was from Beaumont, a graduate of the University of Texas. Quiet, highly competent, and dependable, she took dictation, corrected my terrible grammar, and never complained. I was surprised to learn she was taking flying lessons and had soloed. Jo Anne Gary (later Walton) replaced Virginia Smith. During my last year, Mary Jane Cook was my secretary as well as secretary for a couple or more doctors.

My nurse, Aggie Greer, stayed with me until I retired in 1986. The *Houston Post* ran an article on January 17, 1986, about my planned retirement. The article was illustrated by a photo of Aggie and me at my desk. I cannot say enough in praise of Aggie, one of the most capable persons I ever knew. The Good Lord smiled on me when he brought me Aggie Greer. We still stay in touch and see each other for lunch. Aggie had several assistants at different times, including Jean Murchison Perkins, Margaret Thomas, and Georgianna Arcos.

This core of long-term employees were role models; many became my friends. We had a relatively large turnover in personnel, which was not unexpected. Women had to leave when their husbands were transferred out of town; many young women left to advance their education, get married, or raise a family. Tax-free hospitals in the medical center kept raiding our well-trained staff and offering them advancement in rank and salary, which we could not meet. Even so our personnel were offered a number of opportunities within our large clinic, where there was room for advancement. Training courses were given for all types of positions. Spanish lessons were provided. New secretaries were taught medical terminology. Some technicians were sent to training programs at clinic expense.

On May 1, 1974, our full-time staff numbered 58 physicians and a dentist. On part-time were two each of M.D.s, Ph.D.s, and M.A.s. There were 80 doctors in the clinic in May 1978. In 1979, the Kelsey-Seybold partnership was converted to Kelsey-Seybold Clinic, P.A. (Professional Association). In April 1983, there were 118 doctors, a figure that grew to 150 by 1986, when I retired. In 1974 Bill Seybold reported that there had been an increase of net income averaging about 14 percent for the previous three years. Roughly 57 percent of collections was distributed to the salaried and partner doctors in the form of income and fringe benefits. The clinic companies also realized a nice rental profit. We saw 17,935 new patients and there were 113,288 patient visits in 1971–72. The 1974 report shows 19,086 new patients and great increases in laboratory, nuclear medicine, and radiology bookings. In that year there were about 42 partners, with an average income of about $60,000— good money in those days. It was higher than the average doctor income of other clinics.[4]

Pay distribution never satisfied all doctors, however. The Departmental Cost Accounting–Income Distribution Committee considered sixteen factors when dividing income among the partners. This Committee always had to come up with an empiric distribution which was fairer than the elaborate formula. Squeaking wheels usually got more grease than they deserved. Some doctors left because they felt unfairly treated. Some who liked the clinic left because they did not get enough referrals for their specialty in a general clinic. Others left because they came to the clinic so they could be on a salary while they built a practice of their own. Some I know about left because they couldn't get along with another doctor in their department. We failed to correct some of these personality problems. Several left because the medical schools and hospitals lured them away with prestige and high salaries.

I never could get the partners to invest money in our companies or hold money in reserve in the partnership. I had reserves, but most partners had children to educate and insisted on distributing every penny we made. Finally in 1974, $50,000 was held in reserve, a figure that increased to $140,000 in 1975. This was a pittance, a poor way to face any economic downturn. But we were in flush times. Nothing could go wrong. Our internists were making $10,000 to $20,000 a year more than those at the Medical Clinic of Houston, according to Charlie Armbrust, their chief. Charlie was somewhat jealous of our success. The Mayo staff doctors were making much less than we. We were soon to face a bitter depression, however.

When there were more than a hundred doctors in the clinic and the economy was volatile, there was much diversity of opinion among the partners regarding the many questions that needed answering. Should we build a high rise building? Should we open more branch clinics? How many doctors should we recruit? How do we divide income? Should we open a surgicenter? We attempted to find answers by asking the experts and holding retreats. One expert we consulted for a year or two was David Scoular, who was planning officer for the Baylor University College of Medicine. While at Baylor, he was privileged to do outside consulting. David was an architect who had become well known as a consultant to leading medical schools in this country and abroad. He helped universities such as Harvard, Johns Hopkins, and Stanford. He consulted in Saudi Arabia and Turkey. When the institutions built hospitals and clinics David advised them on architectural design, space allocations, and other plans to meet the changes in medicine. He recognized, for example, the trend for ambulatory surgical facilities and reduced need for hospital beds. David was well aware of medical economics. Too bad Baylor and our clinic did not always follow his advice.

The clinic partners held several weekend meetings and long-range planning workshops. Two excellent retreats were held at the Woodlands in 1981 and Columbia Lakes in 1982. Although I was almost retired, I was practicing in the clinic as a consultant and was invited to participate in the meetings. At these meetings, I always put in a plug for converting the clinic to a foundation like most other clinics our size. Much good came from the meetings, including fellowship among the partners and the wives, who were invited to the Columbia Lakes retreat. A consensus was reached on many, but not all, of the major issues that confronted us. Many partners learned facts instead of rumors about the clinic, and future leaders were discovered. Some people complained that all the Long-Range Planning Committee talked about was present problems instead of long-range plans. Incidentally, of the 1983 Long-Range Planning Committee members, not one of them remained in the clinic for five years. I noted in my appointment diary after one planning committee meeting in March 1983: "We salvaged part of the wreckage, will try to get back on the right track."

We date the origin of the Kelsey-Seybold Clinic from January 15, 1949, the day I began practice in Houston. The patient registration numbers, the patient records file, the bank account, and many other features of the clinic began on that date and have continued without interruption until today. Our partnership agreement was amended several times through the years, including one resulting in a complete change of organization. There were stipulations in our partnership agreement concerning sickness and death benefits, insurance of partners, pay distribution, rules for admission and dismissal, military service and retirement benefits. Some of the rules have held up for nearly fifty years. With so many changes today in managed care, there's not likely to be another partnership like ours in the foreseeable future.

In our agreement was a compulsory requirement for partners to retire at sixty-five years of age. Charlie Dickson and I had separate amendments to the agreement that allowed us to stay on until we were seventy, after which we retired from the association but were allowed to stay on as consultants. On retirement the partners bought our interests by installments over a five-year period. My total interests were a little over $1 million. It became apparent that many partners were still productive, fully competent, and wanted to continue working after sixty-five, so the rule for retirement at sixty-five was eventually abolished. After retirement from the partnership in 1982, I continued to practice in the clinic as always. My pay was determined at 50 percent of my bookings, a very generous benefit considering the high overhead the clinic was then sustaining.

My experiences in the Kelsey-Seybold clinic included a period of conflict among several partners. In 1967 I was still chief of the clinic, as I had been from the beginning, and was in the habit of being the boss. But the job was becoming onerous, and many partners, rightly, believed in term limits. Charlie Dickson was a good administrator. He contributed a great deal to the success of the clinic and we worked well together. I asked Charlie if he would be willing to be chief, while I became chairman of the clinic. Charlie agreed and we were so elected by the partners in 1967. The clinic continued to do well, and Charlie did a great job. He was strong for growth. I admit that he complained to me that I was still trying to run the clinic. My two closest friends, my brother John and Bill Seybold, were leader types and accepted me for a few years but eventually became restive, probably correctly thinking that they knew best. I was too close to John and Bill and very emotional about our relationships. I did a lot of petulant and childish things. We had a number of confrontations.

Bill became chief of staff in 1972. Bill was very conservative, and I felt that he was opposed to expanding the clinic. Actually he favored expansion but at a more moderate rate. We had disagreements on joining Methodist Hospital, on developing branch clinics and NASA contracts. There were disagreements about term limits of office. I certainly stayed in too long, and now that I was no longer chief I favored rotation and term limits of office. Surgeons and internists disagreed about pay distribution. We were unhappy about the younger partners who had made minuscule payments on their partnership interests yet had full voting privileges and wanted to discontinue seniority points in pay distribution.[5]

Partners soon began to take sides. Brother John joined me and the senior internists when we decided to get legal advice. On February 13, 1973, my friend Hugh Liedtke provided, at Pennzoil expense, a lawyer from the Baker Botts firm to discuss our problem and offer advice. Then, in March 1973, on our own, we employed Jim Turley and Finis Cowan, both Baker Botts lawyers. We considered dissolving the partnership and practicing independently in a jointly owned facility. We were still meeting in October 1973 at my house and November at Al Leiser's. The conflicts were finally resolved by our lawyers and the clinic lawyer. Everyone won something and lost something. Some said the clinic was stronger, but it was a bruising experience. My friendship with Bill Seybold was damaged; it is just improving now after twenty-five years. I have always admired Bill, and I'm sorry we had such a serious disagreement. No clinic has ever developed without having controversy, however, and many have had more than we have had.

Changes were taking place in the practice of medicine. Physicians had been very protective of their medical domain. At one time, only a doctor could insert a needle into a vein to withdraw blood or administer fluids or medications to a patient. Only doctors could give injections or immunizations. I remember being called to withdraw blood or start intravenous fluids while I was an intern at Bellevue Hospital in 1936. Soldiers were lined up for the doctors to administer typhoid and other vaccines during World War II. Doctors gave all the vaccines during the first polio immunization drive in Houston. Only a doctor could do a pelvic examination and collect a Pap smear from a female patient. A doctor had to administer a stress electrocardiogram, perform a proctoscopic examination, or suture a wound.

Nurses began taking Pap smears and giving intravenous injections. My nurse, Aggie Greer, had an eagle eye. She never missed a problem when she reviewed a record. She knew the normal range for all the blood counts and chemical determinations. She gave injections, removed ear wax, took Paps, did dressings, and dispensed medications, which were allowed over the counter.

After we reviewed a patient record together, she could call the report to most patients. She could take a history from a patient on the phone and decide whether or not the patient needed to come in to see me, be sent some medication, or referred to another doctor. She could placate a disgruntled patient. She was my right hand. Some of my patients told me they had rather be treated by Aggie, and they might even call her up if they didn't like my diagnoses or treatment. Aggie also kept me on schedule; she was very prompt herself and didn't like for me to be late. Obviously we made a few mistakes. I knew when to refer patients. That was the principle on which the clinic operated.[6]

Medicare arrived in 1965, as a means of providing medical care for the elderly poor. The day after Medicare was announced, two of my wealthiest patients, Governor Hobby and Judge J. A. Elkins, Sr., each had their secretaries call to register them at the clinic as Medicare patients. They were the first two of my patients to request Medicare.

During this period, prepaid medical care—the practice of paying the health care provider a fixed fee in advance—really evolved at the clinic. It grew from zero, when I started in practice in 1949, to about 90 percent of the clinic's patient load. Prepaid medical care developed after World War II, when the Kaiser Shipbuilding Company established such a program for its employees. Within the United States, only a couple of private clinics in California had developed prepaid programs, and these were self-insured. With rising medical costs, however, and increasing demands for health care, employers became interested in preventive care as a means of reducing the costs of providing medical care for their employees. Multiphasic screening examinations became popular in the 1960s and 1970s. Employees lined up for a health questionnaire on a primitive computer program. A technician then conducted tests of vision, hearing, blood pressure, pulmonary function, urinalysis, hemoglobin, and possibly a chest X ray, electrocardiogram, and a blood chemistry profile. A computer spit out the final results of the examination, with recommendations for health improvement. The entities administering these programs were soon called Health Maintenance Organizations, or HMOs. It wasn't long before HMOs expanded into prepaid healthcare. Insurance companies established their own HMOs or underwrote others, while some HMOs chose to underwrite their own programs. A new industry was born, which gradually gained control of American medicine.

The first prepaid program, or HMO, in our clinic was with Rice University. Our relations with Rice began when we contracted to provide a student health program in 1970, and looked into providing a prepaid medical program for faculty and staff. The clinic organized a Health Association to implement our goals, and we went to work. We called on Prudential Life Insurance

Company, and they were interested but felt that using our staff of specialists to deliver medical care would be too expensive. They wanted to change us to a primary care clinic, something our specialists could not accept, so we never made a deal. Eventually, Prudential went to the Magregor Clinic and developed a large prepaid program there. We knew several people in the American General Life Insurance Company. Ben Woodson, the CEO, was a personal friend. In 1973, we obtained approval from the Texas State Insurance Commission for an insurance-funded program and finalized a prepay plan for the Rice faculty and employees. The prepay program with Rice went fairly well. We were actually making money, but only subspecialists and full-time internists were allowed to see the patients. After a year or two of great controversy we dropped the plan. I was very disappointed.

There were many advances in medicine during this period. Beneficial chemotherapy for cancer had begun. The advent of combined chemotherapy, which included cortisone, had not yet been reported. Automated chemical testing of the blood was a remarkable advance. Bob Jordan, our clinical pathologist, installed a SMAC 20 machine in our laboratory. The machine could make twenty different chemical determinations from one sample of blood at a markedly reduced expense: several liver, renal, pulmonary, cardiac, endocrine, hematologic, and electrolyte functions from one blood sample! As a routine test, it uncovered a number of unsuspected diseases, such as parathyroid adenomas, diabetes, gout, and liver failure. Dozens of tests were developed using radioactive isotopes. Even Pap smears and blood counts were done automatically. Tests I never heard of were developed for diseases I never heard of.

In addition to open heart surgery, many new surgical procedures were developed. All sorts of joint replacements were invented. Endoscopic surgery reduced trauma and hospital stays. Anesthesia made amazing advances. There was another development that may or may not have improved medical care overall—alternative medicine. This term certainly included some worthwhile advances, but it also included every imaginable form of quackery.

Lawsuits began appearing more frequently on the medical scene. Doctors were being sued increasingly for malpractice. I saw some fine homes in Houston built by lawyers who had collected large contingency fees for lawsuits against doctors. I was never personally sued for malpractice, but the high premiums for malpractice insurance definitely figured into my later reasons for retiring. The clinic was sued by a lawyer who was one of my best friends. In May 1978, my lawyer friend called me about a patient we once treated who had died in Methodist Hospital of acute meningitis from a sinus or ear infection. The infection occurred after she had not followed treatment or returned for appointments. Her husband, also a lawyer, tried to get various law firms to sue the clinic but they had turned him down, believing there was no case against us. The husband eventually found my friend. I hoped we could settle it out of court and close the case. A few days later, the clinic and Methodist Hospital were sued on seventeen counts for $20 million. The case went to trial before a jury, where the plaintiffs lost on all seventeen counts and had to pay court costs. Later, the daughter of a partner in the involved law firm needed pelvic surgery to be performed by one of our surgeons. The partner called me to inquire whether I thought the surgeon was good. I was surprised that his family were still patients. I told him we would refuse to treat his daughter. If anything went wrong he would sue us. I also told him to take his daughter elsewhere, we would no longer treat his family.

During the 1960s and 1970s, we established numerous company accounts. The patients that really swelled our practice came from two main sources: the oil industry and Latin America. Houston was recognized as the world's oil center, where every major oil company and dozens of independents operated. We provided care to all the giants including Exxon, Gulf, Shell, Mobil, and Texaco. Aramco, formerly the American Arabian Oil Company, later owned entirely by Saudi Arabia, had a large office, as did other foreign oil companies. Conoco, Amoco, Pennzoil, John Mecon, Ernie Cockrell, Signal, Murphy, Sun, McDermott, Huffington, Glassell, Rutherford, Adams, and Phillips were a few of the independents for which we provided medical service. Houston was also the leading center of the gas pipeline industry. We saw patients from El Paso Natural Gas, Transco, Texas Eastern, Tenneco, Texas Pacific Northwest, Columbia, Coastal, Alaska, and Panhandle Pipeline.

We cared for patients in the oil service industries: Schlumberger; Dialog, with Billy McNulty as president; Magobar; Baker; Reed Roller Bit, with John Maher as president; Hughes Tool; and Stewart and Stevenson, to mention a few of the companies. I treated Arch Rowan and executives of Rowan Drilling Company. Other drilling companies we served included Offshore Marine; Western Company, whose president, Eddy Chiles, was my patient; Zapata, George Bush's company; Halliburton; and Monte Christo Drilling, whose president was Russ Birdwell, my white-wing hunting host. I went on an inspection trip to Indonesia for Huffington Oil Company. Most of these companies did business worldwide. We saw sheiks and oil executives from the Arab countries. Many Iranians and Iraqis were patients. One of my patients spent most of his time in Africa in the oil business. It wasn't unusual to get a phone call from Teheran or Singapore saying they were sending us a patient on the next plane with an injury, or fever and jaundice, or intractable diarrhea, or saying that the patient's acting crazy and the local doctor can't find anything wrong. We lost a lawsuit regarding a deranged patient we released too soon. On his way back to Indonesia, he jumped off a wall in Honolulu and fractured his skull, causing brain damage. Patients were also brought in from offshore rigs in the Gulf of Mexico.

We had the largest Latin American practice in the country. The only competitors who even came close were the Oschner Clinic and the Mayo Clinic. We often saw a thousand patients a month from Mexico. Flight attendants called the Sunday night Pan Am flight from Mexico City to Houston the Kelsey-Seybold Special. Carlos Taboado, Al Leiser, and Gene Burke had very large Latin practices. Carlos said he had seen four ex-presidents from Mexico. He introduced me to one elderly ex-president who served before Maderos. One day the wife of the then current Mexican president was going through the clinic incognito. She was being treated like any other patient, until she was recognized by other Mexican patients in the waiting room. Carlos introduced me to the famous Mexican actor Cantinflas, who starred in *Around the World in Eighty Days.* I remember some wealthy Jewish patients from Mexico who came for a thorough examination every year, while on their way to take mud baths in Romania. Latin American patients often left nice presents for the nurses and other employees. I was one of several doctors entertained by them in Mexico. Several of our staff were invited to speak at Latin American medical meetings. In 1967, I spoke at a meeting in Monterrey and met with several doctors to help in their efforts to organize a clinic. Two years later, I met with doctors in Mexico City for the same purpose. Mary and I were entertained at Los Morales restaurant, and I made rounds in the British American Hospital.

In the years before I retired, we were all busy at the clinic. I referred surplus patients to other doctors. On August 12, 1976, I saw a record number of twenty-nine patients, the most I ever saw in a day, Aggie Greer told me. On April 26, 1982, twelve patients for complete examination and numerous office visits filled my schedule. My old lumbar disc popped out, and I had to go home to bed for a week with severe pain. Aggie arranged for other doctors to take care of my patients. I have many pages of information about patients I treated. Rock Hudson, the movie star who was at the top of his career, became a patient, referred by another Houston doctor. Rock came with Tommy Clark, who was introduced as his friend and secretary. He was a very good patient, and he created much excitement among the nurses, receptionists, and technicians who saw him or helped treat him. Once Rock was here when the employees were having their covered dish Thanksgiving dinner on each floor. Rock and his friend joined the group on our floor and ate with us. He was an inveterate smoker, but something else got him sooner. He contracted a galloping case of AIDS and died before we ever saw him again. He had left his friend Tommy

Clark and become promiscuous. His friend, who always had a checkup when Rock came, continued to come to the clinic for his examination. He did not have AIDS. He was very dejected about Rock's death.

Abdullah Aleriza and his secretary, Anne Marie Anders, became patients and great friends. Abdullah was an extremely rich Arabian of Persian extraction. His grandfather was a pearl merchant who sold to the Saudi Arabian royalty. His great-grandfather was once the sheik or ruler of Mecca. As a boy, Abdullah went on a camel caravan encampment with the King of Arabia. He told me many stories of his boyhood. Abdullah grew up and went into business in Arabia and had vast holdings in buildings, shipping, and industrial and building equipment. Well educated and highly cultivated, he went to school in Egypt and Europe. In addition to Arabic, he spoke perfect English with a British accent, French, and possibly other languages. He had houses in Jiddah, Bombay, Geneva, where his son lived, Paris, London, and New York. He built a beautiful apartment in the Warwick Tower and had a Rolls Royce flown in. "I have Rolls Royces at all my houses," he told Mary. He and his wife did not live together. She had a mansion on the Pall Mall of London, he had a marble palace on Grosvenor Square, with a large swimming pool in the basement. His wife also had a pool, which meant that Abdullah and his wife had two of the five basement swimming pools in London. Abdullah entertained us several times in London and Paris, and we entertained him in Houston.

These were my most active years in recruiting. Some partners complained I was recruiting too many doctors. My activities were slowed down by the Long-Range Planning Committee and the Recruitment Committee. Bill Seybold's annual report for 1972 stated, for example, that there were 208 prospects contacted, the majority by letter, but some were by telephone and personal contact. Obviously I was not the only recruiter. There were thirty-eight visits of prospective staff members to the clinic, and six positions were filled that year. After 1982, when I withdrew from the partnership to become a consultant, many doctors were employed whom I never met, especially those for branch offices. The doctors I knew well and who stayed with the clinic through the good and bad years constituted the nucleus of what today is an institution of nearly three hundred doctors.[7]

The clinic's department of internal medicine grew rapidly from 1965 to 1986, when I retired. Every subspecialty of internal medicine became staffed by one or more physicians. There were also several highly qualified general internists. Actually, each subspecialist practiced general internal medicine for the patients who considered him or her to be their family doctor. I was more a general internist than an endocrinologist. If I had been required to take another board examination I probably could have passed the boards in occupational medicine. I had spent more time in that field than any other. As the years went by, my schedule was filled more and more with long-time patients who came on a regular basis to follow a medical condition within my subspecialty, such as diabetes, Addison's disease, or a thyroid problem. I also followed many patients with other kinds of internal medicine problems. The most common cases were cardiovascular diseases, such as hypertension, coronary disease, heart failure, and renal failure. If a problem became severe, I called for a consultation by a cardiologist or referred the patient to a cardiologist for complete care.

Next in frequency were gastrointestinal problems, such as peptic ulcer, irritable bowel syndrome, diaphragmatic hernia, gallstones, and infectious diarrhea. Only the intractable problems required a consultation or referral to a gastroenterologist. The same was true for chest problems, such as asthma, emphysema, and pneumonia. I only referred difficult arthritic problems to the rheumatologist. I treated iron deficiency anemia and pernicious anemia myself, while referring patients with leukemia and serious blood disorders to a hematologist. I treated many gynecologic problems, as well as ear, nose and throat problems without referring the patient to a specialist. I was not alone in this type of practice. The gastroenterologists, the pulmonologists, rheumatologists, the nephrologist, the hematologists, and other subspecialists also took care of routine internal medicine problems for patients who considered them to be their personal physician. Only the cardiologists in our clinic did not see other routine problems. That was a mistake. All of us were board certified internists first and subspecialists second. I believed that staying in touch with general internal medicine made us better subspecialists.[8]

David E. Mouton joined the clinic as director of nuclear medicine in 1972 and developed an outstanding nuclear medicine department. He had graduated from Louisiana State University Medical School in 1965 and received his training in nuclear medicine during his military service. David was a genuine Acadian, born in Louisiana and descendent of General Mouton who fought in the American Revolution. He had a love for life, an outgoing personality, great wit, and high intelligence. A humorist and story teller, David was popular as a master of ceremonies. He was an unselfish volunteer and became a vice president of the Houston Live Stock Show and Rodeo. His energy was unlimited; he carried a heavy caseload of devoted patients, including many prominent people. He brought Bob Millis from Baylor as his chief technician, and in October 1981 David brought Ralph J. Gorten to the nuclear medicine department. Ralph graduated from the University of Pennsylvania Medical School in 1955. He trained and taught at the University Hospital, Baltimore; Duke

University; and the University of Washington in Seattle. He was a board certified specialist in nuclear medicine. Ralph was interested in the uses of isotopes in cardiology, one of the rapidly developing fields of nuclear medicine.

Our psychiatry department dated back to 1954, when Albert Owers left the Menninger Clinic in Topeka, Kansas, and came to Houston to became a partner in the Kelsey-Leary Clinic. In 1957, Owers was joined by Chester Cochran. William Hal Baylston came to our clinic in 1969 from the Menninger Clinic, where he had completed his training. Hal left the clinic in a few years to practice on his own. Overhead was very high for a psychiatrist, and their bookings were much lower than that of other physicians. This left the mainstay and present chief of our psychiatry department, Ricardo Daichman.[9]

Our radiology department finally stabilized when we employed Robert S. Kurth. Bob was completing his twenty years of regular army service and had heard about our clinic from some of our ex-military members. I met Bob in a Dallas hotel room, where we were attending a medical meeting. Bob was very straightforward. He knew all about the clinic, I didn't have to tell him anything. He had decided to come. It was the easiest recruiting I ever did. I wonder if he would have come anyway if I had turned him down. Bob proved to be that direct in running our radiology department. He made a real department of it, as efficient as the Mayo Clinic. The radiology department staff was greatly enhanced when two well-trained Cuban radiologists joined. Eduardo Linares came in June 1972. It is dangerous to say someone is the best of anything, but I believe Eduardo was the best radiology diagnostician I ever knew. He had the eyesight of an eagle, often coming up with a diagnosis that no one even suspected. He was also a true Spanish gentleman. His death from cancer in June 1980 while still in active practice was a tragedy. We were building a new imaging center for a CAT scanner and named it in his memory. The other Cuban was Pedro Raphael, who came in July 1974. He graduated from the University of Havana medical school in 1954. Pedro was a fine radiologist and was still with the clinic in 1996.[10]

Unpredictably, the clinic's fortunes took a major downward turn in the late 1970s and early 1980s. Like many businesses in the city, the clinic fell on financially hard times, as the economy plummeted. The oil business in Houston virtually collapsed, the price of oil having fell from $45.00 a barrel to $8.00, instead of rising to $65.00 a barrel, as W. R. Grace Company predicted when I invested $250,000 in one of their drilling syndicates. We were especially hard hit when the bottom fell out of the Mexican peso and our Latin practice dried up. These events occurred when I was no longer taking a part in administration. In 1983 we had only $1,704,643 in the bank, not enough to meet the monthly payroll. Some partners wanted to sell the partnership leasehold to the pension fund to raise cash. Fortunately that idea didn't pass. St. Luke's Hospital and Memorial Hospital eventually bailed us out. I don't know the details. Apparently $2 million came from St. Luke's and $4 million from Memorial. We were in their debt and losing $1 million a month. We were saved by joining Maxicare Health Plans, Inc., a relatively new HMO from California. Things improved rapidly. Within a year or two we had 100,000 new patients and everyone was busy. But we still were not out of the woods. Maxicare went broke. Things, however, were improving and we were at least meeting the payroll, paying the partners a modest salary, and not incurring more debt. Several doctors retired during this period and had to be paid off. Fortunately, the partnership agreement allowed the clinic to pay off retiring doctors over a period of five years. The real estate holdings of the clinic were overvalued, so the retiring partners got more than they really deserved. I was among the retiring doctors in 1982 but stayed on as a consultant. So did brother John in 1984. Chester Cochran retired to join his wife in practice. Melville Cody died in 1983, and his widow was paid off. There were others who resigned or retired to continue practice elsewhere in Houston. The clinic enforced the no-local-practice penalty, so, at least the clinic did not have to pay those doctors for their accounts receivable.[11]

The tough and determined partners who loved the clinic stayed on and weathered the storm. Jim Kemper, the friendly nonflappable chief of staff, and the executive committee carried them through. They were rewarded when practice recovered and Cigna and other HMOs began using the clinic. Executive director Breaux Castleman improved operations. Breaux quickly learned what was on the horizon. He predicted accurately that HMOs and large health care companies were going to control the practice of medicine and we had better get ready for it. Unfortunately some institutions in the Texas Medical Center didn't get the message.

The clinic leaders considered several options. Since the clinic was back on its feet financially, I promoted selling it to the Kelsey-Seybold Foundation, which, in turn, would pay off its debts with funds raised by the sale of tax exempt bonds. On my son John's advice I called an investment broker at Underwood Neuhaus Company who was an expert on underwriting tax free bonds for municipalities, hospitals, and the like. The broker said there would be no trouble to float a $50 to $100,000,000 tax-free bond for the foundation to buy out the physical properties of the clinic. At various times Dick Eastwood and Dick Wainerdi, executive vice presidents of the medical center, told me they would welcome our clinic—as a tax-free foundation—into the medical center, as it had the Texas Heart Institute and, eventually, the Diagnostic Center. Who knows what would have happened to us? I came to Houston to be a part of the Texas Medical Center, and I would love to see the clinic, developed by many devoted partners, accomplish a dream I've had for many years. The clinic would become a not-for-profit institution and save millions in taxes like other medical center facilities.

Another alternative was to join the Memorial Hospital System, an organization that was well aware of the changing medical scene. Kemper told me that we had not paid back the $4 million we had borrowed from it. Memorial thought it could own us by canceling the $4 million note. The clinic demanded $6 million and Memorial refused, believing the clinic would have to come around. They were in for a surprise. Several health care companies were being considered by the clinic, and the final decision was to join with Caremark, a subsidiary of Baxter Laboratories that was being spun off as a separate company. Caremark bought the clinic's physical assets, paid the debts, and paid the partners cash and stock in the company. They took over management of the clinic and all personnel, except the professional staff. They also financed a building program. I was told they put $100 million into the project just to get it started. Don Wilford, the director of Memorial, told Jim that Memorial made a mistake when it held out for $4 million. The undertaking was successful, but in May 1996, Med-Partners of Birmingham, Alabama, bought out Caremark. It is a scary world. Doctors have lost control of their practice.

I have used many pages telling about my own activities, while neglecting to describe adequately what Mary did during these years. Mary was just as busy as I was, especially in supporting many of my endeavors. She knew many people in Houston when we moved here. Her friends helped me get started in a practice that became the Kelsey-Seybold Clinic today. I could fill pages describing the social events, listed on Mary's appointment calendars, which she undertook on behalf of my medical practice. She entertained out-of-town patients and families with luncheons and dinners; she called on patients in the hospitals and brought them books and flowers. Mary entertained dozens of visiting doctors, often as house guests. She helped new doctors locate houses. She entertained and became friends with many of our NASA doctors, both in Houston and at our out-of-state NASA clinics. We still correspond with several of these doctors and their wives. I must point out that other clinic wives were just as supportive as Mary.

Mary was especially pleased to be appointed to the development board of the University of Texas Health Science Center in Houston. During the 1960s, there was a movement for the University of Texas to open a new medical school in the Texas Medical Center. There were rumors about the university taking over Baylor's medical school, since the medical school was in severe financial straits. Baylor Medical College severed ties with Baylor University, and the Texas legislature appropriated money to Baylor Medical on a per capita basis for medical students. Baylor was saved and was not eager for competition from another medical college in the medical center. Houston was the largest city in America with only one medical college, and some people believed that two schools would create healthy competition instead of duplication of effort. Public meetings were held to promote a new school. People were called on to speak on behalf of a new school. I was asked to talk at a downtown meeting of business leaders and at a meeting in Austin of the Texas Commission for Higher Education.

In 1968, Hermann Hospital was affiliated with the proposed Medical School of the University of Texas. I remember Jack Josey was very active in this effort and made a significant gift for the purpose. He became a regent of the University of Texas and was eventually chairperson of the regents. Another proponent for the new school was A. G. McNeese who, among others things, was prominent as a trustee of the M. D. Anderson Foundation and a regent of the University of Texas. The McNeeses were neighbors. Catherine McNeese and Mary were the closest of friends. They talked on the phone every day; they went to lunch and shopped together at least once a week.

In May 1969, the Texas legislature created the University of Texas College of Medicine in Houston. In 1971, the new school occupied the John H. Freeman Building, adjoining Hermann Hospital. The school opened its doors to thirty-two students in 1971. The first dean was Cheves Smith, a classmate of Jim McMurrey at Harvard Medical College. In November 1972, the six schools of the University of Texas in the medical center were combined to form the University of Texas Health Science Center (UTHSC). The combined institutions were the medical school, the dental school, the school of public health, the school of continuing education, the nursing school, and the school of allied health sciences. The University of Texas M. D. Anderson Hospital and Tumor Institute remained a separate institution.

The first president of the UTHSC was John Olson, recently retired dean of the dental school. John served for two years, 1972–74. We had been friends since I was acting dean of the Post Graduate School of Medicine. He was succeeded by Charles (Chuck) Berry, who had become famous as the doctor for the first astronauts at the Johnson Space Center. I knew him since he was medical director while our clinic provided health care at the Johnson Space Center. Chuck was a competent friendly man who came from the air force Medical Corps. He was not experienced in the operation and intrigue of a medical school. The next president I recall was my longtime friend and former roommate Truman Blocker. Truman had been dean, then president of UTMB in Galveston. After retiring from UTMB, he was sent to organize the University of Texas Medical School in San Antonio. He had also spent some time helping Texas Tech Medical School in Lubbock. The university next sent Truman to Houston as interim president of UTHSC in 1977.

In that year, soon after Truman arrived, Mary was appointed to the development board of UTHSC. Catherine McNeese was appointed about the same time. A. G. McNeese, chairman of regents, and Truman Blocker, president of UTHSC, must have had something to do with it. Mary became secretary of the development board and eventually president of the board. Ed Randall presided at the meetings for Mary while she was president in 1982. I was invited to all the meetings with Mary and was invited individually to a number of committee meetings. Mary and I met many fine people at the university. One of the most interesting was Red Duke, a pioneer in emergency medicine and organizer of the Life Flight helicopter service at Hermann Hospital. In 1978 he took Mary on a helicopter ride to demonstrate the service.

Mary continued on the board for many years and received the agendas for the meetings, something like an emeritus member. Roger Bulger came as president in 1978. His wife Ruth was appointed to the faculty in medicine. Mary and Catherine McNeese gave several parties for the Bulgers. We knew them well during the ten years they were here. I think Roger was responsible for the establishment of the Mary Wilson Kelsey professorship in internal medicine. Herbert DuPont, a specialist in infectious diseases, was awarded the Kelsey professorship. We have stayed in touch with DuPont, who is now chief of medicine at St. Luke's Hospital and directs a program at the School of Public Health. He still holds the Kelsey professorship. We are very fond of him. Mary and I established a charitable remainder trust to partially fund the professorship. John Ribble was dean of the medical school and became acting president of UTHSC, after Roger Bulger retired. Ribble was from Paris, Texas, a friend of my sister Virginia. He was followed by David Low as president of UTHSC. He and his wife came to Houston with a daughter, Kelsey. Dr. Low has been very kind to our granddaughters, who have toyed with the idea of studying medicine.

By far, Mary's greatest achievements were as a homemaker. She was a loving, energetic, conscientious, dedicated, sensible, never-failing wife and mother. Mary tolerated a lot from the five male members of the family. Often Mary said she wished there was a girl in the family. Time after time, she took care of things we had left undone. She assumed many duties we should have performed. Mary was usually in good spirits and always ready for a party. She staged many fine ones and thoroughly enjoyed them as long as she was physically able.

Mary was able to locate and keep good help, Jasper and Lucy Abrams being the most notable. They came in 1949, soon after we moved to Houston.

They were imbued with the culture of southern Louisiana, the place of their birth. Jasper was born and grew up in a cabin in the swamps. He slept on a corn shuck mattress. Water moccasins got in their house during floods. As a young man, he worked in the woods cutting timber with an axe. He knew how to make a tree fall exactly where he wanted. With our power saw and his axe he could convert a big tree into a stack of fireplace wood in a few hours. At one time, he was a professional gambler and, without Mary's or my knowledge, taught our boys how to play poker for money. The children loved him, especially when we took him on hunting trips. He was a good cook and waiter, not the polished type, but he made up for it with his charisma. Our guests always remembered Jasper favorably. Once we had some elegant guests for dinner. Jasper passed the main dish, probably Lucy's shrimp creole. When a guest hesitated to take a second helping Jasper insisted by saying, "Take some more; we's got plenty." That became a favorite saying when Jasper or one of the family passed food at a family dinner. Jasper enjoyed this joke as well as anyone else.

When we sent Jasper on errands, he often came back empty-handed, because he could not read streets signs. We thought he was illiterate, until I had him put on my glasses. Surprising to Jasper as well as to me, he read aloud the label on a can of vegetables without any difficulty. Nevertheless, Jasper would not wear glasses. We didn't know that Jasper could speak French, until we had a French speaking guest. Jasper and the guest conversed in French. He told us he had learned it as a boy in Louisiana.

His wife, Lucy, was a gentle polite woman who grew up in the household of a cultivated white family in Louisiana. She was an excellent cook and housekeeper. Jasper and Lucy owned a house in Port Arthur, a town more Cajun than south Louisiana. Lucy had collected some nice furniture in the house, which they rented out to relatives after they moved to Houston. Jasper and Lucy lived in our servants quarters. Sadly, Lucy suddenly turned up with a rapidly fatal pelvic malignancy and died on February 10, 1973. After she died, Jasper lost control, and he became a hopeless alcoholic. I got mad at him, and he quit. Jasper sold the house in Port Arthur. He crowded Lucy's fine furniture into a little shack in a small enclave near a trash dump off Tanner Road in west Houston. His landlady took his social security check each month and held some back for rent. With the remainder, she bought Jasper groceries and rum, which she rationed out to him. He finally died there, and we buried him in Orange next to Lucy.

Jeff Thompson worked for us for ten or fifteen years after Jasper left. Jeff was very competent, an excellent mechanic, carpenter, and cook. Other fine people Mary employed were Tommy Bryant and her sister Armittie Corkrell from Wharton. They worked for us part time for years. Armittie moved in our servant quarters after Lucy Abrams died. Armittie had a niece and nephew who were head waiters at the River Oaks Country Club. They gave Mary and me special attention when we went there. Armittie died of cancer about 1985. Before Armittie left us, I needed additional help to care for Mary as her health deteriorated. I employed Emelina Cruz, who has been with us now for fourteen years. Six years ago when Mary finally needed around-the-clock companionship and nursing, I employed Maria Olympia (Mari) Pena. Emelina and Maria worked seven days a week taking care of Mary as well as keeping house. When one had to be away, the other took care of Mary on a twenty-four hour shift. The Good Lord sent Emelina and Mari to Mary and me.

Mary belonged to a number of volunteer organizations. When we moved to Houston, she became active in the Junior League, having been a charter member and president of the Beaumont league. Mary was on several boards, including the Heritage Society, the Asia Society, the Botanical Society, the Houston Arboretum, and Planned Parenthood, before they approved abortion. She entertained visitors from the English Speaking Union and the Institute of International Education. The Mayo Clinic held its annual international meeting in Houston in 1971. Mary was in charge of the social program while brother John Kelsey and Nick Hightower of Temple were the general chairmen.

For many years, Mary thoroughly enjoyed membership in the Garden Club of Houston. Many of the members were her friends. She worked hard getting her three daughters-in-law elected to membership. They have also enjoyed membership. Mary grew to womanhood helping her mother and father in their flower garden. She worked hard in our garden. She gave talks on gardening to various club gatherings in Houston, as part of her role in the Houston Garden Club. Mary was pictured in Houston newspapers several times. A news photo dated January 30, 1975, captioned "Mary Kelsey and friends—giant Camellias," shows Mary collecting camellias from a bush in our yard. Mary got her biggest kick in the garden club promoting a fine garden and fountain in the Texas Medical Center adjoining the Institute of Religion. She raised a large part of the money for the garden and was honored at the opening ceremony in May 1984.

Mary was a staunch Republican from the time we came to Houston. She went around town putting up posters for Thad Hutheson when he ran as a Republican for the U.S. Senate. We went to a rally at the Rice Hotel and met Ronald Reagan, the movie star. He was speaking for Goldwater, one of Mary's favorites. Even though we had a personal acquaintance with Democrats such as Senator Lyndon Johnson, she voted Republican. I called myself an Independent and voted for Jack Kennedy and Lyndon Johnson for president and

Bill Hobby for lieutenant governor of Texas. I rarely hear the word "Independent" anymore. Instead, there are Liberal Democrats or Conservative Republicans. Moderates of both parties are ignored. I would like to be known as a Moderate Republican. After Johnson's presidency, I voted the Republican ticket.

The question of abortion has also become polarized, the liberals being pro-abortion and the conservatives being antiabortion. Abortion has gone on, certainly since the days of Hippocrates, who swore he would never do it. Mary took part in Planned Parenthood when it started in Houston. Muggs Leary, who was active, got us interested. Planned Parenthood's goal then was to prevent unwanted pregnancies. Its members supported the laws against abortion. I was strongly in favor of legal abortion to save the life of the mother or when there was a bad conceptus. I even accepted the belief that diabetic women should be allowed an abortion. In those early days, both the diabetic mother and the fetus were at great risk. Many doctors believed the disease, being hereditary, should not be propagated.[12]

Nearly every city had an abortionist who was a clandestine member of the medical profession. We knew this doctor performed safe abortions. We so-called respectable doctors would tell distraught parents to take their daughter to see this doctor if she had missed a couple of periods. The doctor could probably get things straightened out. During my medical residency, one of my classmates referred a girlfriend to this Houston abortionist. I must emphasize to suspicious readers that I was not the resident who sent a girl. My classmate said the girl went in one morning, was given a strong sedative, and the doctor performed a curettement. It was painful, and she rested on a couch an hour or two before leaving the office. This abortionist made a lot of money and gambled a lot in Galveston and New Orleans. There were other medical doctor abortionists in Houston. The daughter of one was my patient. She had no idea what her father did. I knew a very prominent doctor in Houston whose father was an abortionist in another city.

Our family grew rapidly during this period. Our sons got married and had our grandchildren. We are blessed with three fabulous sons and daughters-in-law and six fine grandchildren.[13] One memorable family event occurred in June 1970. Mary and I were about to make an extended trip to Europe, which also included a cruise of the Greek Isles and a visit to Istanbul. Mary's sister Fay wanted to give Mary a surprise present on her sixtieth birthday. Knowing we would be in Istanbul on June 16, Fay secretly bought round-trip tickets to the city for our three sons and their wives. On the night of Mary's birthday in the Istanbul Hilton, we dressed and prepared to go down to the hotel restaurant for dinner. There was a knock on the door. I opened it and our sons and wives burst into the room. Mary was overwhelmed. That night at dinner in the hotel we were entertained by a belly dancer, the first I ever saw. We toured Istanbul together and flew to Belgrade in then-communist Yugoslavia. We rented two Mercedes sedans and traveled through the country, since torn by war. I remember the centuries-old arched bridge at Mostar, which was recently destroyed in the fighting. We visited Sarejavo, where World War I began. This country has been in wars ever since the Huns swept down from the steppes of Russia and expelled the Romans. We drove to Split and visited Roman emperor Diocletian's palace, one of the few intact Roman structures that is still occupied. It is filled with tourist shops.

Other events stand out. Each summer we went to Estes Park, Colorado, where we rented a large house called Aspen Rock, built on a granite outcropping, with a fabulous view of the mountains. There were four cottages on the property. Each family had its cottage, and there was room for at least two additional guest families. Our daily routine was to prepare a backpack lunch and climb one of the mountain trails as a family. We would picnic high in the mountains, rest a while and throw scraps to the chipmunks and camp robber jays.

We got in trouble, unwittingly, with chipmunks. The little creatures had the run of the Aspen Rock house and cottages. They even scurried up on the dining room table for handouts while we were eating. One summer Mavis, Jr.'s, wife, Wendy, started having fever up to 103 degrees every night. We brought her back to St. Luke's Hospital in Houston, where all tests were negative. The pattern of the fever was alarmingly like Pal Epstein fever of Hodgkin's disease. In a few days, Wendy's fever stopped, and she got completely well, with no recurrences. The next summer we spent a month at Aspen Rock among the chipmunks. Mary and I came home, then went on a trip to Scotland with Tommy and Helen Anderson. During the trip Mary began having fever every night up to 103 degrees with chills. We spent a day in the Royal College of Medicine in Edinburgh, where all the specialists examined Mary and found no cause for her fever. We interrupted the trip and returned to Houston, but Mary had no more fever by then.

Later, in Houston, Mavis, Jr., started having the same fever, and his examination also was negative. I began to suspect that members of our family had the same cause for their fever. I then remembered a medical article describing recurrent fever in the Rocky Mountains. The infection is caused by a spirochete called *Borrelia recurrentis* (I think it is now called *B. hermsii*). The spirochete is easily detected in the blood, while the patient is having fever, and is transmitted by a tick that drops off the host after it feeds. I obtained a blood smear while Mavis had fever and took it to Bob Jordan. Mavis' blood was loaded with the spirochetes. A very effective cure for the disease is penicillin. Stuart Riggs, our infectious disease expert, gave Mavis the penicillin, and in about twelve hours Mavis had a raging fever. I hurried to his house and his temperature was at least 107.6 degrees, as high as the thermometer would read. I rushed for ice and wrapped him in a cold sheet and kept applying ice from the refrigerator. He was conscious and suffering. Within a half hour his fever was coming down and within a couple of hours it was normal. Mavis had suffered a Herxheimer reaction, high fever caused by a release of toxins from the spirochetes as they were broken down by penicillin.

When I retired in 1986, at seventy-three years of age, I had practiced medicine for fifty years—thirty-seven years of them in Houston. In 1965, I had resigned from my part time job at M. D. Anderson Hospital, but remained on as a volunteer member of the staff. I continued to send patients there and received referrals from M. D. Anderson, especially from Bob Moreton. Around 1983, I had reduced my practice hours to about four-and-a-half days a week when I was in town. After 1984, I only saw patients at the clinic's Augusta office. I began coming in at nine in the morning and leaving at four in the afternoon. I only went to the hospital for an occasional consultation or for a social visit with a friend. In addition to traveling for the NASA contracts, I took time out of the office for numerous trips. Mary's health was declining; she was suffering memory loss and occasional heart failure. I wanted to spend more time with her. I had lost interest in clinic affairs and often disagreed with what was going on, probably because I was so ill-informed I couldn't make a proper judgment. I told a joke at the fortieth anniversary clinic party about the old man who said, "There's been a lot of changes, and I'm agin em all!"

I announced my intention to retire from practice on January 15, 1986, and saw my last paying patient one month later in mid-February. I tried to make it just like any other day in the office—a full schedule with Aggie Greer preparing the patients for examination and sending them out for tests. Some patients didn't know I was leaving, and I said nothing about it. One patient was Georgette Mosbacher, Bob's wife, and a nationally known cosmetics tycoon. She met Mavis, Jr., at a party a couple of days later and told him she was being examined by me in the Clinic. Mavis said "Why, he just retired two days ago." Georgette was infuriated because I had not told her. She called Aggie and let us know how she felt. I apologized. She and Bob sent me a nice piece of crystal as a retirement present.

I left the office completely in May 1986. The clinic gave me a great retirement party at the Houston Country Club and invited some of my friends. I received many letters from friends and patients and the mayor declared Mavis Kelsey Day. I left many wonderful people in the clinic. I had been closely associated with at least thirty of the doctors for many years. Some were my best friends. As a matter of fact only three of the long-time doctors had retired before I did—Bill Seybold, Charlie Dickson, and Jim McMurrey. I left the clinic in good hands. The clinic was having trouble, but the nucleus of original stalwarts, with the help of some of the younger partners, weathered the storm and saved the clinic. I can say I started the clinic but I can name a couple of dozen who saved it and made it a large, thriving, and highly respected institution.

CHAPTER 17

Areas of Expansion, 1955 to the Present

As the Kelsey-Seybold Clinic continued to grow, three additional areas of expansion emerged in the years after 1955: the establishment of a foundation; the organization of a department of occupational medicine, which won many company contracts, including work at the National Aeronautics and Space Administration (NASA); and the development of branch clinics in and around Houston. All three eventually distinguished our clinical practice from others nationwide.

The formation of the clinic's foundation occurred first. Soon after we entered practice in Houston, grateful patients wanted to give us money to use for charitable purposes. We advised these donors to direct their gifts to institutions of the Texas Medical Center, such as Baylor University College of Medicine and M. D. Anderson and St. Luke's Hospitals. Some patients said they had already given in the Medical Center, and they wanted our clinic to have the money for research or other charitable purposes. We were given several gifts totaling hundreds of dollars. One night in 1955, Mary and I were having dinner with John and Mickey. While John was cooking and I was drinking wine, he suggested that we organize a charitable foundation so that we could receive the gifts, and the donors could obtain a tax deduction. Bill Leary had received several gifts and approved our suggestion.

We called on Tommy Anderson, who was practicing law, running an investment company, and volunteering his time for just about every important cause in Houston. Generous as he was, Tommy agreed to help us organize a foundation. He recommended we enlist the expertise of Marvin Collie, also a friend and patient and a member of the Houston law firm of Vinson and Elkins. He was acquainted with the legal aspects of foundations. We had numerous meetings, and on December 15, 1956, a document of organization of a private foundation was prepared. The trustees were Thomas D. Anderson as chairman, Mavis P. Kelsey, William V. Leary, John R. Kelsey, and Marvin Collie.

We continued to receive gifts and funded a few scholarships at the Baylor medical school. We collected more than $2,000 in 1957. The Kelsey-Leary Clinic bore all the costs for several years, so there was no overhead or operating expenses for the foundation; 100 percent of all gifts would be spent for a charitable cause. Bill Elkins, a generous supporter, became a trustee in 1957. We had almost $1,500 on hand and had made gifts to the Good Samaritan Club; to Baylor for research in the surgical department; and a scholarship for Baylor's freshmen medical students. A grant—given as a memorial to Mrs. Retha Matthews, the mother of clinic business manager Jackie Greer—also had to be allocated. Jackie wanted the memorial to be spent for a piece of equipment for the cardiovascular laboratory at Texas Children's Hospital, where Earl Beard worked. The gift was delayed when one trustee opposed giving any funds to be used in any way which might be beneficial to a member of the Kelsey-Leary Clinic. This was the beginning of a controversy that lasted for years and stunted the growth of the foundation. As the years went, the clinic partners lost interest in the foundation; many partners opposed its existence. They refused to support a foundation which took the money they raised and required it to be spent away from anything they had a part in. Here were our partners, volunteering thousands of hours as teachers and researchers for Baylor, M. D. Anderson, and other medical center institutions—institutions that could receive gifts to support their staff doctors' research, as long as our doctors took no part as nonpay volunteers in the research that our foundation had funded.

By January 1960, the foundation was cleared by the Internal Revenue Service as tax-free. In 1962, Tommy Anderson recommended we add an advisory board. We soon appointed various doctors and administrators in the clinic and generous supporters, including Mrs. Noble Means of East Bernard; Hirsch Schwartz and his wife Felice; the parents of Dr. Gene Burke's wife, Jean; Billy McNulty; and Mrs. Wharton Weems. One year later, the Kelsey Leary Seybold Clinic formalized a student and residency training program with Baylor Medical College, which has continued to this day. At one time, every Baylor medical student spent some time either in our clinic or on our hospital services. We also accepted medical students from other schools for externships. We trained students from England, Scotland, Mexico, and other foreign countries, including Russia.

The financial status of the foundation improved gradually. From the first, we had intended it to be a conduit for gifts from grateful patients. For the first twenty years we had no benefit balls or other public fund raising efforts. We solicited our patients with brochures placed in the waiting rooms. When doctors wanted to pay us for treating them gratis, we recommended they make gifts to the foundation. Jackie Greer was one person who volunteered her time as secretary; she continued with the foundation, even after she left the clinic to work elsewhere. The foundation was approved as a public foundation in 1979. Before 1980, the name was changed to the Kelsey-Seybold Foundation after Seybold rejoined the clinic and Leary resigned. We obtained opinions from accountants and lawyers that our clinic doctors could be awarded foundation grants. The IRS has never questioned our use of foundation funds. It had lean years when it did not get the monetary support it deserved from the clinic doctors. But the clinic did provide space and secretarial help for years.

The foundation had several generous donors. Ernie Cockrell and Pat Rutherford each told us to call when we knew of a special need for equipment or a research project in a medical center institution. We could count on them for several thousand dollars any time we called. About 1977, Pat Rutherford, a diabetic, wanted to make a large gift to our foundation for diabetes, to be used at St. Luke's Hospital. Marvin Collie said the foundation could not accept it. In June 1977, I met with Baylor's Tony Gotto, professor of medicine, and David Scoular, a planning officer. They proposed an endowed professorship in diabetes. In January 1978, I called on Pat at his home and asked for $1,250,000 for an endowed chair to be named for his wife Betty. He accepted and gave the donation for the Betty Rutherford Professorship for Diabetic Research.[1]

The foundation's most important and largest donors were Joe Crump and his wife, Jessie. Originally from Duncan, Oklahoma, the Crumps moved to Midland in West Texas, where Joe Crump continued his career as an independent oil producer. He bought leases and royalties all over the Permian Basin during the early days of the oil boom. The story goes that you could not drill a well in West Texas without Joe Crump's signature. They had many friends and were very generous. Like many self-made westerners, they enjoyed their wealth and shared it with others and were neither pretentious nor arrogant. The Crumps were among the hundreds of people from Midland, Odessa, and other cities of the Permian Basin who became patients at our clinic. They first came in the 1950s and became great friends. Mrs. Crump, known by all as Aunt Jessie, took Mary and me to the best restaurants in Houston. Often we had her and her friends in our home.

The Crumps had no children. They established a trust to distribute their wealth for charitable causes. One-fourth of the trust income was for the treatment of infantile paralysis. This was before the Salk vaccine was discovered. A fourth of the Crump Fund went to the Episcopal Church, and another fourth to the Episcopal Seminary in Austin, funding dozens of scholarships for seminarians. The remaining fourth was for research for the cause and treatment of cancer. Aunt Jessie had been operated on for breast cancer, which was cured.

Almost as soon as the Crumps came to Houston they donated to the foundation and St. Luke's Hospital. In the 1960s, they volunteered an annual gift of $7,500 to the Kelsey and Leary Foundation, to be used for cancer research. After Mr. Crump died, Mrs. Crump became a great traveler in Europe and Latin America. She always traveled with her longtime friend, Fannie Bess Sivalls. Fannie Bess acted as sort of a nurse-companion, adjusting the dosage and administering insulin for Aunt Jessie's diabetes. Aunt Jessie was overweight and enjoyed rich food, but Fannie Bess kept her blood sugar under control. One day, Aunt Jessie and Fannie Bess were in my office preparing to leave for Europe that night. They were in a hurry. Practically as they were leaving the room, Aunt Jessie remarked, "The Crump Trust has $100,000 on hand for cancer research. Could the foundation use it?" "Certainly," I replied. "Okay, we will arrange it when we get back from Europe. Good-by." The Joe and Jessie Crump Center for Cancer Research eventually evolved from that brief conversation. Aunt Jessie then started giving the Kelsey-Leary Foundation about $50,000 a year.

When Aunt Jessie reached her seventies she began to talk about very large gifts. Gilchrist Jackson was a young surgeon in our clinic who had received part of his training at the M. D. Anderson Hospital. He trained there under A. J. Ballantyne who had married Maria Mitchell, niece of Christy Mitchell, owner of the College Inn in Galveston. A. J. and Maria had a large family, and Gil Jackson married their daughter Catina. Gil of his own volition was soon planning an ambitious cancer program for the Kelsey-Seybold Clinic. He presented his proposed program to the clinic research committee the spring of 1982. Unknown to him at the time, his plan was to become the Crump Cancer Center. In July of that year, Aunt Jessie said she was planning to give $1 million for cancer research to us, or possibly to the M. D. Anderson Hospital. She came to Houston and stayed at the Mayfair Hotel (now the Rotary House). On July 29, Tommy Anderson, Gil Jackson, and I called on Aunt Jessie in her hotel suite. Gil presented his plan for a cancer center at the Kelsey-Seybold Clinic which we proposed to call the Joe and Jessie Crump Center for Cancer Research. At that meeting, she gave the foundation $1 million.

The Crump Center was dedicated on January 23, 1983. All of Aunt Jessie's family were there. She wore all her jewels. The gift was described in many Texas newspapers. Reverend Maurice Benitez, Episcopal Bishop of Texas, gave the invocation. I introduced Aunt Jessie, and she made the following statement:

My deceased husband and I set aside one-quarter of the Joe and Jessie Crump Fund for the purpose of curing cancer. We wished that a cure for cancer would occur in our lifetime. It now appears that there will be no single cure for cancer. There are many kinds of cancer and each is a separate disease requiring its own cure. We believe research for the diagnosis and treatment of cancer will go on indefinitely, long after the present trustees are gone.

In gratitude for our long time support and in honor of my deceased husband and me, and in recognition of our decision to join them in forming a permanent research center, the Kelsey-Seybold Foundation and the Kelsey-Seybold Clinic have named the center The Joe and Jessie Crump Center for Cancer Research.

Although my deceased husband and I will not live to see the final solution to the cure of cancer, the Joe and Jessie Crump Center for Cancer Research will perpetuate our original objectives, and will identify our contributions as a permanent institution.

The funds of the Crump Center were channeled into an outpatient center for cancer research, education, prevention, and treatment. The center has focused on early diagnosis by mammography, breast self-examination, and regular surveillance of high-risk patients. A high-risk registry was established jointly with St. Luke's and M. D. Anderson Hospitals. Many papers and presentations have emanated from the program. Identifying high-risk patients has become a goal for numerous health care programs.[2]

Aunt Jessie remained a patient as well as a friend. In September 1977, while at her home in Mission, Aunt Jessie had a coronary occlusion. I flew down to see her in the Valley Hospital at Harlingen. She recovered, but had a pacemaker implanted in April 1978. She was in St. Luke's Hospital in 1980 and 1982. She continued traveling to Midland, Mission, and Houston. Aunt Jessie enjoyed staying in fine hotels. She was excited when some members of the Hunt family of Dallas, whom she knew, opened the Remington Hotel in Houston. It was the finest hotel in Texas, a stay costing $200 a night. On her next trip to Houston, she made reservations at the Remington. Her plane was late. She arrived at night, after the hotel restaurant had closed. When she got to her room she undressed and called for room service. She ordered fried shrimp and a glass of buttermilk. The haughty French chef told her, "Madam, we don't fry shrimp, and we don't serve buttermilk." By eight the next morning Mrs. Crump was out of the Remington Hotel and checked into the Mayfair. I called the manager of the Remington and told him about the incident. He said, "From now on we serve fried shrimp and buttermilk to anyone who orders it." Aunt Jessie never went back.

The other major cancer program of the foundation was the Joe and Madelyn Vercillino Institute for Gastrointestinal Cancer. Joseph Vercillino and Madelyn Stoffel were born in Valier, Illinois, and went to high school together. He became a geologist and she became a nurse before they married. Joe, the son of Italian immigrants, became an international oil developer in America, England, Italy, and Brazil. After seeing several doctors without being diagnosed, Joe came to see our gastroenterologist, John Hughes. John found a cancer of the stomach, which was removed, but metastases to the liver appeared within a few months. Joe knew what his outcome would be. He told John Hughes that he wanted to make a significant gift for gastrointestinal cancer research. John Hughes introduced me to Joe, and we discussed his desires. He and Madelyn had no children and both wanted their gift to honor John Hughes. Since John Hughes was already committed to cancer research, he had no problem developing a program and a tentative budget for clinical research directed toward early diagnosis and treatment of gastrointestinal cancer.[3] Tommy Anderson, John Hughes, and I called on Joe and Madelyn Vercillino in their home. John presented his program, which required $1 million to implement. The Vercillinos were very pleased with the proposal and accepted it during this meeting. The dedication of the Vercillino center was attended by members of Joe's and Madelyn's families. Joe's elderly parents came from Illinois. After Joe Vercillino died, Madelyn and other members of his family continued to support the foundation.

Dr. John Hughes was the first African-American doctor to be taken on the staff of the Kelsey Seybold Clinic. John was born in Florida in 1948 and was graduated from South Florida College of Medicine. He served residences at Florida and the University of California. In 1979 he entered a fellowship in gastroenterology at the University of Texas Health Science Center in Houston, financed by the Kelsey Seybold Foundation. Part of his training was at the Kelsey Seybold Clinic. He was taken on the staff in 1981 and assigned to John Kelsey's section. John Hughes's bright, cheerful personality, his energy and ambition, and his professionalism earned him the respect and friendship of doctors and patients alike.

Two experiences I had with patients will demonstrate how John overcame prejudice. First there was an elderly oil heiress from Midland who had a stomach problem. I told her I was referring her to a brilliant young doctor but I wanted to describe him. The patient's daughter was in the room and said, "I know what you are going to say! He's a black." After some persuasion the lady agreed to see John Hughes. He admitted her to St. Luke's Hospital. Two or three days later I called on her. Without mentioning John's ethnicity, she said,

"That's the nicest, smartest doctor you sent me to. I just love him." She sent her friends to see Dr. Hughes. The second is an example of reverse discrimination. I had, as a patient, the retired African-American leader of the Houston longshoremen. His wife was a retired teacher; they were well-to-do people. The man had a stomach problem. I told him I was referring him to a very competent young stomach doctor but I wanted him to know Dr. Hughes's ethnicity. The patient was surprised. He said, "I didn't come here to see a black doctor." After some persuasion he went to see Dr. Hughes and was pleased. Like the patient from Midland, he did not acknowledge his prejudice once he had seen Dr. Hughes.

Dr. Hughes is active in an illustrious career. He has published numerous articles on his favorite subject, the early diagnosis of bowel cancer. He became a Distinguished Alumnus and delivered the graduation address to his medical school in May 1996.

Another significant donor to the foundation was Mrs. Alice Armer of Fort Worth. Alice was the widow of a successful independent oil producer who died while still in middle age. Alice took charge of her deceased husband's oil business and became known as an outstandingly successful oil operator, something very rare for a woman in the rough and tumble business of finding oil. She was a well-educated, stylish woman who wore beautiful diamonds and gold jewelry. "To Hell with being robbed," she said. She became a patient and reported regularly for her annual examination. Mary and I had a number of mutual friends with Alice and entertained her when she came to town. Once, Mary entertained Alice Armer and Aunt Jessie at the same luncheon. Alice Armer was in her seventies when, one afternoon, she came in and complained of weakness of the right arm. She had a loud carotid bruit and was on the verge of a major stroke. I called Dr. DeBakey who once had operated on her. Before the day was over Mike had done a carotid artery bypass. Alice left the hospital free of symptoms. She said "You and Dr. DeBakey have saved my life, I want to make a gift to each of your foundations. I will give each of you $1 million in oil properties." We arranged for her gift to go into a permanent endowment.

Alice had one son, a very likeable man who was not interested in the oil business but liked fine automobiles and large boats. When Alice turned the business over to her son he drilled one dry hole after another. Alice was very distressed but supported him. Unfortunately, the son developed a rapidly spreading malignancy. Alice developed a large dissecting aortic aneurysm and died, after an operation, in surgical intensive care at St. Luke's Hospital. Her son died a few weeks later. Mary and I went to her funeral in December 1980 and paid our respects to the family. When the estate was settled, we learned that the value of the producing oil properties pledged to the foundation had shrunk from $1,000,000 to $300,000. The foundation has maintained the gift in their endowment fund.

When I review the many accomplishments of the Kelsey-Seybold Foundation, I am impressed with the large volume of work done with such limited funds. As our gifts increased, we made more grants. Dozens of projects have been supported in several fields. In the field of medical education, the foundation began by giving scholarships to many medical students, interns, and residents in the Baylor program and to the University of Texas medical institutions in Houston. When our partner Melville Cody died, his friends established a lectureship in his memory. It is given annually on a gynecologic subject by a leading American authority. Dr. J. Charles Dickson was memorialized by an annual lectureship in otolaryngology. Dr. Shell, one of our most promising young physicians, directed our branch office at Humble. He was killed on his way home from work by a reckless driver. The Kelsey-Seybold Clinic gave the foundation funds for a lectureship in his memory. The James Nall Memorial Award was established in memory of a neurologist in the clinic who also died young.

The foundation has been deeply involved in research. At least half of its grants were seed money to get projects under way so that the researcher could obtain full funding from the National Institutes of Health. Many significant articles have come from its grants. Mrs. Mimi Dompier, for example, has been one of the most generous and consistent donors to the foundation and has served as a trustee for years. Some of the gifts are also from a trust established by her parents, the Bob and Vivian Smith Foundation. Mimi began first by making grants for George Ferry to do research in pediatric gastroenterology. The foundation also funded several of Earl Brewer's pediatric rheumatology projects in the clinic and in Texas Children's Hospital. Through Earl's efforts the Lloyd Bentsen Award, a national award to a young medical achiever sponsored by the senator, has been presented annually for nearly ten years. For twelve years, Earl Beard, chief of cardiology at the clinic, has presented an annual symposium, *Frontiers of Cardiology*, in Winter Park, Colorado. The meeting has been highly successful, attracting nationwide attention.

The foundation joined with M. D. Anderson Hospital in funding dozens of research projects. Some fifteen years ago, for example, the foundation provided M. D. Anderson money to study familial gastrointestinal neoplasia. Louise Strong, a friend of my family, was a young research scientist who initiated the study. Louise made many discoveries and has become internationally famous for her work in familial neoplasia. One of the foundation's major gifts to M. D. Anderson was an electron microscope for use in clinical medicine, the first ever. Before this the electron microscope had been used only for research.[4]

Many research grants went to Baylor University College of Medicine. My brother John was active there and once served as chief of gastroenterology. Studies were for tumors of the small bowel; prostaglandins in esophageal function; esophageal motility; and inflammatory bowel disease. Still other research grants went to the cardiovascular laboratories of St. Luke's and Texas Children's Hospital, beginning in 1958. Projects included: statistical research in ischemic heart disease; research in causes of obstructive lung disease and intraaortic phase-shift balloon counter propulsion in man; studies of echocardiographic analysis with intra-aortic balloon pump; radiation studies in primates; studies of new materials for percutaneous leads; and designing and testing of a mechanical circulatory analog.[5]

The foundation also purchased equipment for a number of projects, beginning with a planimeter for the cardiovascular laboratory at Texas Children's Hospital in 1956. A Micro-gas Analyzer for lung cancer research was given to M. D. Anderson Hospital. To St. Luke's Hospital, we gave a camera system to study malignant tumors, and, to their new nuclear medicine section, a special isotope scanner. The foundation also gave a microscope for renal subsections to St. Luke's. For the Texas Heart Institute we funded the first aortic assist balloon pump. The foundation gave Methodist Hospital a gastroscope and the first gastro-camera in Houston, an instrument that proved to be very effective in teaching. We gave money to the Medical School in Galveston to purchase an early dialysis unit. The Crump and Vercillino Centers, with help from the Kelsey-Seybold Clinic, purchased much equipment to run their research.[6]

The income of the foundation gradually increased from $1,800 the first year to nearly a $1 million a year. By 1980, we had raised about $4 million. Every penny of that money went out in grants. Jackie Greer, Betty Wilcox, and Jo Ann Gary volunteered much time in administration. Later, the work load was so great we had to employ a director. The first full-time paid director I can remember was Mimi Minkoff. Several years ago, one of Mimi's most effective volunteers, Terry Litchfield, left the foundation to be with her husband who was transferred to Singapore. When Terry returned to the states in 1993 she volunteered again. Soon she was employed full time as executive director of the foundation. She turned the place around and put the foundation on a sound financial basis. Terry developed many gifts, grants, and special fund-raising events. She obtained contracts from the Kelsey-Seybold Clinic to do outcomes research and contracts from drug companies, corporations, and medical institutions. She developed a volunteer program. Terry was well organized, intelligent, and a regular fountain of productive ideas. Unfortunately for the foundation, she was hired away in November 1997 by Baxter Laboratories. Her salary was more than doubled and she was made vice president in charge of outcomes research, the same program she had established at the Kelsey-Seybold Foundation.

One loan recipient has been a savior for the foundation. George Ferry graduated from Baylor University College of Medicine in 1964. He was taught by some of our staff while in medical school. While training as a pediatric gastroenterologist at Johns Hopkins in 1968, the foundation provided him a loan of $6,000. After his training, he joined the pediatric section for the Kelsey-Seybold Clinic. He had repaid his loan by July 1975. He had a part-time teaching position in Texas Children's Hospital, but he took time to play an active role in the Kelsey-Seybold Foundation. Eventually he became the voluntary medical director of the foundation. When the foundation expanded, George was given a much earned part-time salary. He has continued as medical director, even though he left the clinic a few years ago to become the full-time chief of gastroenterology at Texas Children's Hospital.

The foundation has also been supported by a dedicated board of trustees. They have all been friends and most of them patients of the clinic. Following the original trustees, the foundation added others, including advisory members: William S. Elkins, J. Cooke Wilson, Jr., Ernie Cockrell, Jackie Greer, Pat Rutherford, Hirsch Schwarz, Maxine Means, Mrs. Wharton Weems, Dick Eastwood, Richard Howe, William D. Seybold, Joseph O. Clark, Mimi Dompier, Edward Randall III, Gibson Gayle, Jr., Mickey LeMaistre, William Harvin, C. Jim Stewart, David Blevins, Randy Smith, Bob Lansford, Fannie Bess Sivalls, Fox Benton, Mrs. Cy (Lissa) Wagner, William Noel, Jim Kemper, Earl Beard, David Mouton, Mike Newmark, Stan Fischer, and Nancy Webb have been especially helpful. Various managers and the accountant of the clinic, as well as certain doctors, have served on the board usually as ex-officio or advisory members.

Thomas D. Anderson was the original chairman and served for twenty-five continuous years.[7] He was honored by a banquet at the Houston Country Club, when he retired as chairman. William Harvin of the law firm of Baker and Botts replaced Tommy as chairman of the foundation. Like Tommy, Bill is a leading Houston citizen. Bill Harwin has served on many boards, usually becoming president or chairman. He has had a very active role at the Texas Medical Center and on boards of the Texas Medical Center, St. Luke's Hospital, and other institutions. He had been a trustee of the Kelsey-Seybold Foundation for a few years. Bill retired in 1995 and was replaced by Stacy Eastland, a Baker and Botts attorney. Stacy has become well known for his work in establishing trusts and foundations. I first met Stacy in 1993, when he established a limited partnership for our family. He has taken the chairmanship in a no-nonsense fashion.

Thanks to the efforts of many people, the Kelsey-Seybold Foundation has attained the critical mass necessary to perpetuate itself. Like the clinic, it has taken a life of its own. Both institutions enjoy an enviable reputation and a world of goodwill. One of the great disappointments of my career, however, was the failure of the Kelsey-Seybold Clinic to become a part of the foundation. The clinic would have enjoyed the many benefits in tax savings and public support and would have become an institution of the Texas Medical Center. Almost from its beginning I proposed converting the clinic from a private business to a tax-exempt foundation. I had seen first hand its advantages at the Scott and White and Mayo Clinics. At these two institutions, the physical properties had long ago been transferred to the respective foundations. Stated in simple terms, the foundations raised large sums of money from gifts and tax-free bonds. With the money, they built large buildings and equipped them for the doctors to practice in—an expense the doctors could not afford. Virtually every general clinic with more than forty doctors had converted to a foundation. Our clinic was competing with the institutions of the Texas Medical Center, every one of which was a tax-exempt institution. The overhead expenses of the medical center doctors were much lower than ours. Across the street from our clinic, Denton Cooley had developed The Texas Heart Institute, built by tax-exempt gifts and tax-free income.

The officers of the clinic were interested enough to send several partners to clinics around the country to study their experience with foundations. I went with Jim Kemper and Ron Rushing to the West Coast to visit several clinics, including the Scripps Institute and the Palo Alto Clinic. Many partnership meetings were held in which I and a few others tried to convince the remaining partners that we should become a foundation. Even after I retired, I continued promoting the foundation as a vehicle for owning the physical assets of the clinic. Milton Underwood, Ernie Cockrell, and Pat Rutherford were among our friends in the business world who strongly supported the foundation idea. Mickey LeMaistre, head of M. D. Anderson and a Kelsey-Seybold Foundation trustee, favored it and wanted to support us. Our new manager, Breaux Castleman, considered the foundation plan, but he said that medical practice would become a giant business under the control of large companies. There is much to support Breaux's views. Nevertheless, the physical assets of the Kelsey-Seybold Clinic were sold to Caremark, a large corporation, then to Med-Partners. Although the move has been successful so far, as obstinate as I am, I still believe the clinic would do better as a foundation, and I believe it can be done even though someone else now owns the plant. Yet, those in the know are very optimistic about the future of the clinic and foundation.

The Department of Occupational Medicine was the next in-house organization to emerge in these years, one inextricably linked to the clinic's contracts with NASA. The origin of these contracts dates back to my service in World War II and my relationship with Randy Lovelace, who had offered me the job at the Aeromedical Research Laboratory at Wright Field in Dayton. After the war Randy was promoted to brigadier general and continued as consultant for space flight to the air surgeon general. In 1945 the idea of a space program inspired the imagination of the general public. People thought Earth already had been thoroughly explored. The Great Western Movement of the last four centuries had been fulfilled. Conquering space became an exciting new frontier. We might even colonize Mars to relieve the crowded population of Earth. There could be space stations and colonies to the moon where we could harvest its minerals or harness solar energy for use on Earth. There were also more immediate and reasonable goals of low orbit satellites: for communication, to carry telescopes, to predict weather, to spy on our enemies, to conduct warfare, and develop stuff in zero gravity. Exploring space was tremendously expensive. The air force was responsible for much of the early development of the space efforts, and they wanted to be in charge of the entire program. In 1958, President Eisenhower signed Public Law 85-568, establishing the National Aeronautics and Space Administration as an entity independent from the air force. Randy Lovelace became chief medical consultant for the Mercury Project for manned space flights, the first major NASA project. A program was soon underway for qualifying and training pilots to be astronauts. Much of this training was developed at the Lovelace Clinic in Albuquerque under Randy's direction. In 1957 simulated space flights were carried out at the School of Aviation Medicine with my friend Paul Campbell in charge. In 1959 the name of the school was changed to the School of Aerospace Medicine. Charles Berry, a flight surgeon, was training and virtually living with the original astronaut trainees.

While space medical research and astronaut training were going on, rockets were being tested both for defense and for space flight. In 1948 a rocket missile in New Mexico reached a height of seventy-eight miles. The next year a guided missile traveled 250 miles. By 1953 a rocket-powered plane flew at 1,600 miles per hour. The U.S.S.R. was still ahead in 1957 when it launched Earth's first satellites, *Sputnik I* and *II*. In 1958 NASA launched the thirty-one pound satellite *Explorer I* from Cape Canaveral while the U.S.S.R. launched *Sputnik III*, weighing 3,000 pounds. In 1959 the U.S.S.R. launched a rocket with two monkeys aboard and sent unmanned *Lunik III* to the moon to take photographs. In 1961 Yuri Gagarin orbited Earth in a six-ton satellite while Alan Shepard made the first American space flight.

When NASA was established in 1958 there was heated competition for location of its numerous facilities. Politics dictated that these centers be distributed around the nation. The Manned Spacecraft Center (MSC) which was to be home for the astronauts and control center for space flights was contested by Massachusetts and Texas. Senator Lyndon Johnson had more political power than the Kennedys. Lyndon's friends Jim and Wesley West had a thirty thousand acre ranch south of Houston which bordered Clear Lake. They sold fifteen thousand acres of the ranch to NASA for MSC, which soon became known as the Johnson Space Center (JSC). The launching center at Cape Canaveral became known as the Kennedy Space Center.

Frantic construction took place around the country in a dozen new NASA centers. While JSC was being built at Clear Lake City, Ellington Field nearby became temporary headquarters for the rapidly expanding facility. An air force flight surgeon was assigned to the temporary headquarters to handle the health problems of the employees. I was a consultant in internal medicine at the Ellington hospital during this time. Randy Lovelace called and asked me to help and advise the JSC flight surgeon with his duties. On June 11, 1962, Randy was in Houston on business for NASA. He invited me to a small dinner party hosted by John T. Jones at the Rice Hotel. There were about eight or ten top NASA officials present, including Robert Gilruth, the new director of JSC. The gathering was a social affair. Randy thanked me for advising the flight surgeon and arranging referrals for him. By this time, Chuck Berry had come to Houston with the astronauts. He was in charge of their health care and was also burdened with trying to handle the expansion of health care, industrial hygiene, and occupational medicine for a work force of eight thousand people. This is when Randy told me that all medical care for nonastronauts would eventually be contracted out and that our clinic should go for it.[8]

At this time, in the early 1960s, our clinic was developing a large practice that we called company medicine. We needed a specialist in occupational medicine. Our friend Valiant Baird, medical director of Humble Oil Company, checked around and located Randolph Hall who had a great record as a colonel in the army. Randy Hall and his wife Josephine came for an interview. When we checked Randy's recommendations, we were told he was remarkably capable but had trouble getting along with people. We employed Randy Hall in 1964, and it didn't take long to learn that both of these traits were very true. Finally, in 1966, the contract for medical care at JSC was put out for bids. Randy, our new chief of occupational medicine, was in charge of preparing the bid. Jim Bakken and John Kelsey were very helpful. We scheduled our own doctors to rotate in delivering medical care. We did not have expertise in industrial hygiene or health physics. We subcontracted these services to the Southwest Research Foundation in San Antonio, whose director was retired general Otis Benson. I first met Otis at the Mayo Clinic before World War II. He was assigned there by the Medical Corps as part of his training to become a flight surgeon.

We won the first contract for a five-year term and began work on October 1, 1966. (Every five years for the past thirty years, we have continued to win the contract.) Randy Hall was project manager and spent much of his time at the space center, but he was so industrious that he maintained practice in the main clinic. He would later start our first branch clinic in Clear Lake City. Several of the clinic internists rotated work days at the center. I remember that Stan Fischer, Maurice Johnston, Ralph Eichorn, and I were among those who rotated until we established a full-time staff. Becoming part of the space program appeared to me as one of those rare opportunities that comes but once in a lifetime. As time went on, our NASA contracts brought many fine people into the clinic, several million dollars in profits, and a national reputation for good work. Several clinic doctors became close friends of the astronauts and their wives. Many astronaut family members became patients in the clinic. It was one of the most gratifying experiences of my career.

The initial contract called for seventeen Kelsey-Seybold employees. We provided coverage twenty-four hours a day, seven days a week, while NASA rushed madly to put a man on the moon. We were blessed with fine dedicated employees. Dowis Atkins, deputy project manager, was in charge of environmental health. He developed the only certified environmental health laboratory in the entire space agency. Vicki Buxton worked at JSC as a secretary. She was the most brilliant employee to come out of the place. Highly educated and stylish, she was so competent in preparing bids that she spent much of her time in the main clinic preparing our bids for NASA and other contracts. Eventually in 1978 she moved to the main clinic full time as an administrator.

Our responsibilities increased dramatically as we proved our capabilities and were asked to provide services for the Apollo Program. We began by providing on-site care for all eight thousand employees and the astronaut families. We did many types of physical examinations, immunizations, laboratory and X-ray examinations, and preventive medicine programs. Soon, there was an extensive industrial hygiene and environmental health program for the center. In 1968, Herb Foss was placed in charge of the aeromedical physiological support (Manned Test Support), which directly involved the astronauts. The equipment included altitude and hyperbaric chambers, a human centrifuge, a water immersion facility, a mock-up Lunar Landing Module, and a simulated splash down retriever ship in Galveston Bay. Our environmental health staff conducted analysis of breathing gases, measured exposure to radiation, developed the system of waste management, and other functions for space flights. One of the most outstanding sights was the solar simulator, the largest known altitude chamber in the world. It would hold the first and second stage capsules of any existing spacecraft. The simulator provided the equivalent of an altitude of 300,000 feet. Mercury lights on one side provided a temperature of +400°F, and cryogenic material on the other side provided a temperature of -250°F. In 1973, 500 flight physical examinations, 6,000 other examinations, and 24,000 patient visits took place.

Randy Hall, our first project manger at JSC, departed the NASA program in 1966. He was replaced by Colonel Paul E. Wright, a graduate of the University of Tennessee Medical College in Memphis who had been a flight surgeon in the air force. He was a man of great energy. When I made my monthly trip to JSC he walked me through our center projects so fast I could hardly keep up. He was talking the entire time. An excellent administrator, Paul knew everything that was going on. He was even tempered and admired by his staff. Paul introduced several important innovations. He expanded the physical examination program to all civil service employees, in addition to those in top management. He designed protocols for all job duties. He promoted Vicki Buxton to the position of administrator, passing over an all-male cast of applicants, and in so doing established a first for NASA. Regrettably, poor health forced Paul to retire in May 1975. The next managing director, Bradley Prior, served until 1979. Colonel Walter R. Hein replaced Prior in February of that year and turned out to be as great as Paul Wright. On Hein's watch the Kelsey-Seybold staff began physical examinations for the Sky Lab astronaut candidates. Walt was a fellow of the American College of Surgeons and a retired air force surgeon. Many of our medical staff at JSC were naval or air force retirees.[9]

Space flight developed rapidly in the 1960s. Russian Valentina Tereshkova, the first female astronaut, made a three-day flight in space in 1963. Gordon Cooper completed twenty-two orbits of the Earth the same year. In 1965, a Soviet astronaut made the first space walk, which lasted ten minutes, followed by a twenty-one minute U.S. space walk by Ed White. In 1966, Edwin E. Aldrin, Jr., stepped out of *Gemini XII* for 129 minutes. There was also tragedy. In 1967, Soviet cosmonaut Komorov was killed on reentry. The Russians landed on the ground while Americans landed in the ocean to be picked up. In January 1967, three of our astronauts, Virgil Grissom, Ed White, and Roger Chaffe, were killed in a training exercise at Cape Kennedy. Several of our friends knew them well.

The *Apollo XIII* flight to the moon was interrupted by an equipment failure and the astronauts narrowly escaped death. Two days into the mission, an oxygen tank explosion in the service module caused a rapid loss of electrical power. The only solution was to turn the lunar module into a lifeboat. The three astronauts crammed themselves into the lunar module, looped around the moon, and made it back to Earth. Ground control personnel were instrumental in getting the space ship back to Earth. As I recall, Frank Borman was on this flight. I saw him at a party and remarked that I thought I would never live to see a man fly to the moon. He belittled my remark by saying, "I never thought I would fly to the moon."

Several space flights circled the moon and came near it. *Apollo XI* landed on the moon on July 19, 1969. Five more manned landings followed, all highly successful. Charles Conrad and Alan Bean returned with 251 pounds of moon rocks in 1969. Two flights, *Apollo XIV* and *XV,* explored the moon in 1971, and *Apollo XVI* and *XVII* landed in 1972 when one crew stayed on the moon surface for seventy-five hours. We had beaten the Russians to the moon, and they gave up trying. One *Apollo* flight orbiting the Earth joined a Russian *Soyuz* satellite 19,240 miles above the earth. The Sky Lab program, following *Apollo,* would place a permanent station in space. The Soviets had gotten ahead of America by developing a space station while we were exploring the moon.

Mary accompanied me on perhaps two of the several launches I witnessed at Kennedy Space Center. Observing the launching of a manned spaceship was an unforgettable experience. Thousands of people attended on the Cape Kennedy grounds. The dignitaries were seated in a grandstand. It was very fashionable for the great and famous to attend. I saw many faces of senators, movie and sports stars, generals, admirals, business leaders, and foreign dignitaries that were familiar to me because they were frequently shown on television. We were a mile away from the launch site. When the countdown reached zero, the skyscraper-sized rocket with its human cargo on the tip rose slowly, as if it would teeter to one side and fall. But it rapidly gained speed and shot into the sky trailing huge flames. It appeared to be directly overhead when it attained several thousand feet, then the rocket turned toward the Atlantic Ocean and soon disappeared.

Our work at JSC continued to expand when Sky Lab and the Space Shuttle were developed. In 1981, the space shuttle *Columbia* was the first spaceship to accomplish a safe ascent into orbit and return to Earth for a safe landing. In 1984, President Reagan announced in his State of the Union message that NASA would build a permanently manned presence in space. Even though there had always been opponents to the space program the decision to build a space station assured the program existence, at least for many years to come.

On January 28, 1986, I was in my car on the way home for lunch, listening to the launch of the space shuttle *Challenger* on the radio, when it exploded seventy-three seconds after takeoff, killing the entire crew. I rushed home and saw a replay of it on television. Millions saw the disaster on television, and our country mourned the terrible loss.

This accident slowed down the program for several years, but it has been put back on track, in spite of many cutbacks in appropriations. Our JSC contract was successful, as measured by the increase of our services and the high grades we received for performance. Our grades were always over ninety, usually the highest of any contractor. Until 1991, we had been awarded a grade of 100 for thirteen years straight. In 1971 we were invited to bid on providing health services to the George C. Marshall Space Flight Center (MSFC), at Huntsville, Alabama. Vicki Buxton revealed her talents again by helping prepare our bid. Through her expertise, we won the contract beginning in 1972 and have won it every five years since. Our MSFC contract provided a medical staff of twenty-three employees, and responsibilities were similar to those at JSC.

In July 1976, we won the contract for medical and industrial hygiene services at the Langley Space Center, located on the grounds of Langley Field at Hampton, Virginia, between Williamsburg and Norfolk. Langley is one of America's oldest airfields. The Wright brothers and Air Corps Officer Langley did early aeronautical research there. There is a museum on the base exhibiting their pioneer work. The base has several wind tunnels, where aerodynamics of experimental planes are tested. I saw several of these strange flying machines in the hangars. The Langley Space Center was studying the aerodynamics of spaceships. I enjoyed visiting Langley Field. The industrial hygienists did well. Epidemiological studies had revealed that people who made model planes were found to have a high incidence of colon cancer. Many model planes were made for testing in the wind tunnels at Langley. Sawdust and fumes filled the model making shops, before our hygienists required that all work be done on tables where dust was sucked under and piped outside where it was cleaned and released.

The medical service program at the Lewis Aerospace Research Center in Cleveland, Ohio, was put out for bids in 1978. We won the small contract. The Lewis Center did research on power engines and meteorology. I was shown a deep hole where the effect of zero gravity could be studied by dropping objects in the hole. The people at Lewis called the hole the Martha Washington Monument, because it was as deep as the George Washington Monument was high. Our next NASA contract was for the Ames Research Center at Moffett Air Field, near Palo Alto, California. We won the four-year contract beginning in 1979, lost the renewal in 1983, then regained it in 1988, two years after I retired. Much of the activity I saw at Ames involved human testing for living in space. Volunteers lived in a boxcar-sized simulated spaceship for three months at a time. Scientists viewed the volunteers through windows. Everything was simulated, except weightlessness. There were other tests using paid volunteers, things I wouldn't volunteer for. I watched as some volunteers, after they had passed the physical, got cold feet and backed out of the tests. The Ames contract also called for supplying medical personnel at Edwards Air Field to receive the astronauts when a space shuttle landed there. The space shuttles landed there occasionally, when weather would not permit landing at the Kennedy Space Center. We bragged that a Kelsey-Seybold doctor was the first person to see the astronauts when they returned from outer space.

I especially enjoyed visiting the contract sites on inspection trips and talking with the many dedicated people of the Kelsey-Seybold Clinic who worked for NASA. I also enjoyed witnessing many of NASA's amazing accomplishments. Our relationship with NASA meant traveling to Washington, D.C., where I had spent so much time during the war. I was able to take Mary on several of the trips. On one trip in May 1982, the daughter of our friend Thad Grundy went to dinner with us. Thad was a senior partner in our son Tom's firm. Thad's daughter was an administrative assistant to Vice President George Bush, and after dinner she took us to Bush's office. Then we went to President Reagan's office. We walked all though the offices of the White House after hours, including the Oval Office, Kissinger's office, and several other presidential assistants' offices.

Apart from its work with NASA, the clinic also developed a great number of other company accounts for the department of occupational medicine. Health examinations by specialists were becoming popular as perquisites for executives. The word soon spread around Houston that the clinic had full-time specialists who performed these examinations. As we grew each internist developed company accounts as part of his practice. We were all specialists. If we lacked a specialty, we referred patients outside for consultation and treatment to other specialists. Some internists at our clinic did not do pelvic exams as part of a routine physical. They referred the patient to a gynecologist who charged an additional fee. This was the beginning of narrow specialization, or overspecialization, that thrived for years before the HMO movement revolutionized medicine.

During the 1950s and early 1960s, companies began asking the clinic to perform various medical services such as preemployment examinations and immunizations. The Houston oil industry asked us to prepare personnel for foreign travel. Our internists were fully occupied with their specialty practices. The company medicine program had expanded beyond doing executive health examinations. This was when we employed Randy Hall as chief of occupational medicine. Tall, handsome, and dynamic, he was well educated and had a broad knowledge of medicine, including his specialty, as well as of medical administration. I thought he would be great to take over preventive medicine and the administration of our company accounts, while the internists could continue their executive health examinations. But the internists in the clinic insisted that Randy not do executive physical examinations. Randy began demanding all the profits from the NASA contract which had been divided among the partners. I tried to mediate between the internists and Randy, and found the experience to be exasperating. But Randy was a highly capable doctor who worked hard and well. He established a department of occupational medicine in our clinic—no easy task, and a pioneering one for a general clinic. Even the Mayo Clinic did not have such a department.

Our contracts were wide-ranging. The Environmental Protection Agency regulations during the 1970s caused a great outcry from industry and created a demand for industrial hygienists and health physicists. We were already doing this type of work at NASA. Companies called on us for advice. We joined with a group of hygienists and physicists from the University of Texas School of Public Health. They organized a company called Tocsin, Inc., for providing this service to companies that were not large enough to have their own hygienists.

In 1980 we were invited to bid on providing medical services to the Naval Regional Medical Center at the Great Lakes Naval Station. This station, famous for training landlocked Midwestern farm boys as sailors during the last two world wars, had a beautiful campus that surrounded old brick dormitories and other buildings. On April 7, 1980, I was on the phone all day in a Chicago hotel room, recruiting doctors. Chicago Medical College had opened a charity teaching clinic almost next door to the naval station. With some of their part-time staff, we put a team together and won the contract, which we held until 1987.

In December 1981, we won the Air Force Health Survey Study, the largest contract in the history of the clinic, bringing a profit of $1,300,000. The purpose of this study was to settle the controversy over whether the defoliant Agent Orange had harmed troops who had been exposed to it during the Vietnam War. There were thousands upon thousands of Vietnam veterans claiming various disabilities from various causes, the largest number claiming exposure to Agent Orange. They suffered a wide range of vague symptoms, yet no one could find genuine organic physical changes attributable to Agent Orange. The air crews and the ground crews who dispersed the defoliant had been exposed to the agent—had sometimes soaked in it for days—and yet many of them had no complaints. These men believed that Agent Orange was harmless. A giant double blind study was developed by the military. Several hundred veterans known to be heavily exposed to Agent Orange were compared with a like number of those who complained. Extensive medical examinations were performed by internists, dermatologists, neurologists, psychiatrists, and psychologists. Extensive chemical tests of blood, liver, kidney function, and cardiopulmonary function were performed. No one knew which group was being tested until the final results were in. No problems were found in either group which could be attributed to Agent Orange.

Our department of occupational medicine expanded gradually. After Randy Hall left, Maurice (Johnny) Johnston took his place as chief. Johnny bragged about our clinic to the U.S. Air Force Medical Department, and several air force medical officers applied. Frank Goss, for example, joined our clinic on Johnny's recommendation in 1971. He had a very successful practice at our Augusta clinic caring for executives and airline pilots. One of Frank's accounts, Sun Ray Oil, was proud of their offshore drilling program in the Gulf of Mexico and invited Frank, Betty Wilcox, who administered the account, and me to see the operation. We left Houston before daylight to board a helicopter at the Galveston Airport. It was a beautiful day. We flew out over the Gulf about seventy miles and landed on the deck of a giant offshore rig, placed high on stilts in a hundred feet of water. A multistory structure, the rig was as tall as any building in Houston. We watched the roughnecks drill the hole several thousand feet into the earth beneath the gulf. The drilling went on twenty-four hours a day; one crew slept while the other drilled. The crews worked on the rigs for a week at a time, before being relieved. They had phone connection with their families; most of them were from Louisiana. The rig had a recreation room, a kitchen, an operations office, and a first aid station. Large watertight life rafts hung over the sides for rapid evacuation in case of fire. Several wells could be drilled from this rig before it would be moved to another site. Crew members cast fishing lines out in the gulf when not at work.

The helicopter took us next to a large rig that served as a gathering station for a number of producing wells. The oil collected there from several wells was then piped ashore in one large underwater pipeline. This rig was permanently installed and had substantial quarters and recreational facilities. We had lunch there. Food and supplies were brought to the rigs by service boats. The crews could have whatever food they wanted, but no alcohol or smoking tobacco. We flew back in the afternoon over the rigs, scattered across the sunny gulf waters as far as the eye could see. It was a wonderful day, something few people get to enjoy.

Pennzoil has been the clinic's most important company account. As Pennzoil's medical director of the account, I helped design the space for the medical office in the Pennzoil Tower, which was being built by Pennzoil and

Zapata. The plans called for a nurse's office, an examining office for the doctor, and some quiet cubicles where ailing employees could rest. By 1970, we had also landed the El Paso Natural Gas Company account. We could not have been so successful in these company accounts without the support of the fine specialists at the clinic. We could refer patients with difficult problems to them. These accounts brought new patients to the clinic, especially the families of the employees. Many clinic physicians handled company accounts. I have only mentioned some of those in which I had a part.

The Kelsey-Seybold Clinic pioneered the extensive development of branch clinics in Texas, a hallmark of our institution, today. During the depression of the early 1980s, patient care at the branches probably saved the clinic. The collapse of the oil industry and the devaluation of the Mexican peso created a devastating drop in practice at the main clinic, while practice at the branch clinics actually increased. Branch clinics didn't come easy, however. In the 1960s very few clinics had branch offices. The only ones I knew of were in California. The Kaiser Permanente Foundation operated several clinics as a part of a prepay medical program, but this organization was different from a fee-for-service clinic. There were doubters among our partners who believed branch offices would detract from our main goal of establishing a specialty clinic in the Texas Medical Center. Others believed branch offices would provide referrals to our doctors in the medical center.

The first time the partners explored the possibility of a branch office was about 1960, at the same time that the Johnson Space Center was being developed in the Clear Lake area. Humble Oil Company, later Exxon, in partnership with the Del Webb real estate company, planned a major land development adjoining the Space Center. Val Baird, medical director at Humble Oil Company, invited me to a presentation of the plans for a new town called Clear Lake City. It would have a complete downtown shopping area, business and professional buildings, research buildings for the space program, and houses for fifty thousand people. At a later one-on-one conference meeting, we were offered space of our choice for a medical clinic in the proposed shopping area. At the time, doctors at our clinic were providing consultations at nearby Ellington Field, and I was advising an air force medical officer at Ellington Field who was assigned to the yet-to-be constructed Johnson Space Center.

I was enthused about the prospect of opening a branch clinic, although none of the partners wanted to move down to Clear Lake to operate it. Events moved slowly over many months while the Johnson Space Center was being built and people were moving into the houses and businesses all over the space center area. Meanwhile, our clinic partners were becoming more interested. Later that November, Jim McMurrey and I drove down to Clear Lake City and interviewed Jim's friend Lawerence Chapman. Dr. Chapman was in general practice and was interested in joining us in a branch clinic project. We made some sort of referral agreement with him.

By November 1964, I was in Clear Lake City working on clinic plans. By this time, we had employed Randy Hall as medical director of our NASA contracts. Randy saw the opportunity for a private practice clinic in Clear Lake City where he could practice while running our JSC operation. The partners finally agreed to a branch office in Clear Lake City in 1967, seven years after I had first become excited by Humble and Del Webb's original proposal. We opened an attractive office in Clear Lake City, with Randy Hall in charge. Stan Fischer, Ralph Eichorn, and I worked part-time there before we employed full-time physicians Lopez and Jonas. The clinic was successful, but we became embroiled in a dispute with Randy about pay distribution. Finally, we settled the disagreement in 1969 by giving him the Clear Lake Clinic. We had owned it for little more than two years, but we suffered no financial loss.

We were already promoting another branch clinic when we opened the Clear Lake City location. Another great real estate project had attracted our attention. Gerald Hines had built the Galleria, one of the nation's first enclosed shopping malls, and an elegant one at that. What a wonderful place for a branch clinic! On my birthday, October 7, 1967, I had lunch with Gerald Hines, Bob Kaim, and Mr. Wahlcott, the top management of Hines interests, to discuss opening a clinic branch in the Galleria. I had already picked the location in the Post Oak Tower, an office building in the Galleria complex. We negotiated over a period of many months. Brother John was active in developing the Post Oak Tower office. On May 5, 1970, the partners voted to open an office in the Galleria. A little less than one year later, in April 1971, we opened the office—Kelsey-Seybold Clinic, Post Oak Tower. Kay Miller was the registered nurse assigned to run the office. John Kelsey, Phil Bentliff, Jim McBee, Will Johnson, Maurice Johnston, and I were some of the doctors who rotated there. It was successful from the start, but not in the way we had expected: Galleria employees were slow to come, while people who lived in Southwest Houston flocked in to see us.

We soon were running out of space at the Post Oak Tower. On January 31, 1973, John found another location at 1900 Yorktown, a project being developed by Mark Lee. An attractive office was designed for us, and we opened in January 1974. John, Phil Bentliff, David Mouton, and I worked there. We also had a pediatrician and a gynecologist there, as well as a clinical laboratory, and X ray. Frank Stransky, a physician's assistant, worked there doing stress electrograms and screening proctoscopic examinations. Norma Alejandro was office manager.

At Post Oak Tower and 1900 Yorktown, the offices were crowded. John started looking for a new location, and in January 1976 we acquired a large tract of about three acres on Sugar Hill between Augusta and Bering Streets. I thought we should have found a more prominent location, but John proved to be right. John almost single-handedly developed this clinic. Ralph Anderson was architect; P. Gervais Bell was the contractor; and American General Insurance Company financed the building. At first, the insurance company was a little reluctant to loan money on a single-purpose building, but financed us because our reputation was so good. The Galleria and Yorktown offices were transferred to the Augusta office, which opened in 1978. An attractive building, it featured a two-level atrium and contained 11,480 square feet. Offices were convenient and provided for internal circulation of the staff. Since John was a gastroenterologist, the branch had complete X-ray facilities for gastroenterology and endoscopic rooms, as well as a fine clinical laboratory. David Mouton opened a nuclear medicine laboratory, including cardiac studies.

The pediatricians and obstetrician-gynecologists at the branch enjoyed a rapidly expanding practice. Frank Goss developed a fine practice in executive health and FAA examinations. The psychiatry, dermatology, ophthalmology, and orthopedics departments opened offices, and the chest and heart sections at the main clinic sent doctors part time. The only service it missed having was otolaryngology. All its patients clamored for an ENT man, so they would not have to fight traffic in the medical center. The branch referred all general surgery to the main clinic. By 1982, the branch had twenty-four doctors. At first I spent two days a week there, and I was at the Augusta branch full time for the last year or two of my practice. Before I retired, the building had already become overcrowded. In 1996, a much larger building replaced the first clinic. I am a patient there now, instead of a practicing physician.

The Kelsey-Seybold Clinic had been doing annual physical examinations on the executives of Texas Eastern Transmission Company and the First City National Bank. In the early 1970s, the two companies undertook a joint building program called Houston Center, which consisted of several high rise office buildings and a hotel joined together by over-the-street passages. Included were a shopping mall and a large parking garage. We were looking for a site for a downtown clinic. In those days, downtown Houston was a delight, boasting fine department stores, shops, banks, major oil company office buildings, and hotels. About 1973, Gene Burke was assigned to develop an office in the elevated passage between the bank and Texas Eastern Company. The Houston Center office opened in September 1974, with Gene Burke and Doris Evans. Nick Nauert worked there part time. Doris was a competent nurse who had been with the clinic for thirteen years. Later, Betty Wilcox ran the office.

This became another successful branch office. I practiced there one afternoon each week, just to see how things were going. I am not bragging about my medical abilities, which I had neglected by not studying and attending medical meetings while spending too much time administering and promoting. But while there, I made a quick diagnosis during a brief office visit on a patient who wasn't feeling well. The examination revealed that the patient had low grade fever. I listened to his heart, and there was an aortic systolic and diastolic murmur. I don't remember whether I found petechiae. I wrote a diagnoses of subacute bacterial endocarditis of the aortic valve on the chart and sent the patient to the hospital in the care of a cardiologist. The final diagnosis confirmed my initial impression. The patient had a positive blood culture and was treated with antibiotics. Regarding my instant diagnosis, "even a blind hog finds an acorn every now and then."

Our next attempt to open a branch clinic did not succeed. This venture began in 1976, when I gave a talk on the treatment of diabetes to the Veterans Hospital staff in Kerrville, Texas. I was invited there by Dr. Y. C. Smith, director of the V.A. Hospital and president of the Kerr County Medical Society. I had known Y. C. since we were AKK brothers in medical school. During this trip, he suggested that the Kelsey-Seybold Clinic should open a branch clinic in Kerrville. That interested me. Before leaving the Mayo Clinic I had visited Kerrville looking for a site to develop a clinic. Now Kerrville offered a chance to open a clinic, to where I and other partners could rotate and enjoy the Hill Country. Some of us might even want to retire there.

Y. C. told me the River Hills Club wanted to open a clinic for its residents and already had a building for the purpose. The River Hills Club was a large new real estate project adjoining the city of Kerrville and developed by the Hunt brothers of Dallas. The brothers were sons of H. L. Hunt, at that time, the wealthiest man in America. The Hunt brothers had purchased a thousand or so acres of land and the magnificent house built by Charles Schriener—a famous early Texas rancher. The property adjoined the city of Kerrville. The Hunts built a golf course and tennis courts on the property and sold lots on which wealthy people built luxury homes for vacation or retirement. I knew several of the people who owned houses there. They included executives of large companies with which we had contracts. The development had room for two thousand houses. A hundred were already occupied, and forty were under construction.

I made several trips to Kerrville. One was on September 30, 1977, by invitation of the club. I was taken on a dove hunt with several of the town's business leaders and a doctor, hosted by the Schriener National Bank. The club management was very persuasive. They would provide a fine building of several thousand square feet. The management promised that we could treat Kerrville residents and other patients outside the club membership. It would be necessary to have these patients to make the project economically sound. The local businesses considered the clinic as an attraction to bring people to Kerrville, which depended on tourism. They promised to send us patients. Partly persuaded by Y. C., the County Medical Society approved the clinic. A few doctors felt threatened, however, and they may have had some influence on our eventual demise.

Maurice (Johnny) Johnston from our Clinic went to Kerrville several times and decided he wanted to move to there and run the branch. He took charge of development and made a successful presentation of the plan to the partners. Several doctors in Kerrville and San Antonio were interested in joining the clinic. We accepted Lloyd W. Sheckles, Jr., an internist specializing in cardiology. He was an AKK who taught at UTMB while I was there and later moved to Kerrville. A local gynecologist and orthopedist agreed to be consultants. In May 1978, Johnny Johnston moved to Kerrville, and, on June 7, he opened our River Hills Clinic. It had all the facilities for executive examinations, including a treadmill ECG and pulmonary function tests, as well as visual and hearing tests required for FAA examinations. Out-of-town examinees were to be given lodging and temporary membership in the club, with golf and tennis privileges.

Business soon turned bad. When the Hunt brothers visited, they nixed the non-member out-of-town and Kerrville patients. Johnston was lucky to see two or three patients a day. We had to close the clinic. The Hunt brothers wanted to charge us for renovations in the building. Bill Seybold and I flew to Dallas one day and met with them. We reached a settlement, but we felt betrayed. The River Hills management had promoted the clinic, made arrangements for out-of-town guests in the club, renovated the building, and paved an entrance for outside patients. The owners then came along and wiped out the whole effort.[10]

We had more success with our next foray. Over the years our clinic had developed a significant practice performing FAA examinations for pilots. We were medical directors for Continental Airlines ever since it was TransTexas Airline. All the pilots were examined in our clinic. The Houston FAA office sent all the air controllers to us for their annual FAA examination. The Airport Authority finally built a clinic outside the passenger terminal but within the airport property. Dr. Duane Catterson, formerly medical director at the Johnson Space Center, had founded a group known as Airport Medical Associates. Their purpose was to operate the Airport Clinic, but some of the partners backed out soon after they took charge of the clinic in February 1983.

I had known Duane since he came to work for the Johnson Space Center. He called me to see if we were interested in taking over the clinic. Jim Bakken, Ron Rushing, and I went out to visit the clinic. It was located in an efficient building, and there was a built-in practice. This was also a very convenient place to examine all the Continental Airline people, the FAA controllers, and other aviation people who had to come into town. Jim and Ron were enthusiastic about it. The partners approved the project, and the Kelsey-Seybold Airport Clinic opened in April 1983. In addition to aviation medicine, the clinic was open for family practice. Drs. Catterson and Ted Trumble ran the operation until Ted's early death from cancer. For a while, I went out for a day or two a month and performed FAA examinations. Under Duane's continued supervision, the Airport Clinic has thrived.[11]

Another wonderful opportunity that proved successful came with George Mitchell's development called the Woodlands, north of Houston. In February 1979, I talked to George about establishing a branch clinic there. He was very much in favor of it. He promoted our clinic and gave us an exclusive right to open a branch in the Woodlands. We picked a location for the new facility. On August 12, 1982, Jim Bakken, Dr. Dudley Goulden, and I met with the Woodlands architects. Dudley had requested directorship of the Woodlands Clinic, and he lived there and operated the clinic for a period before moving to New England. The Woodlands Clinic opening was a fine occasion. A beautiful office had been constructed. An attractive staff welcomed us as visitors. Several doctors I know served there, including Ted Trumble. In 1995, seven doctors were listed on the staff.[12]

Despite our successes with opening branches, several years passed before most of the partners seemed to accept branch clinics as a worthwhile enterprise. Even then, many believed that branch clinics might weaken the main clinic. But we had established a precedent. A few years after Kelsey-Seybold opened its first satellite clinics, the Mayo Clinic and the Scott and White Clinic opened branch offices. My friend H. R. Butt at the Mayo Clinic told me that Mayo's branch clinics were influenced, in part, by our success. Not surprisingly, the decision to open them created controversy at the Mayo Clinic, just as it had at Kelsey-Seybold.

CHAPTER 18

So-Called Retirement, 1986 to the Present

As I look back on it, the celebration surrounding my retirement from the clinic suggested that a great burden had been removed. There was a long article in the paper about my retirement on January 17, 1986, two days after my announcement. The clinic must have hurried to get it in the paper, so I wouldn't change my mind. On February 5, the clinic employees gave me a big retirement party at the Marriott Medical Center Grand Ballroom. Several hundred people were there. The employees raised $1,000 for a Texas A&M scholarship in my honor, to be awarded in the science department to a Texas-born student. The NASA staff at Langley Field, Virginia, sent me a large shining brass crab. I hope the crab didn't have any special meaning. On April 11, the clinic doctors and spouses gave Mary and me a retirement party at the Houston Country Club. About 250 people came. Chief of Staff Jim Kemper made some remarks and presented Mary and me with a large book containing photographs and congratulatory letters from patients and doctors. Sadly, many of our friends who were there have passed away. Employees at each of the dozen branch offices sent me a card signed by the staff.[1]

By far the most important honor I received from the clinic was the establishment of the Mavis P. Kelsey Excellence Award, a cash gift of a year's tuition, to be given each year to a UTMB medical student. Dr. George T. Bryan, dean of students at UTMB, joined with Jim Kemper and me to design the award according to my wishes. I recommended that the award be given to a student without regard of financial need, color, or sex who graduated in the top 10 percent of the class. In addition to high grades, the recipient must have shown qualities of leadership, outstanding character, and ability to handle patients. I stipulated that the student must never have used drugs, since drug addiction has always been a serious problem among doctors. The winner would

Mavis and Mary at retirement, 1986

be selected by a committee of students and faculty. I have met all the recipients and have stayed in touch with several of them.

Mary and I have been invited to many of the annual staff parties. In 1995, I was honored by being made a Fellow of the Kelsey-Seybold Clinic. The citation read: "Through his foresight, courage, perseverance and unswerving commitment to quality medical care the Clinic became a nationally recognized multispecialty medical group. His fine example molded future clinic leaders, both physicians and administrators. Leadership never lessened his faithful dedication and compassion for patients. He set a standard for clinical and administrative excellence. The Clinic, its physicians and employees shall be ever indebted to Dr. Kelsey."

If Mary had been able to attend this function, she would have warned me not to let this flattery go to my head and would have reminded me that a dozen or more doctors contributed every bit as much or more than I in developing the clinic. Members of the original nucleus of doctors are fast approaching retirement. In 1995, Jackie Greer, brother John and I, along with some other long-time trustees of the Kelsey Seybold Foundation joined Tommy Anderson as lifetime members.

Attending the employees' annual parties always reinforces my belief that they are the heart and soul of the clinic. Kelsey Seybold continues to grow. In 1998 there are about thirty offices and nearly three hundred doctors. Brother John and I were invited to the groundbreaking of the Augusta Clinic in 1995. In June 1997 I helped break ground for the new clinic on Bellaire Blvd. Three hundred people attended the event. A 240,000-square-foot clinic is being constructed on a nine-acre tract. The building will be occupied in 1999 with a fifty year anniversary celebration of the Kelsey Seybold Clinic. I'm invited to be honorary chairman of the event.

Doctors at the clinic provided excellent care for Mary and me. David Mouton is our personal physician, and I believe he thinks I have tried to treat Mary and myself. John Kelsey has also been a regular patient in the clinic since his retirement. He was known to have aortic valvulitis, possibly from rheumatic fever in his youth. Since Denton Cooley replaced his aortic valve, John is his old self again.

Retirement has several meanings for me. If retirement means no longer being paid for seeing patients and no longer depending on the practice of medicine for a living, then I'm retired. If retirement means that I have quit work entirely and just goof around, then I'm not retired. There's a joke about retirement which I now hear often. Question: "What are you doing since you

Kelsey-Seybold Clinic, 1998

retired?" Answer: "Nothing, and I never get half-finished when the day is done." That's about the way I feel if I try to do nothing. Doing nothing turns me very restless, almost depressed. I had some definite plans for retirement. I was going to have a lot of free time. I would clean out the garage; fix the yard; get all my papers in order; travel all over the world; go to all the restaurants, museums, and shows; play cards; bird watch; read the daily paper; get rich in the stock market; go hunting and fishing; visit all my relatives and friends; collect more books and art; and do genealogical research. Although I haven't gotten around to playing cards or bird watching, I have occupied myself with some of the things on the list, particularly genealogy, writing, and collecting. I have even spent a little time on boards of charitable and educational institutions.

While in practice, I had neglected UTMB alumni affairs. I had never been to a reunion, but I had paid alumni dues. Nineteen eighty-six marked the fiftieth anniversary of my graduation. I called the alumni office in Galveston to say I would like to attend the class reunion and asked where it would be. As a result of this call, I was immediately appointed agent for the class of 1936 and told to get busy organizing a fiftieth reunion of our class. Of the seventy-eight graduates, forty-four were still alive and accounted for. Twenty-one attended the reunion. Sixteen of the twenty-two survivors came to the sixtieth reunion. We plan a sixty-fifth year reunion in 2001; I will be eighty-eight years old. I am looking forward to it. I probably have about a forty percent chance of still being alive then. In 1987, I received the Ashbel Smith Distinguished Alumnus Award from UTMB. That same year, I was invited to become a member of the university's development board.[2]

I also became more involved with Texas A&M, serving on the advisory committee of the Texas A&M University Press. In August 1988, I was named Houston Aggie of the year by the Houston A&M Club. The following January, I attended the ground breaking ceremony for the A&M Institute of Biological Technology (IBT) in the Texas Medical Center. In 1992, I attended my first alumni reunion at A&M—the sixtieth year since I graduated. I was surprised to see so many healthy, vigorous men who graduated more than fifty years ago. Quite a few had young wives, their second or third. At a buffet breakfast, I watched these old-timers load their plates with eggs, sausage, and biscuits swimming in butter and gravy. I sat down at a table with several of these hardy eaters and commented about how young they looked in spite of eating all that fat. One of the group replied, "Diet doesn't have anything to do with it; it's just good genes." Everyone agreed.

I have spent most of my time during the last ten years writing several books. The total time would represent several years of full-time employment. I often write for twelve hours a day, making many corrections, additions, and subtractions. I struggle away one page at a time, discarding pages of poor writing. I had saved writing chores for retirement. This included completing the genealogy of several families I had spent years researching. I had already published three books on Kelsey family history: *Benjamin Parrott c.1795–1839 and Lewis Stover, 1781–1850/60 of Overton County, Tennessee and Their Descendants* (1979); *The Family of John Massie 1743–c.1830, Revolutionary Patriot of Louisa County, Virginia* (1979); and *Samuel Kelso-Kelsey, 1720–1796, Scotch-Irish Immigrant and Revolutionary Patriot of Chester County, South Carolina* (1984).

Mary and I had accumulated extensive material on her parents' families and were at work compiling books on the Wilson and Thompson families. We completed *Robert Wilson, 1750–1826 of Blount County, Tennessee* in 1987. Mary had worked for many years on the family of her great-grandfather James G. Thompson. She went alone to Washington, D.C., on two occasions and spent a week or two in the National Archives studying the Cherokee Indians of the eighteenth and nineteenth centuries. She located much information about the Cherokee customers at Thompson's trading post on the Canadian River from 1832 to 1836. Mary worked from Thompson's original daybook, which had passed down in the family, Mary having received it from her mother. I went with Mary to state archives and county courthouses in Georgia, Alabama, Tennessee, Arkansas, Oklahoma, and Texas. Mary had several file boxes of material when we started writing. We reproduced the daybook in facsimile, with several illustrations. The book, *James George Thompson, 1802–1879, Cherokee Trader–Texian–Secessionist, His Papers and Family History*, was published in 1988 by the Sterling Evans Library at Texas A&M. It is a beautifully designed book and contains many pages of material about the Cherokees derived from original sources.

I thought we were through writing genealogy, until I received a call one night from Arnold Mitchell in Kingsland, Arkansas. He told me he had found our Kelsey book in a library and read about my great-grandmother Lucy Mitchell. Arnold Mitchell and his sister Helen Mitchell Goggans knew all about Lucy. She was their great-great-great aunt. Arnold and Helen wanted to write a book about our Mitchell family, and I agreed to join in the effort. In 1990 we published *The Mitchell Family of Tipton County, Tennessee, Their Antecedents in Colonial Southside Virginia, including Jones and Bishop and their Numerous Descendants.*

Mary and I spent the equivalent of several full-time years doing genealogy because we enjoyed it. We had a pride of family and a desire to know where we came from. Our Mormon friends and relatives imbued us with the importance of family history. Looking for hereditary disease, we studied the medical history of our ancestors when it was available. Except for finding a rare scoundrel, we came out well on this research. Genealogical research is like solving a giant jigsaw puzzle, the pieces of which are scattered over the country. Every discovery that helps solve the puzzle is a victory. Sometimes we went all over the country and completed an entire section of the puzzle as a result. Other times we came home empty handed. Sometimes a cousin looking over our shoulder put a few pieces together for us. You never finish the puzzle, so you can always go back to it and renew your search for more pieces. There are already about a hundred thousand names, or jigsaw pieces, in the six volumes of genealogy we have published.

When Mary had traveled to foreign countries, she usually wrote entertaining and informative letters home describing her experiences. The accumulated letters serve as a journal of her travels. One year, our children got two volumes of these letters together, had them bound in fine leather covers, and gave them to Mary for Christmas. After she became handicapped, she enjoyed having me read her letters to her. I scraped up every letter I could find and decided to publish them in a book. In 1990 we produced thirty copies of a beautifully illustrated book, *Travel Journals of Mary Wilson Kelsey,* for family and a few of Mary's fellow travelers. We gave two copies to the Library of Congress. We have had requests for the book from the University of Chicago and others, but have not sold any of the few copies remaining.

Perhaps the most fun I had in writing a book was in 1991. For years, Mary and I stopped to look at county courthouses as we traveled through Texas. Occasionally we photographed the outstanding courthouse buildings. After I retired, we traveled around the state more often and stopped to take photos of the courthouse of each county we passed through. We began going out of our way to shoot courthouse pictures. Soon, I had developed another obsession or compulsion, whatever you want to call it, and became determined to photograph every courthouse in Texas. We went to the Rio Grande Valley with our friend Angus Anderson by a zigzag route to photograph as many county courthouses as possible. In 1991, Angus agreed to join me on an extended tour across southwest Texas, through the Big Bend on to El Paso and back up through the High Plains of the Panhandle, to photograph courthouses. Many more trips and ten thousand miles later, we got the job done. Without an accident or a flat tire, we photographed the 254 courthouses. It was a fine experience. We loved to sightsee, and Texas has wonderfully varied scenery. Even the great plains are a breathtaking sight. We saw things we never knew existed and learned a great deal of history. I would love to do it again.

I had all the pictures. I asked Donald Dyal, director of special collections of the Sterling Evans Library at Texas A&M, if they were worth publishing in a book. He thought so, and the A&M University Press was willing to publish it. I wrote the story of my travels and some history and described the architecture of the courthouses. Donald wrote a brief story about each courthouse. I made a gift to the A&M Press, fearing they would lose money on the printing. Donald and I gave our royalties to the A&M Press. If we had known how successful the book would become, we would have kept the royalties. The book came out in 1993 as *The Courthouses of Texas: A Guide* by Mavis P. Kelsey, Sr., and Donald H. Dyal. Well-designed, the book became very popular. Our first signing was at Houston's Brazos Book Store, just before Christmas 1993. The book had received good publicity, which brought a crowd. Donald and I signed 750 books that night and the next day. We had a good crowd at a signing in College Station. The first printing of fifteen thousand was nearly sold out in 1998 and another printing was planned. It received an award for book design, an award from the American Society for Local History, and another from the San Antonio Conservation Society. A courthouse architect from Iowa came down and spent a day with me exchanging pictures and stories. I get phone calls from people who want to tell me their courthouse story.

Aside from our genealogy and book writing, Mary and I spent many years collecting books and art. This continued into my retirement years. It all began back in 1937, when Dr. and Mrs. Paul Brindley inspired me to collect Texana. Before we met, Mary had already collected a number of books, and we had a mutual interest in history. On returning to Texas in 1949 we soon renewed our acquaintance with book dealer Herbert Fletcher, and he introduced me to Palmer Bradley, another Texana collector. We bought more than books, however. We bought collections of books, including a large collection of Remington books and prints; a large collection of Thomas Bewick at a book fair in London; and forty bound folio volumes of the *Illustrated London News* in York, England, during a fifteen minute bus stop. We made three trips to Great Britain in one year to buy books and prints. Among our purchases were near complete collections of periodicals, including two sets of *Harper's Weekly* and *Harper's Monthly*, sets of *Century, Scribners, Appletons' Journal, Harper's Bazaar, Outdoors, St. Nicholas, Ballou's, Gleason's, Leslie's Illustrated News, Texas Folklore Society, American Heritage, Frontier Times*, and *Every Saturday.*

Every cranny in our house and garage storage room was stuffed with books. The servants' quarters became empty, and I covered one entire wall with shelves, which were soon filled. One wall of our study and one long hall has floor-to-ceiling book shelves. The divider between our living and dining room is a double thickness of book shelves. Two of the boys' four bedrooms were converted to book storage. The numerous closets were filled with books. We rented storage space and filled it. We must have had ten thousand volumes. For years,

I had a fair idea of the books we owned and books we wanted to buy. We received many dealers' catalogues. I would check off the books I wanted after going to bed, then order them the next day. I also bought collections at auctions. We were fortunate to buy prints at low prices, before they became valuable. This good luck was pure coincidence. We weren't buying for investment; we were buying to assemble a comprehensive collection. We have never sold a book or print.

There must be hundreds of thousands of books published about Texas and the western states. Texas books are very popular. We collected Texas county histories—a couple of hundred or so of them—especially those of East and West Texas. I was surprised to find that somewhere I had collected an early history of Fannin County valued at $1,500. I probably paid $5.00 for the book in the 1930s. I've had fun reviewing our collection of books, compiled over sixty years, and coming across a forgotten volume, now valuable. Actually, when I started collecting, rare Texas books were not very expensive. There were few books that brought more than $100. After World War II, book prices went up rapidly. About 1953, Dorman David sold to the University of Texas the first book about Texas, *The Relations of Cabeza de Vaca,* for $1,000. Today, this book must be worth $25,000.

We became interested in western travels and collected a set of Rueben Thwaite's *Early Western Travels,* and Josiah Gregg's *Commerce of the Prairies.* I bought Randolph Marcy's travels, including *The Exploration of the Red River of Louisiana,* with the maps in a separate volume, and Frederick Law Olmstead's *Travels Through Texas.* These two books each sold for $5.00. I bought additional copies to give as Christmas presents. Kendall's *Santa Fe Expedition* at $100 was never cheap. Mary bought me a copy as a birthday present. I was fond of books about Indians published by the University of Oklahoma Press. We collected everything Grant Foreman wrote. He described the Cherokee settlements where Mary's great-grandfather had a trading post in 1832. Another favorite was Wilbarger's *Indian Depredations in Texas.* We belonged to the Texas Folklore Society and collected works by Texans J. Frank Dobie, J. Evetts Haley, Walter P. Webb, Noah Smithwick, John Henry Brown, Hubert Bancroft, and Eugene Barker.

We accumulated a fair collection on the Civil War, since our ancestors were Confederate soldiers—books about the Battle of Chicamauga, for example, where Mary's grandfather Hugh Wilson fought and where my great-great uncle Robert Moore was killed. I liked items containing information about General Nathan Bedford Forrest, in whose army my great-grandfather John Kelsey fought. We still have 240 books about medicine.

Cowboys and cattle ranching have been popular subjects since American

pioneers settled the West. Novels of the cowboys were my first favorite read-
ings. Mary's great-grandfather Thompson was ranching in Texas when it was
a Republic; my great-grandfather Massie was ranching in Throckmorton
County soon after the U.S. Cavalry at Fort Griffin had removed the
Comanches and the hunters had destroyed the buffalo. Rupert Richardson
wrote authentic books about this part of Texas, which I collected. I bought
books from Jeff Dykes, who was the leading authority and book dealer on the
range lands.

I found surprisingly few books about the oil industry. For some reason, the
subject wasn't a popular collector's item at that time. One of our favorite oil
books was Boyce House's *Were You in Ranger.* Mike Halbouty and J. A. Clark
wrote the history of Spindletop. Now, there are many stories about oil booms,
both autobiographical and fictional. We were especially interested in the oil
industry, since Mary's father played such an important role in Texas oil. Hunting and nature stories were popular before the environmental movement.
People bragged about their big kills and catches. We had Dodge's *Hunting
Grounds of the Great West;* Theodore Roosevelt's *Ranch Life and the Hunting
Trail;* and Geiser's *Naturalists on the Frontier.* Our collection also included
Branch Douglas's *The Hunting of the Buffalo* and Stuart Lake's *Wyatt Earp.*[3]
Another special favorite was Ellen Schulz's *Texas Wild Flowers.*

We also collected art, particularly wood engraving prints. Mary had bought
a few lithographs and other prints before we married. We received a few prints,
paintings, and art books as wedding presents. Mary had an excellent education in art history in college and had visited many of the great art museums.
We purchased our first oil painting in 1948—a farm scene by Adolph Dehn,
artist laureate of Minnesota—while we lived in Rochester. Our book collecting, however, led us to collecting art prints. Some of our history books contained engravings of landscapes and historic sites and figures, which piqued our
interest. We were especially interested in collecting prints of early Texas scenes.[4]

In about 1968, Mary and I were in Washington, D.C., while I was on business for NASA. We stayed over the weekend to visit museums and book shops.
Our friend Frank Ashburn told us to go to Georgetown. While walking around
there we found a bookstore. We looked at a few books while a slovenly looking clerk with a full beard observed us without saying a word. We didn't buy
anything, but walked next door to a shop called The Old Print Gallery. We
went in and met Jim Blakely, the owner. I asked him who ran the book store
next door. "Don't you know? That's Larry McMurtry, the Texas writer." And
the guy with the beard? "That's Larry," he said. We asked if the Old Print
Gallery had any prints of the Old West and were shown some hand-colored
western scenes done by Frederick Remington, William Cary, and Henry Farny.

For the first time, we learned that scenes like this were wood engravings usually taken from nineteenth-century periodicals. The print dealer had searched old copies of these periodicals and found interesting pictures. He removed the pictures and had them colored by artists. The dealer put the pictures in mattes or frames and offered them for sale. Jim Blakely had hundreds of these prints arranged in bins according to subject matter.

While I was purchasing some western prints, Mary was browsing around and came upon some Winslow Homer wood engravings. We had seen Homer's paintings in museums. His paintings were far too expensive, but here were his original works in wood engravings at prices we could afford. Instead of spending $100 that morning as we had intended, we purchased about $1,500 worth of western scenes and Homer engravings.

This visit to The Old Print Gallery changed our lives forever. It was like becoming addicted to a drug, or being inoculated by a print-collecting virus. With great excitement we brought our prints home and invited our family and friends to see them. Our interest in prints influenced our book collecting. Now we only wanted illustrated books such as *Picturesque America,* Catesby's *Natural History,* Wilson's and Elliott's *Birds,* and McKinney and Hall's *Indians.* We were getting into big-time collecting and we were to meet a young man who could supply our wants, W. Graham Arader III. We frequented print galleries, put ads in art magazines, and engaged buyers. We learned the history of wood engravings, how to identify them and the artists. We looked for old volumes of illustrated nineteenth-century periodicals. Our greatest source of wood engravings was Jim Barber of Dolgeville, New York, a wheelchair-bound cripple who dealt in periodicals. He knew the important illustrators and where they were published. Jim gave us advice and located many important prints for us, particularly Winslow Homers.

Each time we heard of another artist such as A. B. Frost or Thomas Nast we started collecting his works. We collected by subjects that interested us. Winslow Homer illustrated the Civil War, so we were soon collecting other Civil War artists and war scenes. That led to collecting the Mexican War, the Spanish American War, the French Revolution, the Balkan wars, Latin American revolutions and the like. We collected thousands of prints, the entire output of the leading nineteenth-century illustrated periodicals of America, as well as many years of the *Illustrated London News.* We hired a full-time curator, Kemo Curry Franklin, who had worked at the Menil Collection. Later in 1981 we hired Kathleen Wiedower, a fine arts student. I was up past midnight night after night sorting prints by artist or subject. I am a slow reader but have a good memory for pictures. Even today I can identify thousands of prints just by looking at them.

Our collection of Winslow Homer prints, and books illustrated by him, grew rapidly. Many dealers were searching for us. We located every known periodical wood engraving by Homer but two. I am still looking for these two prints from *Leslie's Chimney Corner*. Ours was the most complete collection we knew about. We gave the collection to the Houston Museum of Fine Arts in 1975. The print collection of the museum was rather scant at that time. We also gave the museum our own catalog of the collection and a group of reference books. Katherine Howe, a wonderful curator, edited the catalogue, and the museum published it under the title *Winslow Homer Graphics, from the Mavis P. and Mary Wilson Kelsey Collection of Winslow Homer Graphics*. The collection included about 400 illustrations. In addition to the wood engravings from periodicals, there were examples of sheet music, a few lithographs and etchings, and sixty-five books illustrated by Homer. One of the books was a discovery of additional illustrations by Homer entitled *The Story of our Darling Nellie*. We also obtained the original manuscript of the little book. Two of the greatest authorities on Homer, David Tatham and Philip Beam, were invited to Houston to lecture at the opening ceremony. Mary and I were very pleased and honored. The exhibition was well done, showing the most important engravings. There was considerable publicity and I became an instant authority on Winslow Homer, an appellation I did not deserve. The exhibit was sent on a four-year nationwide tour for showings at about ten museums.[5]

We also made gifts elsewhere. About 1978, Mary and I noticed an advertisement in an art magazine from the U.S. Naval Academy seeking prints of naval and marine scenes for the Robinson Collection at the academy museum. I called the museum and learned that Mr. Robinson was a naval architect who left a fabulous collection of naval prints and a large bequest to the museum for the exclusive use of the collection. Mr. Jeffers was director, Jim Cheevers was a curator (later director) of the museum, and Alexandra Welch was curator of the Robinson Collection. Among our thousands of wood engraving prints I had already enjoyed sorting out several hundred prints of ships, yachts, and sailing vessels. The prints date from the 1830s until 1910 and illustrate the evolution of ships from sailing ships to combination sail-and-steam vessels to the modern steamship. Among the pictures were the famous ships of the Civil War including the *Alabama,* the *Monitor,* and the *Merrimac,* and the battleships of the Spanish American War drawn by famous naval artists. The museum had many colored lithographs but no wood engravings of naval vessels. We offered the prints as a gift, and they were gladly accepted as a part of the Robinson Collection. Mary and I made several trips to the Naval Academy delivering the prints. We enjoyed tours of the Naval Academy and spending time in their museum. Our prints were cared for better there than anywhere else. They were treated by the chief paper conservator of the Smithsonian Institution.[6]

We made our largest donation to the Special Collections of the Sterling Evans Library at Texas A&M. In 1979 Mary and I had several visits with Donald Dyal, who was turning the Collections into a repository for historical books, illustrated art, and books and material of special interests. We wanted to keep our collection intact, since it had taken many years and much hard work to put it together. Although a diverse collection, it had a commonality resulting from our background and interests in literature and art. The collection was too large for any of our children. Furthermore, the children wanted only a few items which appealed to them. We began thinking about a home for the collection.[7] Donald came to Houston and inspected our books. A knowledgeable and passionate bookman, he was enthused about the collection, and we made a deal on the spot. We named it the Mavis and Mary Kelsey Collection of Art and Americana. In 1993, we established a charitable lead trust to support the collection. I am still making annual gifts of books, prints, periodicals, and other art to the collection.

My writing, collecting, and traveling has left little time for outdoor pursuits, such as hunting, fishing, or, indeed, bird watching. This is difficult to excuse, since back in 1964, Mary and I had bought an eight-hundred-acre ranch for recreational purposes and for a tax shelter. Live Oaks Ranch, located on the only wooded area for miles on the Katy Prairie, did bring our family many years of pleasure, however. The Live Oaks was known by that name to travelers before Texas became a Republic. Sam Houston's army and the Texians were said to have camped there during the Runaway Scrape in 1836, when they were fleeing Santa Anna's army. Santa Anna followed them and is said to have camped there on his way to San Jacinto, where he and his army were defeated by the Texians on April 21, 1836. For more than a century, the surrounding land was open range for cattle ranchers. There was an old dipping vat, cattle pens, a bunkhouse, and kitchen on the property. One of the senior members of the Buller family (the former owners) told us that cattle were rounded up there to be branded and dipped in the vat. When cattle were ready for market the cowboys collected and herded them across the open prairie to a stockyard and livery stable in Houston Heights. In 1900, there was no fence between the Live Oaks and the Heights.

The Live Oaks was a wild and beautiful place. John James Audubon came to this area of Texas in the 1840s to collect animals for his *Quadrupeds of North America*. He may have visited the Live Oaks. The setting for his picture of the Texas red wolf is said to be the banks of the Brazos River only a few miles from the Live Oaks. Other animals of the area illustrated by Audubon are the jack rabbit, the weasel (mink), the bobcat, and the prairie chicken. We decorated the walls of the ranch house with Audubon's large folio prints of these animals. When we had overnight guests from the city, I'd stand on the porch and call up a wolf pack by making wailing wolf calls. Soon the wolves would congregate in a pack and respond with weird howlings, as they ran back and forth in the woods around the house. At night we heard big bullfrogs and lots of tree frogs. No one got bitten by the numerous cottonmouth moccasins, but I almost stepped on a large one. There were water snakes. Big chicken snakes got in the henhouse and swallowed eggs, and a seven-foot black snake took residence under our house and kept us free of rats. The most exciting reptile on the place was an eight-foot alligator that lived in the pond, where he subsisted on ducks, fish, and turtles.

The Live Oaks was heaven for bird watchers. Several friends came from Beaumont for a weekend and counted over seventy species of birds, including many migrants. The majority of the birds they identified were those that spent the winter on the Katy Prairie and in our woods. The ducks and geese were the most noticeable. A major flyway from the far north terminates on the Texas coastal region. Thousands of acres of rice fields, pastures, and wetlands on the Katy Prairie provide food and rest for millions of ducks and geese. One of the thrills at Live Oaks was to hear the huge flocks of quacking geese flying over during the night. Such a flock could do a lot of damage, however. We planted oats for winter grazing, and more than once huge flocks of geese, numbering several thousand, made a mud puddle out of our hundred acre oat patch. The vast majority were snow and blue geese. We often saw a few hundred Canadian geese and speckle bellies mixed in with the snow geese.

Other migratory birds were sandhill cranes, curlews, ibises, and egrets. The cattle egret perches on the back of a cow and jumps down to catch insects the cow stirs up. The great blue heron was a permanent resident, always a pleasure to see. Once, I was surprised to see a flight of roseate spoonbills checking out the place. They must have flown over from Trinity Bay to spend the day. Another great bird experience was watching the bald eagles that came down from East Texas and other places to winter in the woods of Live Oaks. We soon learned that the eagles were eating wounded ducks and geese left on the prairie by hunters. At one time I counted twenty-one bald eagles. I once saw a golden eagle sitting on a fence post. It was fun to hide under a tree and watch the eagles exercise by soaring and diving overhead.[8]

After buying Live Oaks, we immediately began spending time there, rambling through the woods, never getting enough of identifying flora and fauna. We found magnificent groves of live oaks, beautiful little dales and coves, hidden ponds, and water holes in the creek. Wildlife was all around. We looked for sites to build a house for ourselves and one for a ranch manager. One day, Mary saw an ad in the paper to sell and move a seventy-five year-old farmhouse. I was at a medical meeting in Rochester, when she came up and surprised me by saying she had bought a house for the ranch. We still have the receipt "For the old Kuehnle house. To be moved within 30 days," dated September 28, 1964, for $250. Mary was bubbling over with enthusiasm. We went antique shopping in Rochester and bought $1500 worth of fine country antiques, some of which was furniture owned by the Mayos when they were pioneer settlers in Minnesota. The house was a one-story nineteenth-century Texas cottage. The exterior was of cypress siding, and the interior walls were of heart pine and had never been papered. The front porch was still intact, with the original chamfered columns. The pine floors were badly worn from many years of traffic, and a back porch had been removed, but we could tell where it had been attached. There were six rooms and an enclosed dog run, but no closets and no bathrooms. It had two front entrances.

We went to work immediately moving the house about forty miles to the ranch. The movers had to remove temporarily the front porch and the roof to move the building—which was about thirty-five feet wide—in the middle of the night along country roads, raising power lines and phone lines as they went. We had raised the ground level of the site about three feet to prevent flooding. The porch and roof were restored exactly as found, and we restored the original yellow color and blue trim. A full-length back porch replaced the original. We screened it in and hung two swinging double beds on the north end and built a large dining table for the south end, leaving room for a folding bed-lounge, chairs, and table in the center of the porch. We built two bathrooms, installed central heat and air conditioning, a modern kitchen, and a Franklin stove in the living-dining room. A large living room was created by removing a partition.

The work cost $35,000 in 1964. Overall there was about 3,000 square feet under roof. The house was furnished with appropriate country antique furniture. A pump organ and a Victrola phonograph in a cabinet supplemented the television and radio for musical entertainment. Mary moved some of her great-grandfather's furniture there. This furniture had been shipped up the Red River from New Orleans to Sherman, Texas, before the Civil War. We had three bedrooms and beds for eleven people, as well as couches and plenty of room on the floor and porch for bed rolls. I've seen times when every square foot of the place was covered with bodies. Large antique armoires were placed in the bedrooms and halls for clothes and linen closets. The family inaugurated the house by spending New Year's night there on December 31, 1964.

We toasted with champagne and inscribed the event on the label of the bottle. We saved and labeled the wine bottles from subsequent major events and New Years parties. Over the years a long row of celebratory bottles accumulated.

Our goal was to produce a herd of registered cattle and sell the offspring for breeding purposes. The woods and ponds were preserved for recreation as well as for protection of the cattle during cold weather. We employed Jim Buller as a part-time manager in July 1964, and then Carl Paben for a couple of years. Ross Wollgast came as ranch manager in 1965 and stayed with us until July 1983. Ross commuted to the ranch for a year while we built a house for him and his family. We were soon spending many thousands of dollars on the hundreds of items, large and small, required to operate a farm and ranch.

I would have done better to be in the stocker business, but I wanted to become a breeder of registered cattle and become successful like Uncle Tom Parrott did years before. In 1964 Charolais cattle were enjoying a great boom. It all started with the publicity about fat in diets causing high cholesterol and heart attacks. Before this, Hereford and Angus cattle had been bred to produce prime steaks, the red meat being marbled with fat. Restaurants served steaks with an inch of sizzling fat on all sides, and the customer ate fat and all. When people were told the fat caused arteriosclerosis, they demanded lean meat. The French Charolais cattle were noted for their lean meat and limited fat. There was a rush to import Charolais breeding cattle to America. By the time I entered the cattle business, the American Charolais Association had been organized, and Charolais breeders had done an outstanding job in promoting their cattle. Charolais were bringing premium prices. One year, Mary surprised me with a fabulous present. It was a young Charolais bull named Sam's Success, a son of the famous Sam 951. We went out to the ranch on Christmas day to see Sam's Success. Neighboring ranchers came over to see Sam's Success and complimented us.[9]

Charolais breeding was popular all over the country for a few years. We sold through ads in the *Texas Cattleman* and the Houston papers. Many ranchers bought our bulls. My cousin Martha Glover bought two. She petted and pampered them. One bull grew to weigh 3,000 pounds and was gentle as a lamb. We named our calves when they were registered. Our white Charolais cows were so lovely, we named many of them after Greek goddesses. We had 377 registered Charolais cattle in January 1976. The situation looked bright, until the worst hazard of ranching descended on us. We were quarantined for brucellosis, which causes abortion in cattle and undulant fever in humans who contract the disease by drinking milk from infected cows. We had been vaccinating for brucella from the beginning. The officials said the vaccine must have been bad. Brucellosis put us out of the cattle business.

We also farmed at Live Oaks: cutting and bailing hay; planting and harvesting corn, maize, sudex (a sort of maize hybrid), soy beans, and peanuts. The Wollgasts were great with animals. They were gentle with the cattle, nursing orphan calves and even taking them in their house. They raised chickens, guineas, ducks, geese, turkeys, and peafowl. We ate guinea eggs (very hard shells but tasted great), duck eggs, even a goose egg or two. When roosters lost their virility, the Wollgasts gave them to us for making Coq au Vin according to the original recipe, which calls for old cocks or roosters. We had roast turkey and roast guinea under glass several times. Once we roasted a peacock—holiday fare for aristocrats and gourmets before the twentieth century. It tasted great. The Wollgasts kept two or three Jersey cows to provide rich milk and butter for the family and often for us, as well as for orphan calves. Jersey cows are the most efficient domestic animals I ever saw. I had forgotten about milking our family cows when I was a boy. The Wollgasts also kept sheep and goats, as well as horses and donkeys, a pet deer, and trained border collies.

We entertained many friends at Live Oaks. We served spring salad and watermelons from the ranch. Several special events were held for school groups. In 1980, Mary invited a group of Bhutanese dancers who were brought to Houston by the Asia Society. We welcomed neighboring farmers and ranchers to the Live Oaks for picnics. Our sons had numerous parties, especially during the hunting season. We eventually gave the ranch to our children and grandchildren. They leased part of it to a sporting club, which subsequently bought much of the land. Our family still owns some 650 acres of it, which is leased to a cattle rancher. Since I've retired our grandchildren have been inviting guests to the ranch.[10]

Mary and I have enjoyed many trips together with our friends during my retirement years. We went to Europe several times and took driving tours in New England, Canada, and the western states. We even went to the Galapagos Islands in 1988. I would have continued traveling if Mary had remained well. In 1996, she was more stabilized and I was able to attend a print society meeting in Fort Worth in May and visit New York in July to see my granddaughter Winifred. Winifred and I spent hours in the Metropolitan Museum looking at the exhibits, including the great Winslow Homer exhibition. The next day I visited old Bellevue Hospital and saw remnants of the buildings that were standing when I interned there in 1936.

After I retired, we made a few new friends but continued to see our longtime staunch friends. Many have passed on. Losing friends is another handicap of old age. Among the people I lost in the medical world since I retired are long-time partner Charlie Dickson, as well as Albert Owers, Bill Leary,

Melville Cody, and Ted Trumble. Sam Haines was one of my best friends and my mentor in Rochester. He lived more than a hundred years. Mary Butt died a few years ago. Ed Rynearson, Mark Coventry, Ray and Priscilla Keating, and George Hallenbeck and his wife, Marion, are other Rochester friends we have lost. M. D. Anderson friends who are gone include Fred Elliott, Cliff Howe, Bob Moreton, Ed White, Gilbert Fletcher, George Ehni, Grant Taylor, and Lee Clark. My wartime friend Pharo Gagge died in 1993. My medical school friends who have died include my fraternity roommate of three years and best friend Ralph Letteer. Another roommate who died is Jim Little. Other AKK brothers who have passed include Carl Goeth, Cooper Conner, Raleigh Ross, Sam Barnes, and George Woodfin.[11]

Many family events have occurred. We have had numerous marriages, christenings, and a few deaths. Mary's sister Fay died on March 3, 1995, after a long illness of pulmonary failure, blindness, and deafness. Her husband, Jamie Griffith, Sr., was failing after her death. He died on July 26, 1996. Long before 1986, our sons had married, had their children, and settled permanently in our neighborhood. We see them frequently, especially during vacations and at holiday dinner parties. The grandchildren have been growing into adulthood and attending college. We can thank God for a happy close-knit family life, which has been free of tragedy during my retirement years.

Mary had health problems as early as 1964. Before I retired in 1986, she began having memory loss. She was very defensive about her symptoms but admitted difficulty in finding her way home in the car. We went to London to buy rare books in 1984. Mary got lost in our hotel, and couldn't find our room. She went out shopping by herself. When she caught a cab to go to the hotel, she couldn't remember its name. The driver wandered around a couple of hours before she was able to identify it. I had become alarmed.

After this Mary declined gradually. She developed severe Parkinsonism and became totally disabled. She could talk very little, but remained cheerful and knew what was going on. She loved to have visits by her children and grandchildren. Her facial expressions told us whether she approved or disapproved what we said. She laughed when someone made a funny remark. She never complained and was cheerful practically all the time. When visitors came she tried her best to project a warm welcome. As long as she was happy I wanted her to stay. I remained ready for whatever God decided to do with her or me. She was a wonderful wife. I was very saddened that she was incapacitated for several years, but became reconciled to our fate and stayed in good spirits writing, working with our books and prints, and watching our grandchildren become adults and face life's challenges.

From the beginning, Mary fought valiantly to overcome her illness. To the very end, and in spite of her disabilities, she wanted to stay alive. Finally, on December 4, 1997, she gave up the battle and passed into the hands of our Lord. All her family was at her bedside, and she was conscious. Reverends Larry Gipson and Peter Thomas came several times to pray for her and our family. Charles Wyatt Brown, our longtime friend and retired Episcopal rector, came from South Carolina to be with Mary for two days. A memorial service was held at St. Martin's Church on December 8. Our granddaughter Kelly sang a strikingly beautiful solo, one of Mary's favorite songs, *Amazing Grace.* The church was filled to overflowing. That afternoon our family attended a service at the Glenwood Cemetery, where Mary's remains were buried next to our son Cooke. Our sons and their wives, although saddened by Mary's death, have helped to bear my deep sadness. Mary and I had been married fifty-eight years. Mary was the greatest inspiration of my life.

I seem to be healthy and look forward to the year 2000 and a new millennium. One July 4, 1998, while editing the final copy of this autobiography, I was hospitalized at St. Luke's Hospital for mild heart failure, apparently caused by hypertension. I developed chest pain in the hospital which prompted my cardiologist, Dr. Sayid Fighali, to arrange for a heart surgeon to stand by while he performed a catheterization of my coronary arteries. Fortunately my arteries were normal. While still in the catheter room I told Dr. Fighali I still had chest pain. "Give him a dose of Mylanta," Dr. Fighali said with a tinge of disgust as he left the room to dismiss the surgeon. I had gone into the room fearing open-heart surgery and came out with a dose of Mylanta.

Our children and grandchildren are healthy and enjoying life. The Kelsey-Seybold Clinic is thriving. At eighty-six years of age I have much to be thankful for. I am pleased to have finished this autobiography. Recently, I read an article by a famous book reviewer in *Pharos,* the magazine of the Alpha Omega Alpha honor medical fraternity. She said there was nothing more boring than reading an old man's memoirs. I should have warned the reader at the beginning, not the end of this book.

Chapter 1. Beginnings: My Family Ancestry

1. My interest in the genealogy of the Kelsey family began when I was quite small, sparked by the memories of my grandfather Joseph Benson Kelsey and the genealogical work of Miss Pearl Kelsey, a relative from Red Banks, Mississippi. In later years, Cousin Pearl gave me a five-cent school notebook full of the genealogy of the Kelseys and related families. A fuller account of my ancestry can be found in chapter one of my *The Making of a Doctor: Early Memoirs from 1912 to 1949* (Houston: privately printed, 1995).

2. Deport's first settlers, around 1874, were John L. and his son Dee Thompson, who installed the first post office and store on the banks of Mustang Creek. The settlers soon learned that the creek was subject to overflow with flooding of all the surrounding area, including Dee Thompson's store. In jest his store was called Dee's Port, and the Post Office Department settled for the official name of Deport. Surprisingly, merchants still built on the banks of the Mustang. Although the main street and the stores of Deport continued to flood, the settlement grew to a town of nearly one thousand and became a trade center for cotton farmers. The trade region had a population of ten thousand.

3. My grandfather's obituary in the *Deport Times*, April 12, 1923, recognized the important role he had played in Deport's growth, as well as his dedication to the practice of medicine, noting the physical toll that the profession took, especially on rural doctors of that era: "Irregular hours and exposure in the practice of his profession put furrows in his face and changed the color of his hair to silver, but he did not allow his mind to become old. He was a great reader and took two post graduate courses later in life to inform himself upon the most modern methods of the treatment of disease."

J. B.'s wife, Jessie, died August 7, 1935, fourteen months after a stroke that had left her aphasic with right hemiplegia. I had finished my third year of medical school after her stroke, and she was always anxious to hear about my training. She smiled and tried to talk, but to no avail.

4. E. T. Parrott was born in Nashville, Tennessee, in 1853, the son of William Giles Parrott and Mary Stover Parrott. The family moved to Eliasville, Young County, Texas, and E. T. grew up as a cowboy and a trader. Virginia Ann Massie's family came to Texas from Virginia via Kentucky in 1872, when she was ten years old.

5. Mary Virginia Kelsey graduated from College of Industrial Arts (CIA), now known as Texas Women's University (TWU), in Denton, Texas, in 1935 with both a bachelor's and master's degree in library science. She and her husband, Marvin Gibbs, a funeral director, rancher, and investor, live in Paris, Texas. They have one son, Marvin Kelsey Gibbs, born January 2, 1945. John Roger Kelsey, Jr., attended the University of Texas at Austin and graduated from Baylor University College of Medicine in Houston in 1945. He trained at Baltimore City Hospital and the U.S. Public Health Hospital in Saint Louis, and from 1948 to 1951 he served a fellowship at

the Mayo Clinic. He and his wife, Margaret (Mickey) Wier Kelsey, had four children: John Roger III (October 8, 1947); Margaret Ann (March 18, 1949); Robert Wier (November 28, 1952); and Virginia Wier (August 30, 1960).

Chapter 2. Texas Country Boy

1. The Choctaw Indian Trail became an important wagon freight road from the Red River steamboat port at Jefferson, Texas, to the Choctaw Nation in southeastern Oklahoma. The Paris and Mount Pleasant Railroad also passed through Deport, until it was discontinued about 1940.

2. At the north end of Main was the American Legion Hall. The front lawn had a croquet court and, later, a miniature golf course. Just north of the hall was the Volunteer Fire Station, and north of it was Central, the telephone exchange run by a lady out of her residence. We rang Central to ask her to connect us with the person we were calling. Central might tell you they weren't at home but were over at another person's house and, "Do you want me to call them there?" The Kelsey families were on a party line. We answered to two rings, my grandfather J. B. answered to one ring, and my uncle Russell answered to three rings.

3. Aside from Aunt Prudence, I had some other wonderful teachers, the most memorable being Miss Dorcas Cameron in the seventh grade. She didn't tolerate foolishness. I mean no foolishness! When sent to the blackboard in her class, one had better perform or risk humiliation. She made a student out of me and gained my deepest respect. I even became the class valedictorian. Aunt Prudence and Miss Dorcas had a profound influence on my entire education.

4. I was also in a Boy Scout troop in Deport, lead by Joe Barham. Our group of boys were wild, raunchy, and uncontrollable. I learned to shoot dice in scout camp. We shot off guns and rambled in the woods. We found the regional scout camp in Paris to be pretty sissy and didn't go back. Uncle Joe Kelsey was thirteen years older than I, however, and his crowd was a lot wilder than ours. There was no limit to their well-organized Halloween pranks, such as leading a horse into the superintendent's office on the second floor of the Deport School. Somehow they got buggies and Model Ts on top of Deport buildings. Everyone waited to see what outrageous pranks would need cleaning up the day after Halloween. There was no trick or treat. It was all tricks.

5. Before repeal of the Volstead Act, people made home brew and no one interfered unless it became a commercial business. Then the police had to be paid off. "Three point two" beer became legal except where local option prohibited it. It was prohibited in Lamar County. I was joined by a group of boys and girls to drive thirty-five miles to Arthur City, Oklahoma, one Sunday afternoon to have my first taste of legal beer, containing 3.2 percent alcohol. We thought it was great. People continued to make strong home brew and buy bootleg whiskey from southeastern Oklahoma, the same area where we often went fishing. Every town had its local bootlegger who could deliver a pint at some rendezvous. Troy Grant was the Deport constable, and if he caught you drunk on Main Street and causing a disturbance he would put you in the calaboose. The calaboose was a one-room building with bars on the two windows and door.

Chapter 3. Texas Agricultural and Mechanical College, 1929–32

1. My wife's family also benefited from the oil industry. Her father, James Cooke Wilson, Sr., came to Beaumont in 1902 and entered the oil business at Spindletop. His first oil well was

a gusher. He spent a highly successful career in oil production and left an estate that has supported and educated three generations of descendants. In 1941, under Cooke's direction, a monument was erected on the site of the Spindletop gusher to commemorate the fortieth anniversary of its discovery.

2. Several buildings added to the campus in the next twenty years were still in use when I was a student at A&M. The original Main Building burned in 1912 but Gathright Hall was not raised until 1933, after I had graduated. Among the nineteenth-century buildings still standing while I was there were Pfeuffer Hall (1887), Austin Hall (1888), Ross Hall (1892), and Foster Hall (1899). The Science Building where I studied was built in 1900. All of these structures were in the stately style of the French Second Empire. The Main or Academic Building was rebuilt in 1913–14; a fine example of beaux arts architecture, it is still the centerpiece of the campus.

3. All kinds of arguments were made to justify hazing, most notably that it led to strength of character and forged teamwork. Proponents cited many examples from history to prove the value of hazing. After all, Wellington used hazing to train his men and saved England at the Battle of Trafalgar. Other examples of history might cut in the other direction, however. General Earl Rudder, A&M class of '32, who in World War II led the assault on Omaha Beach, was opposed to hazing. I doubt he credited his courage to being hazed at A&M.

4. By 1932, student enrollment had dropped to 2,500, even though the state population was growing rapidly. The administration at A&M attributed the decline in enrollment to hazing. Earlier, a Texas senate hearing in 1921 had ordered the college to enforce a strict law against the practice. Every student upon reentering college after his first year was required to sign a pledge that he would not engage in hazing. The commandant suggested segregating the entire freshman class in their own dormitories. The physical education instructors were ordered to report every student with a bruised buttock. These measures had little effect, however. Beginning in the 1960s, only the fear of lawsuits reduced the number of hazing incidents at A&M.

5. My brother-in-law Lt. James Cooke Wilson, Jr., entered A&M after World War II. He had a couple of years of college behind him, and had been a pilot in the U.S. Air Force. A young sophomore came into Cooke's room and announced that Cooke was to be his fish and ordered him to clean the sophomore's room and run some errands. Cooke told him he had already been through hazing and was not about to comply. The sophomore told Cooke that was not the way things were done at A&M, that Cooke would be treated like any other fish. Cooke got mad and told the sophomore: "You little squirt, get out of here or I will beat your ass off." No one attempted to haze Cooke in any way after that.

6. A&M students were called Farmers when I registered in 1929, but rapidly became known as Aggies. There is a camaraderie among Aggies, greater than among any other alumni from any other college I know. While at A&M, students learn to help each other in class work or when in trouble. They learn to defend each other. Aggie jokes only make Aggies more cohesive. They give jobs to fellow Aggies: they vote for Aggies; they buy from Aggies; they send their families to Aggie doctors. They learned the honor code at A&M, and they can depend on the word of a fellow Aggie.

7. After graduation from A&M, I lost contact with many friends, as I became deeply involved in medicine and lived out of state for years. I saw very few Aggies until 1949, many years later, when I moved to Houston to practice medicine. While writing this autobiography, I called Jim Little in Wharton, Texas, where he was retired from practice and we had a laugh over happy memories. Sadly, he died on June 6, 1995, leaving his wife Aletha and two daughters. I attended the funeral. He was buried in the College Station City Cemetery.

Chapter 4. University of Texas Medical Branch, Galveston, 1932–36

1. I was also influenced to some extent by Dr. L. P. McCuiston of Paris, Texas. My grandfather took me to see him when I was a boy. He developed a large practice in Paris and built the Paris Sanitarium. His practice eventually evolved into the McCuiston Regional Hospital, where my nephew Kelsey Gibbs now practices with others in a loosely knit clinic practice.

2. The first medical school in Texas was conceived in Chappell Hill in 1855 as Soule Medical School. It opened its doors as the Galveston Medical College in 1865 but had failed by 1873. Subsequently, the Texas Medical College and Hospital was organized and accepted students from Galveston Medical College. With the strong support of Ashbel Smith and, later, George Sealy, this school managed to have a sporadic existence until 1891, when Texans finally decided to fund a University of Texas medical department in Galveston. The Texas Medical College then went out of existence, and some of its students and faculty and the John Sealy Hospital became a part of the new University of Texas Medical Branch (UTMB). When I entered UTMB in 1932, two of the original faculty members were still alive: Dr. Seth Morris was still teaching ophthalmology and Dr. Edward Randall, Sr., was on the emeritus faculty.

3. Dr. Knight had been on the faculty since 1909. He devoted himself to building the famous anatomy museum, which contained wet and dry specimens, wax models, and row on row of mounted pieces of humans, all minutely dissected and labeled, in formalin filled glass jars. Dr. Duncan began his illustrious career at Galveston in 1932. He developed the section of neuroanatomy and replaced Dr. Knight as professor of anatomy in 1939. Dr. Bute, a neat smallish perfectionist, was a fellow AKK who later moved to Dallas to practice medicine. "Bing" Blassingame was on the anatomy faculty from 1932–36 and later organized an outstanding clinic in Wharton, Texas. He became a lifetime friend of mine.

4. George Herrmann came to Galveston in 1930 as clinical professor of medicine. With an M.S., M.D., and Ph.D. from Michigan, he was the most educated member of the faculty. He was nationally famous for his research on arteriosclerosis and can be credited for proving the role of cholesterol as the cause of atherosclerosis. He was the first subspecialist in medicine at the Medical Branch.

5. The present trend in so-called medical care delivery forces doctors to do brief inadequate examinations on all patients, regardless of how complicated their problems may be. Many patients are now suffering from inadequate examinations, the result of programs operated ostensibly to save medical costs but actually to make profits for entrepreneurs. Billions of dollars are being drained away from patient care. For instance, a March 27, 1995, article in the *Wall Street Journal* announced, "Blue Shield of California has made a $45-a-share, $4.5 billion cash-and-stock bid for WellPoint Health Networks. WellPoint, meanwhile is weighing a purchase of another HMO, Health Systems International." The next day the *Wall Street Journal* reported that WellPoint was about to acquire rival Health Systems for $1.78 billion in stock. These articles make no mention of how doctors and their patients will fare.

6. I also took classes in neurology and psychiatry, under Professor Titus Harris and Adjunct Professor Abe Harris; ophthalmology, under Professor Seth Morris and Instructor C. S. Sykes; otology and laryngology, under Dr. Dick Wall, a 1913 Medical Branch graduate; and pediatrics, under Dr. William Boyd Reading.

7. Dr. Singleton had two sons who became doctors and became my very good friends: Albert O. Singleton, Jr., joined the faculty in surgery and Edward B. Singleton became chief of radiology at St. Luke's Hospital in Houston.

8. The first medical fraternity in Galveston was Alpha Mu Pi Omega, called AMPO. The Phi Alpha Sigma fraternity was well regarded and counted among its alumni several prominent faculty members. My future partner Bill Seybold was a member. Other fraternities were Phi Chi, Phi Beta Pi, Theta Kappa Psi, Nu Sigma Nu, and Phi Delta Epsilon. The women lived in University Hall and belonged to a sorority, Alpha Epsilon Iota.

9. Of my closest friends from medical school, Sam Barnes was the last to die on July 8, 1997. He had returned to his hometown of Trinity, Texas, to become the most competent general practitioner I ever knew, with the possible exception of Dr. Steve Grant in Deport. There are many prominent physicians in the Barnes family. Sam was a leading citizen of Trinity, serving as mayor for many years. Ralph Letteer and his wife, Margaret, had three children and made me the godfather of their daughter Susan. Ralph became a successful internist in San Antonio. He died of coronary disease a few years ago. His widow, Margaret, died in May 1998. Jim Little and I were friends from the time we met at A&M in 1930. Jim married Aletha and joined the Rugeley Blassingame Clinic in Wharton as an internist. He died in Wharton in June 1995. Ross Margraves became a urologist in Houston, but died at a relatively early age from a ruptured aorta. Tom Guthrie, also a Houston urologist, died in 1997. He was a cousin of brother John Kelsey's wife, Mickey. Cooper Conner was a general practitioner in Fort Worth. He died about 1993. Howard Eberle, who died rather young, joined our classmate Steve Williams in the practice of orthopedics in Corpus Christi.

Woody Palmer, Edgar Jones, and Ralph Hamme are retired general practitioners. Carl Goeth did general practice and surgery in San Antonio. He was the son of R. A. Goeth, a member of the first freshman class who registered for the full three-year course and graduated in 1893. Carl died about 1994. Myles Moursund became a dermatologist in Houston and is deceased. Al Hartman, one of my close friends, was an AKK upperclassman. He became a leading surgeon in San Antonio, a brilliant man who died of Alzheimer's disease many years ago. Malcolm Johnson practiced in his hometown of Paris and died years ago. Bob Blount, my commanding officer at Portland Air Base, is described in chapter 9. Frank Ashburn, two years behind me, became one of my best friends; we were also together at the Mayo Clinic. Isaac Lycurgis Van Zandt III was a year behind me. We teased him about his name. He enjoyed a successful career as an orthopedist in Fort Worth. After his first wife died he married the sister of my brother-in-law Marvin Gibbs. He is still around as a good friend.

Chapter 5. Bellevue Hospital, 1936–37

1. Columbia University ran the first division of Bellevue, and Cornell University ran the second division. The fourth division was not affiliated with a medical school. Each division acted virtually as a separate hospital. For many years Bellevue had its own medical school that graduated many of the great physicians of the nineteenth century. Bellevue Medical College was eventually taken over by New York University.

2. Dean Wykoff was a nationally known cardiologist. He edited a useful book on the classification of heart disease. The book was a result of work done in the cardiac clinic at Bellevue. His method of classification is still widely used. While I was at Bellevue, Dr. Wykoff met a tragic end. A fraud was perpetrated on an insurance company when some doctors submitted fake electrocardiograms, allowing healthy people to draw disability benefits. Dr. Wykoff was a consultant for the insurance company and had passed on the electrocardiograms, missing the fraud. Apparently humiliated or depressed by the incident, he committed suicide by giving

himself a fatal injection of morphine in one of the medical school laboratories. He was found dead the next morning.

3. Walker Gill Wylie, another descendent of our emigrant ancestors Samuel Kelsey and Robert Gill, was born in Chester, South Carolina, in 1848. While in his teens he became a captain in the Confederate army. After the Civil War he attended Bellevue Medical College, later to become chief of surgery at Bellevue and a leading surgeon in New York City. Interested in nursing, Dr. Gill went to England to study the Nightingale system and brought it back to Bellevue. He is a member of the South Carolina Hall of Fame.

4. At Columbia, Maurice Moore met his wife, Elizabeth, who was the sister of Henry Luce, founder of Time Incorporated. Maurice became a prominent lawyer in New York with the firm of Swain, De Gersdorf and Moore and lived in a grand apartment at 1000 Park Avenue. I was also invited when Maurice's mother came up from Deport to visit. Maurice wrote recommendations for me on several occasions. Maurice's brother-in-law, Sheldon Luce, became my friend. I attended an all-night party at Sheldon's apartment when the first issue of *Life* was published. During World War II Sheldon and I served together in Alaska and also at Wright Field, Dayton, Ohio, where our wives became friends.

5. In terms of training at Bellevue, those appointed for a second year of internship were assigned to one of the numerous specialties working toward specialty training. A few were selected for a three-year program, the third year to be spent as a resident. From this resident group a few went on to be house staff with faculty appointments.

6. Dr. Ralli had a house on the beach at Stamford, Connecticut. She invited other interns and me out to Stamford and to her apartment in New York City. Once she invited me to visit when the editor, maybe the owner, of the *New York Times,* Mr. Ochs, was there. He and Dr. Ralli enjoyed my Texas accent. Mr. Ochs said I would be great on the radio. He arranged for a man to test me for radio, but the man turned me down. He said I was too uptight and couldn't relax!

7. I lost touch with most of my friends at Bellevue after I left New York. Jerry Flaum was the senior resident in medicine. Harry Fein, a New York University graduate, was my roommate for a while, and we became close friends. He helped me learn my way around New York and Bellevue. Bernie Davison was another close friend. Having never left New York City, Bernie gladly accepted my invitation to spend our vacation together on a bus trip to Texas. Another friend was Dick Jensen of Neenah, Wisconsin, and another from Saint Louis. Ted Bayles, a Harvard graduate, turned up in Alaska with me during the war. Larry Bezier was a fellow intern from Philadelphia. He came to the Mayo Clinic as a fellow in medicine after World War II, then practiced hematology in Philadelphia. My friend Fred Hammond graduated from Galveston in 1937 and followed me to Bellevue the next year for an internship. We spent much time together before I left Bellevue. We met again at Scott and White Clinic two years later.

Chapter 6. Instructor in Pathology, University of Texas Medical Branch, 1937–38

1. Curtis Burge, Jim Cain, and Jimmy Chambers were in anatomy; John Wall and Frank Connally were in gynecology; Charlie Hooks was in urology; Hamilton Ford was in psychiatry and had married my classmate Evangeline Dean; Red Towler was an assistant in psychiatry; Dolph Curb was an instructor in medicine; and Bob Edwards was a graduate assistant in medicine.

2. Dr. Singleton died of a coronary occlusion, as did his son Albert, Jr. Edward retired as chief of radiology at St. Luke's Hospital in Houston in November 1997.

3. Truman was also president at the University of Texas medical schools in Houston and in San Antonio, distinguishing him as having served as president of three of the four medical schools of the University of Texas. Truman's most visible contribution to the University of Texas is the Truman Blocker Collection of rare medical books in the Moody Library of the Medical Branch. He died May 24, 1984. His widow Virginia and I stay in touch several times a year.

4. I patronized Herbert Fletcher for years. He was still in Houston when I came to practice in 1949. He later moved to Salado, Texas, where I still managed to visit his store and buy a few books. Ann Brindley also acquainted me with the Texas Folklore Society. I purchased several of their books by J. Frank Dobie. I subscribed to J. Marvin Hunter's *Frontier Times* and joined the Texas State Historical Society to receive the *Southwestern Historical Quarterly*. I collected several reprints from the Steck Publishing Company in Austin.

Chapter 7. Scott and White Clinic and Marriage, 1938–39

1. The remarks of H. L. Hilgartner at the annual Texas State Medical Association meeting of 1922 were indicative of the profession's attitude toward the formation of clinics. He declared that "the worst fate that could befall our profession would be its evolution into narrow specialists . . . specialization in the practice of medicine is necessary, but it must be guarded against its two besetting dangers—excessive narrowness and the tendency to fall away from the foundations upon which it should ever stand in structural unity."

2. Dr. White died quite young in 1917, and Dr. Scott died October 27, 1940. Dr. Brindley had graduated from the Medical Branch in Galveston in 1911. He had a tremendous practice and garnered many honors. Soon after I returned to Texas in 1941, he was named president of the Texas State Medical Association. He had three sons who became doctors; one, Valter, Jr., trained with me at the Mayo Clinic and shared a fourplex apartment with us. We are still friends. Valter, Jr., followed his father in becoming a leading physician.

3. Quite a few people underwent unnecessary operations for "chronic appendicitis," while the death rate for removal of an acute appendix was high. Surgeons were often criticized for operating too often or not operating soon enough. It was a tough decision which confronted surgeons nearly every day. In other instances, many patients were given thyroid extract for virtually every complaint. We had no reliable test for thyroid function. The basal metabolic rate was measured by an unreliable and laborious test, the B.M.R. Only years later, after I had joined the Mayo staff in 1947, were better tests developed. In those days the only effective treatment for hyperthyroidism was surgical removal of the offending goiter. Today these patients can be spared surgery by giving drugs or radioiodine.

4. The family continued to use the house for nearly thirty years. Unfortunately, Hurricane Carla destroyed Le Caprice in 1961. Several hundred feet of beachfront eroded away, and no effort was made to rebuild the house.

5. This stress-related fever would later occur again as a young staff member at the Mayo Clinic. I came down with high fever when I was scheduled to address fifteen hundred people in Cleveland. Charles W. Mayo was in Cleveland for the same program. He read my speech.

6. Mary and I always had a warm feeling for the Lamar Hotel. When we moved to Houston in 1949, Dr. Bertner arranged for me to take night calls at the Lamar. In the 1970s, the

Lamar was leveled to make way for a parking lot. After the implosion of the hotel we drove down to see the pile of rubble that once had been the palace of our wedding night. The Majestic Theater disappeared many years ago.

Chapter 8. The Mayo Clinic, 1939–41

1. The building was dedicated in 1928. Complete with all its equipment, the tower cost the Mayo Properties Association $3 million.

2. The Wilsons became our friends. They had an apple orchard and would invite us up to pick apples when they were ripe. So our misadventure turned out in our favor, even if we did miss meeting the new fellows at the Wilson Club.

3. One of the patients I examined was Paul Meserve. While in Rochester, he met and married Ruth Mayo, the widow of Joe Mayo. Joe Mayo, son of Charlie Mayo, interned at the Scott and White Clinic before returning to join the Mayo Clinic staff. He was killed accidentally in 1936, when his car was struck by a train, leaving his wife and two children who lived at Mayowood. After Paul Meserve married Ruth Mayo I continued seeing him. The marriage was a stormy one, ending in Ruth Mayo's suicide in February 1942. One of Joe's sons developed diabetes and I treated him later while I was on the staff.

4. After we moved to Houston we still got together at medical meetings with the Butts. Mary Butt died in 1991. Red has become an artist working in metal and has had some successful exhibitions. We have several pieces of his work, including one called *George Washington and the Cherry*. Red has received about every honor an internist can receive. He has been named president of the American College of Physicians and the American Society of Gastroenterologists; fellow of the Royal College of Physicians; and member of the governing board of the Mayo Clinic. He has been on the Mayo Clinic's payroll in some capacity for sixty-four continuous years, more than any other doctor.

5. Within a month of our arrival Dr. and Mrs. Palmer Woodson came from Temple. Mary had them to dinner and served a roast pheasant I had killed on a patient's farm. Hugh and Laurita DeLaureal, Dr. and Mrs. A. C. Scott, Jr., Dr. and Mrs. Sherwood, Mrs. G.V. Brindley, Sr., and C. J. Simpson also came from Temple. From Beaumont came Mr. and Mrs. Y. D. Carroll, Mr. B. D. Orgain, Sr., Mr. T. S. Reid, Mr. Rothwell, Carol Kyle and Lamar Cecil. We entertained all these people while they "went through the clinic." Mary's mother and father also visited.

6. Dr. Giffin, a graduate of Princeton University and Johns Hopkins medical school, completed a two-year residency as William Osler's last resident. When I was assigned to his service, he was nearing the compulsory retirement age of sixty-five. He was still proud of his training under Osler. I can take some pride in being a second-generation student of Sir William Osler. Dr. Giffin came to the clinic about 1912 as assistant to Christopher Graham, an original partner of the clinic and a brother-in-law of Charlie Mayo. Other members of the Giffin section included Charlie Watkins, Byron Hall, Mel Hargraves, and Joe Pratt.

7. The title of my thesis is "The Role of Sclerosis and Chronic Thrombophlebitis of the Portal Vein and its Tributaries in Splenomegaly." The work made few ripples and no waves in the world of medicine, but the results were published in various forms in leading medical journals. I presented it to the staff of the Mayo Clinic. I ran out of reprints, and I was quoted widely by hematologists and gastroenterologists. But I received more from the effort than anyone else. I would never have completed that thesis if I hadn't been so stubborn. I fear that doing the thesis only reinforced my stubbornness.

8. Jim Cain emerged from the war a full colonel. After his fellowship, he went on the staff in the Snell section. He and Ida May were friends of President and Mrs. Lyndon Johnson. Jim became the Johnsons' personal family physician. When Lyndon needed a cholecystectomy, Jim assembled a team of Mayo Clinic doctors and flew to Washington to remove the president's gall bladder, all this done with great TV publicity. I saw Jim on national TV as he issued progress reports on the president's operation. Jim died a few years ago. I visited Ida May in Rochester in September 1997.

Other Texans I knew in Rochester were Pete and Mary Pearson, John and Martha Thomas, Jim and Natalie Kriesle, Ben and Minnie Wells, John Bagwell, Mildred Cariker, Ed Clarke, Gene Ellingson, Everett Lewis, Tom Melton, Earl Yeakel, Jack Upshaw, Don Paulson, Compere Bason, Alex Doss, Bob Elliott, Albert Fischer, Oliver Gooch, Walt Hasskarl, Nick Hightower, John Hinchey, Jack Lee, Jim Pridgeon, Burgess Sealy, Ira Skinner, Luke Vaughn, John Webb, and Ella Zuchlag.

Chapter 9. Military Service, 1941–45

1. My friend Al Owers from Scott and White was in my class at Randolph. After the war he trained at the Menninger Clinic in Topeka, Kansas, and came to Houston to join the Kelsey-Seybold Clinic, becoming my partner and personal psychiatrist.

2. I have reproduced much of this wartime correspondence between Mary and me in chapter 10 of *The Making of a Doctor*.

3. Other pilots of the Fifty-fourth Fighter Squadron whom I lived with were: Major Frank Pope, who replaced T. W. Jackson as C.O. of the Squadron (Pope was also shot down); Captain Tawlk, who replaced Pope; Lieutenant Ambrose, who shot down a Japanese PBY then later disappeared flying to Seattle on leave; Captain Laven of San Antonio; Bud Husted, a premed student; Bob McDonald; and Lieutenants Bean, Mills, Hasenfus, Kaufman, Anderson, Stevens, Millard, Strenkowsky, Hodges, and Gardner. All of these men won medals. They were of the original crew, and I knew everyone of them well.

4. The Army had R&R officers to boost morale. They drafted and assigned artists and entertainers. An opera conductor from the Boston Symphony once organized a thirty-one piece band at Cold Bay, for example. Major Kermit Roosevelt, son of President Teddy Roosevelt, visited the pilots and recounted his experiences as a Canadian pilot who had helped evacuate Dunkirk by carrying a passenger in his single-seat Hurricane Fighter. As another morale booster, I was issued a whiskey allowance and gave each pilot an ounce of whiskey when he returned from a mission.

5. Other medical colleagues in Alaska included Dr. Moore, surgeon of the XI Army at Fort Richardson, and Colonel Albreight, C.O. of Fort Richardson Hospital who lived in Palmer, Alaska. After the war, Albreight became Governor of Alaska. Major Peyton Moffitt was a regular army flight surgeon in the Fighter Command. Others in the command were Major Milo Fritz, an Alaskan ophthalmologist who flew in his plane to Eskimo villages and fitted eye glasses; Captain Bob Mooney, squadron flight surgeon at Umnak; Captains Kaycoff and Ted Bayles from Bellevue; Major Walter Stager, group surgeon who followed me at 343 Fighter Group. At the base hospital on Umnak, Colonel William Katz became C.O., and Captain Amos Gillsdorf was base flight surgeon. Major Seargent Billy McNulty, regular army, was his assistant and sent a $5 bill to my new born son Cooke.

6. During the last few months of 1994, while researching my family genealogy, I noticed

that Cooke's birth certificate recorded his name as Cooke Randolph Kelsey. Apparently, he was first named Cooke Randolph but as discussions went on, his name was changed to Cooke Wilson, and his registered name was not corrected.

7. On another occasion, I flew up to Anchorage with several of our pilots, and we were put in jail a second time. Dodging Anchorage cops was child's play compared to life in the Aleutians, however. Service men claimed to be able to smell women when they came up to Anchorage after several months in the Aleutians. It wasn't that women smelled differently; the reason was the powder and perfume. To this day, at eighty-five years of age, I can still smell powder and perfume where women have been, something I learned in Alaska.

8. In addition to having a leading role in pilot selection, I was made chief of the gastroenterology section that filled three wards in the huge temporary hospital. I was very busy.

9. Mavis P. Kelsey, "Acute Exposure of Flyers to Arctic Waters," *Air Surgeon's Bulletin* 1 (February 1944): 7–10; and "Flying Fatigue in Pilots Flying Long-Range Single-Seat Fighter Missions," *Air Surgeon's Bulletin* 1 (June 1944): 14–16.

10. Mary's delivery deserves special mention. She was due to deliver about June 15. She went to Dr. Ricketts, a highly recommended obstetrician in Dayton, who scheduled her for a cesarean section in the Miami Valley Hospital. I asked Dr. Ricketts if he would invite Willard Cooke of Galveston to do the cesarean. Dr. Cooke had taught me obstetrics in medical school and was nationally famous, and Dr. Ricketts thought it would be an honor to have him. Dr. Cooke was to be nearby in Pittsburgh, Pennsylvania, giving American Board examinations, when Mary came to term. I called Dr. Cooke who agreed to come on Dr. Ricketts' invitation. He arrived on June 13, and the next day he performed a cesarean on Mary and delivered Tom. I took Dr. Cooke to the officers club for meals, and he seemed to have a wonderful time.

11. Another friend was Harvey Savely. Our common interest was amateur botany. We went to the woods, when we could get off from seven-day work schedules. Harvey taught me to identify many plants I had never seen. When we moved to Dayton, I looked forward to seeing a Kentucky coffee bean tree. Like a bird watcher, I wanted to add another specimen to my list. The Kentucky coffee bean tree, a member of the legume family, only grows in a small area of Kentucky and adjoining Ohio. A few of these rare trees grew in a nature preserve near Dayton. Harvey and I went to the preserve and identified a few of these trees. The tree is characterized by double compound leaves and very thick twigs and branches. It may reach a height of eighty or more feet. We visited Major Ernie Pinson and his family who lived in Yellow Springs, about twenty miles from Dayton. Mary was fond of Captain D. W. Pierce and his wife. They knew Mary's relatives in Saint Louis. I have mentioned knowing Sheldon Luce when I interned in New York and when we served in the Aleutians. Sheldon was stationed at Wright Field. They had children the age of ours, so we picnicked together. Captain John Hickam of the aeromedical laboratory married one of the technicians at there. Hickam Field in Hawaii bears John's father's name. We went to the wedding at Patterson Field Officers Club. It seemed that every general in the air force came to the wedding. John Hickam became a professor of medicine at Harvard. Unfortunately, he died young, at the height of his career. Other scientists I remember at the aeromedical laboratory were Loren Carlson, Greg Hall, Ernie Pinson, William Bachrach, and E. M. Sweeney; E. J. Baldes, Charlie Code, E. H. Wood, and William Boothby were among those doing aviation research at the Mayo Clinic. I knew General David N. W. Grant, Herman Wigodsky, Charlie Kossman, and General Malcolm Grow in the air surgeon's office. Colonel Harry Armstrong was the father of aviation medicine. He and Gen-

eral Eugene J. Reinatz, Paul Campbell, and Otis Benson were at the School of Aviation Medicine at various times.

12. Randolph Lee Clark, who trained with Randy Lovelace at the Mayo Clinic, was also attached to the service liaison section in 1945. Before coming to Wright Field, he had done surgery in an air force hospital. I met him for the first time in Dayton. As I recall, Lee had undertaken writing a history of the air force medical department, including the aeromedical laboratory and the school of aviation medicine. We became friends, not knowing that we would meet again in Houston four years later. Lee stayed in the service after the war to complete his history. He spent several months on the project at the school of aviation medicine in San Antonio before coming to Houston as chief of M.D. Anderson Hospital.

Chapter 10. Return to the Mayo Clinic, 1946–47, and Staff, 1947–49

1. Founding families of the clinic had been in Rochester for almost a hundred years, and many were kin. Our other neighbor, George Hallenbeck, was a grandson of Christopher Graham, one of the original partners of the clinic. Dr. Graham's sister Edith married Charles Mayo. Another early clinic partner, David Berkman, Sr., originally a veterinarian, married Gertrude, sister of William and Charles Mayo. Dr. Berkman's daughter Daisy married Henry Plummer and daughter Helen married Starr Judd. Mr. Harwick, business manager of the Mayo Clinic, married Dr. Graham's niece, Margaret. Dr. Rankin, a Mayo surgeon, married Charles Mayo's daughter, Edith.

2. I always wanted Frank Ashburn to join us in forming a clinic in Houston. He visited Houston, but a chest surgeon told him there was no room for another in the city. Frank decided to go to Washington, D.C., and join a well-established partnership of surgeons.

3. The loss of their sons was so traumatic that Randy Lovelace resigned from the Mayo Clinic. He moved his family back to their hometown of Albuquerque, New Mexico, where his uncle had started a clinic.

4. I told other people in passing that aspirin may cause surgical bleeding, but I was too dumb to follow up on it. I should have started an investigation. With the resources of the Mayo Clinic, I could have soon proven my theory. Over a period of a few years, doctors began to realize that aspirin could cause surgical bleeding. Today, aspirin is withdrawn for several days, and the blood is tested for bleeding tendencies before surgery is undertaken.

5. Sam encouraged me in many ways. He was disappointed when we left Rochester, but he and Emily visited us in Texas and we always visited them in Rochester and had long telephone conversations during the Christmas holidays. Sam did nice watercolors, and we have two farm scenes done by him. We were invited to his hundredth birthday celebration. I was in Rochester a month before to be with my brother John who was in surgery. I had a great visit with Sam and Emily and Olivia, but I missed the birthday celebration. Sam died soon before he reached 101 years. Emily died a about a year later.

6. Our friendship with Ray and Marion Keating continued after we moved to Houston. We visited them in Rochester and at various medical meetings. A terrible tragedy befell Ray and Marion. One night they were driving from the Rochester airport in their Volkswagen. A Vietnam veteran, drunk while on leave from the army and driving a large·car at nearly a hundred miles an hour, rear-ended the Keating car, killing Ray and Marion instantly.

7. Also in this section was Randall Spargue, who specialized in diabetes, and Alexander

Albert, Ph.D., a biochemist in charge of the endocrine laboratory. Through patient referrals, I met most of the surgeons of the Mayo Clinic, especially those who did thyroid surgery: Marden Black, Ed Judd, Charles W. Mayo, Jim Priestly, and Howard Gray. I could easily write a large book about the fine doctors I knew in Rochester.

8. Another distinguished visitor was Houston mayor Oscar Holcombe, who came to my office, introduced himself, and invited me to come to Houston. I don't know how he got my name, but I was flattered.

9. Other patients from Houston were Mr. and Mrs. Tom Monroe and Mr. and Mrs. Tom Hunt. Mr. Monroe was on the board of Hermann Hospital. Mr. Hunt, owner of Hunt Tool Company, was an old-timer in the oil business who knew Cooke Wilson, Sr., at Spindletop. He urged us to move to Houston. The Hunts entertained Mary and me at their ranch near Houston at Simonton and later would tell their friends they brought Mary and me to Houston. Mrs. Thomas D. Anderson of Houston also became a patient. Her husband, Tommy, was a nephew of M. D. Anderson. The Andersons welcomed us to Houston. We have been close friends ever since.

10. Mary is fifth generation through her great-great grandmother, Anne McDonald Thompson (1780–1857), who is buried in Grayson County, and I through my great-great-grandfather, Reverend William Martin Massie (1802–75), who is buried in Parker County.

Chapter 11. Settling in Houston, 1949

1. We had a wonderful welcome when we moved to Houston. I can rightfully be accused of name dropping when I list the people who entertained us and helped us get established in Houston. Tommy and Helen Anderson gave us a party at their house. As I recall we met Ben and Mary Anderson and Leland and Essamina Anderson. I had met Tommy's brother James in Rochester, while he was a patient of Mandred Comfort. Also at the party were Mark and Elizabeth Crosswell, Dr. and Mrs. Robert Johnston, Sr., Ernie and Virginia Cockrell, the Thad and Palmer Hutchesons, Buddy and Jean Lykes, Griff and Virginia Lawhom, Bob and Blanche Strange, Marvin and Nancy Collie, the Lovett Abercrombies, and the Victor and Billy Carters.

2. Cooper Ragan collected Texana and Americana. We enjoyed many evenings together with our books. He and Susie willed their books to the A&M library. Cooper recommended me for membership in the Texas Philosophical Society and the Committee on Foreign Relations. I remember meeting Cooper and Susie Ragan, the Syndor Odens, Judge Hannay, Albert and Nettie Jones, David and Catherine Searles, Bob and Lib Whilden, and Tommy and Jean Robinson.

3. Even though I was a Methodist, I had been attending the Episcopal Church in Rochester with Mary. In Houston, we attended St. John's Church and Christ Church, where Bishop Quin often preached. Christ Church was the oldest church in Houston, started in 1839 as I recall. The church was designated a cathedral soon after we came to Houston. Reverend Hamilton Kellog from Minneapolis was made dean of the cathedral. We had mutual friends with the Kellogs in Minnesota and soon became friends. In the cathedral, he held a large adult confirmation class, which I attended. At the confirmation ceremony, in front of a full house, Dean Kellog called on me to tell why I was being confirmed an Episcopalian. I rose and said that my wife had been after me to join the Episcopal Church since we married and I finally agreed. The Dean was disappointed. He expected some inspirational remarks. Mary wasn't very happy about it either. After we came back to Texas, Reverend Charles Wyatt-Brown became the rector of St. Mark's Episcopal Church in Beaumont, where all the Wilsons went.

Mary's brother Waldo was chairman of the search committee who invited him. We soon became good friends of Charley and his wife, Shep. Charley later headed up Palmer Episcopal Church in Houston, so Mary and I moved our membership to Palmer and stayed there until Charley retired. In 1995, we moved to St. Martin's Church, which is near our house. This church was started as a mission by Reverend Tom Bagby with the help of his wife, Mary Louise. Reverend Larry Gipson is now rector.

4. Later Miss Ima gave her house to the Museum of Fine Arts. Mary was a docent there and wrote a brief history of the Hogg family, which pleased Miss Ima a great deal.

5. Most of my information comes from my good friend Tommy Anderson. For years he has told me stories about his uncle Monroe. For additional information, see N. Don Macon in association with Thomas Dunaway Anderson, *Monroe Dunaway Anderson, His Legacy: A History of the Texas Medical Center*, 50th anniversary ed. (Houston: n.p., 1994).

6. In addition to its many contributions to medicine, the M. D. Anderson Foundation has made many large gifts to other charitable and educational organizations in Houston and elsewhere.

7. In early 1913, Jesse H. Jones, owner of the *Houston Chronicle* and national business leader, was a surgery patient at St. Vincent's Hospital in New York City. There, he met a young resident, Ernst W. Bertner, who gave the anesthetic for Jesse Jones's surgery. Impressed with his skills and personality, Jones urged Bertner to move to his newly completed Rice Hotel as house physician and establish a practice in Houston. Dr. Bertner told me this widely known story when he explained why he and Mrs. Bertner lived in the Rice Hotel. A few years after Dr. Bertner established his local practice in gynecology and general practice, he departed for a year's study at the Johns Hopkins Hospital in Baltimore. This experience imparted to him a lifelong interest in cancer, which became particularly relevant in his efforts to organize M. D. Anderson Hospital and Research Center in the early 1940s.

8. Dr. Bertner's dedication was a great inspiration for those who helped develop the Texas Medical Center. He was active in many civic and charitable affairs, served as president of the Harris County and Texas Medical Societies, as national trustee of AKK, and as a professor at Baylor University College of Medicine. A successful investor in ranching, real estate, and oil production, he became a very wealthy man. He and Mrs. Bertner established a significant medical foundation.

9. Fred Elliott was one of the first people Bertner introduced me to when I came to Houston. Fred liked to cook. We cooked for each other several times. His wife Anne became my patient. After retiring as dean of the dental college, Elliott became the medical center's first full-time director in 1952, with the title executive vice president of the Texas Medical Center. Under his leadership the Texas Medical Center prospered. He resigned the vice presidency in 1962, but continued on the board of directors until December 1986. I saw him after he moved to Kerrville, where he died in his nineties.

10. Walter H. Moursund describes this event in his book, *A History of Baylor University College of Medicine, 1900–1953* (Houston: n.p., 1956).

11. In 1948, when trustee Horace Wilkins of the M. D. Anderson Foundation Board drove me around the Medical Center, he was surprised that the Baylor building was named the Roy and Lillie Cullen Building, instead of being named for Mr. M. D. Anderson. The Anderson Foundation had paid for the move from Dallas and made the move possible; however, that name had already been selected for the cancer hospital. Mr. and Mrs. Cullen had donated $2,250,000 for construction of that first Baylor building. I knew many of the Baylor faculty

soon after I arrived in 1949 including: Dr. John C. Haley, professor of anatomy; Dr. Culver M. Griswold, professor of dermatology; Dr. Walter H. Moursund, the dean; Dr. Herman W. Johnson, professor of obstetrics; Drs. Don W. Chapman, James A. Greene, Alvis E. Greer, Robert A. Hettig, Daniel E. Jenkins, John H. Moyer, and Ellard M. Yow in internal medicine; Drs. Berne L. Newton and Stuart A. Wallace in pathology; Drs. John K. Glen, Russell J. Blattner, and George W. Salmon in pediatrics; Drs. Hebbel E. Hoff in physiology and Peter Kellaway in neuro-physiology; Dr. Herbert T. Hayes in proctology; and Drs. Warren T. Brown in psychiatry and associate dean, James Greenwood, Jr., in neurosurgery and William S. Field in neurology. Others in surgery were H. Jack Ehlers, James G. Flynn, Elliott B. Hay, Herbert F. Poyner, and Edward T. Smith, orthopedics and Hermann Hospital chief of staff. I knew Joseph Johnson, the business manager, for many years; we served on a bank board together.

12. There were several other smaller facilities in Houston at this time. The Houston Tuberculosis Hospital was established in 1918 at Shepherd and Buffalo Drive. It contained 150 beds in 1950. I was never in this hospital, but my future partners, Bill Seybold and Bill Leary, were very active there. The hospital closed years later for lack of patients. The Greenwood Sanitarium had been established by Drs. James Greenwood, Sr., James F. Dibrell, and Thomas E. Greenwood in 1912, and was located way out on old South Main Street at Oak Hill. The facility served patients with nervous diseases, alcoholism, and drug addiction, and handled selected cases of pellagra. The sanitarium was closed shortly before Greenwood's death in March 1949. We once thought about buying it as a future home for our future clinic.

The Houston Eye, Ear, Nose, and Throat (EENT) Hospital was located downtown at the corner of Caroline and Walker streets. In the days before antibiotics, infected tonsils were responsible for throat abscesses (quinsy), otitis media, acute mastoiditis, rheumatoid arthritis, and endocarditis. Those infections were a major cause of hospitalization. Nearly everyone had their tonsils removed to prevent these complications. After the advent of penicillin, these complications virtually disappeared. Many EENT hospital beds were closed down. The Houston EENT Hospital was closed in 1958, when the group moved to the Memorial Professional Building. Hedgecroft Hospital had just moved to the old Masterson mansion on Montrose Avenue when I arrived in 1949. Mrs. Nell Harris Schwartz opened the institution in 1942 for the rehabilitation of children and adults physically affected or crippled by poliomyelitis. After poliomyelitis was controlled through the Sabin and Salk vaccines, Hedgecroft became a mental hospital for a few years and was ultimately razed.

The Houston Negro Hospital was built in 1927 as a three-story stucco structure with fifty beds at 2900 Elgin Avenue. In 1951, new equipment was obtained and building improvements were made. Baylor University College of Medicine consulted with the staff of twenty-two black doctors, and cancer care was provided by the staff of M. D. Anderson Hospital. I was called or sent there several times to see patients, probably as a member of the Anderson staff. The hospital was later renamed Riverside Hospital.

St. Elizabeth's Hospital, also an institution for African Americans, was opened in 1947 at 4514 Lyons Avenue. It contained fifty-five beds and was operated by the Missionary Sisters of the Immaculate Conception. The Turner Urological Institute was built at 506 Caroline Street in 1924 by Dr. Weems Turner. He was soon joined by his younger brother Harold. Both were active AKK alumni. Dr. Weems Turner had trained at the Brady Urological Institute in Baltimore. He built the Turner Urological Institute as a small model of the Brady Institute. It was the most up-to-date urological facility in Houston.

The Medical Arts Professional Building and Hospital opened in 1926 downtown near St. Joseph's Hospital. There was a small general hospital in the building. The Houston Clinic was another downtown facility which operated as a general clinic. The Heights Clinic and Hospital was opened in 1923 as a six-bed hospital by Dr. Thomas A. Sinclair.

One night when I was checking on one of my patients, I parked my car in the Memorial Hospital lot. To my chagrin, someone broke a car window in my absence and took my medical bag. Thereafter, I kept my bag in the trunk and removed the M.D. sign from the car. For years the M.D. sign gave doctors special privileges such as parking in a no-parking zone or speeding, supposedly to see a patient in emergency.

Dr. Jimmy Hill was my great friend at Memorial Hospital. He was famous locally as a thyroid surgeon. He always had several patients in the hospital recuperating from thyroidectomy and asked me to see a few.

In the 1970s Memorial's management adopted a satellite system of care. The downtown hospital was closed and three area hospitals opened. These included a large six-hundred-bed hospital in the southwest section of the city and two smaller ones in the northwestern and southeastern areas.

13. Methodist began as a three-story hospital established by O. L. Norsworthy, a prominent surgeon who gave the building to the Methodist Church in 1919. The name changed to the Methodist Hospital in 1922, and, in 1924, moved to a new building. Mrs. Walter Fondren, Sr., was a major contributor to Methodist Hospital. Her daughter and son-in-law, Catherine and Milton Underwood, were my patients. Once, Milton told me the family wanted to dispose of the Fondren house on Montrose Avenue. Mrs. Fondren Sr. had moved to River Oaks. I suggested they give it to Methodist Hospital. Ted Bowen had become director of the hospital and gladly accepted the house. He credited me with getting the Fondren family interested in Methodist Hospital. Could be!

14. The Junior League of Houston's Health Clinic for Indigent Children started in 1927. In 1942, the Junior League for Memorial Fund was established and, in 1947, gave $42,000 in seed money to establish the Texas Children's Foundation and Hospital. Other contributors included Mr. and Mrs. J. S. Abercrombie, Wesley and Neva West, and the Anderson Foundation. Soon after we came to Houston, Mary became active in the Junior League, which continued to operate its clinic in the Texas Children's Hospital. Mary's activity led to an unusual gift to the Junior League Clinic. Miss Lillian Moore was first employed as an English governess for the Wilson children in Beaumont, when Mary was a child. After the Wilson children grew up, Miss Moore became the governess for the children of Governor and Mrs. Will Hobby in Houston. When these children grew up, Miss Moore came back to the Wilson family as a babysitter for our children as well as for Fay's. Miss Moore had been very frugal. Before she died, she named Mary and Fay executors of her will. Miss Moore loved children and had no heirs, so at Mary's and Fay's recommendation she willed her estate to the Junior League Clinic in Texas Children's Hospital. The clinic erected a plaque in the lobby in Miss Moore's memory.

Chapter 12. Solo Practice, 1949–50

1. Dr. Bertner had a very stable practice and referred many patients to me while he was alive. George Waldron had trained at the Mayo Clinic. George was said to have the largest practice in Houston, grossing $300,000 a year. Valvular heart disease prevented him from

serving in World War II and eventually led to his early death at the height of his career. Open-heart surgery for valvular defects was yet to be developed.

2. Buck Schiwetz became my patient for several years while he was in Houston. I soon met Buck's wife who was a temperamental, accomplished artist in ceramics. She destroyed a lot of her beautiful work, because it didn't come up to her expectations. I stayed in touch with Buck until his death at eighty-five years of age on February 3, 1984. Mary and I collected his pictures, prints, and the books published about him.

3. A few years later, Julia Bertner married Ed Naylor, himself a widower. He chided me for calling her Mrs. Bertner, but admitted introducing her as Mrs. Bertner to guests at the hotel where they spent their honeymoon. Mrs. Naylor continued to be interested in the Texas Medical Center and participated in the ceremonies of building the M. D. Anderson Hospital and the Jesse Jones Library. The Naylors invited Mary and me to the ranch at Monaville. They had several happy years together before they passed away.

4. Unfortunately, Mrs. Kendall was killed in an automobile accident a year or two later. The numbering of patients in our register began with #1, the first patient I saw when I arrived in Houston, followed by #2, and continuing in uninterrupted sequence. I am patient #513 in what became the Kelsey-Seybold Clinic. Mary is #504. Some of the first patients are still around and will give me their clinic number when they greet me. Today, the clinic claims more than a million patients.

5. Randolph Lee Clark was born into a family of prominent Texas teachers who founded Add-Ran College, which became Texas Christian University. Lee was proud of being a national amateur wrestling champion. He attended the Medical College of Virginia, where he met and married Bertha Davis, his classmate. After graduating in 1932, the couple later became residents in the American Hospital in Paris, France. After serving a fellowship at Mayo, Lee joined the Shands Clinic at Jackson, Mississippi. He served in the Air Corps in World War II as a consultant to the air surgeon general. Later in the war, he was transferred to the aeromedical laboratory, where we became friends.

6. Paul Yoder, Frances Goff, Anna Hasselmann, Art Kleifgen, Zuma Krum, John Musgrove, Roy Heflebower, Marga Sinclair, Margaret Sullivan, and Robert Kolvoord were some of the other important people at Anderson Hospital whom I also knew well. Some of them became my private patients.

7. Mary Lou King refreshed my memory on the early years of the Harris County Unit of the American Cancer Society. Every Christmas she delivers her annual gift of mayhew jelly, which she makes from the fruit that grows in the Big Thicket swamps of East Texas.

8. Soon after I arrived, a Texas Mayo Alumni Society was organized. One of the first meetings was held at a dude ranch in Bandera. The president, John Thomas, was a champion hog caller who kept all the guests awake at night. That party was about as wild as the Texas party we had in Rochester, Minnesota, when Bill Seybold hit Andy Rivers. Another great meeting was held at Fort Clark. Jim Cain came from Rochester as guest speaker and arranged for Lyndon Johnson's barbecue cook to serve us.

9. Jack Jones was a general practitioner in Galveston. Ralph Hamme was in the Rio Grande Valley. In Fort Worth were Cooper Conner, the Terrells, the Grammer brothers, and Tildon Childs, who married a woman from Rochester. Raleigh Ross was a general surgeon in Austin.

10. Other Texas graduates included Jasper Arnold, Selwyn Hutchins, Ty Robinson in urology, Manuel Bloom in dermatology, and John Karnaky, the expert in trichomonas. Kenneth Von Pohle, Art Faris, Jimmy Clapp, Ruth Heartgraves, and Mildred Cariker were in gynecol-

ogy and obstetrics. Eugene Ellingson, my student at Galveston, trained with me at the Mayo Clinic and practiced surgery. Homer Prince taught physical diagnosis in the department of internal medicine when I was a sophomore in medical school. He moved to Houston and practiced as an allergist for years, then moved to Crockett to live in the country. John Kennedy practiced general surgery with Dr. Wooters. He later joined our clinic for a few years before he retired. Elizabeth Stripling Crawford became a leading ophthalmologist. General practitioners I knew from Galveston were Ed Crocker, Lynn Bourden, Ben Knolle, and Nathan Cotlar. Dolph Curb, the resident in internal medicine at John Sealy Hospital while I was in pathology, joined the Lummis Reece group of internists, as did Bill Donahue.

11. Hermann Hospital neurosurgeon R. C. L. Robertson sent me many referrals. Claude Pollard practiced with him for several years before moving to Austin. Robbie's son joined him in neurosurgery. Other Houston neurosurgeons included Jim Greenwood, Marshall Henry, William Cheek, and Randolph Jones.

12. Other internists I knew were Bob Wise, chief of medicine at the Veterans Hospital, and Sidney Schnurr in the Postgraduate Graduate School of Medicine. Also there were Bill Owen, Ted Groff, Bill Brown, John Bunting, Bernie Farfel, Edmond Doak, Ed Ory, Hugo Engelhardt, Julian Silverblatt, George Zeluff, Henry Cromwell, Lynn Bernard, Lucille Robey, and LeRoy Dugan. Belton Griffin and Fred Dorsey joined the Diagnostic Clinic. Herbert Allen was an internist who became a specialist in nuclear medicine and had a long career in Houston. Still more internists were Harold Dobson, Stanley Zimmermann, Rodney Rodgers, and Carlos Hamilton, whose son and grandson became doctors. Some early cardiologists were Bob Leachman, Bob Hall, Bill Winters, and Don Chapman. Otolaryngologists included Herbert Harris, Fred Guilford, Bill Wright, and the group at the Houston Eye Ear Nose and Throat Hospital. Another, J. Charles Dickson, later joined our clinic and became chief.

13. The DeBakey-Cooley competition is well known: two people with identical goals and egos who have at times drawn criticism for their drive and aggressiveness. I admire both men greatly. They will be remembered in history as two of the world's greatest surgeons. Both are also great leaders and philanthropists. It is truly amazing that two such men should appear at the same time in the same place. They stand among the other fine giants in the Texas Medical Center, including Monroe D. Anderson, Ernst W. Bertner, and Lee Clark. Other men who have made large gifts to the medical center institutions include Hermann and George Brown (Brown Foundation), Hugh Roy Cullen (Cullen Foundation), and Jesse Jones (Houston Endowment).

Chapter 13. Kelsey, Seybold, and Leary Partnership, 1950–53

1. Dorothy Teall, Bill Seybold's secretary, collected most of the correspondence between Bill and me. In 1970, she compiled the letters from 1949–50, along with some photographs of the Texas Medical Center during its early years, into a single volume, *History of the Kelsey-Seybold Clinic/Dear Pardners*. A copy of her book is in the McGovern Archives of Medical History at the Houston Academy of Medicine Library. I also abstracted and included these letters in the appendix to the second volume of my memoir, *Doctoring in Houston and My Story of the Kelsey-Seybold Clinic and the Kelsey-Seybold Foundation* (Houston: privately printed, 1996). The following account is based on this source.

2. In several of my letters to Bill Seybold, I mentioned making mistakes with patients and doctors. I had lost patients by not explaining that I was doing an examination that was differ-

ent than what they might have been accustomed to in brief office visits with other doctors. Often I thought they were coming for a complete examination, when they really had come for an office visit. I soon trained my secretary-receptionist to make sure what type of examination the patient wanted when he or she made an appointment.

3. Frances Randolph Rather was born in Austin, Texas, on July 16, 1916. Frances and my wife, Mary, are descended from Henry Randolph, the first Randolph to come to America in 1643.

4. Margaret Pierson Leary was born September 29, 1916. She is a descendent of the famous colonial painter Charles Wilson Peale and of Reverend Abraham Pierson, first president of Yale University.

5. Jacky provided me an official copy of the *History of the Post Graduate School of Medicine,* submitted to the Regents of the University of Texas, April 1958. I was saddened to read her obituary in the *Houston Chronicle* on February 26, 1996, just a few months after she provided me this information.

6. Grant Taylor died in Houston in 1995 at ninety-four years of age. His wife Pat became my patient and their sons Grant, Jr., and Worth went to school with our sons.

7. Our Anderson friends included: Lee and Bert Clark, Gilbert and Mary Fletcher, Cliff and Eleanor Howe, Cleon and Betty Lou Shullenberger, John and Millicent Wall, and Dr. and Mrs. Robert Johnston, and Bill Russell, who was not yet married. Other medical friends were Lynn and Elizabeth Zarr, Val and Mary Louise Baird, F. O. and Joyce McGehee, Ike and Eleanor Reynolds, Steve and Lucy Foote, Dr. and Mrs. Peyton Barnes, Melville and Barbara Cody, Claude and Muriel Cody, John and Lela Hull, Everett and Mary Seale, Herbert and Elsie Hayes, and Maury Campbell and Jack Staub, who were not yet married. In addition, there were many people moving from Beaumont to Houston who knew the Wilson family. They included the Blaffers, Fondrens, Farrishes, Sterlings, Cullinans, Hobbys, and Kennedys.

Chapter 14. Kelsey-Leary Clinic Years, 1953–61

1. John enjoyed an illustrious career. He was chief of gastroenterology at Baylor and Methodist Hospitals in the early days. He was very active in teaching and served on the American Board of Gastroenterology for years. He was on the Mayo alumni board and served as its president. He served as an officer in several national societies. He won a traveling scholarship to England. He published a couple of books and a hundred medical articles. John was an active sportsman, a near champion golfer. After retirement he became an artist. He loved to build his own residences and vacation homes.

2. Al and his wife, Marge, were fond of their Swiss heritage and made many trips to visit their relatives in Switzerland. The entire family established Swiss citizenship, which can be held concurrently with American citizenship. Al was a violinist and belonged to a chamber music group. He and Marge collected butterflies and went to Belize and other places to do their collecting. He traded butterflies and moths with people all over the world. One night we had an invasion of hundreds of rare giant moths at our yard. Al and Marge came over and collected many of these, which he traded with other collectors. Al and Marge became experts in making jewelry. They raised rare tropical fish and plants. I wondered if they ever got any sleep.

3. Jackie was born Alice Matthews in Palestine, Texas, in 1909. She graduated from CIA, later named Texas Women's University (TWU). She was an ardent supporter of TWU, eventu-

ally being honored as a distinguished alumnus. Although Jackie was hired away from the clinic in 1963, she remained a trustee of the Kelsey Leary (later Kelsey-Seybold) Foundation.

4. When our clinic was small, the doctors and employees knew each other well. We knew all the spouses by first name and the number of children in each family. We had parties for the entire staff and their spouses. I remember several parties at our house when the total group numbered less than fifty. As our numbers increased, we had parties after hours in the clinic and later in clubs or restaurants. Finally, in the 1990s, our parties became so large that the doctors and spouses filled the Houston Country Club; a whole park had to be rented for the annual picnic, and a very large meeting hall could hardly accommodate the employees' Christmas party.

5. I became the Cody family doctor. Sadly, Melville developed a highly malignant cancer of the stomach, killing him within a few weeks. He died in 1983. The Kelsey-Seybold Foundation established the Melville Cody Memorial Lectureship in 1983. This fund brings a leading gynecologist to the Texas Medical Center each year. Melville's hobby was woodcarving; his subjects were birds and animals. His work was refined and beautiful, the result of fine detail. We displayed his wood sculptures in our waiting rooms and at the February 15, 1996, Kelsey-Seybold Foundation benefit art exhibition in the new Houston Museum of Medical Science. Melville's widow, Barbara, attended this exhibition.

6. The NASA contract is discussed further in chapter 17.

7. I also remember a lovable, philanthropic Jewish couple who had realized their American Dream. We had a common bond: the wife saw my certificate of internship at Bellevue Hospital in New York and exclaimed that she was born in Bellevue. She was the daughter of immigrants who lived in a Jewish ghetto in New York. The family received all their medical care at Bellevue and loved the institution. I didn't know them then, but they were patients of Bellevue while I was there.

8. The original pathologist was soon replaced by Carl Lind and his associate Bill Hill and both served well for many years. Carl Lind became chief of staff. Edward B. Singleton was chosen in 1953 as chief of radiology. He developed an outstanding department and became internationally famous. Ed was born in Galveston, the son of Albert O. Singleton, who was professor of surgery at Galveston, while I was there. Ed graduated from the medical school in Galveston in 1946 and trained at the University of Michigan. He served in the air force for two years, before spending the rest of his career as chief of radiology at St. Luke's and Texas Children's Hospitals. Ed's brother Albert Singleton became a surgeon on the faculty at Galveston. His wife Joan was an accomplished artist. Mary and I became close friends of the Singletons and enjoyed being with them on many occasions. Albert and Joan died at a relatively early age.

9. After Ben Taub Hospital was opened, an obstetrics program was continued at Jeff Davis. At this time Winnie Wallace, mother of my daughter-in-law Wendy Kelsey, was on the Harris County Hospital District Board. She was a tireless volunteer who contributed a great deal to the womens' program. The obstetrics program at Jeff Davis, the Winnie Wallace Maternity Pavilion, was named for her. Eventually, Jeff Davis was closed, abandoned, and left to vandals who stripped out the copper pipe and stole from the surplus medical equipment stored there.

10. The Texas Institute of Rehabilitation (TIRR) was organized in the Texas Medical Center about 1955. Its original purpose was to treat the victims of polio. William Spencer from Texas Children's Hospital became the director. He was a good-natured man, always smiling and enthusiastic. His optimism was just what polio victims needed. Bill Spencer went on to develop numerous rehabilitative modalities for all kinds of physically handicapped people.

11. Our clinic has since done many thousand mammograms and the Crump Cancer Center is based on the use of the mammogram.

Cliff Howe was an inveterate smoker who denied that smoking caused lung cancer. He was proved wrong when he developed lung cancer and died from it at age sixty-six in 1980. He left a wife and five children. Ruel Stallones, dean of the University of Texas School of Public Health, was another heavy smoker who denied smoking caused lung cancer; he met the same fate.

12. In 1958, the Texas Society of Architects awarded our house first place in a statewide contest for the best designed house of the year. Mary opened the house and grounds for benefit tours on numerous occasions, allowing thousands of people to walk through. When we moved here, Buffalo Bayou was a slow clearwater stream in which we could wade and pick up mussels. There was a swimming hole at one spot. Our boys could swing out on a rope tied to a limb of a huge sycamore tree. They could drop into the pond or swing to land on the opposite side. This hole was home to some big catfish, large soft shell terrapins, and water moccasins. Now the Buffalo Bayou has been scoured out; its banks have eroded, and the volume is tenfold as a result of heavy building and water use upstream. Environmentalists are trying to reduce its pollution.

13. We visited Europe numerous times and the Middle East and the Orient three times. We have traveled over much of South America and Africa on several trips and made one trip to New Zealand and Australia. Mary and I went to England three times in one year to buy rare books. When we traveled, we always shopped the rare book dealers of the large cities we visited. We even bought Nepalese documents and prayer books in Katmandu. We made a point of seeing the great architectural wonders of the world. In addition to the treasures of Europe, we have seen the Great Wall of China, the formal gardens of Japan, the Taj Mahal in India, the Pyramids of Giza, the Kremlin in Moscow, the Acropolis at Athens, St. Sophia in Istanbul, St. Peter's Cathedral in Rome, Christ's manger in Bethlehem, and the Opera House in Sydney.

14. Father Henry Magill from Dallas was a Catholic priest, the friend of the John Maher family. Through son John's friendship with Albert Maher, Father Henry became a friend of our family. He often came and stayed with us and was very fond of the boys. The summer of 1959, Father Magill had planned a trip to Ireland, the land of his birth. He invited several boys to go with him, including Cooke. Mary and I approved the trip, but Cooke did not care to go. Billy Woodfin did go with Father Magill. Ironically, the two were in Ireland the night that Cooke was killed. If only Cooke had gone with Father Henry. When Father Magill returned he came to Houston immediately and was a great comfort to me.

Chapter 15. Kelsey Leary Seybold Clinic, 1961–65

1. While attending the University of Texas, one daughter was killed in an auto accident between Austin and Houston. I have known too many young people who were killed in auto accidents on that road. Irving's wife Laura died of breast cancer while quite young, and he eventually married again.

2. Frank Anderson and his wife Velma had children. They had never lived in a large city and grew homesick for College Station. I hated to see them go, but we have remained friends. They entertained Mary and me when we went to A&M as members of the development council for the Texas A&M College of Medicine and the Sterling Evans Library. Frank has been an important teacher and supporter of the A&M College of Medicine. Jim McMurrey's

wife, Odette, and Mary became great friends through their participation in the Houston Garden Club. Jim and Odette also lost a child. They had a son who died suddenly on a high school playing field. Jim was a great quail hunter and kept fine dogs. A gentleman and intellectually honest, Jim was an exceptionally competent surgeon. I had the fullest confidence in him when I referred him patients with life-threatening problems. Jim operated on me for an intestinal obstruction in 1977.

3. Charlie's son Jessie joined us as an orthopedist for a few years. His other son, Jay, became a medical administrator. The Dicksons became family friends. His wife, Ruth, and daughter Roseanne were my patients. Charlie died a few years ago, but I still see Ruth at Luby's Cafeteria with her friends. During his career at the clinic, Jim Smith served on many committees and was once chief of staff. He has been very active in the Otolaryngology Department at Baylor as associate professor and senior attending at Methodist Hospital. He also served at St. Luke's, Texas Children's, M. D. Anderson and UTMB. He was president of the UTMB alumni, and in 1995 was named an Ashbel Smith Distinguished Alumnus.

4. Earl became a full clinical professor under Russell Blatner, professor of pediatrics at Baylor and director of Texas Children's Hospital. Earl served on numerous state and national advisory programs on child health and education and received many awards, including the U.S. Surgeon General's Exemplary Service Award Medal given to Earl in 1988. He was honored in the former Soviet Union, where he made several lecture tours behind the Iron Curtain. Earl published over two hundred articles, books, abstracts, pamphlets, and movies. His books on children's arthritis were published in several languages. Now retired, he writes novels. If one is published, I'm sure it will be a good one.

5. When Bill Gray retired from the clinic, he found another dentist for us, David Teasdale, a young Texas Dental School graduate. Also a very fine dentist, he stayed at the clinic until it moved out of 6624 Fannin to the Doctors Center on South Main. David has continued to be our family dentist. He now has offices in the Texas Medical Center. The clinic dentists have taken care of our family for years, a major reason why I still have good teeth. All good clinics should have a dental department.

6. The dermatologists employed an electrologist, Nancy Mitchell, who was a fine woman. She removed unwanted hairs from a number of my female patients with endocrine problems. Nancy went into practice by herself. Mary Clark came to the clinic as a physical therapist and was very popular with patients and clinic personnel. Her father, M. T. Briggs, was a retired professor of pediatrics at Harvard Medical School. The family became my patients. Our patient records grew so rapidly that we became overwhelmed with the numbers and lost some records. Finally, in 1963 we employed Zelda Rudin, a certified medical record specialist. She did a wonderful job and stayed with us until she retired in April 1975.

7. In later years Alfred Glassell bought a large cattle ranch between Hebronville and Falfurrias called Buenos Suerte. In addition to cattle he developed the property for quail hunting. He obtained expert advice in wildlife conservation and limited hunting to his family and friends. For the past fifteen or twenty years Alfred has invited me on an annual hunt. Mary was invited several times with the ladies. My sons have been invited for father and son hunts to be with Alfred and my godson Alfred III. I was a poor shot and got worse as the years went by. I felt it was a shame to waste such fine shooting opportunities on me. But I was never teased or criticized. I entered into the conversations as if I were a great hunter, and expostulated on the qualities of various guns and dogs.

8. There were many other hunting trips, including dove hunts at the Maher ranch in Falfurrias

and quail hunts with Dr. High in Cuero. Soon after I arrived in January 1949, Jamie Griffith invited me on a duck hunt with Jack Garrett. A thin layer of ice had formed around the decoys. The ducks flew in to land and skidded across the ice. I thought my toes would freeze off. It was the coldest duck hunt I ever attended.

Chapter 16. Kelsey-Seybold Clinic, 1965–86

1. There were other memorable events. In 1970, for example, we had to evacuate the building—at least on two occasions—because of bomb threats. Careful searches of the building turned up no explosives.

2. At one time the Hannahs agreed to sell us the land our Clinic was on. We had the money. Earl Beard reminds me that we tried to convince the partners to buy it. After I had dropped out of management, we had growing pains again. We had built branch offices. We moved many services to rental space in the Medical Tower, where the clinic spent large sums remodeling space for pediatrics, neurology, psychiatry, and business offices.

3. After Breaux left, Mike Fitzgerald was made director. Mike Condit became chief of staff replacing Jim Kemper who, by clinic rules, was required to step down. Mike Condit developed into a great administrator, and both Mikes have done a fine job. Through the years, members of the clinic management team included Everett C. Wilkie and Greg Polley, accounting; David Bell, director of employee relations; Mike Childers, McNeil, and William Ancelle, administrators; and Lastie Villien, supply officer. Several secretaries, nurses, and receptionists worked their way up to management positions, including Bill Jo Reiske, Vicki Buxton, Joyce Burch, Betty Wilcox, and Ruth Jordan.

4. Our staff members continued on the faculty and carried a large teaching load in clinical practice for Baylor medical students and house staff. While he was chief of the Kelsey-Seybold Clinic, Bill Seybold was responsible for a teaching affiliation, signed in June 1974, between Baylor University College of Medicine and the clinic. The agreement called for all Baylor students, as part of their curriculum, to spend eight weeks in a department of the Kelsey-Seybold Clinic. Baylor wasn't nearly so large then. They needed clinical staff to teach their students.

5. During this time, the clinic was often faced with attractive offers and propositions, beginning in 1970 with Memorial Hospital's offer to join them in their new hospital on the Southwest Freeway. A few years later, Methodist Hospital wanted to buy the clinic, an offer the partners also rejected. In September 1983, we declined an offer to invest in a home health care company.

6. There was a great deal of resistance from some partners when we added Frank Stransky, a physician assistant, to the staff at the Kelsey-Seybold west office in June 1973. Stransky knew his limitations, as well as his qualifications, and did not attempt procedures he was not trained to do. He did a more thorough proctoscopic examination than some of the doctors. He also performed stress electrocardiograms, under a doctor's supervision, something technicians do routinely today.

7. Jim McMurrey became chief of surgery when Bill Seybold retired. Jerry Doggett became the next chief of surgery in 1981. Gilchrist L. Jackson, born in Kentucky in 1948, graduated from the University of Louisville in 1974. He completed his residency training in general and oncologic surgery at the M. D. Anderson Hospital, before he joined us on July 1, 1981. Gil and his wife, Catina, have a fine family, and have been friends of our family for three generations.

Another outstanding surgeon was Marion Jack Williams who came about 1985. James A. Wolf came to the clinic as a general and oncologic surgeon after I retired. Melville Cody was chief of gynecology and obstetrics until he died in May 1983. William A. Johnson came to the department in July 1967 and served until August 31, 1994, when he and his family moved to Virginia. Don Pranke came to the clinic as chief of urology in May 1964 and remained in the clinic until he retired in 1996. He only did office practice during the last few years. Robert A. Renner came first as a resident, then joined the staff in 1981 after he completed his residency. He is now chief of the urology department at the clinic. Thomas H. Crouch joined on October 9, 1972, after his military retirement. He stayed with us until his second retirement on February 28, 1992. We are now blessed with a fine orthopedist, Glenn C. Landon, who trained at the Mayo Clinic. He was chief of orthopedics at the V.A. Hospital in Houston before joining the clinic.

8. Ralph D. Eichorn joined the gastroenterology section on May 1, 1966. Francisco J. Garcia-Torres, born in Puerto Rico in 1945, joined the Clinic on July 9, 1979. Frank has been an outstanding gastroenterologist and endoscopist and chief of gastroenterology at the Clinic for several years. About 1993, Frank performed a full colonoscopy on me, and I watched the procedure on a television screen. Looking inside your own intestines while you are lying on a table is, indeed, a strange experience. Frank was instrumental in saving the life of my sister-in-law Betty Wilson. Vincent Friedewald, a native Texan, came to the clinic on brother John's recommendation in August 1982 from the Honolulu Clinic. Vince produced medical programs for national television. This occupied so much of his time that he virtually stopped practice and left the clinic on June 29, 1984. John Hughes came in 1981. He was the first black doctor to be taken on the staff of the Kelsey-Seybold Clinic. Earl Beard has been chief of cardiology in our clinic since he arrived in 1954. Thanks to Jim Kemper the section of rheumatology has been stable. Jim continued an active practice even while bearing the responsibilities of chief of staff and taking a role in national rheumatology organizations. He turned the section over to John M. (Mike) Condit but is still seeing patients today. Mike Condit joined the rheumatology section in 1966 and the clinic in 1978; he is now chairman of the clinic board, a very demanding job overseeing nearly three hundred physicians. Martin S. Fischer joined the clinic as a rheumatologist on August 3, 1970. Al Leiser joined me in the section of endocrinology in 1956 and retired in 1997. Phillip K. Champion joined us on July 12, 1971. Irving Schweppe came to the clinic in 1961 and later became chief of medicine at St. Luke's, finally retiring in 1995 to be replaced by Herbert DuPont, who holds the Mary Wilson Kelsey professorship at the University of Texas Health Science Center. Stanton P. Fischer joined in 1965. Stuart Riggs joined as a specialist in infectious diseases in 1969. In April 1972, Elihu N. Root joined our Clinic as an oncologist. One outstanding general internist to join our clinic was Carlos F. Taboada. David C. Wilkinson II and Kathleen H. Ryan were general internists. Ophthalmology in our clinic was served intermittently by a number of doctors before it was finally stabilized by Nancy Webb and Ruben Lemos. George Ferry joined the clinic as a pediatrician on July 8, 1970. In December 1981, he left to work full time at Baylor in Texas Children's Hospital. Later, George became part time at Baylor and part time as executive director of the Kelsey-Seybold Foundation. Other outstanding pediatricians include F. James Boland. Wilson Fraser was our first dermatologist. He was joined in July 1966 by Donald W. Owens, a native of Trinity, Texas, and a friend of my classmate Sam Barnes. Don has been chief of dermatology for years. He is also certified in dermatopathology. Jerry H. Stephens also joined the clinic in dermatology.

9. We wanted a neurologist too, but there was a great shortage in this specialty. Harris Hauser had left us to join his father and two brothers. I thought our needs were permanently

settled when Bill Seybold's son William Randolph joined us in 1976. Mike Newmark also came to the neurology department in January 1983. Mike runs an important epilepsy program in the clinic, supported by the Kelsey-Seybold Foundation through the charitable gifts of Mimi Dompier. Mike has taken a leadership position in the professional and education committees of the clinic and is a director for the Kelsey-Seybold Foundation.

10. Next came Patrick M. Conoley in July 1980. In 1967 we employed Lawrence McCarthy, a board certified clinical pathologist, but he only stayed a year. Robert A. Jordan came on January 1, 1968. He was a board certified clinical pathologist who got his medical degree from Tulane in 1958. Bob was highly competent and installed all the newest procedures in the laboratory. He was one of the first to install a SMAC 20 in a private clinic.

11. New York Life bought Maxicare and took over our prepay program. The program has continued to this day. The clinic contracts with several other HMOs, companies, and government entities for prepaid health care and is thriving today.

12. The situation has changed. Mary and I dropped out of Planned Parenthood when it began to support abortion. Our daughter-in-law, Wendy Kelsey, became president of Planned Parenthood for two years. We have close friends on both sides of this issue. I wish the issue would go away and moderation would prevail. I wish there was a new Moderate Political Party that the majority of American people could join. It seems that now all parties take an extreme position.

13. Our son John Wilson Kelsey married Karen Ashley Arthur Thomas in 1977. John legally adopted Karen's daughter Kelly Elizabeth (born February 18, 1969) from a previous marriage. John is an investment management consultant and is a director in the consulting group of Solomon Smith Barney in Houston.

Thomas Randolph Kelsey married his childhood sweetheart, Margaret Ann Heinzerling, in 1966. They have three children: William Randolph (born May 18, 1969); Margaret Heinzerling (January 17, 1973); and Mavis Parrott III (April 14, 1978). Tom is a partner in the law firm of Liddell, Sapp, Zivley, Hill and LaBoon in Houston.

Mavis Kelsey married Winifred (Wendy) Wallace in June 1970. They have two children: Winifred Wallace (born March 12, 1973) and Cooke Wilson (January 4, 1977). Mavis is a commerical real estate broker and investor in Houston.

Chapter 17. Areas of Expansion, 1955 to the Present

1. Our friends Hugh and Bill Liedtke with Pennzoil Company, and Pennzoil Company itself, have also been very generous to the foundation, supporting many of its projects. The Murphy Baxters, friends of the Liedtkes since they were together in the Permian Basin, made a gift of $130,000 to the endowment fund.

2. The Crump Center joined with the Pennzoil Company in developing a Cancer Awareness Program. A joint research program with M. D. Anderson Hospital involving 532 women revealed that nonprotein bound estradiol and estradiase bound albumen was found to be significantly higher in breast cancer patients than in disease-free women. Among other programs of the Cancer Center is a program for the study, diagnosis, and treatment of head and neck malignancies. There were also chromosome studies of patients with cancer and many more projects at the forefront of studies to control the most serious cancer affecting women. Thousands of people have benefited from the Crump Cancer program.

3. John Hughes, the first black doctor at the Kelsey-Seybold Clinic, in 1981 joined the

gastroenterology section, whose chief was my brother John. Hughes was born in Florida in 1948 and was the first black to graduate from the University of South Florida College of Medicine in 1975. His bright personality, energy, ambition, and professionalism earned him the respect and warm friendship of doctors and patients alike. John Hughes has instituted a number of joint research projects between the Kelsey-Seybold Foundation and M. D. Anderson Hospital, particularly regarding the genetic basis and heredity of bowel cancer. He has promoted early diagnosis and cure of colon cancer, the most common cancer to attack both men and women.

4. Other grants to M. D. Anderson were for studies of esophageal cancer; genetic studies in cancer; investigations into B and T cell lineage; chemotherapy of solid tumors; development of immunoglobins; virology studies in luekemia; studies of cell wall proteins in renal cancer; tissue culture of breast cancer; human lymphocytes; antitumor drugs; breast and lung cancer; familial collagen vascular diseases and cancer; mitochondria of breast cancer cells; DNA and breast cancer; familial gastrointestinal neoplasia, aging, and cancer; and many others.

5. Grants were made to Dr. McPhearson's Retina Research Foundation for a study of ocular melanoma. The Houston Independent School District received a grant for kindergarten screening for school failure. The Texas Institute for Rehabilitation received two grants. The University of Texas School of Public Health received a grant of $10,000 to develop a fellowship program in occupational medicine. Grants were made to the new University of Texas School of Medicine in Houston. The University of Texas at Austin received funds to study Type A behavior patterns.

6. In 1968, the Kleberg Family Trust gave the Kelsey-Leary Foundation $1,000 to establish a chapel in the clinic for patients and staff. When we became overcrowded and the space was not making a profit, the chapel was closed, and the $1,000 was returned to the Kleberg Foundation. I believe this could have been handled in a better way. Our psychiatrist Chester Cochran and I had confidential knowledge of why the chapel was given. We failed to generate the support which the chapel deserved. Regardless of one's religion, or even if one has no religion, there is a spiritual side of life that the medical profession should recognize. Spiritual strength has sustained people through physical and emotional crises and has saved many a life. I have experienced it. Most of us don't recognize spirituality unless we are in a major crisis or in deep sorrow or sublime happiness. At one time memory was considered to be a spiritual quality. Now we have a physical basis for it. Someday we may discover a physical basis for spirituality. Then we will have to give it a new name.

7. Tommy was born in Oklahoma City in 1912, one of five sons of Mr. and Mrs. Frank Anderson. The family moved to Houston in 1928. Tommy attended Rice Institute and the University of Texas. He received his law degree from Washington and Lee University. He was initially associated with the law firm of Andrews and Kurth. After stints in the banking and investment fields, he returned to law in 1965 and organized his own partnership. Tommy had served in naval intelligence in New Orleans during World War II and obtained the rank of commander. He married Helen Sharp, whose father was a Texas Supreme Court justice, and their children grew up with our children. Tommy and Helen have spent much of their life in service. He has served as president of Houston's Museum of Fine Arts and the Houston Grand Opera; chairman of the board of visitors for the M. D. Anderson Hospital; president of the Council of the Diocese of the Episcopal Church of Texas; and a trustee of Washington and Lee University. To me, Tommy's most important titles have been chairman of the Kelsey-Seybold Foundation and president of the Cooking Club. Mary and I made several wonderful trips with

Tommy and Helen before Mary became disabled. We have enjoyed many good times together.

8. Randy Lovelace had lost two sons to polio in 1946. But that was not the end of tragedy for the Lovelaces. They had an apartment in Aspen, Colorado, and often flew up there in their plane on weekends to ski. One Monday morning Randy and Mary, with their pilot, took off from the Aspen airport for Albuquerque without filing a flight plan, so there was no record of them leaving. The plane did not arrive in Albuquerque. The doctors at the Lovelace Clinic thought Randy had decided to spend another day or two in Aspen, so they were not alarmed by this absence. After a couple of days and no Randy, they called Aspen to learn that the Lovelaces were not in Aspen and the plane was not at the airport. The weather was terrible; the dreaded fear was that the plane had crashed in the mountains. Our friend Billy Rubey, then living in Aspen, was a member of a volunteer air rescue team. Billy knew that a certain canyon near Aspen had trapped other planes which had flown into it and could not generate enough power to fly over it. The canyon was too narrow to make a 180 degree turn and fly back out. He predicted that Randy's plane would be found in the canyon, and rescue teams were sent out to the canyon immediately. They found the Lovelace plane. All passengers had died, but not before one or more had climbed from the wreckage and had frozen to death while awaiting rescue.

9. Paul Wright was a true gentleman. He and I became close friends. There was a strong history of hypertension and early death from coronary disease in his family. Unfortunately, he had severe hypertension and suffered a coronary occlusion in 1972. He returned to work, but in February 1975 he was hospitalized for another coronary occlusion. After retiring, he bought a house near Kerrville, where he lived for two or three years before he died, leaving his wife Janet and two daughters. Mary, Vicki Buxton, and I went to Paul's military-style funeral in San Antonio. His widow, Janet, died early in 1996.

10. Johnny Johnston got a job in the Kerrville V.A. Hospital and continued to live in Kerrville. He is retired there today. On February 19, 1996, he sent me a clipping about an organization that has moved into Kerrville and is building a 30,000 square foot building as a clinic for twenty-four doctors. Johnny wrote: "Indeed we were looking ahead. This is the second facility to be opened here. The other is a type of HMO which we too would have sponsored. But I'm not bitter. Life in the Hill Country is great."

11. In 1945, I became a certified FAA medical examiner for class I airline pilots. I kept my certification up to date by attending FAA refresher courses. I was asked to teach in several of the them. In 1986, just before I retired, I received my last FAA Examiners Certificate. Ever since my days a squadron flight surgeon in the Aleutian Islands, I enjoyed being with professional pilots.

12. The Kelsey-Seybold Clinic has many branch clinics today, including the Quail Valley Clinic, which opened in Missouri City in December 1980 under the supervision of Spencer Berthelsen, and the Humble Clinic, originally staffed by Stephen Shell. Before I retired, other branch clinics opened in Clear Lake City, Pasadena, Katy, Cy-Fair, Spring, Copperfield, Cornerstone, and Kingwood. There were so many that I never saw all of them.

Chapter 18. So-Called Retirement, 1986 to the Present

1. Many friends wrote letters when I retired. One was from Bob Moreton at M. D. Anderson, which quoted an 1807 letter written by Thomas Jefferson: "I would wish the young practitioner, especially, to have deeply impressed on his mind, the real limits of his art, and that

when the state of his patient gets beyond these, his office is to be a watchful, but quiet spectator of the operation of nature." Thomas Jefferson's remark holds true today.

2. Bill Levin was president of UTMB at the time. Bill was supported strongly by his wife, Edna. The two dedicated their lives to UTMB and led the school through trying times. In 1988, it became time for Bill Levin to retire at age seventy. His replacement was Tom James. Tom and his wife, Gleaves, also dedicated themselves fully to UTMB. They retired in 1997 to be replaced by Dr. and Mrs. John Stobo.

3. One Christmas, I gave Mary a collection of three hundred nineteenth-century childrens' books, some printed in the early 1800s. Many of these books were illustrated with exquisite little wood engravings. Mary was especially fond of collecting her favorite authors. Her favorite was Anthony Trollope, whose works have become hot collectors' items in the last few years. We had about two hundred Trollope volumes. Jane Austen, the Mitfords, and Georgette Heyer also were some of Mary's favorites. We also collected books by Ben Green, George Catlin, Charlie Russell and Frederick Remington.

4. Other art collecting began in 1954, when we purchased a circus scene by Jean Dufy in Paris. We decided to buy a work of art each time we made a significant trip. We made many trips to Mexico and bought pictures from Ines Amor's gallery. In 1955, just before we left Mexico City, we bought a Diego Rivera painting of a peasant woman climbing a mountain with a large pottery vessel on her back. Jamie Griffith, Fletcher Pratt, and I toured Mexico in 1959. We rushed by Ines Amor's gallery and I bought a beautiful Carlos Merida duco called *The Fortune Tellers.* In 1963, Mary and I lucked into the Belles Artes Palace while we were just walking around. There was a government sponsored sale of well-known artists. We bought two Fannie Rabels, one titled *La Nina,* which had been widely illustrated in art magazines. At this exhibit we obtained oil paintings by Artura Estrado *(The Aqueduct in Chapultapec Park)*, Roberto Montenegro, Trinidad Osorio, and Nicolas Mareno *(El Sembrado,* which had been on a world tour of Mexican art). While visiting the Robert Strausses in Morelia we bought an Alfredo Zalce. On another trip, we purchased a typical volcano scene by Dr. Atl (born Geraldo Murillo, a revolutionary who spent much time in prison) and several drawings by Alfredo Siqueros. In Mexico City, we purchased a fine Andrea del Sarto engraving, and a nice still-life oil by Luc Hueber, a French artist. At a Christmas time in the 1950s, we bought nearly a dozen small paintings and drawings from Mexico. The most valuable item of the lot was a line drawing, signed by Pablo Picasso in 1943, showing the head of a bull, entitled *Los Toros Son Angeles Que Lleuven Cuernos.* In 1969, we began buying nineteenth-century oils by American artists from Meredith Long. The most important painting in our collection was purchased by Mary. It is a characteristic Frederick Freiseke showing a woman in a blue striped dress standing obliquely in front of a mirror.

5. Mary and I also supported the museum in other ways. We made several gifts of art, including Remington prints, the Gentling brothers' *Birds of Texas,* a complete set of bound volumes of *Harper's Weekly,* and, of all things, a Hunzinger side chair.

6. We delivered the prints to the Naval Academy before they had been appraised. Alexandra recommended a print authority, W. Graham Arader III, who had appraised some prints for the academy. He completed the appraisal in a few days. He visited us in Houston in October 1979, and we found him to be a bright, enthusiastic young man. He had recently graduated from Yale, where he made extra money by selling art prints in his room. After graduation he opened his own business as a dealer in art prints. Graham had an amazing ability to recognize fine art. He knew intimate details about all the great illustrators of animals, birds, and flowers of the

eighteenth and nineteenth centuries. I should have known that in a few years he would become the greatest dealer in America of art prints and books of natural history. We became close friends and remain so to this day. Graham located the fine nature books for our collection. Within a few years we owned most of the major large American natural history volumes.

7. We had collected so many Thomas Nast prints, for example, that we gave collections to Texas A&M, the Menil Museum, and the Museum of Fine Arts, Houston. There are probably a hundred or so still around the house. We also arranged to give to Landau, Germany—Nast's birthplace—a collection of his engravings from *Harper's Weekly*. Our prints are still housed in the Landau Public Library and have been on several exhibition tours in Germany.

8. Human settlements are rapidly taking over the prairie. I guess about half of it has been destroyed since we bought Live Oaks. The ranch is still the most secluded area on the prairie. For years I had wished to see the Live Oaks converted to a game preserve. In 1996 our sons did exactly that. A few miles from our ranch is a protected game refuge on the Warren Ranch. Thousands of birds rest there.

9. We joined the Performance Registry International and sent semen from Sam's Success for a breeding performance program. Breeding cows by artificial insemination (AI) was becoming very popular. In 1969, Ross Wollgast and I attended an AI course. I bought the equipment, and a veterinarian at A&M obtained semen from Sam's Success and Uranium and froze it in vials. We did AI for several years with semen from our bulls and semen from famous bulls of other breeders. Sam's Success produced calves that weighed 500 pounds at weaning, and we sold his semen to other ranchers.

10. In 1982, Mary and I gave a $5,000 grant to Texas A&M University, College of Agriculture, Department of Wildlife and Fisheries Services, to finance a fellowship for a M.S. degree in wildlife management. The grant was awarded to Ellen King, a lovely young lady from El Paso. She had a B.S. degree in zoology from A&M and had worked in her chosen field of wildlife conservation in New Mexico. Ellen spent the summer of 1982 at the ranch. She stayed in our house while she performed a remarkable survey of the ranch. She earned her master's with an eighty-four page illustrated thesis entitled "A Wildlife Management Plan for the Live Oaks Ranch, Waller County, Texas." The thesis contains pages of scientific lists of the fauna and flora, colored photographs of plants, maps and diagrams. Some of her recommendations have been carried out.

11. Some other friends we lost were Shirley and Justa Helm, Lovett Abercrombie, Jim Walsh, Borden Tennant, John Lynch, Joe Vercillino, Bill Noel, Percy Arthur, Hermann Pressler, Ben Powell, Louise Maverick, Stan Shipnes, Raybourne Thompson, Buddy Lykes, Howard Boyd, Barry Hunsaker, Roy Rather, Burris and Jean Head, Cooper and Susie Ragan, Madison and Betty Wright, Maxine Means, Marvin Collie, Ed Andrews, David Blevins, Ted Law, Camilla and Tex Trammel, Milton Underwood, Ed Smith, J. T. Armstrong, John Olson, Max Levine, Eddie Chiles, Bob Moroney, Margaret Symonds, Alene Bachman, Aurellia Comfort, Frank A. Smith, and Mrs. Frank Smith at 102 years. These are just a few of the friends that I can call to mind.

Note: Pages with illustrations are indicated by italics.

Anderson, Angus, 344

Anderson, Frank G., Jr., 37, 185–86, 270–71, 376–77n 2

Anderson, Frank G., Sr., 37

Anderson, Helen, 171

Anderson, Monroe Dunaway, 185–87. *See also* M. D. Anderson Foundation

Anderson, Ralph, 241, 245, 261–62, 272, 289, 335

Anderson, Thomas D., 186–87, 263–65, 313, 322, 381–82n 7

Anderson and Clayton Company, 186–87

anesthesia, 297

anesthesiologists, 209

Anson Jones Press, 91

antibiotics: medical practice prior to, 89; penicillin testing, 240; and revolution in medicine, 212; sulfa drugs, 82, 90, 120, 131; and tuberculosis, 164

antiseptics, early 20th C., 58

appendicitis, 363n 3

Arabia Temple Crippled Children's Hospital, 196

Arader, W. Graham, III, 348, 383–84n 6

Arcos, Georgianna, 292

Arkansas Ozarks, 29

Armbrust, Charlie, 293

Armer, Alice, 319–20

Armhurst, Charley, 217

Armstrong, J. T., 214

Army Air Corps, U.S., 139–48, 154–61

Arnold, Hugh and Hiram, 214

Arnold, Tommy, 214

art collection, 347–50, 383–84n 4, 6–7, 383n 4

Asbury, Samuel E., 46

Ashburn, Frank: career path of, 367n 2; and Fay Wilson, 162; friendship of, 132–33, 156–58; marriage of, 163; at Mayo, 130; singing voice of, 71

aspirin, anti-coagulant properties of, 169, 367n 4

Assembly Ball, 183

astronaut training, 324

athletics at Texas A&M, 37, 42, 45

Atka Island, 143

Atkins, Dowis, 326

atomic weapon research, 156

Attu Island, 141, 151

Audubon, John James, 350–51

Augusta branch clinic, 335

automobile dealerships, 9–10

automobiles, as ticket to adventure, 70–71

autopsies, 85, 88–89, 126

availability of medical care, early 20th C., 79, 95–96, 118. *See also* costs, healthcare; managed care revolution

Aves, Fred, 214

bacteriology, 64

Baird, Bill, 217

Baird, Valiant, 325, 333

Baker Botts law firm, 295

Bakken, James A., 277, 290, 338

Baldes, E. J., 155

Balfour, Donald, 98, 119, 162–63, 171

Ballantyne, Alando J., 208, 316

Banta, Ray, 77

Barber, Jim, 348

Bargen, J. A., 131

Barker, John and Pearl, 138

Barkley, Howard, 215

Barnard, Christian, 280

Barnes, Sam, 110, 152, 218, 355, 361n 9

Barnes Hospital, 130

Barnette, Nell, 277

Barr, H. B., 218

Barta, Capt. James, 134

Barthelme, Don, 261

Bates, Col. William, 182, 187, 220

Battle of Midway, 142

Baughn, Ford, 28

Baxter Laboratories, 304

Bayer, Alvin, 214

Baylor University, 45

Baylor University College of Medicine: and advent of UTHSC, 305; brother John's tenure at, 158, 193; K-L clinic participation, 256–57; K-S Foundation grants to, 314, 321; and Methodist Hospital, 195; transfer to Houston, 185, 191–93, *192*

197; Mavis's plans to organize own, 173–77; solo doctors' objections to, 94, 363*n* 1. *See also specific clinics*

Cloud, Tom, 215

Cobalt 60 radiation, 260

Cochran, Chester and Jamie, 244, 303

Cockrell, Ernie, 281, 315, 323

Cody, Melville, 248, 303, 320, 355, 375*n* 5

Cold Bay Harbor, Alaska, 142–46

Coleman, S. D., 218

collection of books and periodicals, 345–47

collections: artwork, 347–50, 383–84*n* 6–7; books and periodicals, 91, 158, 345–47, 383*n* 3; county courthouse photos, 344–45; stamps, 129; start of, 4; Texana, 91, 184, 345–46

College Inn, 61, 87

College Station, Tex., 36

Collie, Marvin, 313–14, 315

colon cancer, 381*n* 3

Colonial Hospital, 115

colonic irrigation, 211

Comfort, Aurelia, 129

Comfort, Mandred, 129, 130, 171, 175

Communist Party, 80

company medical accounts: and branch office opportunities, 334–36; K-L Clinic, 249–51; NASA, 250, 324–30; oil industry, 298–99, 330–31, 332–33; solo practice, 206–207

computer facilities, 279

Confederacy, 3–4

Connally, John, 281

Conner, Cooper, 71, 76, 355

consultations, 280

Continental Airlines, 337–38

Cook, Mary Jane, 291

Cooke, Willard R., 66, *67*, 87

Cooking Club, 263–65. *See also* food

Cooley, Denton, 59, 213, 218, 243, 341

coronary artery disease, 6, 204, 213, 259, 280

corporal punishment, 20

corporate medical accounts. *See* company medical accounts

cortisone treatments, 166, 170–71, 212

costs, healthcare, 205–206, 251–52, 254–55, 274

cotton production, 4, 14, 17–18, 22–23, 186

county courthouse photo collection, 344–45

Cournand, Dr., 83

Coventry, Mark, 355

Cowan, Finis, 295

cowboy books, 346–47

Coyle, Mildred, 246

Crager, Jay, 218

Crank, Harlan, 214

Crigler, Cecil, 215–16

criminals, Mavis on, 84

Cronin, Tom, 213

Crowe, Lt., 144

Crump, Joe and Jessie, 315–18

Crump Cancer Center, 316–17, 321

Cruz, Emelina, 308

Cullen, Roy, 188, 193

Cullen Nurses Building, 195

Cupadero Ranch, 219–20

Curmley, Russ, 208

Curtis, Raleigh, 110

Cushing Memorial Library, 38

Daichman, Ricardo, 302

Daily, Louis, 215

Dale, Seaborn, 209

Daly, Jed, 214

Damon Hospital, 115

David, Dorman, 285, 346

Davilla, Beatrice "Bea," 244

Dawson, W. T., 65

Dayton, Ohio, 154–61

D-Day memories, 160

DeBakey, Michael, 94, 195, 218

DeBerry, Tom, 28

Dee, Mrs., 98, 100, 110

Dehn, Adolph, 117

DeLaurel, Hugh, 110

demand oxygen mask, 155

dentists, 276, 377*n* 5

Deport, Tex.: Civil War traditions in, 3; early 20th C. medical care in, 57–59; J. B. Kelsey's role in growth of, 5–6,

fungus diseases, 65, 155

Gagge, Pharo and Eddie, 158, 355
Galleria clinic, 334
Galton, Francis, 40
Galveston, Tex., 59–60, 71, 90. *See also* University of Texas Medical Branch (UTMB), Galveston
Galvez Hotel, 71
gambling in Galveston, 60
games and activities, children's, early 20th C. rural, 27–30
Gandy, Joe, 215
Garcia-Torres, Francisco J., 379*n* 8
gardening, 156, 256, 262, 308
Gardner, Bob, 216
Gardner, Herman, 214
Gary, Jo Ann, 291, 321
gas pipeline industry, company accounts with, 298–99
gastroenterologists, 240, 270
gastroenterology: cancers, 318, 321, 381*n* 3; colonic irrigation, 211; familial gastrointestinal neoplasia, 320; Mavis's preference for, 128–29, 131, 167
gastrointestinal fluoroscopy, 240
Gatura, George, 217
Gayle, Gibson, Jr., 322
Gehrig, Lou, 118
Geiss, Dr., 149
genealogical work, 342–44, 357*n* 1
general practice, Mavis's work in, 204, 235, 301
general practitioners: need for more in clinic, 173, 278; opposition to group practice, 94; referrals from, 217, 232; vs. specialists, 184–85
genetics, 38, 40
George C. Marshall Space Flight Center (MSFC), 329
George Washington University, 102
Gibbs, Mary Virginia (née Kelsey) (sister), 7, 11, 31, 357*n* 4
Giffin, H. Z., 126, 172, 364*n* 6
Gillsdorf, Capt., 150
Gilruth, Robert, 325

Gingrich, Wendell, 64
ginning season, cotton, 23
Gipson, Larry, 356
Glassell, Alfred, 283–84, 377*n* 7
Glassman, Arthur, 216
Glenn, Frank, 216
Goar, Everett L., 215, 259
goat gland injections, 59
Gober, Olin, 95
Goeth, Carl, 75, 213–14, 355
goiter diseases, 168–69. *See also* thyroid problems
gonorrheal salpingitis, 84
Goodheart, Dr., 83
Goodloe, Max, 216
Good Samaritan Club, 314
Gorten, Ralph J., 248, 301–302
Goss, Frank, 332, 335
Goulden, Dudley, 338
Graduate School of Biomedical Sciences, 232–35
Graham, Evarts, 130
Graham, Mavis, 7
Grant, Maj. Gen. David N. W., 154
Grant, James, 152
Grant, Mahlon, 11, 31, 48–49
Grant, Stephen, 10, 57–59
Gray, Bill and Millie, 276
Gready, Tom and Donald, 213
Greenwood Sanitarium, 74, 370*n* 12
Greer, Agnes "Aggie," 220, 246–48, *247,* 291–92, 295–96
Greer, Alice M. "Jackie," 245, 276–77, 314, 315, 321, 374–75*n* 3
Greer, Alvis, 213, 217
Greer, Boyd (Jing), 246
grief, magnitude of, 268–69
Griffey, Ed, 215
Griffin, Belton, 239
Griffith, Jamie, 162, 260, 282, 355
Grimmett, Leonard, 209
Grindlay, Jack, 220
Griswold, Culver, 210
Groshong, Sgt. James, 154–55
group medical practice, debate on, 38–39, 94, 363*n* 1. *See also* clinics

Grundy, Thad, 330
Guadalcanal, 152
Guerra Ranch, Mexico, 285
Guest, Leonard, 22
Guion Hall, Texas A&M, 36
Gunn, Ralph, 262
gynecologists-obstetricians, 214, 215, 216,
    248–49

Haigler, Sam, 215, 218
Haines, Sam, 166, 167, 169, 171, 177, 355
Hall, Randolph, 325, 326, 327, 330–31, 334
Hallenbeck, George and Marion, 158, 160,
    163, 355
Hallman, Grady, 213
Hammond, Fred, 100, 110, 111
Hankamer, Roy, 193
Hannah, John and David, 241, 245, 271–72
Hanselman, Anna, 189
hardware business, 5–6, 7, 9–10
Hargis, Huard, 75, 98, 118, 130, 213, 257–58
Hargis, Lucylle, 98, 258
Harle, Tom, 273
Harrington, M. T., 40
Harris, Brantley, 74
Harris, Titus, 74, 91
Harris, Wade, 215
Harris County Medical Society, 193, 196,
    257, 259
Harris County Unit of the American
    Cancer Society, 210
Hart, James, 234
Hart, John, 167, 218
Hartman, Al, 213
Harvin, William, 291, 322
Haskall, Walt, 218
Haun, Prudence (Mrs. James R. Kelsey)
    (aunt), 19–20
Hauser, Abe, 214
Hayes, Herbert, 213
Haynie, Tom, 208, 281
hazing, 37, 43–44, 359n 3–5
health insurance, 254–55, 296–97
Health Maintenance Organizations
    (HMOs), 296–97, 303
health physics, 325, 331

heart bypass surgery, 259
heart disease, 6, 204, 213, 280
Heartgraves, Ruth, 216
Hedgecroft Hospital, 370n 12
Heflebower, Roy, 189
Hein, Col. Walter R., 327
Heinzerling, Ann (Mrs. Thomas Kelsey)
    (daughter-in-law), 214, 218–19, 267
Heinzerling, John and Margaret, 218
Helm, Shirley and Justa, 183
Hench, Phillip, 170, 171, 244
Hendrix, Byron M., 63
Hermann, George, 68, 193–94, 360n 4
Hermann Hospital: charity service at, 193–
    94, 207; clinic move away from, 255;
    growth of, 185; and KSL Clinic, 235;
    origins of, 193–94
Hermann Professional Building, 177, 185,
    186, 199, 241
Herxheimer reaction, 311
Herzog, Carl, 200
Hewitt, Richard, 166–67
Hickam, John, 270
High, Harold, 218
high blood pressure, 249
Hild, Jack, 216
Hill, Annette, 206, 242
Hill, Stratton, 208
Hines, Gerald, 334
Hines, John, 219
Hinshaw, Corwin, 164
hitchhiking, 46–53
HMOs (Health Maintenance
    Organizations), 296–97, 303
Hobby, William P., Sr., 193, 247, 254, 281,
    296
hobo adventure, to California, 48–53
Hogg, Ima, 184
holiday traditions, 26–27, 122–25
Hollywood Club, 60
Holton Arms School, 101
home delivery of babies, decline of, 66–67
Homer, Winslow, 80, 348, 349
honeymoon, 111–13
hormone therapy, for cancer, 260
hospital privileges, 185, 198, 271

hospital rounds, 203, 207–10, 255–57. *See also specific hospitals*

house calls, 203–204, 236, 250, 287

housing: Dayton, 156; Houston, 181–82, 261–62; Mayo Clinic, 118, 162–63, 172

Houston, Tex.: general practitioners vs. specialists in, 184–85; Kelsey family move to, 181–83, 368*n* 1; social life, 183; Texas Medical Center development, 185–96, 370–71*n* 12–14; tour of, 183–84

Houston Academy of Medicine Library, 196

Houston Country Club, 236

Houston Eye, Ear, Nose and Throat (EENT) Hospital, 370*n* 12

Houston Garden Club, 256, 308

Houston Municipal Hospital, 194

Houston Museum of Fine Arts, 349

Houston Negro Hospital, 370*n* 12

Houston Society of Internal Medicine, 185, 210

Houston Tuberculosis Hospital, 236, 370*n* 12

Howe, Cliff, 224, 260, 355, 376*n* 11

Howe, Richard, 322

Howe, Wright, 158

Hudgins, Edgar, 198

Hudson, Rock, 254, 299–300

Hughes, John, 318–19, 380–81*n* 3

human centrifuge, 160

Humble Oil and Refining Company, 106, 333

Hunt brothers, 336, 337, 368*n* 9

hunting and fishing: and Cooking Club, 264; in Minnesota, 117; during solo practice, 219–20, 221; with sons, 265–66; white-wing dove hunt, 283–86; as youth, 10–11, 13, 14, 28–29

hunting and nature stories books, 347

hurricanes, 61, 283

hypertension, 249

hyperthyroidism, 170, 363*n* 3

hypoplasia of the aorta, 90

hypothermia, 125, 148

hypothyroidism, 170

income distribution for clinic partners. *See* pay distribution for clinic partners

incomes, physician, exponential growth of, 280

indoor plumbing, rural lack of, 15

industrial hygiene, 325, 326, 329, 331

infection, as most common cause of death, 89

infectious diseases: decline in deaths from, 212; lack of subspecialty in, 120; malaria, 15; polio epidemic, 164, 165–66, 194–95, 257–59; tuberculosis, 164, 259; venereal diseases, 66, 69, 73, 84, 240. *See also* antibiotics

insane asylums, 74

Institute of Experimental Medicine, 116

Institute of World Affairs in Mondsee, Austria, 101

insulin, 82

insurance: health, 254–55, 296–97; malpractice, 126, 252, 274, 297–98

internal medicine: Bellevue training in, 81–82; chest section at Mayo, 164–65; at K-S clinic, 300–301; Mavis's experience level in, 134; residency in, 120, 126; revolution in medical knowledge, 211–13. *See also* internists; *specific subspecialties*

International Thyroid Congress, 257

internists, 214, 217–18, 238–40, 243–44, 244, 249, 270

internship. *See* Bellevue Hospital, New York

interscholastic competition, 20

Introduction of Physiological Chemistry (Bodansky), 63

investments, business, 260–61

iodine deficiency, 168

Irvine, Virginia, 90

Isoniazid, 164

isotopes, 169–70, 208–10, 212–13, 248, 297

Jackson, Gilchrist, 209, 316, 378*n* 7

Jackson, Capt. T. W., 139, 142, 144

Japan, in Aleutian Islands, 140–41, 146–47, 150–51

Japanese Americans, government treatment of, 135–36

McAlexander, Mary Emma "Jessie" (Mrs. J. B. Kelsey) (grandmother), 3–4, 6, 357*n* 3
McCauley, Lt. Col., 139
McComb, Bill, 209
McCord, Jacqueline, 232, 233–34
McDonald, R. P., 84
McDonough, Francis and Kay, 119
McEwan, Currier, 79, 86
McGehee, F. O., 216
McGovern, John, 217
McKeever, Duncan, 216
McMurrey, James D., 271, 333
McMurty, Larry, 347
McNamara, Dan, 216, 243
McNeese, A. G., 305, 306
McNulty, Billy, 250, 314
McNulty, Sergeant, 150
McWilliams, Hamlin K., 218
Means, Noble and Maxine, 220, 314
meat inspection duty, 134
Mecom, John, 217
Medical Arts Professional Building and Hospital, 371*n* 12
medical breakthroughs. *See* advances in medicine
Medical Clinic of Houston, 217
Medical Computer Company, 279
Medical Corps Reserve, 132, 229–30
medical practice: and dangers of radioisotope experiments, 170; early 20th C., 4, 6, 57–59, 69; fads of the 1930s, 96–97; pharmacology, 65; pre-antibiotic treatment of infections, 89–90, 164; psychiatry, 74, 165; specialization development, 79; wartime limitations in, 149. *See also* clinics; doctor-patient relationship; specialization
medical profession: decline in prestige of, 211; post-WWII doctor glut, 196–97; and power of spirituality in healing, 381*n* 6; rise of non-physician practitioners, 295–96; rise of specialists, 185. *See also* clinics; physicians
medical school. *See* University of Texas Medical Branch (UTMB), Galveston

medical societies, membership in, 169, 171, 185, 210, 211, 257
Medicare, 296
Med-Partners, 304
Meisler, Irving, 217
memberships, professional, 169, 171, 185, 210, 211, 257
Memorial Hospital system, 195, 303, 304, 371*n* 12
Menninger Clinic, 241
menopausal symptoms, 97
mental hospital, Mavis's externship in, 73–74
mental illness. *See* psychiatry
Merriman, George, 217
metabolic medicine section at Mayo, 166–71
Methodist Church, 10, 30, 93
Methodist Hospital, 195, 255, 321, 371*n* 13
Mexico, as source of patients, 299, 302
Mickens, Annie, 162
military life, Texas A&M College, 36, 41–45
military service: *Air Surgeon's Bulletin* assignment, 154–61; Alaska assignment, 140–52; call to duty, 132–33; as interruption of clinic organization plans, 173; Portland Air Base duty, 134–36, 138–39; Randolph Field Aviation Medicine School, 136–38; Sheppard Field, 153–54
Miller, Kay, 334
Miller, Ralph, 245
Millis, Bob, 248, 301
Mills, Susannah, 3
Milton, Tex., 4–5
Minkoff, Mimi, 321
Minnesota, 113
miscarriages, 131
Mitchell, Arnold, 343
Mitchell, George, 260, 338
Mitchell, Layne, 216
Mitchell, Maria, 208–209, 316
modernization in Texas, effect on local businesses, 9–10
Moersch, Herman, 164–65
Monterrey, Mexico, 263
Mooney, Capt. Bob, 142–43
moonshine, 11, 51, 70, 71–72, 358*n* 5

Portland Air Field, Oregon, 132–36, 138–39

Post Graduate School of Medicine in Houston, 232–35

Post Oak Tower location, 334–35

Potter, Claudia, 95

poverty, in early 20th C. Texas, 17

Poyner, Herbert, 215

Pranke, Donald W., 276

pre-employment exams, 207, 330

pre-medical education, importance of, 59. *See also* Texas A&M College

prepaid medical care, 296–97

preventive medicine, 64, 210, 252, 330–31. *See also* company medical accounts; examination, physical

Price, Katherine, 111

print collection, 347–50, 383*n* 6–7

Prior, Bradley, 327

private practice: challenge of opening, 196–97; flourishing of Mayo-based, 171–72; searching for Texas location, 166, 167. *See also* solo practice; *specific clinics*

professional associations, 169, 171, 185, 210, 211, 257

Prohibition, 11, 51, 70, 71–72, 358*n* 5

prostitution, 38, 42, 60, 66

psychiatrists, 214, 244

psychiatry: evolution in practice of, 74, 165; and externship at Wichita, 73–74; at K-S clinic, 302; Mavis's solo work in, 204; at Mayo, 165; patients' reluctance to seek help, 203

psychoanalysts, 241

public health, and Texas Medical Center development, 190

Pullen, Al, 261

Quin, Bishop Clinton S., 109, *110,* 158, 183, 195–96, 219

Quonset huts, 149

racial prejudice, overcoming, 14, 17, 318–19, 370*n* 12

Radcliffe, Mrs., 156

radio, advent of, 19

radioiodine experiments, 166, 169–70, 212–13

radioisotopes, 169–70, 208–10, 212–13, 248, 297

radiologists, 215, 241–42, 271, 273

radiology department, 302

radio program, Mary's, 102

railroads, and transformation of rural Texas, 5

Ralli, Elaine, 82, 362*n* 6

Randall, Edward, III, 306

Randall, Larry, 131

Randall, Laura, 270

Randolph Field, Tex., 137–38

Rankin Bell's hamburger stand, 26

Raphael, Pedro, 302

rare book collection, 91, 158, 345–47, 383*n* 3

Rather, Roy, 261

rationing, wartime, 136, 152, 156, 163

rauwolfia serpentina, 249

Reading, Boyd, 72–73, 87

real estate investments, 260–61

recruitment of associates, 238–44, 270–71, 273–74, 275–76, 300–302

red light district of Galveston, 60

Reece, Charles, 217

Reed, Ruby, 111

referral network, 213–20, 228, 231–32, 235–37, 279–80

refugees from Pearl Harbor, 137

Reiske, Billy Jo Farris, 277

religion: and Baylor medical school, 192; children's reaction to, 220; as contributor to healing, 381*n* 6; early exposure to, 17, 20, 30–32; Mavis as Episcopalian, 368–69*n* 3

renal necrosis, 90

renal transplants, 280

research, medical: aeromedical, 148, 154–55; cancer therapy developments, 259–60; endocrinology, 170; K-S Foundation contributions to, 320–21; Mavis's thesis, 127–28, 364*n* 7; sulfa drug testing, 82; and viruses, 258. *See also* advances in medicine

reserpine, 249

Reserve Officer Training Corps (ROTC), 41–45

Waldron, George, 176, 371–72n 1
Walker, Breckenridge, 129
Wall, John, 209, 210, 214
Walters, Waltman, 214
Walton, Vic, 147–48
Warner, Clyde, 255
Washington, DC, 157–58
weather and climate: Aleutian Islands, 143–45; in early 20th C. Deport, Tex., 15; Rochester, Minnesota, 125–26
Webb, Nancy, 322
Weems, Mrs. Wharton, 314
Weigand, Col., 154
Weight Watchers Diet, 83
Weiss, Mr. and Mrs. Harry, 111
Welch, Alexandra, 349
Welch, Hugh, 215
Wells, Ben, 209
West, Jim "Silver Dollar," 219–20, 246–47, 325
West, Neva, 174, 182–83
West, Wesley: and brother Jim, 219; and Manned Space Center project, 325; as network contact, 182–83; and professional meeting attendance, 211; and snake bite treatment, 205; support for clinic idea, 228; wealth of, 174
western print collection, 347–48
western travel books, 346
White, Ed, 355
White, Raleigh, Jr. and Aleene, 130
White, Raleigh R., Sr., 94
white-wing dove hunt, 284–86
Wichita Falls, Tex., 73–74, 153–54
Wiedower, Kathleen, 348
Wier, Mary Margaret "Mickey" (Mrs. John R. Kelsey, Jr.) (sister-in-law), 158, 172, 239, 240
Wigodsky, Maj. Herman, 159
Wilcox, Betty, 321, 335
wildcat drilling projects, 260
Wilder, Russell, 98, 213
Wilford, Don, 304
Wilkins, Horace, 174, 187
Wilkins, Lawson, 217
Williams, Jarrett, 88

Williams, Steve, 253
Wills, Seward, 216
Wilson, Charles, 281
Wilson, Charlotte (née Strong) (sister-in-law), 101, 111
Wilson, Claude, 103
Wilson, Fay (sister-in-law): courtship of, 130, 162; and courtship of Mavis and Mary, 100, 101, 102, 103, 109, 111; death of, 355; as neighbor, 282
Wilson, James Cooke, Jr. (brother-in-law), 82, 250, 282, 359n 5
Wilson, James Cooke, Sr. (father-in-law), 105, 107–108, 110, 158
Wilson, John (brother-in-law), 132
Wilson, Louis B., 115
Wilson, Mary Bradley (née Randolph) (mother-in-law), 100, 104, 177, 262, 282
Wilson, Mary Randolph (wife). See Kelsey, Mary Randolph (née Wilson) (wife)
Wilson, Morris and Crain, 241
Wilson, Waldo (brother-in-law), 101, 105, 109
Wilson Club (House), 115
Windrow, Frank, 216
Winston, Elizabeth Rice (Mrs. John W. Kelsey) (daughter-in-law), 282
Withers, Henry, 217
wives, social network of, 121
Wollgast, Ross, 353, 354, 384n 9
women: as employees of clinic, 291–92; low numbers in med school, 69
Women's Army Corps (WAC), 152–53
Woodbine Lodge, 111
wood engraving print collection, 347–50
Woodfin, George, 355
Woodlands branch clinic, 338
World War I, veteran's protest during Depression, 52
World War II. See military service
Worrall Hospital, 115
Wright, Madison (cousin), 35
Wright, Orville, 156
Wright, Col. Paul E., 327, 382n 9
Wright-Patterson Field, Dayton, Ohio, 154–61